THIRTEEN CLOCKS

Thirteen Clocks

How RACE United the Colonies and
Made the *Declaration of* Independence

ROBERT G. PARKINSON

Published by the
OMOHUNDRO INSTITUTE OF
EARLY AMERICAN HISTORY AND CULTURE,
Williamsburg, Virginia,
and the
UNIVERSITY OF NORTH CAROLINA PRESS,
Chapel Hill

*The Omohundro Institute of Early American History and Culture
is sponsored by the College of William and Mary.
On November 15, 1996, the Institute adopted the present name
in honor of a bequest from Malvern H. Omohundro, Jr.*

Cover illustration: *American Musket*, c. 1760–1776.
Courtesy George C. Neumann Collection, Valley Forge National Historical Park;
flag © iStock.com/smartstock.

Library of Congress Cataloging-in-Publication Data
Names: Parkinson, Robert G., author.
Title: Thirteen clocks : how race united the colonies and made
the Declaration of Independence / Robert G. Parkinson.
Other titles: 13 clocks
Description: Williamsburg, Virginia : Omohundro Institute of Early American
History and Culture ; Chapel Hill : The University of North Carolina Press, [2021] |
Includes bibliographical references and index.
Identifiers: LCCN 2021004004 | ISBN 9781469662565 (cloth) |
ISBN 9781469662572 (paperback) | ISBN 9781469662589 (ebook)
Subjects: LCSH: Racism — United States — History — 18th century. |
United States — History — Revolution, 1775–1783 — Propaganda. |
United States — History — Revolution, 1775–1783 — Social aspects.
Classification: LCC E209 .P343 2021 | DDC 305.800973/09033 — dc23
LC record available at https://lccn.loc.gov/2021004004

To the memory of

JERRY L. PARKINSON

(1939–2020)

Preface

Thirteen Clocks: How Race United the Colonies and Made the Declaration of Independence is an abridgement of *The Common Cause: Creating Race and Nation in the American Revolution* (2016). Sort of. It isn't a traditional abridgement; only three chapters from that original appear here, and those are heavily revised and in new forms. The argument is the same, but that book, which topped out at seven hundred pages, detailed the continuity and prevalence of the stories that began to circulate first in 1775 and 1776. *The Common Cause* covered the entire Revolutionary War and its aftermath, whereas *Thirteen Clocks* focuses on the fifteen months between the start of the Revolutionary War and the Declaration of Independence. It has a new introduction and conclusion and new material exploring all the myriad problems patriot leaders faced when they began the nearly impossible task of constructing a durable union in the 1770s. There is also a new essay for further reading.

I began work on the project that would become *The Common Cause* in 2001. I knew I wanted to work on race and the American Revolution but had no real sense of where I was going, so I figured I'd begin where so many others had: with the newspapers. I had no idea what I would actually find there. For more than a year, I sat in front of a microfilm reader in a corner of Alderman Library turning squeaky wheels to look at colonial newspapers page by page, frame by frame. I started where *Thirteen Clocks* starts—with the news of Lexington and Concord—and went through each of the dozens of American newspapers serially, taking detailed notes, through the end of 1783. A few months into my research, I developed the ability to predict what I was going to see next. This was an unanticipated, somewhat baffling new skill. After I had studied several titles, I began to wonder why I was able to know what was coming next—and, more important, what that experience of reading the same story, whether the paper was published in Connecticut or Carolina, might mean for the patriots' mobilization campaign. It took me a while to understand, but I had stumbled across the political power of the newspaper exchanges. Once I began to grasp its importance, I wondered whether I had actually discovered the Revolutionaries' secret.

My mind also reeled at all the material I was finding about enslaved and Native peoples in the middle pages of those newspapers. How many other people had started their research on the Revolution with the newspapers? Dozens? Hundreds? Why was I so surprised at the tremendous amount of evidence? The thickness of the archive still astounds me. One of the main reasons *The Common Cause* reached seven hundred pages was because it was the best way to honor and convey the sheer size — the amount, the bulk — of the stories I had found in the papers.

Patriot leaders thought about enslaved and Native people *all the time* during the Revolution. When patriots weren't working daily in assembly halls trying to formulate policy about these groups, they were working closely with publicists in print shops to broadcast any news, whether rumored or real, about British agents whispering to African Americans, Indians, and (at first) German mercenaries to subvert the Revolution. Patriot leaders not only embraced fear and prejudice to convince Americans they needed to resist British tyranny but weaponized them for the new republic by making those stories the basis of the "common cause" appeal after Lexington and Concord.

This was the interpretation of the American Revolution and the founding I mulled over from 2001 until the publication of *The Common Cause* in 2016. Naturally, when I began to talk about what I had discovered (at conference receptions or job interviews), listeners were quick to say this was sheer presentism. The events of the fifteen years in which I researched and wrote that book witnessed repeated instances of politicians' using fear to stoke racial prejudice. I first heard that my project was really all about the September 11, 2001, attacks and their aftermath, including the demonization of Muslim peoples and the passage of the Patriot Act. Then I heard that it was really a project about how the U.S. government sold, justified, and prosecuted the war against Iraq. And then I heard that these themes were really about the backlash to the election of Barack Obama — especially the rise of the Tea Party in 2010 and the public's willingness to tolerate divisive, racist rhetoric about immigrants and people of color that, in part, led to the presidency of Donald Trump and the terrible, deadly white supremacist rally in Charlottesville, Virginia.

It was about none of those things. My interpretation had one source of inspiration: that squeaky microfilm reader. Then again, that *so many* such episodes happened over the first two decades of the twenty-first century is a reminder of how powerful the combination of fear and prejudice remains as a force for political mobilization in American society. Although they seem to be a permanent part of our culture, the political uses of fear and their influence on how Americans think about race are not simply our contemporary problems. They are as old as the United States. In fact, I am convinced they made the states united in the first place.

It does not give me joy to write these words. But I believe we must try to understand not only *why* patriot leaders decided to broadcast these particular stories and cement words like "merciless Indian savages" at the heart of the Declaration of Independence but also *how* they did it. *Thirteen Clocks* is a book about process, about how abstract things that seem to be just "in the air" become real. It is about how ideas that float like clouds get tethered to the ground and become fixtures of cultural discourse. Racism seems an especially difficult cloud. We know it is out there somewhere, but many people complain it is difficult to find, because it is either everywhere — perpetual, permanent, and ubiquitous in current American life and throughout its history — or nowhere, a figment of imagination. There is a notion that has pervaded American society of yesterday and today. It is an impression, a nagging sense, a feeling: Some people belong in this country and some people don't. No matter what their birth certificates say. But what is that notion? What is it based on? Where did it come from? Why is it so powerful?

Thirteen Clocks is about the origins of this particular ideological cloud, this shapeless feeling, and how it came to be anchored at the heart of the American republic at the very moment of its founding. This work seeks to understand how abstract ideas such as these are made concrete. By examining the historical development and use of tangible things (like the exchanging of news stories through communications networks), we can see how things that appear intangible, and therefore intractable, got that way. And, perhaps, by uncovering how these things got buried, we can face the task of dealing with them.

But we do need to face them. Criticism of patriot leaders' choices at the moment of independence is not treason. We have to be willing to be critical, to grapple with these difficult problems and processes. We need to plumb their depths and realize just how entrenched the challenges are that lie before us. To avoid doing so will not make those problems disappear, nor does it mean we are bound to fail. Some charge that, if we admit how deeply white supremacy is buried at the heart of the American republic, our will to change will be diminished. That understanding this can only lead to a throwing up of hands. If it's always been this way, why try? That is only the case if we think our capacity is too shallow — our spirit too brittle — to handle this information.

Those news stories about so-called "merciless savages" and "domestic insurrectionists" that circulated throughout America in 1775–1776 may seem dead and gone, entombed inside forgotten reels of microfilm, but they exist. They were put there by patriot leaders whom we revere for other words they said and wrote. If we are to understand America's origin story — if we are to grasp fully what Jefferson, Franklin, and Adams meant in the opening lines of the Declaration — we must also come to terms with that same document's final grievance and the consequences of those words for millions of people in North America in 1776 and for generations after.

When I first approached Nadine Zimmerli and Cathy Kelly with the idea of adapting the tome, they were all in right away. Nadine was instrumental in getting *The Common Cause* across the finish line, and Cathy, who was a marvel in championing this project, more than matched her enthusiasm. It is a distinct pleasure to be a second-time author with the books program of the Omohundro Institute of Early American History and Culture. Many thanks to Karin Wulf, Virginia Montijo Chew, Emily Suth, and, especially, my veteran copyeditor, Kathy Burdette. This is simply a superb team of people. My express thanks to Gerry Krieg and Beatrice Burton for reprising their roles as mapmaker and indexer extraordinaires.

After the publication of *The Common Cause,* I was lucky enough to be invited to talk about my findings at multiple venues, including George Mason University, the University of Richmond, the Ohio State University, Siena College's McCormick Center for the Study of the American Revolution, Historic Sotterley Plantation, Fraunces Tavern, the David Library for the American Revolution, the Virginia Festival of the Book, and several scholarly conferences. All these audiences asked very engaging, thoughtful questions and gave me opportunities to distill the presentation of my interpretation. That process is evident in *Thirteen Clocks,* and for that, I extend my sincere appreciation, especially to the historically curious members of the public who take the time to attend events like these. Much thanks to Chris Pearl and his students at Lycoming College for road testing an early draft.

I have to thank, in particular, Peter Onuf and Annette Gordon-Reed for their generous, unflagging support of the book and its author. Having those two in my corner, along with friends and colleagues Brad Jones, Brian Murphy, Johann Neem, Honor Sachs, Molly Warsh, Brett Rushforth, James Lewis, Charlene Boyer Lewis, Diane Sommerville, and Steve Ortiz, is more than I deserve. Thank you, friends.

That list should be a bit longer. The very untimely losses of two dear friends, Leonard Sadosky and Jan Lewis, make the appearance of this book a "happysad," in my daughter's turn of phrase. That bittersweetness was compounded by the loss of my father just before this book went into production. He fought a long and valiant battle with heart failure, which is ironic because his heart was his greatest feature. These were three people the world couldn't afford to lose, and we are much the poorer for it. I miss them very, very much and always will.

Finally, to the women who occupy the inner rooms of my heart. Thank you to my mother and sister, who are always on my team. My girls, Abby and Carly: it is fantastic to watch you grow into such fabulous young women. You make a father proud. And Julia, who knows.

Contents

Preface *vii*

List of Illustrations *xv*

Abbreviations *xvii*

Introduction *1*

CHAPTER 1
Newspapers on the Eve of the Revolutionary War *13*

CHAPTER 2
The Long Odds against American Unity in the 1770s *36*

CHAPTER 3
The "Shot Heard round the World" Revisited *68*

CHAPTER 4
"Britain Has Found Means to Unite Us" *82*

CHAPTER 5
A Rolling Snowball *101*

CHAPTER 6
Merciless Savages, Domestic Insurrectionists,
and Foreign Mercenaries *128*

CONCLUSION
Founding Stories *164*

Notes *187*

Guide to Further Reading *217*

Index *223*

ILLUSTRATIONS

FIGURES

1	Outer sheet of colonial newspaper	22
2	Inner sheet of colonial newspaper	24
3	Print shop in 1774	26
4	Franklin "Join, or die" cartoon	38
5	"A Compleat Map of North-Carolina from an Actual Survey"	90
6	Guy Carleton	95
7	Lord Dunmore	103
8	Colonel Guy Johnson and Karonghyontye (Captain David Hill)	125
9	"Map of the Maritime Parts of Virginia"	134
10	Map of Gwynn's Island, Virginia	152
11	Letter from "Armatus"	154
12	John Dunlap's broadside of the Declaration of Independence	159
13	"The Murder of Jane McCrea"	166
14	"A Scene on the Frontiers as Practiced by the *Humane* British and Their *Worthy* Allies"	170

MAPS

1	Places of Newspaper Publication, 1775–1776	19
2	Distribution Routes for *Pennsylvania Journal,* 1775–1776	33
3	Sites of Colonial Conflict, 1760s–1770s	44
4	Massachusetts, April 1775	71
5	North Carolina, 1775	87
6	Virginia, 1775–1776	104
7	Canada and New York, 1776	145

Abbreviations

BOOKS AND PERIODICALS

4 *Am. Archives*
M. St. Clair Clarke and Peter Force, eds., *American Archives,* 4th Ser., *Containing a Documentary History of the English Colonies in North America . . .* , 6 vols. (Washington, D.C., 1837–1846).

5 *Am. Archives*
Peter Force, ed., *American Archives,* 5th Ser., *Consisting of a Collection of Authentick Records, State Papers, Debates, and Letters and Other Notices of Publick Affairs . . .* , 3 vols. (Washington, D.C., 1848–1853).

DHFFC
Linda Grant De Pauw et al., eds., *Documentary History of the First Federal Congress of the United States of America, March 4, 1789–March 3, 1791* (Baltimore, 1972–).

Early American Imprints
Charles Evans, ed., *Early American Imprints, Series I: Evans, 1639–1800* (1903–1959; rpt. New York, [1983?]–).

JAH
Journal of American History

JCC
Worthington C. Ford et al., eds., *Journals of the Continental Congress, 1774–1789,* 34 vols. (Washington, D.C., 1904–1937).

JER
Journal of the Early Republic

LDC
Paul H. Smith et al., eds., *Letters of Delegates to Congress, 1774–1789,* 26 vols. (Washington, D.C., 1976–2000).

PBF
Leonard W. Labaree et al., eds., *The Papers of Benjamin Franklin* (New Haven, Conn., 1959–).

PGW: RW
W. W. Abbot et al., eds., *The Papers of George Washington: Revolutionary War Series* (Charlottesville, Va., 1985–).

PHL
> Philip M. Hamer et al., eds., *The Papers of Henry Laurens,* 16 vols. (Columbia, S.C., 1968–2003).

PJA
> Robert J. Taylor et al., eds., *The Papers of John Adams* (Cambridge, Mass., 1977–).

PJM
> William T. Hutchinson and William M. E. Rachal et al., eds., *The Papers of James Madison,* 17 vols. (Chicago, 1962–1991).

PNG
> Richard K. Showman et al., eds., *The Papers of General Nathanael Greene,* 13 vols. (Chapel Hill, N.C., 1976–2005).

PTJ
> Julian P. Boyd et al., eds., *The Papers of Thomas Jefferson* (Princeton, N.J., 1950–).

PMHB
> *Pennsylvania Magazine of History and Biography*

Rev. Va.
> Robert L. Scribner et al., eds., *Revolutionary Virginia: The Road to Independence; A Documentary Record,* 7 vols. (Charlottesville, Va., 1973–1983).

VMHB
> *Virginia Magazine of History and Biography*

WMQ
> *William and Mary Quarterly*

NEWSPAPERS

American Gazette
> *The American Gazette: or, the Constitutional Journal* (Salem, Mass.)

American Journal
> *The American Journal and General Advertiser* (Providence, R.I.)

Boston Gazette
> *The Boston Gazette, and Country Journal*

Boston News-Letter
> *The Massachusetts Gazette; and the Boston Weekly News-Letter*

Boston Post-Boy
> *The Massachusetts Gazette, and the Boston Post-Boy and Advertiser*

Cape-Fear Mercury
> *The Cape-Fear Mercury* (Wilmington, N.C.)

Connecticut Courant
   The Connecticut Courant (Hartford)
Connecticut Gazette
   The Connecticut Gazette and the Universal Intelligencer (New London)
Connecticut Journal
   The Connecticut Journal (New Haven)
Constitutional Gazette
   The Constitutional Gazette (New York)
Continental Journal
   The Continental Journal, and Weekly Advertiser (Boston)
Dunlap's Maryland Gazette
   Dunlap's Maryland Gazette; or, the Baltimore General Advertiser
Essex Gazette
   The Essex Gazette (Salem, Mass.)
Essex Journal
   The Essex Journal and the Massachusetts and New-Hampshire General Advertiser (Newburyport, Mass.)
Freeman's Journal
   The Freeman's Journal, or New-Hampshire Gazette (Portsmouth)
Gazette, of the State of South-Carolina
   The Gazette, of the State of South-Carolina (Charleston)
Georgia Gazette
   The Georgia Gazette (Savannah)
Independent Chronicle
   The Independent Chronicle (Boston)
Maryland Gazette
   The Maryland Gazette (Annapolis)
Maryland Journal
   The Maryland Journal, and the Baltimore Advertiser
Massachusetts Gazette
   The Massachusetts Gazette, or the Springfield and Northampton Weekly Advertiser
Massachusetts Spy
   The Massachusetts Spy (Boston)
New-England Chronicle
   The New-England Chronicle: or, the Essex Gazette (Cambridge)
New-Hampshire Gazette
   The New-Hampshire Gazette, and Historical Chronicle (Portsmouth)
New Hampshire Gazette (Exeter)
   The New Hampshire Gazette, or Exeter Morning Chronicle

New-Jersey Gazette
   The New-Jersey Gazette (Trenton)
Newport Mercury
   The Newport Mercury (Rhode Island)
New-York Gazette
   The New-York Gazette; and the Weekly Mercury
New-York Gazetteer
   New-York Gazetteer, or, Northern Intelligencer (Albany)
New-York Journal
   The New-York Journal, and the General Advertiser
New York Packet
   The New York Packet
North-Carolina Gazette
   The North-Carolina Gazette (Newbern)
Norwich Packet
   The Norwich Packet (Connecticut)
Pennsylvania Chronicle
   The Pennsylvania Chronicle, and Universal Advertiser (Philadelphia)
Pennsylvania Evening Post
   The Pennsylvania Evening Post (Philadelphia)
Pennsylvania Gazette
   The Pennsylvania Gazette (Philadelphia)
Pennsylvania Journal
   The Pennsylvania Journal; and the Weekly Advertiser (Philadelphia)
Pennsylvania Ledger
   The Pennsylvania Ledger: or the Virginia, Maryland, Pennsylvania, &
   New-Jersey Weekly Advertiser (Philadelphia)
Pennsylvania Mercury
   Story & Humphreys's Pennsylvania Mercury, and Universal Advertiser
   (Philadelphia)
Pennsylvania Packet
   The Pennsylvania Packet, or the General Advertiser (Philadelphia)
Providence Gazette
   The Providence Gazette; and Country Journal (Rhode Island)
Rivington's New-York Gazetteer
   Rivington's New-York Gazetteer; or the Connecticut, New-Jersey,
   Hudson's River, and Quebec Weekly Advertiser
Royal Gazette
   The Royal Gazette (New York)

Salem Gazette
    The Salem Gazette, and General Advertiser (Salem, Mass.)
South-Carolina and American General Gazette
    The South-Carolina and American General Gazette (Charleston)
South-Carolina Gazette
    The South-Carolina Gazette (Charleston)
South-Carolina Gazette; And Country Journal
    The South-Carolina Gazette; And Country Journal (Charleston)
Virginia Gazette (Dixon & Hunter)
    The Virginia Gazette (Williamsburg; Dixon & Hunter)
Virginia Gazette (Pinkney)
    The Virginia Gazette (Williamsburg; Pinkney)
Virginia Gazette (Purdie)
    The Virginia Gazette (Williamsburg; Purdie)
Virginia Gazette (Purdie & Dixon)
    The Virginia Gazette (Williamsburg; Purdie & Dixon)
Virginia Gazette, or the Norfolk Intelligencer
    The Virginia Gazette, or the Norfolk Intelligencer (Holt)

THIRTEEN CLOCKS

INTRODUCTION

On a winter's day in 1818, an eighty-three-year-old John Adams sat down at his desk in Quincy, Massachusetts, to compose what would become one of the most important reflections on the American Revolution. He was writing to Hezekiah Niles, publisher of the prominent political magazine *Weekly Register,* and he had a great deal to say. "What do we mean by the American Revolution? Do we mean the American War?" Adams began. Clearly, the answer in his mind was: No way. "The Revolution was effected before the war commenced. The Revolution was in the minds and hearts of the people . . . *this radical change in the principles, opinions, sentiments, and affections of the people, was the real American Revolution.*" Niles and his readers needed to know that this had already happened before the shooting started.[1]

These thoughts had not just come suddenly to Adams on a dreary February day. Three years before, with a late summer sun warming his aging bones, Adams had written almost the exact same thing to Thomas Jefferson. In that letter, too, he had expressed his firm beliefs that the real revolution had been completed "in the course of fifteen years, before a drop of blood was shed at Lexington." In both letters, Adams told his correspondents, if they didn't believe him, he hoped the "young men of letters in all the States" would "undertake the laborious, but certainly interesting and amusing task, of searching and collecting all the records, pamphlets, newspapers, and even handbills" to find out just how "the temper and views of the people" were so suddenly and thoroughly changed.[2]

Adams thought this miraculous transformation was the essence of the American Revolution. "The colonies had grown up under Constitutions of government, so different, there was so great a variety of religions, they were composed of so many different nations, their customs, manners, and habits had so little resemblance, and their intercourse had been so rare, and their knowledge of each other so imperfect," he wrote to Niles, "that to unite them in the same principles in theory and the same system of action, was certainly a very difficult enterprise." "The complete accomplishment of it, in so short a time and by such simple means, was perhaps a singular example in the history of mankind. *Thirteen clocks were made to strike together—a perfection of mechanism which no artist had ever before effected.*"[3]

Adams's letter to Niles has shaped how Americans have thought about their Revolution ever since. It perfectly sums up the celebratory interpretation of the heroic American Revolution. It makes the Revolution an intellectual fight about political ideas like liberty, natural rights, and the righteousness of republican government. Those ideas were so appealing to so many people, Adams argued, that they overwhelmed every other jealousy, disagreement, and division that had been the hallmark of America's now-erased colonial history. Adams denied that the Revolution needed any violence, least of all a war: republicanism alone made those colonial clocks chime together. Those united bells announced the founding of the United States, a new hope for mankind the world over.[4]

Thirteen Clocks offers a different interpretation of the American founding. I argue patriot leaders weaponized prejudice about African Americans and Indians to unite the American colonists and hammer home the idea that the British were treacherous and dangerous enemies. Immediately after Lexington and Concord, patriot leaders seized any story they could lay their hands on that hinted British agents might be using Natives or enslaved people to put down the American rebellion. They publicized these widely in weekly newspapers, telling and retelling stories about any involvement between British military officers, royal governors, or any government agents who might be encouraging slaves to rise up against their masters or Natives to slaughter backcountry settlers. Republicanism wasn't enough to keep the thirteen colonies united in the first year of the Revolutionary War — or so patriot leaders, especially John Adams, Thomas Jefferson, George Washington, and Benjamin Franklin, actually believed in the moment. No matter what they said later on, throughout 1775 and 1776, these men spent a great deal of time, money, and effort broadcasting stories about what the Declaration referred to as "domestic insurrectionists," "merciless Indian savages," and "foreign Mercenaries" working with the king (and therefore against the "common cause") to as much of the colonial public as they could reach. Once the war began, the commitment of patriot leaders to the amplification of these particular stories reveals their conviction that this was the best way to secure American unity. Race made the thirteen clocks chime together; the consequences would last long after 1776.

Thirteen Clocks explores how the men who orchestrated the creation of the United States justified that new nation by excluding some people they thought unworthy. The so-called "founders" might have believed that all men were created equal, but they also arranged things so the United States would not belong to everyone. Believing unity to be the highest priority, they traded away equality to secure the union. From its first inception, the exclusion of African Americans and Native peoples was what allowed the states to be and stay united. Since that new republic would be one based on citizenship — a form of political belonging that acts much like a club, where the members get to decide who's included and who's not — the argument that some people didn't belong as Americans would endure after the Revolution. Whether they intended to do so or not, through the stories they sponsored, the words they used, and the statements they made, those founders buried prejudice deep in the cornerstone of the new American republic in 1776. There it remains. *Thirteen Clocks* is about how this came to be.

The thirteen mainland North American colonies had never seen themselves as having much in common with one another. Religion and economics drove them apart during the seventeenth and eighteenth centuries, creating jealousies and hard feelings. As we will see, this was actually getting worse on the eve of the Revolutionary War. When Benjamin Franklin was frustrated by the colonies' lack of sympathy for one another in 1754, as war seemed to threaten them all, he famously drew an American rattlesnake severed into several pieces to represent their disunity with the caption "join, or die." But, as Franklin came to realize, the colonies much preferred the latter, right up until shots rang out on Lexington Green.

American patriots faced an almost impossibly steep mountain in 1775. The task of making "the cause" common was rendered even more difficult by their having to make their pitch to the *American* people. On a macro level, the English colonists who lived in North America during the second half of the eighteenth century paid the lowest taxes, profited from the widest distribution of land ownership, and enjoyed the most social mobility and prosperity of any people in the western world. This made many of the free men among them touchy about losing such an advantageous position. New British policies threatened these achievements; fighting imperial interference could secure America's bright future. On a micro level, these experiences might run in the opposite direction. The farmers of Concord, Massachusetts, felt embattled years before they exchanged musket fire with British redcoats. They saw their farms becoming less productive and watched their children leave for new frontiers. They worried that their best days were long gone. These New Englanders thought about the imperial crisis differently: fighting British interference might regenerate their failing society, restore the good old days, and put a stop to all this troubling change. Some embraced the idea of revolution as a leap forward; others wanted it to be a turn back. Protecting the future or renewing a glorious past may be why many colonists rallied to the patriot cause, but in no way could their commitment be taken for granted, certainly not after the bullets began to fly. We must remember how high the stakes were for everyone involved. Many settlers had a lot to lose by participating in something that had never been done before: the largest-scale colonial rebellion in human history. There were plenty of reasons for plenty of people not to take these risks.[5]

Moreover, Americans had to take up arms against their cultural cousins, the very people most of them modeled their lives on. To fight the powerful British army and navy, patriot leaders had to convince the colonial public that the people whose books, clothes, dinner tables, parlors, gardens, faiths, language, and art they emulated and shared were actually foreigners — that British culture was not their culture. In order to make the cause common, patriot political leaders had to destroy any feelings of British nationalism in colonists' hearts and minds. Only then could the seeds of American patriotism grow. When abstract political ideas and keywords came into play — such as "liberty," "rights," and "representation" — patriots had to make an airtight case that American definitions of those words were better than British ones. They had to hold the high ground: that their movement was one led by freedom fighters, true defenders of the ancient British inheritance of representative government and human liberty. Their enemies were going to call them bad names, such as "rebels," "traitors," and "insurrectionists," so they had to convince enough of the American public that they were none of those things. It was the British, in truth, who were trying to not only destroy but enslave them.

John Adams would long after say these were the years that mattered the most: from the early 1760s to 1775. During this period, as Parliament passed more and more legislation regulating and taxing American commerce, patriot writers and political leaders framed their resistance in terms of masculine, virtuous, selfless action. Good patriots would reject these attempts to take away their rights through what they argued were perfectly lawful campaigns. They organized petition drives and sponsored boycotts of British consumer goods. They started new political clubs and gave them unassailable names such as the Sons of Liberty or committees of correspondence. Good patriots, their leaders argued, would recognize tyranny on the horizon and take proper steps to defend their rights and their families.

At bottom, these resistance campaigns were fights over constitutional questions that arose out of ideological reconsiderations about what representation and consent really meant. How did the colonies fit into the political structure of the British Empire? Patriots labored to argue this had nothing to do with tea or stamps: the transcendent issue was their legal standing in the empire. This was not, as British critics alleged, just a way to dodge the tax collector. There was yet another reason patriot leaders kept focus on the constitutional argument in the 1760s and 1770s: the imperial crisis was also a period of disturbing conflicts inside several colonies and between others, amid a rising chorus of antislavery. As we will see, underneath patriot leaders' feet lay fault lines that might just swallow them up if they didn't make their arguments carefully.

Print, therefore, would be essential to their success. In his 1818 letter to Niles, Adams suggested researchers needed to get their hands covered in ink by scouring printed items — pamphlets, handbills, and newspapers — if they wanted to find out what had really happened. Printer's ink was indeed the Revolution's lifeblood; it, too, carried essential nutrients of the rebellion, traveled along paths leading out from core to peripheries, and kept vital organs alive. There was no common cause without print. Whether colonists gathered in assembly houses or taverns or on city streets to protest imperial reforms, their victory depended on ink. Had British authorities done a better job in recognizing print's function and used tourniquets to shut off the supply of print in their locales, perhaps the resistance movement might have suffered a sudden death. Adams was right about that: we cannot understand the American Revolution without print.

The most advanced method of communication of the eighteenth century, newspapers were the patriots' best chance to make the cause common. Ever since another patriot leader observed in 1789 that, "in establishing American independence, the pen and the press had merit equal to that of the sword," newspapers have been acknowledged as critical to the patriots' mobilization campaign. The colonial press had expanded greatly in the mid-1700s, thanks in part to both the Great Awakening and the Seven Years' War. The number of prints published in English had doubled in the decade before the Stamp Act, and they would increase by more than 250 percent over the next ten years. The years of the "imperial crisis" (1763–1775) saw the founding of a dozen papers, with printers themselves taking increasingly more partisan stands either for or against the emerging resistance movement.[6]

As the former printer of the *Pennsylvania Gazette,* Benjamin Franklin grasped perfectly newspapers' essential role in clarifying such a messy, confusing affair as a civil war or colonial rebellion. "By the press we can speak to Nations," Franklin wrote a friend in 1782. Thanks to newspapers, he concluded, political leaders like himself (or Adams or Jefferson) could not only "strike while the Iron is hot" but also stoke fires by "continual Striking." The bundles of newspapers distributed throughout American cities and the countryside had the capacity to serve as potent instruments of mobilization. They connected people, organizations, and ideas and helped build trust among fellow colonists who were not only strangers but often suspicious ones.[7]

This was the scene in the spring of 1775: the patriots claimed the constitutional high ground and had made their pitch to as many colonists as they could, especially through print. They had convened a Continental Congress and established a sweeping boycott of all British goods. It was the climax of the first phase of the Revolutionary conflict.

Then came what Ralph Waldo Emerson would later call the "shot heard round the world." With the battles of Lexington and Concord, the American Revolution underwent a fundamental transformation. Now, a war with the powerful British state loomed over the thirteen colonies. As the stakes rose, the pressure on the common cause appeal increased exponentially, too. British redcoats and warships threatened the patriots' very survival, not just politically but personally. Everything depended on the colonies' sticking together. When the American Revolution became the Revolutionary War, it evolved into something different than abstract ideas about political ideology. The colonists didn't know it, but they were on the cusp of a grueling, wrenching experience. As it turned out, the Revolutionary War's eight bloody years would become one of the longest wars in American history. The war transformed the American Revolution. It was not just an outgrowth or aftereffect of the constitutional crisis; rather, it changed everything.

It stands to reason that patriot leaders' intentions underwent a profound change, too. Their explanations why Americans should resist became much darker — and much less concerned with consent or representation. In 1775, the common cause appeal all but stopped being about rights. Instead, patriot leaders started talking a lot about Native and enslaved people.

This abrupt turn — from arguments about constitutions to warnings about Indians and the enslaved — was in part because British agents in the colonies tried their best to put out the fires of rebellion by any means available to them. Remember that Parliament's reason for trying to reform the empire was to have colonists share the financial burden of the now-massive British realm. If a royal governor or naval captain could figure out a way to bring an end to this potentially crippling rebellion before the cash-strapped crown had to incur the astounding costs of recruiting, training, and equipping an army, then transporting it across the ocean, that imperial officer would receive endless adulation in Britain. The rewards one stood to gain — statues, parades, honors, the king's lucrative gratitude — surely danced through the minds of many.

From that perspective, Native and enslaved peoples might well play roles as allies in the growing conflict. Army and navy officers, royal governors, Indian superintendents, and other imperial officials all over America made plans and wrote home asking permission to engage Native peoples and / or emancipate and arm enslaved people to help in putting down the rebellion. This was the lever that stood, many believed, the best chance to bring a sudden halt to this unwelcome civil war.

That particular lever wasn't without its hazards. Patriot political leaders and publicists seized on the tactic immediately, using it to galvanize support. For them, Britain's embrace of Native and enslaved people presented a golden opportunity, a way to solve several difficult political problems all at once. First, it was something they truly had in common. Fear of Indian massacres and slave rebellions had been a staple of colonial nightmares for generations. Colonists all over North America had these terrors in common even more than they shared a British identity. Second, it was not controversial. Stories about British plans to "excite" Native peoples or "tamper" on slave plantations stayed far away from nettlesome grievances in particular colonies that might foster jealousies between them. Finally, it was the perfect way to destroy public faith in their cultural cousins. If British officials were willing to inflict upon the colonists the most terrifying things imaginable, then the colonists could not possibly turn away from or settle this rebellion. There could be no compromise. These were the actions of bitter enemies, not of people who aspired to the return of peaceful relations. So, when imperial officials got anywhere near that lever, patriot political leaders and publicists howled with shock and betrayal — but they did so with a glint in their eyes, for they knew this was the best way to build a new wartime common cause.

Howl, they did. As we will see, starting a few weeks after the battles at Lexington and Concord, patriot publicists and political leaders put any evidence of British plans to arm Native and enslaved people before as many colonial readers as they could reach — again, especially through print. Nearly every week, colonial newspapers began to report stories of rumored or actual slave insurrections and worrisome signs coming from the backcountry.

These stories had added power because they were not concoctions. Most of them had some basis in truth. Thousands of African Americans and Native peoples were, indeed, paying close attention to the dissolution of the British Empire in America. Many took action. Thousands of African Americans, free and enslaved, saw war with Britain as an opportunity to challenge the legal, social, or economic obstacles that bound their lives. They made the Revolutionary War the largest slave rebellion in America until the Civil

War. Native peoples across the trans-Appalachian backcountry greeted the imperial conflict in a similar fashion, often by playing the two sides against one another in a complex diplomatic game. Thousands of Natives tried to improve their situation by aiding the Americans, allying with the crown, or trying to stay neutral — or a combination of all three.

The stories patriot leaders told about these strategies described enslaved and Native peoples — without explicitly calling them so — as George III's proxies. A proxy is someone who acts on another's behalf. In a way, this wasn't a change from how the patriot leadership had justified their resistance to imperial reform starting in the 1760s. Their constitutional argument had always been about the issue of proxies: how would the American colonies be represented in the empire? "No taxation without proxies" doesn't have the same ring to it as "no taxation without representation," but the meaning is the same. When the American Revolution transformed into the Revolutionary War, the centrality of proxies did not disappear. It, too, transformed. Now the patriot leadership told stories about what soldiers who fought on the king's account might do to the American public. Substitutes (not in red coats) who might aid the crown, whether they came from the slave quarter, Indian country, or Europe, were almost constantly on the minds — and in the news — of patriot political and publicist leaders.

Thirteen Clocks is about how these stories made America independent. Benjamin Franklin — the man who, twenty years earlier, had bemoaned that his countrymen would rather die than join — wrote a few weeks into the war, "Britain has found means to unite us." He meant that the news of bloodshed in Massachusetts had "extinguish'd" any differences among patriot leaders. But, beginning in the summer of 1775, war stories that he helped spread about rebellious slaves, hostile Natives, and threatening foreign mercenaries produced a similar effect on enough of the colonial population to sustain unity throughout the mainland. Patriots first referred to themselves as the "united colonies." A year later, they renamed themselves the United States of America. As the delegates to the Continental Congress put it in the Declaration of Independence, they had become "Free and Independent States" who had "full Power to levy War, conclude Peace, contract Alliances, establish Commerce, and to do all other Acts and Things which Independent States may of right do." These were the tolls of the thirteen colonial clocks ringing as one.[8]

Those united clocks did not wind themselves, however. Adams later referred to this "perfection of mechanism" as the work of an "artist," which was probably a reference to God. But he knew who those artists really were.

Adams and his colleagues, especially Franklin, Jefferson, and Washington, calibrated those clocks. They watched and listened intently and tried to keep them all ticking. They had thousands of partners in this effort, including members of local and provincial committees, militia officers, Continental army soldiers, and, perhaps most critically, the several dozen people who produced and distributed colonial newspapers.

The internal mechanisms of those clocks were extraordinarily complicated. Some of the ticking parts were Enlightenment ideas about natural rights, some were republican ideas distilled from eighteenth-century British politics and literature, some came from the Puritan past or the ancient world. Other gears weren't molded from books, at all. Some were forged by economics, by issues involving land, labor, or opportunity. The reasons millions of Americans in New York or Maryland or South Carolina or Pennsylvania reached individual decisions about whether to support or oppose the Revolution — or do both, or do neither, or go back and forth — are too many for any historian to fully grasp.

But we have been unable — or unwilling — to see one of the most prominent gears that lay at the center of each clock's mechanism. It has been hiding in plain sight. Americans' prejudices about enslaved and Native peoples were also part of why colonists participated in the Revolution. Patriot leaders did not create these prejudices — the bundle of ideas that would coalesce into a system of thought called "race" in the years after the Revolution — but they did employ them to cement the American union starting in 1775. As we will see, they told the colonial public again and again, in the months leading up to independence, that they must oppose British efforts to "tamper" on slave plantations or "excite" Natives to make war in the American backcountry. They spent time and money broadcasting stories about enemies who did not wear red coats — including the looming threat of foreign mercenaries — week after week after week in the fifteen months between Lexington and independence.

Those leaders featured the king's proxies in every official patriot statement of purpose, from the Declaration of the Causes and Necessity of Taking up Arms to the Declaration of Independence one year later. In fact, the issue of proxy enemies is the only explanation for why those leaders felt compelled to take the fateful step of declaring American independence in the summer of 1776. Ship captains crossing the Atlantic spotted thousands of German troops standing on British transport ships headed to New York in May. As soon as these captains landed and related such important information, the process of independence began. Reports of the Hessians' imminent arrival comprised the final twist; at that moment, the thirteen clocks were wound. It was the news of proxy enemies that brought the colonies to the edge of independence.

A central theme of *Thirteen Clocks* is contingency. Nothing about the start of the Revolutionary War was inevitable. For a long time, no one understood that it actually *was* the start of "the Revolutionary War." The battles at Lexington and Concord could have easily been the first — and only — fighting in a colonial rebellion that elements of the British army squashed and ended with the arrest and execution of a few malcontents from Boston. We know how things turned out, but they could not have known. It was not inevitable that the Revolution would become what it did: a continental effort that would throw away monarchy and establish an extended republic based on the universal rights of citizens.

The incredible story of those fifteen months deserves our close attention. We have grown too satisfied with certain scenes from 1775–1776. They have become our founding legends: Paul Revere's frantic ride through the Massachusetts countryside; the heroic minutemen who responded to the call and lined up on Lexington Green and at the Concord Bridge ready for sacrifice; colonial farmers waiting until they saw the whites of British soldiers' eyes before blasting away on Bunker Hill; George Washington hurrying north to take command of a Continental army; Americans sitting in taverns or parlors racing through the pages of Tom Paine's pamphlet *Common Sense;* the stirring, unanimous vote to declare independence; John Adams and Benjamin Franklin convincing Thomas Jefferson to write the Declaration of Independence; and John Hancock scratching his enormous signature across the bottom of it. It is a story of men (almost exclusively men) making heroic acts and writing heroic words.

There is much more to the story. We need to break out of the confines of this founding mythology and restore a fresh sense of contingency to see the desperation, panic, and anxiety of those confounding days, weeks, and months. We will find these same people performing less heroic feats and writing less heroic words. Since patriot leaders could not know what news the next express rider might deliver, let alone how things would turn out, they grabbed hold of the safest, most secure tactics they could find and clung to them for dear life. This flotsam and jetsam was composed of colonial Americans' prejudices about enslaved and Native peoples. But patriots did more than just grasp onto those ideas; they crafted them into durable narratives that drove the American Revolution forward. They turned stories about British officers' working with proxy enemies into compelling reasons for American independence. They did not have to do so. We should examine why they did and consider what that choice means for us.

In the climax of the Declaration of Independence, Jefferson referred to those proxies as "merciless Indian savages," "foreign Mercenaries," and "domestic insurrectionists." We need to understand how that language got into the Declaration, what its appearance there meant, and how it competed with other words in that document—especially the statements about life, liberty, happiness, and equality. Focusing on only the opening paragraphs of the Declaration has left us with an incomplete understanding of the founding. We need to come to terms with the Declaration's final grievance to understand what the Continental Congress meant in 1776 by *"we"* when they said, "We hold these truths to be self-evident." That expression did not include everyone then, and it has not done so yet. *Thirteen Clocks* explores the contingent story of how that sense of exclusion—some people belong in America and some people don't—occurred at the birth of the United States.

Finally, a word on race. The reader should notice that I avoid using the word "race" in the text of *Thirteen Clocks* but employ words like "prejudices," "stereotypes," or "attitudes." The system of thought that would develop in the nineteenth century as "race" or "racism" was under construction during the Revolutionary period. Historians differ on whether they believe that racism caused millions of Africans to be enslaved throughout the Atlantic world or whether the economic desire for unfree labor necessitated a legal and cultural justification that, in turn, created race and racism. Some scholars have recently identified the eighteenth century as the starting point for racialized thinking about Natives' being seen (and seeing themselves) as "red." The decades before the American Revolution were a gestation period for ideologies about race that, by the early 1800s, would be thought of as conventional wisdom—or "natural." In those decades, nearly all colonists who came to America from Europe in the eighteenth century arrived with, grew up with, or learned attitudes and prejudices about Native and enslaved peoples, much of it suspicious and negative.

By the last quarter of the eighteenth century, therefore, the interpretation that race was a biological construct, with skin color predicting and determining all sorts of human attributes, was well under way. Political change gave it its final push. Republican revolutions in America and France—and, especially, the massive uprising of enslaved peoples in Haiti—ironically helped bring this biological explanation of race to the surface in much of the western world. We have traditionally given the founders a pass on this, citing those opening phrases of the Declaration and the abolition of slavery throughout the North as evidence that the Revolution in America either tried to derail the oncoming train of racism or, at the very least, slowed it down. *Thirteen Clocks* shows, instead, how the American Revolution and the founding of the United States contributed to the institutionalization of modern racism. American independence did not slow that train; it accelerated it.

The events recounted in this book would drive those arguments forward in the American context, but in 1775 and 1776, most people still believed that one's behavior (not skin color) determined whether one could be eligible for inclusion in society or the body politic. As the book's subtitle indicates, readers in the twenty-first century can understand that race could make America independent, but patriot leaders would not have conceived of the situation in precisely those terms. During the early nineteenth century, around the time an elderly John Adams wrote his influential letters to Hezekiah Niles and Thomas Jefferson (reflections that erased this darker side of the common cause appeal from the movement for independence), "race" as we might distinguish it — with "Black" and "red" people judged reflexively as inferior and "white" people assumed as superior — was a recognizable construct. In 1775, however, that hadn't happened yet. *Thirteen Clocks* argues that Adams and Jefferson contributed — whether unintentionally or unwittingly — to the creation of, indeed, the Americanization of, modern racism and white supremacy. But they didn't have to. This is why the reader must always remember the importance of contingency: things did not have to turn out this way.

CHAPTER 1

NEWSPAPERS *on the* Eve of the
REVOLUTIONARY WAR

Bostonians were on edge at the end of 1767, for more reason than the onset of yet another bitter New England winter. The Townshend Duties, Parliament's second attempt at asserting its authority to tax the American colonies, had just gone into effect, and the Sons of Liberty were having a hard time convincing Bostonians to fight it with all their might. They wanted merchants to adopt a sweeping nonimportation boycott, but they were struggling to find support. Samuel Adams, James Otis, John Hancock, and their fellow patriot leaders were on the defensive.

So, when printers John Mein and John Fleeming brought out the premier issue of the *Boston Chronicle* on December 21, patriot leaders could not afford for it to be hostile to their sputtering resistance movement. When they saw that page one included an article from an English paper attacking William Pitt, they knew it spelled trouble. Pitt was a hero of the Sons of Liberty, and this was powerful evidence that the *Chronicle* was not going to be friendly to their political point of view.

Three weeks later, Otis and Adams responded in the *Boston Gazette,* the most radical patriot paper in Boston (and in America). *Gazette* printers Benjamin Edes and John Gill counted themselves as integral members of the patriot leadership, with Edes playing an active role in the Sons. The January 18, 1768, *Gazette* featured a provocative essay written by "Americus" that defended Pitt and heaped abuse on the *Chronicle*. Mein (pronounced "mean") did not take this criticism lightly.[1]

He burst into the *Gazette*'s shop on Queen Street, demanding to know who "Americus" was. Edes retorted that Mein, as a fellow printer, ought to know he would never reveal his sources. This did nothing to calm Mein down; the *Chronicle* printer returned that, if Edes wouldn't name names, he must be "Americus," and Mein threatened to do him harm. When Edes again refused, Mein stormed out. The next morning, as Edes arrived at work, he found Mein already skulking at the door, still seeking justice for the perceived slander against him and his paper. Edes again refused to divulge his sources; Mein came back again that evening and took his frustration out on the more diminutive John Gill by thrashing him in the street with a cane. Sam Adams, writing as "Populus" in the *Gazette,* would soon refer to the attack on Gill as a "Spaniard-like Attempt" to restrict the freedom of the press.[2]

This was only the start of John Mein's combat with Boston patriots. Gill would sue Mein for damages, and, represented by John Adams, he forced Mein to pay a substantial fine for his violent outburst. During the year that Adams prepared for *Gill v. Mein,* political tensions in Boston went from bad to worse. Sporadic violence against imperial officials convinced the crown to send troops to occupy the city. In October 1768, twelve hundred British redcoats tramped up the Long Wharf and set up their tents on Boston Common, a block away from John Mein's print shop on Newbury Street. This escalation convinced the city's merchants that the Sons of Liberty were right: they should boycott all British imports for the entirety of 1769.[3]

Rather, it convinced some merchants. By the summer, there were more British goods on store shelves than there should have been. This was suspicious. Someone was breaking the boycott. Boston patriots began interviewing merchants and printed a handbill that admitted 6 of the 211 merchants had not been properly attentive to the boycott. John Mein blew his stack. This was a cover-up. He had information that 190 of the 211 merchants were violating the nonimportation agreement, and he boasted he would prove that Boston's patriots were liars and hypocrites. For the rest of the summer of 1769, Mein and his partner Fleeming splashed dozens of ships' manifests across the front pages of the *Chronicle,* giving documented evidence that patriots like John Hancock were not to be trusted.

This affront made the *Chronicle* printers marked men, and they knew it. As the summer faded, Mein and Fleeming stuffed pistols in their pockets everywhere they went. By October, the city's town meeting condemned Mein as an enemy of his country. In early November, a large crowd confronted the printers on King Street, and a fight broke out. In the scuffle, while Mein was getting roughed up, Fleeming managed to draw his gun and pull the trigger. Luckily, he did not hit anyone, and the printers fled to hide out in the shelter of a British guardhouse. When Lieutenant Governor Thomas Hutchinson refused to come to Mein's aid, Mein decided he wasn't safe in Boston anymore. In the middle of November, he sneaked aboard a ship bound for England. The feisty, confrontational loyalist printer was gone forever.[4]

John Mein's clash with Boston patriots tells us several important things about newspapers and the American Revolution. First, it illustrates the increasing politicization of colonial newspapers in the 1760s. Earlier in the eighteenth century, printers in England and America boasted that "freedom of the press" meant their pages were open to all points of view. The Stamp Act changed all that. In 1765, Parliament placed a tax on paper in the colonies. Anyone who wanted to print anything on paper, from playing cards to legal documents, had to do so on sheets that bore the king's stamp. Newspapers were right in the center of the controversy. The Stamp Act did more than politicize paper; the subsequent storm that the hated tax touched off also transformed what a "free press" meant. Newspapers in America became more overtly partisan, most siding with the infant patriot movement, and they also became progressively more polarized. Over the decade between the Stamp Act and the outbreak of the Revolutionary War, any printers who tried to maintain a neutral or moderate stance on the imperial crisis failed. In every city, not just Boston, newspapers took sides either for or against the burgeoning patriot resistance movement. A "free press" was becoming one that claimed it was free from political pressure or force, not one that was open to both sides of this imperial debate.

The Mein episode reveals one important reason for the increasingly intense politicization: printers were becoming political actors themselves. Because publishing a newspaper by itself wasn't the most lucrative business in the colonial marketplace, all printers angled to have the governor appoint them official printer of the colony's laws and dollar bills. This was where the money was. In fact, it was the appointment to this position that eventually allowed Benjamin Franklin to retire from printing and enter politics. Printers, therefore, had long watched for sudden shifts in colonial politics. At the outset of the imperial crisis, many began to play leading roles in the resistance.

Benjamin Edes was not the only printer who joined the Sons of Liberty. Several other leading printers were also members of their local branches of the Sons: *Pennsylvania Journal* printer William Bradford in Philadelphia and *Providence Gazette* printer William Goddard, to name two. In 1766, when debts forced John Holt to stop operation of his *New-York Gazette; or, the Weekly Post-Boy,* the New York City Sons of Liberty helped him secure new equipment and start a new paper, the *New-York Journal.* Like the *Boston Gazette,* the *New-York Journal* would become one of the most important patriot papers in America.

If printers were becoming patriots, Mein's clash also shows how patriot leaders were acting like printers, too. Mein was right to suspect that "Americus" was James Otis. Patriot leaders throughout the colonies understood how important print was to the success of their political efforts, and they made print shops sites of revolution. If we revisit those two shops on Boston's Newbury and Queen Streets in the late summer of 1769, we find Mein and Fleeming working hard at the *Chronicle*'s press, publishing their run of fifty-five ship manifests and customs records to undermine the public's confidence in nonimportation. They printed four thousand copies of the lists and sent them gratis all over North America. On the first Saturday of September, John Adams detailed in his diary how he, his cousin Sam, James Otis, and the *Boston Gazette* printers responded to the *Chronicle*'s assault. They passed long hours working in the *Gazette* print shop: "The evening [was] spent in preparing for the Next Days Newspaper. A curious Employment. Cooking up Paragraphs, Articles, Occurrences etc. — working the political Engine!" Adams gives us a remarkable glimpse into the interconnectedness of political leaders and printers in the American Revolution. This was a symbiotic process; printers and political leaders needed one another.[5]

What did John Adams mean, exactly, by the phrase "cooking up"? Was this "fake news"? Perhaps. That term, one of the present day, has a pejorative connotation. But that should not keep us from seeing what the Adamses were doing in the *Gazette* offices that evening. They were manipulating the news. They would contend that they did so for serious reasons and that John Mein was a dangerous threat. According to one historian, Mein's "cleverness, courage, resourcefulness, and journalistic skill made the task of silencing him both necessary and difficult." His elimination was critical. If it took doctoring — or even fabricating — items in the newspaper to destroy the public's confidence in Mein and his lists, they showed few qualms about doing so.[6]

"Cooking up" could mean many different things. One option would be to pen a scathing essay (today it would be called an op-ed) under a pseudonym. Doing so under the protection of a false name offered writers several advantages. They often adopted disguises from ancient Rome or Greece that allowed them to appear as public defenders (such as "Populus") or ancient guardians of liberty or virtue (such as "Nestor" or "Cato"). Pseudonyms enabled them to deny authorship and maintain their ability to say that they would never get down in the political muck. Anonymity also increased the printer's social and political power. Only Edes and Gill knew the identity of "Americus," as John Mein found out the hard way. Printers were secret keepers. And by managing secrets well, they gained credibility with political leaders. Trust was a critical element in this burgeoning, fragile political movement.

But "cooking up" might not only include what we would call opinion items. The front page of the *Boston Gazette* that Otis and the Adamses helped to "cook up" did not feature an extended opinion essay but petitions and excerpts from English newspapers. The back page was full of notices of runaway servants and apprentices, as well as items for sale (not from Britain!), including Madeira wine, choice chocolate, and, jarringly, a "Likely Negro Girl," for which interested buyers should "Inquire of Edes and Gill." The printers were the keepers of many secrets. None of these things, however, seems to qualify for Adams's notion of "cooking up." Inside the *Gazette* was a different matter. Readers found an assortment of private letters, closely crafted "news" about Lieutenant Governor Hutchinson's recent importation of tea, and poems attacking Governor Francis Bernard. All of these items constituted the fare that patriots scrupulously prepared the evening before. Were they accurate? They appeared in the *Gazette* as bare-bones facts and allegedly reliable accounts. Nonetheless, we should be wary. Adams wrote that he cooked up all sorts of dishes: "Paragraphs, Articles, Occurrences etc." The deep and thorough interaction and mutual dependency between patriot leaders and printers meant that even these benign items we would judge as facts—as "news"—could be unreliable.[7]

The Mein episode reveals one final, crucial thing about the patriots' resistance movement: it was fragile and did not convince everyone all the time. Even in Boston. Men who had a platform like John Mein were real threats. They needed to be silenced or discredited. Trust was an essential commodity that had to be continually monitored; even in the most radical place in America, it was a resource that could not be taken for granted. The Adams cousins tried to maintain public opinion via the pages of Edes and Gill's *Boston Gazette,* but if that didn't work, crowds could drive the point home with force or threats of force. Physical violence lurks all around the verbal sparring between the *Boston Chronicle* and the *Boston Gazette.*

The fragility of the patriots' cause was even more evident when they thought about how their movement might be received outside Boston. How might colonists far away perceive their actions? How dependable were people who called themselves friends in Pennsylvania, Virginia, or South Carolina? How powerful were their enemies? Did every colony have its own John Mein? As the stakes of the resistance movement increased, they realized their partnership with printers would have to be rock-solid in order to secure the essential resource of public trust. There were going to be a lot of late nights in the print shop to make the cause common.

Thanks to the ten years of protest known as the imperial crisis, when the shooting started, patriots enjoyed almost a monopoly on print throughout the thirteen mainland American colonies. Thirty-three American newspapers printed the news of the battles at Lexington and Concord. Twenty-nine papers would carry the news of independence fifteen months later. Ordinary calamities (fire and health) and extraordinary ones (war and politics) would close down several shops over those frantic months, while four new ventures started. Nearly all of these papers were pro-patriot.

One-third of America's newspapers in 1775 were printed in New England. None of the newspapers in Boston that supported the crown survived the beginning of the war. The most pro-patriot printers, Isaiah Thomas of the *Massachusetts Spy* and Edes and Gill of the *Boston Gazette*, sneaked their presses out of Boston just before British troops occupied the city's streets in April. There was more upheaval in Massachusetts, with one Salem paper, now called the *New-England Chronicle*, relocating closer to the scene of action to join the growing army camp in Cambridge. There were eight other newspapers in New England outside of Massachusetts: the *Providence Gazette* and the *Newport Mercury* in Rhode Island; the *New-Hampshire Gazette* and the *Freeman's Journal* (both Portsmouth) in New Hampshire; and the *Connecticut Courant* (Hartford), *Gazette* (New London), *Journal* (New Haven), and *Norwich Packet*. All of these leaned toward the patriot cause.

Papers in the mid-Atlantic colonies were located only in Philadelphia or New York City during the first year of the Revolution. Philadelphia had a robust print market. Three of its papers rivaled the *Boston Gazette* for the most staunch patriot papers in the colonies: John Dunlap's *Pennsylvania Packet*, William and Thomas Bradford's *Pennsylvania Journal*, and David Hall and William Sellers's *Pennsylvania Gazette*. The Continental Congress would turn to these printers most often when they wanted stories to reach the broader American public. Benjamin Towne's *Pennsylvania Evening Post* was the most unusual of colonial newspapers in 1775, in that it appeared three days a week, on Tuesdays, Thursdays, and Saturdays.

Three newspapers in New York City published the news of the start of war. One was *Rivington's New-York Gazetteer*, published by the infamous loyalist James Rivington. He was even more talented and dangerous than John Mein. Rivington's reputation for publishing items hostile to the rebellion was so notorious that patriot authorities in one community voted to burn every copy that came into the town. Inhabitants in another village hanged him in effigy. In March 1775, a young, snarling James Madison wrote to William Bradford, Jr. (brother and son to the *Pennsylvania Journal* printers), that he wished Rivington would spend just twenty-four hours in

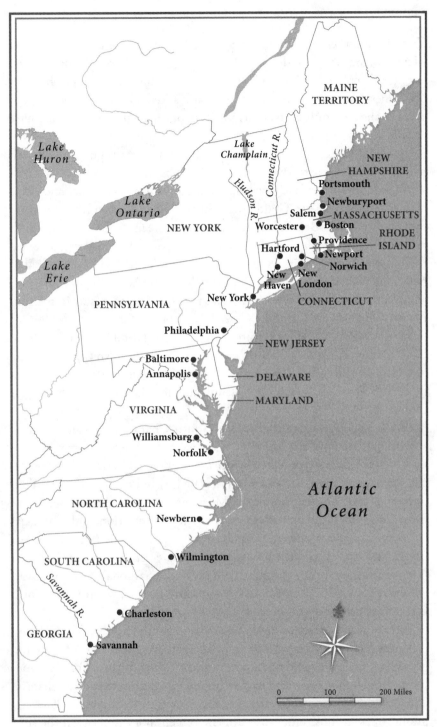

MAP 1. *Places of Newspaper Publication, 1775–1776. Drawn by Gerry Krieg*

Virginia, and then he "would meet with adequate punishment." Like John Mein, violence would indeed cut Rivington's career short. Before 1775 was out, hostile crowds had invaded his shop, stolen his press, and put him out of business. Patriots far preferred John Holt's *New-York Journal,* long sponsored by the Sons of Liberty. Two more patriot papers started over the course of 1775 and 1776 in New York City.[8]

Until the 1770s, the only newspaper in Maryland was published in Annapolis. The growing town of Baltimore soon boasted two new papers, William Goddard's *Maryland Journal, and the Baltimore Advertiser* and *Dunlap's Maryland Gazette.* Goddard's politics took him away from his print shop so often that he put his sister Mary Katherine in charge. It was as much her paper as his. In Virginia, there were four separate newspapers, all named the *Virginia Gazette.* (Since the law stipulated that the financial windfall of becoming the colony's official printer would go only to the *Virginia Gazette,* all printers confusingly gave their paper that same name to stay in the running.) Williamsburg had three *Gazettes:* one printed by Alexander Purdie, one by John Pinkney, and the third by the team of John Dixon and William Hunter. In Norfolk, John Hunter Holt brought out his own *Gazette,* which, as we will see, brought on the wrath of Virginia's royal governor, Lord Dunmore. All of these papers in Maryland and Virginia supported the patriot cause.

As the principal seaport in the Deep South, Charleston was also a central spot for colonial printing. In 1775, there were three newspapers published in the city, led by Peter Timothy's *South-Carolina Gazette.* Timothy was the southern version of Benjamin Edes; he boasted to Benjamin Franklin in 1777 that he was "continually in Motion from Congress to Committee, from Committee to Council, from Council to Inspection, and so on." As for the rest of the South, few copies remain intact of the two newspapers printed in North Carolina, the *North-Carolina Gazette* (Newbern) and the *Cape-Fear Mercury* (Wilmington), and the one in Savannah, Georgia *(Georgia Gazette).* The *Georgia Gazette* stayed fairly neutral, whereas the North Carolina papers were pro-patriot.[9]

Patriots thus controlled nearly all the news for the first year of the Revolutionary War, and that monopoly was heavily weighted toward New England. This control would not last forever: British occupations of New York City, Philadelphia, Newport, Savannah, and Charleston would eliminate or, at best, disrupt patriot networks and facilitate the establishment of several loyalist ones in those cities. But, for the fifteen months between the start of the war and the Declaration of Independence, patriots could count on reaching as wide an audience as they ever had enjoyed, or ever would. The political engines hummed along then as smoothly as they were ever going to during the long Revolutionary struggle.

We have seen how printing and the concept of a "free press" had shifted as a result of the turbulent politics of the imperial crisis. Now let us look closely at what a newspaper in colonial America was in 1775. What did it look like? How was it made?

A typical weekly newspaper in colonial America was one single sheet of paper folded in half to make four printed pages. The paper's design was a result of the mechanical production of each week's issue. Put more simply, since the ink had to dry on one side of the sheet before the printers could use the other, the outer side wasn't really "news." Printers filled what would become the front and back pages with items that they could prepare ahead of time or ran for multiple weeks. Each word had to be assembled (or "composed") by the printers and their assistants one letter at a time, in reverse. This meant thousands of arduous reaches into upper and lower cases to grab letters to slide into place (types used the most often were kept in the lower cases; the others, like capital letters, in harder-to-reach places — thus the origin of "upper case" and "lower case" letters).

Colonial printers composed the front and back pages of newspapers during the beginning of their workweek. For the back page, where the advertisements normally appeared, they would arrange whatever already-assembled sticks of type they could hold over from the last week's issue and fill out whatever new material would be needed to complete the page. The same time schedule went for the front page. Unlike today, little "news" actually appeared there; there was no such thing as putting the most important news on the front page. Because printers had to complete it first, normally the material that filled the three columns on the front page consisted of content pulled out of a magazine or periodical from England or news from London and the European continent that was already approximately two months old. Even John Adams's "cooked-up" *Boston Gazette* featured older English news on the front. Another option for the outer sheet was an essay. As the imperial crisis deepened in the 1770s, printers placed argumentative essays on contentious political or constitutional issues by writers like "Populus" or "Americus" here. If those essays or items of European news ran longer than the three columns on the front page, often they would continue on the back with the ads. Thus half of the work of assembling the weekly paper would be complete.

Imagine that the archetypal colonial newspaper comes out every Wednesday, as the *Massachusetts Spy* did in Boston, the *Pennsylvania Gazette* in Philadelphia, and the *Georgia Gazette* in Savannah. As soon as bundles of

SEPTEMBER 1, 1775.　　THE　　NUMBER 31.

VIRGINIA  GAZETTE.

Always for LIBERTY,　　AND THE PUBLICK GOOD.

ALEXANDER PURDIE, Printer.

At a meeting of the COMMITTEE of SAFETY, in the town of *Richmond*, the 26th day of *August*, 1775.

Ordered, THAT the chairmen of the several committees in this colony do deliver the publick arms, to be by them collected, pursuant to an ordinance of Convention, to the captains who shall be appointed to command the companies of regular troops to be raised from their respective districts, taking their receipts for the same; and that the said captains take proper measures for their safe conveyance to the place of rendezvous. And it is farther ordered, that the said chairmen do respectively correspond with the President of this committee, informing him of their progress in the minute service, and when they shall have completed each the number of regulars required from their respective districts.

(a copy)
JOHN PENDLETON, jun. clerk.

AUGUST 26, 1775.

THE COMMITTEE of SAFETY, at a meeting appointed at *Hanover* town on the 18th of next month, intend to proceed to the choice of all officers within their appointment, particularly a *comissary* of *provisions*, or *contractors* for each of the regiments to be raised pursuant to an ordinance of Convention, previous to which all persons inclined to contract, or to be appointed *commissary*, are desired to send their proposals, in writing, to EDMUND PENDLETON, esq; President of the committee, enclosed and sealed. At the same time, the committee will be ready to deliver the commissions, and administer the oaths, to the field-officers of the regulars chosen by the Convention; and all captains and subalterns, who may be chosen by the district committees, are also to attend, to receive warrants for the money necessary in recruiting, and their instructions.

By order of the committee.
JOHN PENDLETON, jun. clerk.

CAMBRIDGE, *August* 3.

SOME very late intelligence hath been received at head-quarters this week from Canada, the substance of which is, that the Canadians and Indians cannot be persuaded by governour *Carleton* to join his forces, but are determined to remain neuter; that there are but 500 regulars in Canada, and near all those stationed at St. John's, in order to make a stand against the provincials expected down the lake; and that consequently Quebeck and Montreal have been left quite bare of troops, except a small guard at each place.

Last monday morning, near *Charlestown* neck, a warm fire began between our advanced parties and those of the enemy, attended with cannonading from the enemy's works on Bunker's hill. We took two marines prisoners, and killed several of the regulars, with the loss of one man belonging to *Marblehead*, who was killed with a cannon ball.

Parties of rifle-men, together with some Indians, are constantly harrassing the enemy's advanced guards, and say they have killed several of the regulars within a day or two past. One of the rifle-men is missing, and is said to be taken prisoner.

Last monday morning about 800 men went from *Roxbury* to the spot where the light-house lately stood, where they found 40 of the enemy, 28 soldiers, and 12 tory carpenters and labourers, who were sent from Boston to erect a building for fixing up lights. Our people, before they surrendered, killed four of them (among whom, it is said, was the lieutenant) and took the rest prisoners, being 24 regulars and the 12 workmen, with the loss of one man on our side. The same day the whole number were brought to head-quarters in this town, and the day following sent off to Worcester. On thursday last notifications were posted up in the town of Boston, to inform all such of the inhabitants as were desirous of quitting the town that they might give in their names to the town-major. Great numbers immediately applied, and several have had permission to come out. The reason of this permission is owing to the scarcity of provisions, Gage thinking he must be obliged to furnish them out of the king's stores, or let them starve. They were not permitted to bring out their effects.

PROVIDENCE, *July* 29.

A GENTLEMAN from *Cambridge* informs, that advice had been received there, by several regular soldiers who have deserted, that it had been determined to attack the lines of the American army on *sunday* last, but that not more than one quarter of the troops destined for the attack could be prevailed on to come out, the others declaring they would much rather die within their own lines than turn out to be slaughtered; and that *Gage* has, in consequence, been obliged to lay aside the project. Some movements made at Bunker's hill, and the landing of a number of troops at Charlestown, on *sunday*, corroborate this intelligence.

NEWPORT, *July* 31.

LAST thursday a large schooner came into this harbour, supposed from Boston, inquired for the men of war, and finding they were gone out, she immediately tacked and stood out again, in pursuit of them.

Last saturday the ships *Rose*, Swan, and *Kingfisher*, with the above schooner, returned into this harbour, and brought in two brigs and three sloops from the West Indies. They have released one brig.

NEW YORK, *August* 7.

LAST thursday capt. Patrick Sinclair, lieutenant-governour and superintendent at Michillimachinack, who lately arrived from North Britain at some port in *Maryland*, and after passing through Pennsylvania and New Jersey, was apprehended by order of our provincial congress, and sent to Suffolk county on Nassau island, there to reside on his giving his parole of honour that he will not take any part in the present unhappy controversy between Great Britain and the colonies, and that he will not depart from or go out of the said county without permission of the Continental Congress, or of this or some future provincial congress, until the present unhappy controversy between Great Britain and the colonies shall be determined.

August 10. By a return express, who left the camp at Cambridge last friday evening, we are informed that six sail of transports sailed from Boston, under convoy of a man of war, some time ago, for the eastward of Caso Bay, for forage; that they landed a number of men for the purpose; that while the men from the ships were landed, a number of men from the shore possessed themselves of five of the ships, made the seamen and soldiers prisoners, and secured the ship out of the reach of the men of war.

Last monday an express arrived from East Hampton, with the following intelligence! That several vessels were seen cruising off Fisher's island and Long island, with an intent to carry off some of the stock from the east end of Long island and Gardiner's island, for the use of the army and navy at Boston; and that the inhabitants were assembling under arms to oppose their landing, and to drive the stock from those places where they were most likely to be taken off. Our provincial congress immediately ordered four companies of general Wooster's forces, in conjunction with the men now raising in Suffolk county for the continental service, to repair thither to the assistance of the inhabitants. General Wooster moved accordingly, from his camp at Haerlem, last tuesday. By an express, which arrived on tuesday, we learn the number of ships was 13.

Last tuesday the first division of col. M'Dougall's battalion of provincial troops sailed, under the command of lieutenant-colonel Ritzema, to join major-general Schuyler at Ticonderoga. They will be soon followed by the second, under major Zedwitz, and their colonel is preparing immediately to follow with the third and last division.

PHILADELPHIA, *August* 10.
Extract of a letter from New York, August 7.

TEN carpenters, going to repair the Boston light-house, were taken by the Americans.

" Yesterday we were informed that the two men of war, and three transports, which left Boston some time ago, had arrived at Montauck point, the east end of Long Island, and were getting provisions. Some of the Long Island companies, I am told, are gone to oppose them."

Extract of a letter from Cambridge, July 31.

" Last friday we were informed, by our out sentries at the foot of Bunker's hill, that the enemy had cut down several large trees, and were busy all night in throwing

FIGURE 1. *The outer sheet of a colonial newspaper. Special Collections, John D. Rockefeller Jr. Library, The Colonial Williamsburg Foundation*

WOODSTOCK, *August* 4, 1775.

THE gentlemen who purchased the sale of the estate of col. *John Carter*, deceased, are desired to discharge their bonds immediately, either by payment to the subscriber, or capt. *William Carr*, merchant in *Dumfries*.

CATESBY WOODFORD, executor.

SURRY, *August* 15, 1775.

THE commanding-officers of the southern district are requested to appoint the general musters in *September* next on the following days, when they will be waited on, by their obedient servant.

COLIN CAMPBELL, adjutant.
September.

SURRY, friday	1.
PRINCE GEORGE, monday	4.
CHESTERFIELD, tuesday	5.
CUMBERLAND, thursday	7.
PRINCE EDWARD, saturday	9.
AMELIA, monday	11.
BRUNSWICK, wednesday	13.
DINWIDDIE, friday	15.
SUSSEX, monday	18.
SOUTHAMPTON, wednesday	20.
ISLE of WIGHT, friday	22.
NANSEMOND, monday	25.
NORFOLK, wednesday	27.
——— BOROUGH, thursday	28.
PRINCESS ANNE, saturday	30.

STOLEN from *Amelia* courthouse, the 22d of *June* past, a BRIGHT BAY MARE about 4 feet 10 inches high, short switch tail, hanging mane, a narrow blaze in her face, and branded on the near buttock x or nearly so; had on, a good hogskin saddle with a blue cloth housing and leather stitched on round it. Whoever will contrive me the said mare, &c. near the lower church in *Amelia*, shall be well satisfied for their trouble; and if the thief be convicted, the reward shall be 20 dollars.

(2ß) JAMES CHAPPELL.

THREE POUNDS REWARD.

RUN away from *Fredericksburg*, on the 7th instant (*August*) JOSEPH SMITH, a *Scotchman*, by trade a painter, appears to be about 33 years of age, 5 feet 9 or 10 inches high, very fleshy, much marked by the smallpox, has light brown hair, which he commonly wears plaited behind, curled at the sides, and fastened with pins. He took with him two coats, one of them a dark brown pretty much wore, the other a light brown, very short, with buttons at the sleeves, a nankeen and a gray cloth waistcoat, two pair of brown linen and a pair of black silk stocking breeches, three check and two white shirts (he commonly worked in his check shirts, therefore it is probable they may have some paint on them) two pair of stockings, one of them mixed yarn, the other ribbed thread, two pair of shoes, one of them old, the other almost new, country made. Whoever takes up the said servant, and secures him in any jail, so that he may be had again, or delivers him to col. *Fielding Lewis* in *Fredericksburg*, or mr. *Lund Washington* at *Mount Vernon*, in *Fairfax* county, will be, by either of those gentlemen, paid the above reward, exclusive of what is allowed by law. (6)

NORTHAMPTON, *August* 11, 1775.

RUN away from the subscriber, on wednesday the 14th of *June* last, a negro man named *Jonathan*; he is a low black fellow, with a round face and thick lips, his clothes uncertain, as he may have exchanged them. He is a cunning artful fellow, loves card-playing, but otherwise sober. Whoever takes up said negro, and secures him in any jail, so that I may get him, shall be well rewarded by

ANNE TOMPKINS.

COMMITTED to *Nansemond* county jail, the 3d day of *August* 1775, a negro man who calls himself WILL, and says he belongs to *William Bibb* of *Prince George* county. He is a black fellow, about six feet high, and appears to be about 35 years old; had on, when taken, a cotton jacket, and black cloth breeches. The owner is desired to take him away, and pay charges.

WILLIAM WHITFIELD, jailer.

RUN away from the subscriber, in *Peytonsburg*, *Pittsylvania* county, the 24th of *June*, an *English* convict servant man named JOHN WILLIAMS; he carried with him a claret coloured frieze coat, a light coloured *Newmarket* do. either bearskin or beaver coating, two osnaburg shirts, and a pair of osnaburg trousers, a pair of leather breeches, and a raccoon hat lined with green persian. He is a thick well set fellow, about 5 feet 9 or 10 inches high, light hair, a brazen look, and is very fond of spirits, has several large warts on his hands, and a very remarkable scar on his upper lip, right under his nose, thus X. He formerly teached a reading school at this place, for about six or eight months past. As he understands the *Prussian* exercise very well, I expect he will endeavour to pass for a deserter from general *Gage*, or some of his majesty's troops. I will give 5l. reward for him if taken in *Virginia*, and 10l. if taken in *Carolina*, *Maryland*, or *Philadelphia*, or secured in any of his majesty's jails, so that I get him.

(6) HENRY WILLIAMS.

HANOVER, *July* 25, 1775.

RUN away from the subscriber, on the 19th of this instant, PETER WILSON, an indented servant man, about 24 years old, 5 feet 5 or 6 inches high, has short yellow hair, a very down look, is well set, and round-shouldered; he is a native of *Scotland*, and speaks broad, is a butcher by trade, a good hostler, and a tolerable good weaver. It is supposed he rode a likely black horse about 4 feet 11 inches high, with a switch tail; and he carried away with him a black coat of superfine broadcloth, half worn, a jacket and breeches of white fustian, and a jacket of dark do. a new felt hat, a pair of country made pumps, and an old great coat. Whoever will secure the said servant, so that I get him again, shall have 40s. reward, besides what the law allows.

(tf) JOHN SYME.

RUN away from the subscriber, at *West Point*, in *King William* county, the 21st of last *December*, a very likely *Virginia* born negro man, named MIKE, about 22 years old, six feet high, and stutters much; had on, when he went away, a suit of negro cotton, but may probably change his clothes. I forewarn all masters of vessels from carrying him out of the colony. Whoever brings the said negro to me shall have 3l. reward, besides what the law allows, and if taken out of the colony 10l. (tf) JOHN WEST.

TAKEN up in *Orange*, a DARK BAY MARE about 12 years old, about 4 feet 7 inches high, has some saddle spots, and branded on the nearbuttock with the figure of 9. Posted, and appraised to 8l.

ISAAC CROSTHWAIT.

TAKEN up in *Halifax*, a DARK BAY MARE about 4 feet 9 inches high, 5 years old, has three small saddle spots on the left side and one on the right, is crest-fallen, and had on a bell about 2s. 6d. price, with a leather collar, fastened with a large iron buckle, paces slow, and branded on the near buttock WF in a piece. Posted, and appraised to 15l. ‖ JOHN WADE.

TAPPAHANNOCK, *August* 10, 1775.

INTEND to leave the colony for a few months. In my absence, mr. *George M'Call*, or mr. *William Shedden*, will transact my business, and the business of mr. *John M'Call* of *Glasgow*.

ARCHIBALD M'CALL.

RUN away from the subscriber, in *Gloucester* county, on the 14th of this instant (*May*) a negro man named NED, about 19 or 20 years of age, five feet two or three inches high, rather of a tawny complexion, has some ringworms on his face, and some white hairs in his head; his clothing was an old brown coat, and a yellow striped cotton waistcoat. I bought him last *March* at the sale of mr. *John Shershee* in *James City* county, for *Mann Page*, junior, esquire. He was brought from one of his quarters in *King William* county, and I have reason to believe that he will go to those parts, or to his mother, who lives with mr. *Thomas Booth*, in *Richmond* town. Any person who will take up the said slave, and secure him so that I get him again, shall be paid 40s. by *Mann Page*, junior, esquire, to whom the negro belongs.

(tf) JAMES JONES.

FOR SALE,

A TRACT of LAND, containing 3000 acres, whereon is a plantation which has employed, for some years past, twelve or fourteen slaves; this tract lies in the upper end of *King William* county. Also a tract lying in the lower end of the said county, containing 1100 acres, and pleasantly situated on *Pamunkey* river; a brick dwelling-house, with necessary offices, a fishing shore, and a lively fertility of soil, recommend the latter tract to any gentleman who may be about to settle in life. Possession will be delivered on the 25th of *December* next, to the purchaser, or purchasers, who will have liberty of sowing fall grain. Mr. *Benjamin Grymes*, jun. of *Orange*, will make known particulars to any person who may be inclined to purchase the whole, or any part of the said tracts. Credit till the first of *January* 1777 will be allowed, by

JUDITH ROBINSON.
(tf.) LUCY ROBINSON,
BENJAMIN GRYMES, jun.

To be SOLD in *Amherst* county,

FOUR THOUSAND acres of exceeding good tobacco LAND, being part of a large tract formerly advertised, together with a very valuable gristmill, upon *Buffalo* river. This land is equal to any that has yet been sold of the tract. The time of payment will be made agreeable to purchasers. Mr. *Gabriel Penn*, who lives near the land, is authorised to bargain for it, and will show it to any person inclinable to purchase.

(tf) CARTER BRAXTON.

For SALE,

A TRACT of LAND in *Caroline* county, near *Newmarket*, containing about 3000 acres of well timbered land, having thereon two plantations, in good repair, with proper and convenient edifices for farming, or making tobacco. For terms apply to the subscriber.

(tf) JOHN BAYLOR.

For SALE,

A TRACT of LAND in *Caroline* county, contiguous to *Mattapony*, containing about 2000 acres of well timbered land, the property of mr. *Robert Baylor*. The terms may be known by applying to mr. *Nathaniel Burwell* in *King William*, mr. *John Armistead* in *Caroline*, or mr. *John Baylor*, executors. (tf)

ARTICLES of Intelligence, Essays, Advertisements, &c. are thankfully received for this Paper, the Price of which is 12s. 6d. per Annum, Advertisements inserted as usual. PRINTING WORK done with Care and Expedition, and on reasonable Terms.

up a line and abbatis in front of it. In the evening, orders were given to the York county rifle company to march down to our advanced poft on Charleftown neck, to endeavour to furround the enemy's advanced guard, and to bring off fome prifoners, from whom we expected to learn the enemy's defign, in throwing up the abbatis on the neck. The rifle company divided, and executed their plan in the following manner: Capt. Dowdle, with 39 men, filed off to the right of Bunker's hill, and, creeping on their hands and knees, got into the rear of the enemy's fentries, without being difcovered; the other divifion, of 40 men, under lieutenant Miller, were equally fuccefsful in getting behind the fentries on the left, and were within a few yards of joining the divifion on the right, when a party of regulars came down the hill to relieve their guard, and croffed our rifle-men under capt. Dowdle, as they were lying on the ground in an Indian file. The regulars were within 20 yards of our rifle-men before they faw them, and immediately fired. The rifle-men returned the falute, killed feveral, and brought off two prifoners and their mufkets, with the lofs of corporal Creufe, who is fuppofed to be killed, as he has not been heard of fince the affair.

"In return for this, the enemy alarmed us laft night in their turn. At 1 o'clock this morning, a heavy firing of fmall-arms and cannon occafioned our drums to beat to arms; the army was immediately ordered under arms to their pofts. The firing continued in three different quarters, Roxbury, Sewell's Point, at the mouth of Cambridge river, and at the advanced pofts on Charleftown neck. Some hours elapfed before we knew the defign of the enemy, which was this: We had furrounded fome of their out-guard the night before, which induced them to ferve our fentries in like manner.

"They fent two flat-bottomed boats to Sewell's Point, to attack our redoubts there; fallied out at Roxbury, and fet fire to the George tavern, our advanced guardhoufe. Our people attacked, beat them, and took one prifoner, who is expected here every minute. The flat-bottomed boats, after an ufelefs fire of many hours, retired; the piquet guard of the enemy, on Charleftown neck, attacked and drove in our advanced guard of 60; who, being reinforced by general Lee's order, recovered their ground, and beat off the enemy, killed feveral, and brought off feven mufkets, without lofing a man, although our men engaged them under their guns, within point-blank fhot of their lines. We are juft informed, that 250 of the Marblehead failors have formed on Plowed hill, near Bunker's, and have drove in all the out-guards of the enemy. The enemy do not appear to be very fond of coming out. We fhall harrafs them continually, and for this reafon want the aid of the riflemen. Only one company, as yet, come in."

Auguft 12. We hear from Cambridge, that captains Percival and Sabine of the marines, Johnfon of the Royal Irifh, Lemoin of the train, and a number of privates of the minifterial troops, in all about 30, were killed laft week; alfo a captain mortally wounded, who is a fon of lord Chedworth's.

Corporal Creufe of the rifle-men, now prifoner at Bofton, has fent a letter to his comrades in the camp, informing that he was treated kindly by the regulars.

The exprefs who was fent by the Congrefs is returned from the eaftward, and fays he left the camp laft faturday; that the rifle-men had picked off ten men in one day, three of whom were *field-officers*, that were reconnoitring; one of them was killed at the diftance of 250 yards, when only half his head was feen.

NEW YORK, *Auguft* 21.

A GENTLEMAN belonging to Philadelphia arrived here laft friday evening from Bofton, by way of Rhode Ifland. The 25th of July he was taken by the Glafgow man of war, 150 leagues from the land, in the fhip *Charming Sally*, capt. Doman, with 2200 barrels of flour, from Philadelphia for Lifbon, and carried into Bofton the 4th inftant. He informs us, that general Gage was difmantling Caftle William, and removing the cannon, with the garrifon, up to town; that near 400 of the wounded foldiers had died fince the battle at Bunker's hill; that there was not the leaft appearance of any embarkation among them, and that it was the general opinion among the military that nothing farther would be attempted by general Gage until he had other accounts from England; that provifions of all forts were fcarce and dear, mutton 18d. per lb. geefe 8s. and every other thing in proportion, notwithftanding a fhip had juft arrived from Ireland with falt provifions.

BALTIMORE, in *Maryland, Auguft* 24.

BY a veffel juft arrived at Philadelphia, from Ireland, in a fhort paffage, we have advice of the arrival of John Watts and Roger Morris, efquires, two of his majefty's council for the province of New York, at London; and that they had been examined touching American affairs by the miniftry and the lords of the privy council, who were fo greatly alarmed by their reprefentations that the orders which had been defpatched to Ireland, for fix regiments more to embark for this country, were countermanded. His majefty was alfo advifed to call the parliament together immediately, which he did accordingly; and it was faid it was either fitting, or was convening, when the laft accounts came away. The miniftry are, it appears, in the *horrors*, and the whole nation under the moft direful apprehenfions of feeing " *the wide arch of the raifed empire fall.*" Such has been the folly and madnefs of British councils, that the *great empire*, which was wont to conquer others, hath made a fhameful conqueft of itfelf. *Extract of a letter from general* Washington, *dated camp at Cambridge, Auguft* 10, 1775, *directed to the Provincial Congrefs at* New York.

"We have had no occurrence in the camp, for feveral days, worthy of notice; but by fome advices from Bofton, and feveral concurring circumftances, we have great reafon to fufpect that a part, or the whole, of the minifterial troops, are about to remove. New York is the place generally talked of as their deftination. I give you this intelligence as it came to me, but do not vouch for its authenticity."

A fchooner with arms and ammunition was lately feized by the Nautilus man of war, near Newcaftle, on Delaware.

WILLIAMSBURG, *September* 1.

SINCE our laft, the hon. PEYTON RANDOLPH, efq; col; THOMAS NELSON, and GEORGE WYTHE, efq; fet out for Philadelphia, to attend the General-Congrefs on the 5th of this inftant, accompanied by their feveral ladies.

This day WILLIAM GODDARD, efq; furveyor, &c. to the conftitutional poftoffice, arrived in this city, on a tour through the feveral united colonies, to eftablifh offices in the principal towns and other commercial places, under the authority of BENJAMIN FRANKLIN, efq; who is appointed poftmafter-general by the Hon. the Continental Congrefs; and as foon as the officers are commiffioned, and the routes fixed, the eftablifhment will immediately take place.

NORFOLK, *Auguft* 30. Lord Dunmore has lately made feizure of another veffel belonging to meff. Eilbeck, Rofs, and co. for government fervice forfooth!

The goods imported in the fnow Unicorn, feized by lord Dunmore as above-mentioned, were ordered by the Norfolk borough committee to be immediately returned in the fame veffel; but his lordfhip has taken care to prevent that, by laying his hands upon the goods, and converting them to his own ufe; and the veffel, we hear, is intended for St. Auguftine, to bring the remainder of the 14th regiment.

It appearing that the above goods, imported in the Unicorn, had been countermanded by meff. Eilbeck, Rofs, and co. the committee of this borough have acquitted them in this inftance of any breach of the affociation.

We are affured, from good authority, that general Howe is appointed to the command of the troops at Bofton, fuppofed to be at the requeft of general Gage.

A correfpondent writes, that a certain floop of war, not 100 miles diftant, was lately kept in conftant alarm a whole night, with her matches burning, tomkins out, guns loaded with grape fhot, and all hands at their quarters, till day-light difcovered the formidable enemy, which had caufed fuch terrible apprehenfions, to be only one of the neighbours with his negroes catching mullets! A certain governour, it is faid, was in all hafte fent for, to affift with his fage advice at the council of war that was held on this mighty occafion.

This day arrived from London the famous major Rogers, formerly of the rangers.

IN CONVENTION, FRIDAY, *Auguft* 25.

Refolved, THAT it be recommended to the committees of the feveral counties and corporations in this colony to call all collectors and receivers of fines heretofore impofed by any courtmartial, and all other perfons who have any money in their hands arifing from fuch fines, to an immediate account for the fame, and, after paying any arrears which may be due for arms or trophies formerly purchafed, apply any fuch money for providing arms and ammunition for the ufe of their refpective counties and corporations, in fuch manner as they fhall think beft.

Extract from the ordinance for regulating the pay of the MILITIA.

AND be it farther ordained, that William Langhorne, Henry King, John Scafbrooke Wills, William Norvell, Champion Travis, or any three of them, be, and they are hereby appointed commiffioners to examine, ftate, and fettle an account of the pay and provifions of the volunteer companies who have been lately called into actual fervice for the defence of the lower parts of the country, during the fame allowance as is fettled by this Convention for the regular forces; and under the regulations of the late invafion law as to the number of men which is to entitle officers of a certain rank to pay, excepting that mr. Charles Scott, commander in chief of the faid volunteers at Williamfburg, fhall be allowed 12s. 6d. per day from the time he was chofen to that command, and certifying the fame as is directed in the cafe of the militia on the frontiers; and upon fuch certificate, the treafurer, by warrant from the Committee of Safety, is required to pay the money fo certified to be due. And each of the faid commiffioners fhall be allowed 15 s. per day, for the time they fhall be employed in fettling the faid accounts.

To the honourable the PRESIDENT, *and the reft of the* DELEGATES *of the* PEOPLE *of* VIRGINIA, *now fitting in Convention: The petition of fundry* MERCHANTS, *and others*, NATIVES *of* GREAT BRITAIN, *and refident in this colony,*

HUMBLY SHEWETH,

THAT your petitioners being chiefly agents, factors, and perfons who, from their youth, have been bred up to and employed in the business of commerce, have at no time interfered with the civil institutions of the country, but have always acted in conformity to the laws under which they have enjoyed the best security for their persons and property. With this experience of the protection derived from these salutary laws, as well as from the happy intercourse they have enjoyed with the inhabitants, many of your petitioners have formed connections of the most endearing nature, and have invested considerable proportions of their property in real estates, with a view of continuing their residence among a people with whom they have hitherto lived in such harmony. Your petitioners beg leave to represent, that their fears are much awakened from the ill-grounded prejudices which they are informed actuate the minds of some of the people of this colony against your petitioners, as a body, who are not natives of the land; a circumstance which, being accidental, cannot be imputed to them as a fault, and therefore, on that account, they hope to stand in the same light with other subjects who conform to the laws. They are sensible the unhappy differences subsisting between the parent state and her colonies have given rise to distinctions to their prejudice among the natives of the country, and excited jealousies of them which otherwise had never existed. Discriminated from the rest of the society, and placed in a suspicious point of view, they presume to lay before this Honourable House the hardship of their situation, and, in the sincerity of their hearts, to declare, that they hold this people in the highest estimation, as friends and fellow-subjects; and that, in war or peace, they will cheerfully contribute with them to the exigencies of this their common state: That in all internal commotions, or insurrections, they pledge their faith, at the risk of their lives and fortunes, jointly with their fellow-subjects of this colony, to defend the country; and that in case of an attack from the troops of Great Britain, they will not aid in any manner or communicate intelligence to them by letter or otherwise. Permit your petitioners to assure this Honourable House, that they wish not an exemption from the hardships and burthens to which the people of this country are exposed, from the civil contest subsisting with the parent state; but are willing, and ready, to participate in all instances, except taking up arms against those people among whom they were born, and with whom perhaps they are connected by the nearest ties of consanguinity. To this circumstance they entreat your impartial and favourable attention; and that you would be pleased to mark out a line of conduct by which your petitioners, in this dangerous crisis, may move as useful members to the community, without being held to the necessity of shedding the blood of their countrymen; an act at which nature recoils, and which every feeling of humanity forbids. This allowed your petitioners, they again repeat their readiness to stand up with the foremost in defence of the country against internal insurrections, and in its support by the most liberal and cheerful contributions.

That the supreme director of the universe may inspire you with wisdom to put a period to this unnatural contest, and restore this once happy land to peace, safety, and union with its parent state, is the ardent wish of

Your respectful and dutiful petitioners.

FRIDAY, *August* 25, 1775.
THE foregoing petition was presented to the Convention, and the following resolution thereupon unanimously agreed to:

Resolved, that the said petition is reasonable; and it is recommended to the committees of the several counties and corporations, and others the good people of this colony, to treat all such natives of Great Britain resident here, as do not show themselves enemies to the common cause of America, with lenity and friendship: To protect all persons whatsoever in the just enjoyment of their civil rights and liberty; to discountenance all national reflections; to preserve, to the utmost of their power, internal peace and good order; and to promote union, harmony, and mutual good-will, among all ranks of people.

Resolved also, that the said petition, together with this resolve, be forthwith published in the Virginia gazettes.

Ro. C. NICHOLAS, president *pro tempore.*
(a copy)
John Tazewell, clerk of the Convention.

** On TUESDAY will be published, The JOURNAL of the CONVENTION.

49

FIGURE 3. *A print shop in 1774. Tab. XXI, Einige Arten nützlicher Beschäftigungen. c) Die Arbeit in der Buchdruckerei. (Beschreibung lt. Quelle). J. B. Basedows,* Elementarwerk mit den Kupfertafeln Chodowieckis u.a. Kritische: Bearbeitung in drei Bänden . . . (Leipzig, 1909). *This German print shows a working print shop in the late eighteenth century. The division of labor is clear: the master printer is in the back at his table choosing content, the journeyman on the left is assembling the types, and the beater and puller are at the press producing the printed sheets.*

fresh papers went out to the public, printers in those shops would begin that Wednesday preparing the next week's issue. They would spend the remainder of Wednesday, all of Thursday, and perhaps part of Friday preparing the essays and advertisements that would appear on the front and back pages. Then, the apprentices would lock those sticks of type onto the press, and two of them would begin the physically demanding work of producing the newspaper. One was known as a beater. His job was to take two animal skin-covered balls soaked in ink (a combination of soot and varnish) and pound the types until they were saturated. His partner, the puller, would then attach a blank sheet to the wood frame, maneuver it under the ink-soaked types, and pull the heavy lever to impress the ink into the paper. The process had changed little since Gutenberg's day: it was still dirty, sweaty, boring work.

A good beater and puller team could churn out more than two hundred pages (one hundred outer sheets) per hour. By the 1770s, newspaper subscription numbers were on the rise in the colonies. In order to make ends meet, printers needed at least 700 reliable subscribers. Printers were doing better than that during the imperial crisis. According to the one subscription book that has survived, William Bradford's *Pennsylvania Journal* had 2,200 subscribers on the eve of the Revolution. That meant Bradford's team of beaters and pullers had to work at maximum capacity for twenty-two hours to get half of the paper produced for that week. Increasing numbers of subscribers might have been good for Bradford and his colleagues, but it only translated into longer hours and sorer muscles for his apprentices.

By Saturday night, the apprentices working for the *Massachusetts Spy, Pennsylvania Gazette,* and *Georgia Gazette* (the last probably being enslaved workers) hung their completed outer pages up to dry in the rafters of the print shop and rested their weary shoulders and elbows. While the apprentices were hard at work producing the outer pages, the printer and his journeymen set about planning the typically six columns of print that would appear on the inside.

Usually, the inside of a colonial newspaper was where to find the news. Gathering the information that would appear there was not an easy task. Just as there were no headlines or illustrations in eighteenth-century newspapers, there were no reporters. Printers were passive receivers of news: they depended on others to provide them with stories. The news could come from a few sources. One way was from the water. Nearly all colonial newspapers on the eve of the Revolution came from print shops in port cities. The nearly three dozen newspapers in production on the verge of the Revolutionary War circulated from nineteen American towns, all but three of them on the water. Ship captains were among the most important suppliers. They carried letters, gathered intelligence from other ships traveling the high seas, and transported print all over the Atlantic. *Pennsylvania Journal* printer William Bradford sought to corner the market of information coming into Philadelphia. Not only did he work his way into becoming the city's postmaster, and therefore the primary receiver of all the mail coming into town, but he also became the proprietor of the London Coffee House across the street from the city's main wharf, and therefore the primary receiver of many thirsty mariners coming into town.

News also came from individuals who made a trip to the print shop for the specific purpose of having a portion of their private correspondence inserted into the newspaper. Usually, these were elite gentlemen who wanted the news conveyed to the public but their name kept out of it. Letters appeared with generic attributions such as "A letter from a gentleman in New York City to his friend in this place" or "A letter received from a friend in London." Only the printer knew who the correspondents really were, and it was essential for him or her to keep those secrets well or else risk betraying trust and losing this important avenue of information.

The third and most widely used method of filling the inside sheet of the weekly newspaper was by clipping articles that appeared in other printers' newspapers and reprinting them in one's own. This system was called the "exchanges," and it was the lifeblood of the eighteenth-century newspaper business on both sides of the Atlantic. Colonial printers did not see this as theft or plagiarism. In fact, they sent issues to their colleagues free of charge as a courtesy. Printers would peruse these free copies, select an article or several, and then copy them into their own paper under a heading that listed where the information was from and how old it was.

To see how the exchange system worked, and the changes it went through as a result of the Revolutionary War, we will compare two issues of the *Virginia Gazette*, chosen at random and published one year apart.

On Thursday, September 1, 1774, printing partners Alexander Purdie and John Dixon sent out another weekly *Virginia Gazette* from their Williamsburg shop, located next to the post office. It was the 1,204th time they had done so. In that particular paper, the front page did not feature an essay but, instead, was covered with news from Europe. The first column was an exchanged story from The Hague, dated May 27, followed by two columns of news from London dated early June. Inside the exchanged stories that originally appeared in a London paper were anonymous letters from Vienna and St. Petersburg. News from London bled over to the second page, which was filled with more letters from Madrid, Paris, Genoa, and various English towns. On the third page, there was a single, small paragraph of local news, under the dateline Williamsburg, that related how a ship had sailed from Virginia's Eastern Shore to Boston to take food to that beleaguered city (then suffering under the restrictions of the Coercive Acts). After that came one sentence announcing that three ships had arrived nearby from Liverpool, a short statement that a well-esteemed member of a North Carolina town had suddenly died at age twenty-three, and another informing readers that Virginia's delegation to the First Continental Congress had departed for Philadelphia. Purdie and Dixon filled the remaining two-and-a-half columns of the third and the entire back page with advertisements, as well as a poem celebrating the king's birthday.

One year later, a great deal had changed in Alexander Purdie's world and in the world he presented to readers in his *Virginia Gazette*. His long-standing partnership with John Dixon had dissolved early in 1775, and he carried on solo, boasting that his paper was "Always for LIBERTY and the PUBLICK GOOD." A few months after that business decision, the Revolutionary War broke out in Massachusetts, and the news swept over the North American continent. By September 1, 1775, the battles at Lexington and Concord and on Bunker Hill were months old, and General George Washington was in command of the rebel army in Cambridge. As we will see, lots of other people had spent the summer calculating their response to this earth-shattering news.

How different was Purdie's newspaper of September 1, 1775, from the one he and Dixon had published exactly one year earlier? The number of columns dedicated to advertisements was roughly the same, with ads taking up half of the third page and the entire back. The content of those notices, however, reflected the deepening unrest of the moment: in the 1774 issue, there were six advertisements for runaways (three for indentured servants, three for enslaved people); in the 1775 issue, there were nine (three for servants, six for the enslaved). The front page in 1775 was also atypical in that it was full of exchanged news rather than an essay or speech. But, whereas the news a year before was from all over the continent of Europe, this issue was almost wholly American. Purdie clipped stories from the *New-England Chronicle* (Cambridge, Mass.), *Providence Gazette, Newport Mercury, Maryland Journal, and the Baltimore Advertiser, Virginia Gazette, or the Norfolk Intelligencer,* and multiple stories from the *New-York Gazette: and the Weekly Mercury* and *Pennsylvania Evening Post.* As a year earlier, readers would find surprisingly little local news—a single paragraph, again, of original content—but what they did learn was a flurry of information from reports across North America (see Figures 1 and 2).

This book focuses on the news in the newspapers, on the material that usually appeared on the inside sheet rather than the political essays from the front page or the advertisements on the back. At first glance, it is easy to overlook these deceptively simple items. Much of the news came in the form of bare bulletins; terse, declarative sentences in short paragraphs that lack much attraction to the historian's eye. Purdie and Dixon gave their Williamsburg readers this tiny morsel of local news on September 1, 1774: a ship landed, a young person died unexpectedly, and a party of political leaders had left town. That is all. It hardly seems worthy of our attention.

But we should not be so quick to underestimate the power of these short sentences—and especially the exchange system—in the building of a Revolutionary movement. The exchanges were essential to the earliest construction of "an American people" and, subsequently, "an American nation." In the

1700s, people living far away from one another began to think about their connectedness in new ways. Thanks, in part, to the growth of print culture (especially the rise of the novel and the newspaper), people started to imagine that they were living together in the same community. This meant a new conception of the idea of "nation" and "national identity." The newspaper exchanges were a crucial ingredient in making these fictional connections: colonists in Virginia read stories about what was happening hundreds of miles away in the Canadian backcountry, and Connecticut readers learned that similar things were happening in the Carolina backcountry. Moreover, because printers simply cut and pasted paragraphs from one paper into their own, these readers in Virginia and Connecticut learned the exact same things because they read the exact same words.

Let us return, one last time, to the news that John Adams "cooked up" in the offices of the *Boston Gazette* in 1769. Who else read the items James Otis and the Adams cousins fabricated to discredit John Mein and loyalist supporters? Lots of people. Their cooking-up went far beyond Boston's city limits. Readers all over America learned of the news they managed, manipulated, and, in part, invented that Saturday night in the Queen Street offices of the *Boston Gazette.* Eleven other newspapers outside Boston included some part of their handicraft. The "facts" the Adams cousins and James Otis fashioned in the waning September daylight on the *Gazette's* type tables found their way to hundreds of other tables, in public and private houses throughout New England, New York, Pennsylvania, Virginia, and Georgia. What happened in Boston did not stay in Boston. This was essential to making the cause common. The exchange system was a powerful weapon that could make or break a political movement; the patriots understood this intimately and acted accordingly.[10]

The exchanges helped colonists conceive of themselves as fellow Americans who shared similar experiences. Patriot leaders tried to create institutions that fostered these feelings, like the committees of correspondence, but the exchanges did so far more effectively, in part because they were informal and unassuming. Colonial readers in America consumed these newspapers in their own, local context, interpreting and translating them into settings that were familiar to them: their homes and hearths, their villages and towns, their fields and stores. But the exchanges called upon colonists to make an imaginative leap, to cast their minds to places far away that they had never before considered. They had never met John Mein, but they knew him through the exchanges. More important, they might have known people like him and projected their own frustration onto tories in their communities.[11]

The exchanges encouraged them to think continentally and, crucially, to empathize with fellow colonists whom they would never meet. This was the essential first step to conceiving of one another as living in the same nation and, as such, the critical ingredient to winding the thirteen clocks to chime together. The exchanged stories — mundane as they may seem on their face — made the United States.

All this depended, however, on thousands of literate colonists thirsty for their weekly newspapers. How many actually read these newspapers? What was the size of these newspaper runs? How many people *could* read them, and how many did?

It is difficult, but not impossible, to gauge the saturation of colonial newsprint on the eve of the Revolutionary War. Thanks to the survival of two subscription books for one newspaper, William Bradford's rabidly patriot *Pennsylvania Journal,* we can get a tantalizing glimpse into how far print penetrated into the colonial countryside as war loomed.

When William Bradford reported the news of the Boston Tea Party in early January 1774, he sent copies of his *Pennsylvania Journal* to 1,703 subscribers. Next to 286 (16.8 percent) of these names, Bradford noted a title that reflected an elite status: militia officer, physician, minister, or gentleman. At least 24 women had their own *Journal* subscriptions. Bradford sent issues to the colonial governors of Virginia, New Hampshire, and New Jersey. Another 13 men who took the *Pennsylvania Journal* would sign the Declaration of Independence, and 3 more would serve as the first governors of their independent state.

One-third (551) of these papers remained in Philadelphia, which meant the bulk of Bradford's support lay outside the city. There were a nearly equal number of subscribers in New Jersey and Delaware as in the city: 568, with another 246 going to the rural Pennsylvania hinterland. Another 338 papers had farther to go, to the Chesapeake, the Carolinas, New England, the West Indies, the British Isles, and Europe.[12]

Then, as it did with everything, the war transformed William Bradford's business accounting. By the end of the summer of 1775, Bradford — now in partnership with his son Thomas — started a new ledger to document *Journal* subscribers. Business was booming, after all. This second book not only showed the growth — by early 1777, they enjoyed nearly a 30 percent rise in total subscriptions — but it was organized differently. They divided this second book up by delivery routes, showing where they sent papers every week. The routes, depicted in Map 2, spiral out in all directions from Philadelphia. There is much more detail in the second book; we know exactly where the papers went and how they got there.

Here is one example of what we can learn from this subscription book. Peter Withington lived in Reading, Pennsylvania, in 1775. At some point during the 1770s, he had become the Bradfords' most important distributor to the Pennsylvania frontier. By the early months of the Revolutionary War, the Bradfords were sending 184 issues of the *Journal* up the Schuylkill River to Withington's house in Reading every week, a large number nearly equal to the amount of papers they were sending to the entire Chesapeake region in the early 1770s. Withington's neighbors in Reading would receive 13 of those issues; the rest would be stacked in a corner in his house, waiting for delivery rider William Carheart to arrive and pick them up. Carheart, loaded down with about 170 papers, would then set off down the road west from Reading to the Paxton settlement on the Susquehanna River (now Harrisburg), where thirty subscribers were waiting. Then he turned north, where the Juniata River flows into the Susquehanna, to deliver 13 more papers. He continued to ride up and down the Susquehanna, delivering papers for Conestoga, East Pennsboro, and Carlisle. By the first days of independence, seventy-eight customers in Carlisle depended on Carheart for their weekly news from Philadelphia (at least in the form of the *Pennsylvania Journal*). The Revolution had been good for business there, with forty-five new customers signing on in 1775, thirty-seven more in 1776, and only four lost along the way. Carheart still had to gallop down the wagon road to Shippensburg and Chamberstown (now Chambersburg) before turning his horse back in the direction of Withington's house, a tiring one hundred miles to the east.

Peter Withington and William Carheart are not deemed "founding fathers." They have no memorials or protected heritage sites. But the success of the American Revolution depended on their efforts in small, yet essential, ways. They were the protectors and carriers of the news, which made them nurturers of the patriot movement. They did the dirty work.

In September 1776, Withington would be commissioned a captain in the Twelfth Pennsylvania Regiment and serve in the desperate defense of New Jersey, but his military career would be cut short by camp fever, from which he would not recover; he died at his Reading home in May 1777. But Withington's record of service to the common cause was far more extensive than these few weeks in uniform. In fact, the contribution he made by working with Carheart and the Bradfords before he joined the Continental army was just as important, if not more so. After all, Pennsylvania military recruiters' ability to fill up the regiment in which Withington would serve stemmed, in part, from his other job as distribution agent of the *Pennsylvania Journal*. Withington and Carheart were an essential part of the common

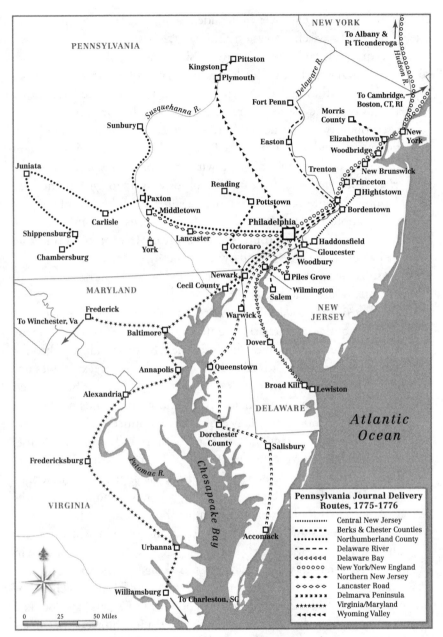

MAP 2. *Distribution Routes for* Pennsylvania Journal, *1775–1776.*
Drawn by Gerry Krieg

cause. Without their hard, yet unheralded, work, the thirteen clocks very likely would not have chimed as one in July 1776.

The second subscription book can also show us the political response to the events of war and the Bradfords' navigation of those stormy revolutionary seas. In 1775, they added 436 customers; in 1776, they added another 470; and, in 1777, they added a further 100. During that time, they suffered few losses: only 119 wrote the Bradfords to cancel their subscription (21 in 1775, 79 in 1776, and 19 in 1777). The Bradfords' gains exceeded their losses by tenfold. Clearly, the public agreed with the stories they inserted in the *Pennsylvania Journal*. The larger number of losses in 1776 (79) might seem to undermine this interpretation, but here, again, the war helps explain some of the dislocation. The largest number of the Bradfords' losses in 1776 came from the central New Jersey route, specifically from Trenton and Princeton. That area would be a battleground by year's end.

These subscription books, dutifully protected by the Historical Society of Pennsylvania, reveal to us the Bradfords' network of subscribers as it grew with the start of the Revolutionary War. They raise intriguing, but mostly unanswerable, questions. First, the Bradfords list only the people who made the effort to write to them to establish service. These individuals asked for the *Journal,* and the Bradfords sent them one issue every week. It does not tell us what happened to the papers once that original subscriber finished with them. What other family members, neighbors, or friends might have read them secondhand? How many eyes actually scanned each newspaper? Second is the issue of literacy and oral communication. The Bradfords' lists included deliveries to taverns in the Pennsylvania countryside. Did people read them out loud in public houses there? How big might those gatherings have been? Researchers have told us that literacy rates among eighteenth-century American colonists were much higher than among English men and women. One scholar states that, on the eve of the Revolution, white male literacy in New England was "nearly universal." In 1775, 60 percent of men in England could sign their will instead of just marking "x," whereas 90 percent in Vermont, 87 percent in Virginia, and about 70 percent in the Pennsylvania countryside could. Among women, 38 percent in England also marked legal documents with their signature, but 83 percent in Connecticut, 67 percent in Massachusetts, and 56 percent in Virginia could. Nevertheless, information conveyed orally remained a force in colonial culture. As one scholar has noted, in the 1700s, the idea of "publication" meant reading texts aloud to gatherings of townspeople. How many ears heard the exchanged stories in the *Pennsylvania Journal?*[13]

We cannot know the total for certain. Although the Bradfords' books shed important light on where their newspaper headed every Wednesday, who received the papers, and how they got there, the books still do not provide a complete picture. We can say with confidence that at least two thousand colonists across the mid-Atlantic and beyond received a weekly issue of the *Pennsylvania Journal* in 1775 and 1776 and that many more very likely knew what it said.

But this is just the web spun out of one Philadelphia print shop. If we were luckier, thirty-two other subscription books would have survived for us to analyze. As much as we can learn from the Bradfords' books, they show us only one of the nearly three dozen newspaper networks at the start of the Revolutionary War. Had subscription books from the *Massachusetts Spy, Virginia Gazette, Connecticut Courant,* or *South-Carolina Gazette* had been as well preserved, they would illustrate the webs as they actually were: overlapping, extensive, and thick, with multiple strands crisscrossing the same towns and often the same residences. We could connect and overlap our map of *Pennsylvania Journal* deliveries to thirty-two others just like it. If we had those books, then — and only then — could we have a full accounting of how many colonists received newspapers in 1775.

Print, especially the exchanges, was essential if there was any hope of thirteen clocks' chiming together. Newspapers held the potential to establish stories — the same stories — to a wide audience across a wide spectrum of a remarkably literate colonial society. The tiny stories inside the fold of the weekly newspaper could do astounding work: the exchanges could promote trust, the most fundamental element in establishing the patriot cause. Some astute political leaders, like the Adams cousins and their Boston printer allies, realized this early on, as the confrontation between them and John Mein illustrates. "Cooking up," they knew, was an essential craft if the resistance movement stood any chance of success.

For those patriot leaders who weren't as quick to grasp the importance of newspapers and the exchanges, the troubling clouds of discord that threatened the mainland American colonies in the early 1770s helped to convince them. Those conflicts signaled the need to find a reliable way to make the cause common. In several different areas — internal conflicts, border fights between colonies, protests over slavery, and, worst of all, the loyalist counter-argument — colonial America did not seem at all to be trending toward unity. The odds against the thirteen clocks' striking together were getting longer and longer in the half decade before Lexington and Concord.

CHAPTER 2

The LONG ODDS *against*
AMERICAN UNITY *in the* 1770s

The first order of business was to clear the galleries. After all spectators had been escorted out of the chamber on this "day of such importance," late in the afternoon of March 14, 1774, Parliament opened debate on how to punish Boston for destroying thousands of pounds of East India Company tea. A week before, the king had informed the House of Commons of the "violent and outrageous Proceedings" that had taken place in Boston Harbor the past December and asked them to pass legislation "for better securing the Execution of the Laws, and the just Dependence of the Colonies upon the Crown and Parliament of *Great Britain*." For the remainder of March, Parliament debated the Boston Port Bill, the first of what would later be known as the set of punitive measures collectively called the Coercive Acts. The sticking point was whether Boston should be singled out. Lord North insisted that Boston alone was the "ringleader in all riots" and therefore "ought to be the principal object of our attention for punishment." Despite Edmund Burke's warnings that discontent was "universal . . . throughout all America," those who advocated making an example out of Boston won the day.[1]

Focusing their wrath on Massachusetts alone made sense. After all, despite the many things they did not understand about the colonial complaints, the North administration was certain that American unity was impossible. The prevailing wisdom in Britain, continually reinforced by colonial correspondents, imperial officials, military officers, returning travelers, and Atlantic merchants, was that the resistance movement in America was anything but universal. The mainland American colonies, they were sure, could never sustain a united front. Since Boston could not count on any steady friends, there was no need for a general interdiction. Or, as another member of Parliament suggested, it "appears to be wise, first, to single out Boston as the principal ringleader of the whole disturbance, and begin this punishment there, in order to see what effect the proceedings will have." Few anticipated how widespread, how continental, those effects would be. This underestimation turned out to be Britain's biggest blunder of the American Revolution.[2]

Wrong as their prediction turned out to be, the British government had very good reasons to anticipate American disunity. Patriots in America would label the Coercive Acts as "intolerable." But even they had no way of knowing how many Americans might, in fact, tolerate them. As the son of one Boston patriot put it fifty years after the Revolution, "The real cause of wonder is, that a harmony so perfect, and a union, as it respected the end and means of opposition, so general, should have been effected at such an early period." "The real cause of wonder" is right.[3]

A brief survey of the obstacles standing in the way of intercolonial unity on the eve of the Revolution reveals all that had to be overcome to make the cause common. Not only had all previous efforts of colonial unity failed miserably, but the odds against the thirteen colonies' sticking together were incredible in the 1770s. These worsening problems ranged from intercolonial disputes that threatened violence to a growing criticism of slavery and a dangerous loyalist counterargument. Taken together, these powerful divisions, whether simmering from the colonial past or boiling in the present, jeopardized the chances that thirteen clocks could ever chime as one. British officials could be confident that the American rebels stood little chance of success.

Two decades earlier, the first attempt at colonial union had ended in disaster. With war clouds looming in 1754, representatives from seven colonies met at Albany to discuss a defensive alliance and coordinate Indian policy. The lesson learned by nearly all who attended the abortive Albany Congress was that, even when they were threatened with utter destruction, jealousy and provincialism trumped unity. Benjamin Franklin, one of the prime movers at the conference, was disillusioned by the refusal of any colonial legislature to ratify the Albany plan. A few years later, he confessed that the colonies were far too different — they had "different forms of government, different laws, different interests, and some of them different religious persuasions and different manners" — to form an effective union. "If they could not agree to unite for their defence against the *French* and *Indians,* who were perpetually harassing their settlements, burning their villages, and murdering their people," he predicted five years before the Stamp Act, "can it reasonably be supposed there is any danger of their uniting against their own nation, which protects and encourages them, with which they have so any connections and ties of blood interest, and affection, and which 'tis well known they all love

FIGURE 4. *Franklin "Join, or die" cartoon.* Pennsylvania Gazette, *May 9, 1754. Library of Congress, Prints and Photographs Division. https://www.loc.gov/item/2002695523*

much more than they love one another?" In the end, the most lasting product of the Albany Congress was Franklin's "Join, or die" illustration of a severed colonial snake. At midcentury, it seems, most Americans preferred death over one another.[4]

This animosity, of course, was hardly new. Over a century and a half of settlement, few colonists showed any interest in building intercolonial bridges. Because the thirteen colonies were, in fact, four distinct regional provinces, they had little need or desire to get along. Reputations, formed long ago in the seventeenth century, held sway: for southerners, New England was a land of intolerant, democratic religious zealots; for New Englanders, their southern neighbors were immoral, lazy sinners who earned their living through the toil of others. One outspoken Anglican parson from Virginia warned southern delegates to the Second Continental Congress to be on their guard against the "Goths and Vandals" from New England. "O 'tis a monstrous and an unnatural coalition," he predicted, "and we should as soon expect to see the greatest contrarieties in Nature to meet in harmony, and the wolf and the lamb to feed together, as Virginians to form a cordial union with the saints of New England." Listening to the descendants of Puritan dissenters would only lead to civil war, he lamented.[5]

Regional divides, moreover, ran along both North-South and East-West axes. Colonists did not valorize frontier hunters or celebrate hardy pioneers living in the backcountry before the American Revolution. The opposite was true. For many people living in Philadelphia or Newport or Williamsburg, the farther one lived away from the Atlantic and its connections to Europe, the more "savage" one became. As anxious as American inhabitants were about Europeans' perceiving them as "going native," they immediately applied those prejudices to their own backsettlers.[6]

In the late 1760s, Anglican minister Charles Woodmason kept a journal of his travels throughout the Carolina frontier. His opinions about the inhabitants there reflect a similar tension between popular attitudes that easterners were "civilized" and westerners "savage." The aggravated itinerant preacher sneered that the backcountry was "without Law, Gospel, Trade, or Money." Although Woodmason despised the patriot movement, he summed up in one description of a "vast Body of People assembled" what many future patriots probably thought about frontier settlers. "Such a Medley! Such a mixed Multitude of all Classes and Complexions I never saw," Woodmason confessed to his diary. "After Service they went to Revelling Drinking Singing Dancing and Whoring — and most of the Company were drunk before I quitted the Spot — They were as rude in their Manners as the Common Savages, and hardly a degree removed from them." After the Revolution, men and women like these would be mythologized as true-blue Americans. But, on the verge of conflict with Britain, that redemption was impossible to foresee. The backcountry was, for many easterners in 1775, hardly a land that fashioned heroic types like Daniel Boone but, rather, a place where savages of all sorts lived. Worse, they might all be bloodthirsty killers like the Paxton Boys.[7]

Then again, the people on the frontier found plenty of fault with their eastern peers, as well. Resenting being slighted by misappropriated government services — especially after suffering repeated Indian attacks throughout the 1750s–1770s — frontier settlers across the backcountry bristled against coastal power centers. In the pamphlet war that followed Pennsylvania's infamous Paxton crisis in 1763, frontier writers rebuked eastern claims to civility or superiority. One tract laid the blame for "Screams of Children," "fruitless Sighs of the disconsolate Widow," "Groans of a broken hearted Father mourning for a darling Son or Daughter," and "whole Families butchered while they are asleep" at the feet of inattentive Pennsylvania authorities who cared more for Indians than for them. Another sarcastically reproached Philadelphia's Quakers as "compassionate and merciful Christians, so easily affected with Pity for Indians, would not grant a single Farthing (as a Society) for the Relief of their Fellow Subjects." Hardly the murderous "CHRISTIAN WHITE SAVAGES" that Benjamin Franklin branded them, frontiersmen increasingly argued that they were the true representations of masculine courage and pure liberty.[8]

Ethnic, religious, and cultural prejudices divided not only East from West but North from South. In truth, those provincial attitudes really stemmed from sheer ignorance. Colonists simply lacked information about each other. Communication networks ran more reliably across the Atlantic than they did up or down the mainland coast. Invariably, colonists in New Haven or Salem knew more about the courts of St. Petersburg or Versailles than they knew about their neighbors in Williamsburg or Savannah, certainly before the middle of the 1700s.[9]

This provincialism extended to even the most prosperous colonists. Before they attended the first Continental Congress in Philadelphia, neither Samuel nor John Adams had ever left Massachusetts. In early 1773, one of their patriot colleagues, Josiah Quincy, Jr., decided to find out what other colonists were like. Ostensibly seeking warmer climes to soothe his tuberculosis, Quincy also had political motives in his plan to tour the American continent: he wanted to learn what others thought about the Boston radicals. Boarding ship just a few weeks after joining the newly formed Boston committee of correspondence, Quincy would eventually travel from the Carolinas to Rhode Island throughout the spring. Along the way, the twenty-nine-year-old served as Boston's ambassador: a one-man committee of correspondence making connections and arguments that furthered the patriot cause in the quiet months before the Tea Party.

After a harrowing sea journey, he arrived in Charleston, "traversing the town from one end to the other," meeting new friends. Some of those new acquaintances, including Edmund Rutledge, Thomas Lynch, Jr., and Charles Cotesworth Pinckney, would soon become leading patriots. For now, Quincy had some work ahead of him to convince Carolinians that Boston was worth supporting. At a dinner party held in his honor, Quincy noted how one guest grumbled that Britain "would do wisely to renounce the Colonies to the North and leave them prey to their continental neighbors or foreign powers." After listening to accusations that "Boston aims at Nothing less than the sovereignty of the whole continent," Quincy responded that the "Inhabitants of the Massachusetts paid a very great respect to all the Sister provinces, [and] that she revered, almost, the leaders in Virginia and much respected those of Carolina." His opponent was hardly placated. "When it comes to the test," he returned, "Boston will give the other provinces the shell and the shadow and keep the substance." This was dangerous talk, and it would not be the last time Quincy heard his fellow colonists question the virtue of Boston patriots.[10]

For his own part, Quincy found South Carolina a foreign—and, perhaps, hostile—place. "Cards, dice, the bottle and horses engross prodigious portions of time and attention," he concluded. During another social occasion with "about 20 or 30" "more elder substantial gentlemen," Quincy related that the conversation revolved mainly around "negroes, Rice, and the necessity of British Regular troops to be quartered in Charlestown: there were not wanting men of fortune, sense and attachment to their country, who were zealous for the establishing such troops here." Even outside these disturbing social gatherings, Quincy was nervous. "The whole body almost of this people," he decided, "seem averse to the claims and assumptions of the British Legislature over the Colonies; but you will seldom hear even in political conversations any warm or animated expressions against the measures of administration. Their fiercer passions seem to be employed upon their slaves and here to expend themselves."[11]

The grip of slavery on South Carolina astounded the young man from Braintree, Massachusetts. He recognized the anxiety that such vicious bondage created. "A few years ago," he wrote, "it is allowed, that the Blacks exceeded the Whites as 17 to 1. There are those who now tell you that the Slave[s] are not more than 3 to 1, some pretend not so many. But they who talk thus are afraid that the Slaves should by some means discover their superiority; many people express great fears of an insurrection, others treat the idea as chimerical." In the end, Quincy must have been concerned that, given this focus on maintaining security among their slaves and how "prevalent" the "general doubt of the firmness and integrity of the Northern Colonies" was in South Carolina, any predictions of a political union between his old friends in Boston and his new ones in Charleston were foolish.[12]

As Quincy began his overland journey north, his health might have improved, but his unease probably did not. In North Carolina, he met more potential allies, including William Hooper, Robert Howe, and Cornelius Harnett (whom he referred to as the "Samuel Adams of North Carolina"). Here, he found "the plan of Continental correspondence highly relished, much wished for and resolved upon, as proper to be pursued." But he also acknowledged that it was "very apparent" there was "no great friendship or esteem" between the two Carolinas. "There is very little, if any kind, of commerce or intercourse between the No[rth] and So[uth] prov of Carolina, and there is very little, if any more, of regard in the Inh[abitan]ts of the one Colony for those of the other."[13]

Traveling north that April—exactly two years before war would break out—Quincy must have found the notion of unity laughable. Noting a "very bitter, and important" contest between religious groups in Virginia and Maryland, he proceeded to Pennsylvania. In Philadelphia, he dined with some of the city's leading political lights, including Joseph Galloway, George Clymer, William Allen, Benjamin Rush, and John Dickinson. He heard whispers that Benjamin Franklin was "a very trimmer—a very courtier," a fact that Quincy had already "ever believed." Allen, Pennsylvania's chief justice, gossiped that Franklin was "the first proposer of the Stamp Act," leading Quincy to the conclusion that "men who are very great foes to each other in this province, unite in their doubts, insinuations and revilings of Franklin." Despite this backbiting, Quincy decided that Pennsylvanians "as a body of people may be justly characterized as industrious, sensible, and wealthy." He celebrated the "benevolence, hospitality, sociability, and politeness" of the "excellent city" of Philadelphia. Still, although the middle colonies might be better matched to Quincy's home region than the slave plantations of Carolina, they faced big problems, too. "There is a general disliking," he related, "not to say antipathy among the Quakers against N[ew] Eng[lan]d: and this aversion has its influence in their judgment on the men and things of that country, and especially in their opin[ion] concerning the public transaction of the Massachusetts Bay." The source of this disaffection was Massachusetts's history of religious intolerance. "They are frequently calling to mind and often relating little anecdotes of the severities used towards their ancestors in that province.—No doubt the story is exaggerated, but they give it credit, and feel accordingly."[14]

What might Quincy have reported back to his Boston patriot colleagues in May 1773? What predictions might he have made about the chances of unity? Any honest briefing could not have been positive: South Carolinians were more troubled about their slaves than anything else. The Chesapeake was preoccupied with its own religious controversy. Pennsylvania was equally self-absorbed with internal politics, making it difficult to distinguish friends from enemies. Furthermore, many Pennsylvanians still held a grudge against the New England Puritans who had hanged Quakers more than a century ago. People in different provinces who nevertheless had a lot in common, such as those in the two Carolinas, could not stand one another— which did not bode well for their prospects with strangers a thousand miles away. And, above all, the distrust and disagreement about Boston's public proceedings was the most worrisome: if the crisis continued and the crown singled Massachusetts out, forthcoming sympathy and aid could not be considered automatic. Although all was not lost, Quincy was surely not optimistic about the chances of a common cause just a few months before the Boston Tea Party.[15]

Historians of eighteenth-century America would offer that, contrary to

Quincy's conclusions, the colonies were not nearly as different as these reports suggested. Throughout the American continent, colonial societies, economies, and cultures were actually converging in the middle decades of the 1700s, in large part because the Atlantic itself shifted from a barrier to a bridge. As a result of maturing communication and trade networks, more and more ships laden with goods, information, and people — whether by choice or by force — traversed the ocean. Merchants offered greater variety; discerning consumers could be particular about the texture of their imported cloth, the glaze of their tea set, or where their enslaved person came from. Widespread religious revivals also widened horizons and brought American provincials into contact with other colonial ideas, writings, and people. Still, Quincy wasn't entirely off-base: even though underlying factors might have been bringing the colonies together, the perception of difference remained powerful.[16]

It stands to reason the British would also find the prospect of American unity laughable. By the middle of the 1770s, the British government could consult a thick catalog of predictions reassuring them that any actions taken against Massachusetts would not create continental sympathy. But, more than informants' reports, events also offered distinctive proof of widespread disunity.

Internal conflicts and jurisdictional tensions surfaced throughout the continent from the New Hampshire frontier to South Carolina in the 1760s and 1770s. Clashes over land rights, political access, or good government flared up during the imperial crisis with Parliament. As Quincy recognized, religious dissenters challenged both the Anglican establishment and the social hierarchy of Virginia's planter elite. Men and women of the lower class in Philadelphia, Boston, and New York City demanded economic and political reforms. In New Jersey, disgruntled yeoman farmers renewed their decades-old struggles against large land proprietors in 1769, when a group calling themselves the Liberty Boys protested debt collection and exorbitant lawyers' fees by blockading the Monmouth County courthouse and burning one prominent landholder's barn.[17]

There were "regulators" everywhere in the late 1760s. On the frontiers of Pennsylvania, angry settlers who called themselves the Black Boys attacked trade caravans heading west from Philadelphia. Those wagons carried goods and weapons sent from urban merchants and bound for Indian country, and frontier vigilantes intercepted and destroyed the matériel — before it could be used against *them*. In South Carolina, backcountry planters also took justice into their own hands during those years. Angry that the provincial

MAP 3. *Sites of Colonial Conflict, 1760s–1770s. Drawn by Gerry Krieg*

government's failure to establish a proper system of courts and jails in the backcountry hindered slavery expansion, aspiring interior planters called themselves "Regulators" and initiated a vigilante crime-fighting campaign from 1767 to 1770. They were not the only ones to invoke the law-abiding name of "regulator." Settlers in North Carolina's piedmont, too, used it to refer to their fight against a provincial government dominated by coastal elites. The North Carolina Regulation began in 1766 with the formation of a political reform movement in Orange County. This group, which also likened itself to the Sons of Liberty, petitioned the Newbern government to repeal regressive taxes, end skyrocketing legal fees, and investigate corrupt local officials who wantonly embezzled funds. Their grievances, too, fell upon deaf ears. Over the next few years, the crisis escalated until the spring of 1771, when Governor William Tryon, believing that the entire backcountry might revolt against his government, marched a small militia force into the interior. On May 16, 1771, Tryon and 1,185 soldiers engaged and defeated more than 2,000 Regulators at Alamance, a battle that resulted in thirty fatalities, two hundred casualties, and seven executions for treason.[18]

These internal clashes would pose significant challenges for the common cause once the war began. Friends in the early 1770s could be enemies a few years later. Often, despite wrapping themselves in the mantle of the Sons of Liberty, many of the insurgent leaders and their adherents would take different sides during the Revolution. Conversely, the opponents of New Jersey's Liberty Boys were, in fact, in the vanguard of the Revolutionary movement. A shared feeling of intercolonial trust and unity would require some forgetting.[19]

The necessity of collective amnesia was most evident in the case of the North Carolina Regulators. The battle of Alamance was one of the rare times before the Revolution that colonial events crowded out news from Europe in American newspapers. Throughout the continent, printers published accounts from both sides during the summer of 1771. From early reports out of Carolina, readers learned that the Regulators were "lawless desperadoes" whose "dangerous and daring conspiracy . . . threatened to overwhelm this once flourishing province in one scene of horrid confusion and lawless fury!" But some in Boston viewed Alamance through the lens of the clash with Britain and hatred for their own royal governor. Three of the leaders of the Boston resistance movement — Dr. Thomas Young, Joseph Greenleaf, and printer Isaiah Thomas — published a series of articles in the *Massachusetts Spy* that vilified Tryon and his Newbern supporters. Young called Tryon a bloodthirsty tyrant and charged the militia force with acting like a medieval *"Posse Commitatus."* Greenleaf referred to Tryon's friends as a "banditti of robbers" and retorted, "What shall we in future think of the term Loyalist, should it continue any time to be exclusively applied to extortioners, traitors, robbers, and murderers?"[20]

Naturally, supporters of Tryon's government — including future patriot leaders like Samuel Johnston and Josiah Quincy's future friends William Hooper and Robert Howe — were outraged when copies of the *Spy* reached the capital of Newbern a month later. On July 29, in a public meeting in Newbern, they voted to indict Thomas, Greenleaf, and Young and conduct a public "execution" of the Massachusetts printer. Issue number 17 of the *Spy* was then taken to the county sheriff to be "publicly burnt under the gall[ow]s by the common hangman . . . as a testimony of the utter abhorrence and detestation in which that infamous production and its still more infamous authors are held by the people of this government."[21]

Fewer than four years later, these theatrical condemnations could be added to the list of all the ways the Revolution turned the world upside down. In the wake of the Coercive Acts, when Young and Greenleaf—who had since gone on to become principal organizers of the Boston committee of correspondence—sought assurances that the colonies south of Massachusetts backed Boston's protests, they appealed to the same men who had burned them in effigy. When Quincy's tour brought him to North Carolina in the spring of 1773, he found that, after talking to the very people his Boston friends had condemned, he was forced to "change my opinion of the Regulators and Governor Tryon." A few days later, he dined with "the most celebrated lawyers," whom he now referred to as "sensible Tryonists." Those "sensible" men were the "banditti of robbers" Greenleaf and Young had condemned only a few months hence and the same group who burned the *Spy* in retaliation. To make matters worse, almost a year after Lexington, Greenleaf's aggrieved Regulator heroes turned out in large numbers to fight against the patriot cause. As Quincy found out in person, any predictions in 1772 that put the Boston Sons of Liberty and the Regulators on the same side in the conflict with Britain would turn out to be false just a few years later.[22]

Forgetting recent disagreements or rivals might have been uncomfortable, but it was not impossible. Nor was it the most serious threat to union. Violent competition between colonies, however, might be. British economist Josiah Tucker dared to suggest in 1776 that it was in the crown's best economic and imperial interest to recognize American independence because "the moment a separation takes effect, intestine quarrels will begin: For it is well known, that the seeds of discord and dissention between Province and Province are now ready to shoot forth." Once true civil war erupted among the thirteen colonies, Parliament would be considered their "protectors, mediators, and benefactors." Again, evidence in the years leading up to the Revolution buoyed Tucker's confidence that America would need Britain to play umpire between the provinces.[23]

In the middle years of the 1770s, while Boston leaders begged other provinces to create correspondence committees, border controversies between Pennsylvania and Virginia, New York and New Hampshire, and Connecticut and Pennsylvania threatened to undermine the infant notion of a common cause. Unclear colonial charters, imperfect geographic knowledge, and the bureaucratic muddle of the British Empire led to competing land claims that lurched toward violence as imperial authority increasingly collapsed in the 1770s. Tensions simmered throughout the middle colonies. Settlers from Connecticut and Pennsylvania fought over the Wyoming Valley region surrounding the upper Susquehanna River, land agents from New York battled with New Hampshire squatters in the Green Mountains, and, in the most serious clash, the competing claims of Pennsylvanians, Virginians, and Shawnee Indians to the Ohio Valley surrounding Pittsburgh led to open warfare in the summer of 1774.[24]

Both Connecticut and Pennsylvania believed the Wyoming Valley, a twenty-mile stretch of arable flatland surrounding the north branch of the Susquehanna River, belonged to them. In 1753, authorities in Connecticut organized the Susquehanna Company to promote settlement to what they believed would be a new colony; their purpose was to found "a New Connecticut in institutions, laws, and people." The Seven Years' War temporarily delayed the Susquehanna Company from fulfilling this vision. Pennsylvania leaders, however, denied the Susquehanna claim. After successfully pressing the Iroquois to sell them those same lands at the 1768 Treaty of Fort Stanwix, Pennsylvania authorities opened their own land office in January 1769. Soon, settlers from both colonies, armed with guns and axes, converged on the valley.[25]

The Pennsylvanians got there first. When the first forty families from Connecticut arrived, the Pennsylvania settlers had their leaders arrested for trespassing. Tensions escalated as more settlers arrived in the spring of 1769. By the summer, there was war. According to one Pennsylvanian's account of the fighting, "Two Hundred Miscreants, composed of the Dregs of [Connecticut] . . . Horse-stealers, Debtors, and other Runaways, . . . came likewise armed into this Province" led by "Captain's Cowardice," but these *"fierce Warriors"* were soon forced to surrender "with Tears in their Eyes." The Connecticut "cowards" would have their revenge, however, when new Susquehanna president Zebulon Butler recruited a few dozen of the notorious, outlawed Paxton Boys to help them fight in exchange for free land. One of them, Lazarus Stewart, would murder a deputy and become a fugitive from Pennsylvania authorities. Together, the Connecticut settlers and Paxton Boys routed the Pennsylvanians in early 1770. For the next several months, raids—involving hundreds of men and resulting in casualties on both sides—ravaged the valley.[26]

After thirteen months of bitter fighting, by the end of 1771, Butler's Connecticut Yankees and his hired guns held Wyoming. From 1772 to 1775, there was a tentative, anxious peace in the valley, but ill feelings remained. How those frustrations and vengeful impulses might surface once the colonies found themselves at war was a troubling thought. The Connecticut settlers, at least, signified that they backed the patriots by naming their town after two of the colonies' most fervent English supporters, John Wilkes and Isaac Barré. Still, what consequences this violent episode might have for intercolonial relations were unknowable in the spring of 1775. And, more important, the potential for a damaging renewal of the conflict was a grave concern for patriot leaders.

Connecticut and Pennsylvania were not the only colonies with boundary fights just before the Revolution. The Green Mountains controversy began in the 1740s, when the ambitious first governor of New Hampshire, Benning Wentworth, creatively read his colony's charter and subsequently began selling lands to the west of the Connecticut River, which he called the "New Hampshire Grants." New York governor George Clinton, believing these lands belonged to his government, appealed to the king for justice. It took fifteen years to get an answer. In 1764, the crown ruled in favor of New York. Over the next decade, New York governors sold patents for more than two million acres in the Green Mountains. But, because it took so long to reach a settlement in this case, by 1765, there were more than fifteen thousand people already living there, families from New England who had settled in the Grants at Wentworth's encouragement. In the late 1760s, the landlords from New York began to demand rents from people they deemed squatters. When they refused, the landowners filed nine ejectment suits in New York courts in 1770. The eviction cases — which were adjudicated by future Continental Congress delegates James Duane and Robert Livingston — convinced the settlers they needed to organize a paramilitary unit to defend themselves. Like the North Carolina Regulators and New Jersey Liberty Boys, the Green Mountain Boys, led by Ethan Allen, also equated their struggle with the Sons of Liberty. They argued that their defense of their lands was the same, justifiable act as those taken by Bostonians against parliamentary tyranny. "If the Grants equaled America," one historian has argued, "then New York was its Britain."[27]

New York authorities, of course, rejected this interpretation. They saw the Green Mountain Boys as an illegal gang, referring to them instead as the "Bennington Mob," and repeatedly called for their arrest. Just a few days before the House of Commons began debate over the Boston Port Act, Governor Tryon — whose reassignment from North Carolina gave him certain insights on how to deal with backcountry uprisings — proclaimed that the real object of the "Bennington Mob" was to "spread Terror and Destruction through that part of the Country which is exposed to their oppression." The provincial assembly, following Tryon's call, passed a special riot-and-treason law that explicitly sentenced Allen, his cousin Remember Baker, and six other Green Mountain Boys to death if captured. The "Bloody Act," as the Boys would call it, generated a great deal of ill will between leaders like Allen and George Clinton — who chaired the committee that passed the bill of attainder and who would soon uncomfortably find themselves on the same side.[28]

Although no blood would be spilled in this confrontation, the pressure of property destruction, hurt feelings, and worry was building. Patriots did not know how Allen and the Green Mountain Boys would respond to the news of war. Just as with Tryon's former opponents in North Carolina, because the imperial conflict was superimposed upon this separate but just as vital internal struggle, many colonists wondered what side the Boys would support. Allen had continually justified his cause by conflating the attempts by New York landlords to seize their property with Parliament's efforts to do the same. But, as in the Wyoming Valley, there was potential for internal conflict in the New Hampshire Grants. If the Green Mountain Boys saw war in New England as an opportunity to attack their enemies in New York, this would be a distressing development to the common cause. Or, also as in the Wyoming controversy, the degree to which the Green Mountain conflict might poison relations between New York and New England could also be a problem for mutual feelings of trust.

The most dangerous intercolonial border dispute, however, was the competition between Virginia and Pennsylvania over the Pittsburgh region of the Ohio Valley. Late in 1772, the British army garrison at Fort Pitt packed up and retreated east. Representatives from both Virginia and Pennsylvania rushed to fill the political vacuum they left behind. For a decade, families from all over the mid-Atlantic had flouted the Royal Proclamation of 1763 that forbade new settlement west of the Allegheny Mountains. But their ambition paled in comparison to land speculators in Philadelphia, Williamsburg, and London who eyed the Ohio country with delight.[29]

Prospective speculators pooled their resources to gain influence over the region, forming competing land companies that jockeyed for royal permission to access the Ohio. They lobbied for the king to form a new inland colony. Pennsylvania governor John Penn laughed that this was a huge waste of time. There was no controversy: that land belonged to his colony. Penn moved to cut off these lobbying efforts by creating Westmoreland County and deputized local landowner Arthur St. Clair to supervise affairs there for Pennsylvania. Virginia, on the other hand, claimed the Ohio belonged to them. Virginia governor Lord Dunmore took matters into his own hands—he went there personally. Confident that Virginia's charter rights would triumph in the legal contest for the Ohio Valley, Dunmore toured the region in late summer 1773. When he returned to Williamsburg, he issued a proclamation calling on any settlers living west of the mountains to rally to Virginia and in early 1774 sent Dr. John Connolly as his agent in Pittsburgh.[30]

For the next two years, while Penn and Dunmore sparred with one another, each issuing official proclamations that denounced the other's actions, St. Clair and Connolly themselves battled for support among the surrounding settlers in Pittsburgh. In this high-stakes political game, Connolly was the more ruthless. He organized a militia force, declared himself "captain commandant" of Pittsburgh, threw St. Clair in jail, and encouraged surveyors to go down the Ohio. When those surveyors came into conflict with another group who believed they had rightful claim to the region, the Shawnee Indians, this building tension spilled over into violence. As soon as word reached Pittsburgh that a number of Shawnees attacked a surveying party, Connolly moved swiftly to capitalize on this opportunity to bolster his authority by circulating notices alerting settlers to Shawnee raids. By the end of April, premeditated, cold-blooded attacks touched off a series of escalating raids that quickly became a full-fledged war between Virginia and the Shawnees, known as Dunmore's War.[31]

Dunmore's War, which ended after an inconclusive engagement at Point Pleasant on October 10, 1774 (the same day John Adams marveled in his diary about the "Wit, Sense, Learning, Acuteness, Subtlety, [and] Eloquence" of his new associates at the First Continental Congress), was equally inconclusive in settling the intercolonial controversy. Whereas Dunmore saw Point Pleasant as a decisive ratification of Virginia's claim, Pennsylvanians were aghast at the actions of the governor and his agent in Pittsburgh. Suspicions persisted, east and west of the Allegheny Mountains. Chaos continued to reign out West, especially after both Dunmore's and Penn's authority collapsed a few short months after Point Pleasant. What would come of that disorder, more important, could not be ascertained at the start of war with Britain. Whoever could stabilize the region and bring an end to the violence would have a significant advantage in earning the backcountry's allegiance.[32]

But the reaction to frontier violence in 1774 reveals another latent weakness that threatened continental unity in 1775. When eastern colonists read in their newspapers about the brutal attacks perpetrated by the men associated with Virginia, their sympathies often ran to the aggrieved Natives. Widely published reports about Ohio violence consistently invoked concepts of civility and savagery—but the barbarians were not Indians. Philadelphia printers, though hardly objective, vilified Connolly and the Virginians as a *"gang of* worse Savages."[33]

The border fight over the Pittsburgh region did more than just alienate Pennsylvanians from Virginians; it showcased the deep cultural divide between East and West. But the line between civility and savagery was reversed. When newspaper reports maligned Dunmore's men as "worse savages," they exposed the disdain of many along the Eastern Seaboard for "frontier banditti." When war broke out with Britain, it would seem a reasonable forecast that the patriots would not seek the assistance of those "worse savages." This posed a not-insignificant problem for future patriots: Connolly aside, the people castigated and denounced in the frontier violence of 1774 turned out to be some of their warmest friends in the approaching conflict with Britain. Hard work, selective remembering, and collective forgetting would be necessary to change public perception.

Internal conflicts, intercolonial disputes, long-standing and still-raw cultural disparities between East and West, North and South: each of these factors narrowed the chances of the colonies' coming together in a durable union. There was another risk in the 1770s. Agitation against the institution of slavery was rising to unprecedented levels in the early years of that turbulent decade. An antislavery movement began to emerge from evangelical and dissenting religious circles in Britain and America in the 1760s. A few Quaker, Methodist, and Baptist luminaries began to prick the public's conscience about the evils of the African slave trade by preaching sermons, publishing tracts, petitioning legislatures, and filing lawsuits. The imperial controversy with Britain helped antislavery sentiment gain traction in the colonies because many political writers invoked the metaphor of slavery to illustrate what was at stake if they complied with parliamentary reform. Together — albeit with different motives — religious activists like Samuel Hopkins and Anthony Benezet and patriot polemicists like James Otis and John Dickinson brought increasing attention to the slavery problem and its relationship to colonial society. As Josiah Quincy heard directly from slavery-obsessed South Carolinians, if the common cause was also one that threatened their precious institution, they might well decide the Revolution wasn't worth it.[34]

Decades before the American Revolution, some Quaker leaders reminded their brethren that slavery was a sin. Benjamin Lay and John Woolman argued, in the middle years of the eighteenth century, that their fellow Quakers should purge themselves of the curse of bonded labor. Although some of this antislavery sentiment did reach the general public, especially Woolman's 1754 tract *Some Considerations on the Keeping of Negroes,* it was mainly directed internally as an effort to purify the Society of Friends. At the same time, however, Anglo-American religious revivalism also contributed to a slow, steady turn against slavery. As the final quarter of the eighteenth century approached, there was an increasing and unprecedented protest on both sides of the Atlantic against the trading and keeping of slaves. Soon Quaker Anthony Benezet and New Light Congregationalist Samuel Hopkins began to ask colonists of all faiths to rethink their keeping of slaves and, especially, their importation of new people from Africa. Benezet became the leading colonial campaigner against the slave trade. Beginning in the middle of the Seven Years' War, he authored a series of pamphlets that exposed the horrors of the Middle Passage, recruited other sympathetic Pennsylvanians to go on the record against the practice, and cultivated a correspondence network.[35]

Yet, despite this increasing criticism, slaveholders did not have to worry about Benezet's fire catching. Though genuine and passionate, eighteenth-century antislavery sentiment — whether the sources were radical Protestantism or Enlightenment rationalism — lacked political organization and was largely inconsequential. It was, as one historian has put it, "antislavery without abolitionism." When and if this dissent could be located in a political context, however, those arguments might be quite effective.[36]

By the eve of the American Revolution, this was increasingly the case. From the passage of the Sugar Act in 1764 until the outbreak of war, colonial opponents of Parliament consistently argued that they were being enslaved. Slavery, they shouted, was the worst of all possible political fates; it resulted from unchecked power. Enslavement was defined by various measures: when one was taxed without his or her consent, provinces were ruled without representation, the populace was left to the mercy of standing armies, ancient charters were amended or abridged, decisions for compensating court and government officials were taken out of local hands. For colonial polemicists like John Dickinson, when these political rights are stripped, *"We* are therefore — SLAVES." Pamphleteers and essayists incessantly invoked the metaphor of slavery to describe what lay in store for America throughout the imperial crisis. Of course, the presence of thousands of enslaved people — especially in the 1770s, when the percentage of African Americans as a proportion of the total population was greater than it had ever been before or since (21.4 percent) — reinforced these arguments, but most patriot writers ignored or sidestepped the plight of actual slaves and focused on the victims of parliamentary conspiracy.[37]

Not all did. Four years before he became John Mein's tormentor, James Otis famously stated in a 1764 pamphlet that, by the law of nature, all men, white or Black, were freemen. "Does it follow," he wrote, "that 'tis right to enslave a man because he is black?" Otis pulled actual and metaphorical slavery together, cautioning, "It is a clear truth that those who every day barter away other men's liberty will soon care little for their own." Nearly a decade later, Benjamin Rush, at Benezet's behest, published *An Address to the Inhabitants of the British Settlements, on the Slavery of the Negroes in America.* "Ye men of Sense and Virtue," Rush implored, "ye Advocates for American Liberty, rouse up and espouse the cause of Humanity and general Liberty." After a West Indian planter living in Philadelphia challenged Rush point by point, the physician responded in turn with a second edition, all in the hectic year of 1773. Rush's amended tract deepened his call for the patriots to live up to their ideals: "Where is the difference between the British Senator who attempts to enslave his fellow subjects in America, by imposing Taxes upon them contrary to Law and Justice; and the American Patriot who reduces his African Brethren to Slavery, contrary to Justice and Humanity?" "Blush ye pretended votaries for freedom! ye trifling patriots!" chastised Massachusetts minister John Allen in a 1774 pamphlet. "For while you are fasting, praying, non-importing, non-exporting, remonstrating, resolving, and pleading for a restoration of your charter rights, you at the same time are continuing this lawless, cruel, inhuman, and abominable practice of enslaving your fellow-creatures, which is so disgraceful to human nature." Allen, who began his tract by defining political and civic slavery, implored his fellow patriots not to be hypocritical. Most, however, did not make the connections to Africans that Rush, Otis, and Allen did. Nevertheless, whether or not they included real bondsmen and -women in their critiques, patriot polemicists deliberated on, appealed to, worried about, and talked openly regarding the concept of slavery during the decade before Lexington. This was new — for everyone.[38]

By incessantly talking, writing, and thinking about slavery, people on both sides of the imperial controversy began to "see" the institution anew. In the 1770s, a wave of legislative and legal reform was indeed gathering momentum. In the spring of 1772, the Court of the King's Bench heard testimony on the case of James Somerset. He was a man born in Africa, sold into slavery in Virginia, and taken to England as his master's personal servant. When Somerset escaped in London, his master, Charles Steuart, recaptured him and arranged for transportation to the West Indies for resale. British abolitionists, led by Granville Sharp, saw in Somerset an opportunity to test whether the British legal system would support slavery or freedom. Britain's chief justice, Lord Mansfield, decided for Somerset, supposedly ruling that slavery was "so odious, that nothing can be suffered to support it, but positive law." What this meant for slaves at home and in the larger empire was unclear. Since England had no positive law legalizing slavery, Sharp and his colleagues boasted that Mansfield's edict had swept England of slavery and emancipated all of the 14,000 bonded men and women residing in the British Isles. Although this was not the case, *Somerset*'s implications for slavery in the Americas was the subject of wide speculation.[39]

"A Correspondent says, This Cause seems pregnant with consequences," summarized one account of the decision that appeared in several colonial newspapers. But how pregnant? The confusion over what the ruling really signified in London—fueled in large part by abolitionists who broadcast the case as the "great negro cause"—was reflected across the Atlantic. Various news reports from England informed colonists of the progress of the "much talked of cause of Somerset," a case that "concerns the whole British nation," and a few American printers found space for speeches, including final pleadings and a summary of Mansfield's decision once the case concluded. Still, what *Somerset* would mean for slaves and slaveholders in the British Empire was unclear. Nor was it obvious that this would be roundly denounced in the colonies. Some English correspondents surmised Mansfield's decision would have a negative effect. One report opined, "The late decision with regard to Somerset the Negro . . . will occasion a greater ferment in America . . . than the Stamp Act itself." Then again, an English abolitionist commentary published in Philadelphia and Williamsburg reflected the ubiquitous natural rights discourse about freedom and slavery. Parliament simply could not make positive law on this topic because "the laws of nature are the laws of God." If they did, where would it end? "If Negroes are to be slaves on account of colour, the next step will be to enslave every Mulattoe in the kingdom; then all the Portuguese; next the French, then the brown complexioned English; and so on till there be only one free man left, which will be the man of the palest complexion in the three kingdoms!" After the dust settled on the "great Negro cause," it was apparent that the decision did not challenge property rights in the Americas—yet. That relief had to be tempered with concern among slaveholders that, with all this discussion of slavery set in the context of other complaints about abridged political rights, perhaps their property was not truly secure.[40]

At any rate, the larger perception that emerged from the *Somerset* case for Britons at home was a popular notion that Britain was different from its colonies; unlike its territorial possessions, Britain itself was "a unique asylum for liberty." Antislavery activists in the colonies, though, were trying to close that gap. During the same years James Somerset was becoming an Atlantic celebrity, several colonial political bodies—influenced partly by rights talk, partly by economic interests, and partly by public pressure—made plans to decrease the number of slaves in their communities. The year before *Somerset,* the Massachusetts General Court approved a bill to prohibit the importation of slaves from Africa. It failed when Governor Thomas Hutchinson refused to sign it, citing it as unnecessary given the paltry demand for slaves in the Bay Colony. In 1772, the House of Burgesses tried to prohibit new Africans from being sold in Virginia. Slavery had been so successful in the Old Dominion that the slave population was now growing steadily on its own, and, by the 1770s, with soils beginning to wear out and planters' debts climbing, continued imports made little financial sense. Patriots in Virginia merged this economic self-interest with their protest of the Townshend Duties when they added slaves to the list of items they chose not to import in their 1769–1770 boycotts. On April 1, 1772, just a few weeks before opening arguments began in *Somerset*, the burgesses drafted an address to the king begging his "paternal Assistance in averting a Calamity of a most alarming Nature." They stated that the sale of African slaves "hath long been considered as a Trade of great Inhumanity" and, if not prohibited, "we have too much Reason to fear will endanger the very Existence of your Majesty's *American* Dominions." Like the Massachusetts bill of the previous year, the Virginia burgesses' 1772 address did not impress the king or his administration.[41]

The year following the "great Negro cause" saw a wave of antislavery fever building in several mainland colonies. In New York, Quaker petitioners successfully lobbied the legislature to approve a £20 duty for bringing slaves into the province, but it, too, failed when the royal governor did not assent. Benezet, who helped impress the consciences of New Yorkers by sending them Benjamin Rush's new pamphlet, also pressured political leaders in New Jersey. During its 1773 session, the New Jersey Assembly moved to amend the slave code to ease the procedures for masters to manumit as well as outlaw the slave trade. After a few proslavery petitions challenging these amendments arrived on the steps of the legislature, the whole affair was put off until next year's session, when it was postponed again. Colonial governments were not the only institutions that tried to take action against slavery in 1773. Four slaves, citing the "divine spirit of *freedom* [that] seems to fire every humane breast on this continent," appealed to the Boston committee of correspondence that they would lobby the General Court to "again take our deplorable case into serious consideration, and give us that ample relief which, *as men,* we have a natural right to." One Massachusetts town, Medfield, did not need to see this petition, which the Boston committee circulated widely throughout the province; they had already instructed their representatives to vote for legislation against slavery. Other towns followed suit, drafting resolutions against the slave trade in 1774. In their town meeting that year, the inhabitants of Providence also instructed their representatives to the Rhode Island Assembly to draft a bill against the slave trade and for gradual emancipation. Seeing the steps their neighbors were taking, the Connecticut Assembly also cut off slave importations in 1774.[42]

The pinnacle of the antislavery wave occurred when the First Continental Congress met in the fall of that year. In their deliberations about how to respond to the Coercive Acts, the Congress included slaves as part of the enumerated "goods" that would not be received in the mainland colonies. The second article of the boycott they crafted, known as the Continental Association, stipulated that the mainland colonies would "neither import nor purchase, any slave imported after the first day of December next; after which time, we will wholly discontinue the slave trade, and will neither be concerned in it ourselves, nor will we hire our vessels, nor sell our commodities or manufactures to those who are concerned in it."[43]

The Association put into policy the sentiment Thomas Jefferson had expressed just before the delegates sat in Philadelphia. "The abolition of domestic slavery is the great object of desire in those colonies where it was unhappily introduced in their infant state," he wrote his widely circulated tract *A Summary View of the Rights of British America.* Jefferson, apparently stung by the failure of the burgesses' 1772 plea to close the slave trade, considered the king's rejection of "our repeated attempts to effect this by prohibitions . . . so shameful an abuse of a power trusted with his majesty" that it was another significant reason to resist crown authority. A few months later, the town of Darien, Georgia, underscored Jefferson's sense of the colonies' desire. In the first few days of 1775, the inhabitants of Darien drafted a set of resolutions that included their "disapprobation and abhorrence of the unnatural practice of Slavery in *America* . . . a practice founded in injustice and cruelty, and highly dangerous to our liberties, (as well as lives,) debasing part of our fellow-creatures below men, and corrupting the virtue and morals of the rest; and is laying the basis of that liberty we contend for (and which we pray the Almighty to continue to the latest posterity) upon a very wrong foundation."[44]

Clearly, in the years right before the outbreak of war, a campaign against slavery was growing across Anglo-America. Influenced in part by the considerable discussions of political slavery and a deepening discourse of natural rights, by the end of 1774, there was an almost rapturous feeling of expectation that slavery might disappear from America, and soon. This was, at least, how Benjamin Rush interpreted events swirling about him. "We have now *turned from our wickedness,*" Rush rejoiced after Congress ratified the Association. "I venture to predict there will be not a Negro slave in North America in 40 years." The Philadelphia physician and pamphleteer concluded with an observation that lay at the root of why this dream would never come to fruition: "I now feel a *new* attachment to my native country, and I look forward with *new* pleasure to her future importance and grandeur."[45]

Tragically, predictions that slavery was doomed in America or that Americans would apply their assertions of natural rights to Africans quickly turned out to be illusions that dissolved right before the eyes of antislavery advocates. As powerful as that 1770s antislavery wave became, it crested in 1774 and receded even faster. The peak year for antislavery publications was 1773; according to one historian, that year saw more pamphlets attacking slavery than any other single year until 1819. It would be almost half a century before antislavery returned to this height. In a speech at the House of Burgesses in January 1773, Patrick Henry held forth that, if Virginians ended the slave trade and then maintained a "pity for [the slaves'] unhappy Lot and an abhorrence for Slavery," the time would soon arrive for complete abolition. Fewer than two years later, Henry received a letter from Samuel Allinson, a New Jersey Quaker unknown to him. Allinson begged Henry "to consider, that a fairer time never offered, to give a vital blow to the shameful custom of Slavery in America."[46]

That "fairer time" would be lost. In fact, the leading writers against slavery, especially Anthony Benezet, would be silent for nearly a decade after 1774. Throughout the first several years of the Revolution, only one significant pamphlet surfaced, Samuel Hopkins's *Dialogue concerning the Slavery of the Africans,* published in the spring of 1776. Although sentiment against slave imports continued through the 1770s, they did not translate into a consensus for abolition. Just a few days before the battle of Lexington, ten Philadelphians met at the Rising Sun Tavern to organize the Society for the Relief of Free Negroes Unlawfully Held in Bondage, the first abolitionist society in America. But, after four meetings, the group dissolved. What happened to the "great object of desire?"[47]

Historians have offered several reasons why what seemed like a growing public chorus against slavery collapsed. Some deny that it did. Scholars of a previous generation contended that abolition, especially in the North, remained a central thrust of the Revolution. Others, more recently, indict the patriots, especially in the North, for a lack of political will in letting this "fairer time" slip away. Still others cite practical elements, including a "serious paper shortage" that "reduced the number of all publications, including antislavery tracts," during the war. But Rush's personal reflection on what the antislavery wave made him feel about his country reveals a larger problem that must be taken into account: the drive for union.[48]

By no means did all colonists agree that ending actual slavery had anything to do with defending themselves against Parliament's efforts to enslave them. Rush might have felt "a new attachment" to America because he was sure the colonies were on the verge of giving the lie to Dr. Samuel Johnson's 1775 barb that "the loudest yelps for liberty" came from "among the drivers of negroes"; many others, plainly, did not. Johnson's quip would stand as a withering critique of the patriots because principled stands against slavery flew in the face of colonial unity and were, therefore, a significant threat to the entire resistance movement. As the New Jersey Assembly found out when a number of proslavery petitions arrived to challenge the Quakers' argument, there was no consensus on how to deal practically with the details of abolition, such as property rights, compensation, or the extension of political, economic, or legal rights to freed peoples. Especially since abolition arguments seemed to be gaining such traction both in Mansfield's England and in the halls of colonial legislatures, no matter what they personally felt about trading or keeping slaves, patriots needed to be concerned about a backlash. They had to consider what effect a wholesale embrace of abolition might have on the depth to which the populace trusted them and saw them as legitimate alternatives to the king's authority. Like the border controversies, slavery was a potential fault line undermining unity. Josiah Quincy's sarcastic observation that South Carolina's slave laws were "more of the policy of Pandemonium than the English constitution" shows how slavery could alienate, rather than unify, the colonies. Antislavery was antiunion, and this was no small problem. Hypocrisy and silence, in other words, were increasingly necessary evils as the patriots moved toward open conflict with Britain.[49]

War would, indeed, heighten public concern. When British officials began threatening, in the summer of 1775, to emancipate and arm slaves, patriots would encourage their fellow colonists to forget Johnson's gibe about drivers of negroes, instead calling attention to his insidious proposal a few paragraphs earlier "that the slaves should be set free" and thereby "furnished with fire arms for defence, and utensils for husbandry, and settled in some simple form of government within the country, [that] they may be more grateful and honest than their masters." The actions of resistant slaves and the at-least-rumored willingness of British authorities to sponsor those actions profoundly altered this wave in the summer of 1775. Behavior, and representations thereof, against the "benevolence" of self-congratulatory American political bodies who claimed they were putting slavery on the road to extinction directed the building antislavery sentiment into a completely different channel. The unity imperative quieted calls — when they should have been loudest — to extend rights to all. But that was not the only effect it had. The threat of slaves' attacking their masters had always been one of the darkest nightmares haunting the colonial imagination. When that fear was connected to British "proposals," like Dr. Johnson's "hints," it substantiated arguments that slavery needed to be protected, secured, and extended — not abolished. But patriot leaders did not know that before Lexington. On April 18, 1775, slavery was another serious threat to divide the colonies.[50]

The issue of slavery throws light upon the greatest weakness of all. Accusations of hypocrisy from across the Atlantic on the slave question were one thing; such claims could be much more distressing when they came from more proximate voices. Another outspoken Anglican minister, Samuel Seabury, rector of St. Peter's Church in Westchester, New York, addressed the slavery metaphor — and the patriot reticence to include actual slaves — in a 1774 pamphlet. Seabury wrote,

> Slavery under a republican Congress is as bad, at least, as slavery under a *King, Lords* and *Commons:* And upon the whole, that *liberty* under the supreme authority and protection of Great-Britain, is infinitely preferable to *slavery* under an American Congress. I will also agree with you, "that Americans are intitled to freedom." I will go further: I will own and acknowledge that not only *Americans* but *Africans, Europeans, Asiaticks,* all men, of all countries and degrees, of all sizes and complexions, have a right to as much freedom as is consistent with the security of civil society.

Seabury's contention — that colonists had far more reason to fear slavery from the patriots than from Parliament and that patriot lamentations about infringed natural rights were not to be trusted — underscores the largest threat facing intercolonial unity: the loyalist counterargument.[51]

Loyalists, too, saw conspiracy, illegality, and doom all around them in the mid-1770s. But, for them, the sources of that tyranny lay in committees and congresses. Yes, evil and designing men threatened liberty, but those men were Samuel Adams and Patrick Henry, not Lords North and Mansfield. Yes, a corrupt legislative body promised to destroy their way of life, but that institution was the Continental Congress, not Parliament. Supporting law and order was the true test of British patriotism. Loyalist writers, especially as the crisis accelerated after East India tea mixed with the waters of Boston Harbor, increasingly claimed that local committees did not express the people's voice; they were, instead, run by ambitious men who sought to elevate themselves at their country's expense. John Mein might have been forced out of Boston, but he was far from the only dangerous voice that proclaimed the patriots to be liars and hypocrites. A loyalist sent *New-York Gazetteer* printer James Rivington lyrics to a song that he said described the "portrait of an *American* Whig":

> He's a *rebel* by nature, a *villain* in grain
> A *saint* by profession, who never had grace:
> *Cheating* and *lying* are puny things,
> *Rapine* and *plundering* venial sins,
> His great occupation is *ruining nations,*
> *Subverting of Crowns,* and *murdering Kings.*[52]

Many loyalists argued, in the months before the outbreak of war, that Britain was the true fount of liberty and prosperity. The patriots were making disastrous choices to sever imperial institutions, commercial ties, a shared Protestant history, and a beloved royal family. Unity should include the British Isles in the shape of a reformed Anglo-American empire, not an independent America — which is what the traitorous faction from New England had secretly been after all along.

The patriots' position on Parliament, consent, colonial rights, and allegiance was just that: an interpretation. It was an argument with another side. And that counterargument was a legitimate one. Patriot leaders fashioned themselves "whigs," appropriating the celebrated example of the Glorious Revolution, but a not-insignificant percentage of the colonial public rejected this line and those who espoused it. For these people, a diverse group in class, geography, and outlook — ranging from upcountry settlers in the Deep South and Anglican parishioners in the Chesapeake to urban merchants in northern cities — the whigs were anything but the heroic defenders of the English constitution: they were rebels or insurrectionists or traitors. These labels could spell disaster for those who denied parliamentary sovereignty. If the common cause was to be at all successful, the public had to recognize the difference between actions taken by patriots in defense of their natural rights and those taken by traitors who subverted the constitution. Because the Revolution called upon people to decide who was legitimately in charge of America, whoever could win the battle over names had a significant advantage in legitimizing their side.

Hindsight tells us that the loyalists would lose the critical battle of public opinion for a number of reasons. Many loyalists held a political and cultural conservatism that led them to view "the people" as inherently unreliable and potentially licentious; prominent loyalists were naturally reticent to beg that the public reconsider their resistance to crown authority. They did not think the law needed defending out loud; it spoke for itself. Raising their voices — and patriot leaders sensed that their arguments were indeed changing people's minds — could be dangerous. Patriot leaders were not above encouraging retribution against loyalist writers and their publishers. Recall what happened to John Mein and to Rivington. Threats of violence to loyalist bodies or property also stymied their argument. A complicated mixture of factors caused the loyalists to fail.

But no one could predict who would win that battle on April 18, 1775. The specter of "rebel" or "traitor" was always at the door, haunting those who, it should be recalled, attempted to conduct the first large-scale colonial rebellion ever. Not only did the patriots have to be concerned that their actions might solidify the opposition and convince many colonists to support the king's arms; the larger worry was that people might not volunteer to fight against the British, participate on committees to raise money and supplies for that effort, or support the boycotts. They instead could vote against political candidates who supported resistance, or they could quietly undermine the authority of the patriot governments by shrugging off their stories at home or in the taverns and coffeehouses. It would take constant management to limit this dangerous sort of disaffection.

That the cause would not be common after all: this was the definitive threat to unity. Effective loyalist counterargument was at its most dangerous in the winter of 1774. After the First Continental Congress adjourned and local committees began enforcing the new Continental Association, loyalist writers vented their spleen as never before to undermine these steps. Every week for six months, Rivington's *New-York Gazetteer* and Draper's *Massachusetts Gazette* — two of the most popular papers in America — included poems, songs, notices, and essays that dripped with satire and sarcasm against the patriots. Loyalist pamphlets flooded the bookstalls in unprecedented numbers that winter. Their arguments, too, focused on the unlikely prospects of unity.[53]

"Rouse, my friends, rouse from your stupid lethargy," Samuel Seabury wrote as "A Westchester Farmer." "Mark the men who shall dare to impede the course of justice. Brand them as the infamous betrayers of the rights of their country." Seabury labeled patriot organizations "a riotous mob; — for a number of people, be they Committee-men, or who you please, assembled to do an unlawful action, especially in the night, deserve no better name." Two weeks later, Seabury produced another pamphlet, "The Congress Canvassed," which concluded with a dire prognosis if the "venomous" actions taken by Congress led to war. If independence was achieved, "we should

presently turn our arms on one another; — province on province, — and destruction and carnage would desolate the land." But, in the more likely case,
Britain would subdue the rebellion and then "the most dreadful scenes of
violence and slaughter — CONFISCATIONS and EXECUTIONS must close
the HORRID TRAGEDY." Finally, in a third pamphlet that explored the
slavery problem, Seabury contended that the Continental Congress was
"founded in sedition" and its resolutions "supported by tyranny."[54]

"A Westchester Farmer" directly challenged the patriots' scorecard of who
was right and wrong, who was justified and abusive, and who were the true
defenders of English liberties. He had a legitimate point. The Continental Congress was an illegal body without jurisdiction, and its authority was
based simply on the consent of the people as expressed in extralegal conven-
tions. But if people listened to Seabury, that consent might dissipate.

More worrisome for the patriots, Seabury's paper assault was hardly alone.
Other loyalist writers, including Myles Cooper, Jonathan Sewell, Jonathan
Boucher, and Thomas Bradbury Chandler, published pamphlets or wrote
lengthy newspaper essays during the winter of 1774–1775. When the First
Continental Congress passed the Association, especially with its creation of
local "committees of observation and inspection" to maintain compliance
in the nonimportation boycott, it also crossed the point of no return in the
eyes of many loyalists. As one historian has shown, those winter months witnessed the launching of a "British common cause." They were having their
own "Loyalist moment," convinced that now was the time to speak out.[55]

That was certainly the view of Daniel Leonard. Aged thirty-four in 1774,
Leonard was a member of one of the wealthiest families in Massachusetts.
After graduating second in his class at Harvard, Leonard practiced law, served
four terms in the Massachusetts House of Representatives, and, in the words
of close friend John Adams, "had been as ardent and explicit a patriot as I
was, or ever pretended to be." But that was before the Tea Party. Leonard's
break would become irreparable once he agreed to become a Mandamus
Councillor, one of the thirty-six crown appointees who replaced the elected
assembly under the new and hated Massachusetts Government Act. In the
final few weeks of a turbulent year, Leonard took up his quill, writing a series
of essays under the pseudonym "Massachusettensis."[56]

Because so "little has been published on the part of government," Leonard
began in the first of what would be seventeen letters published in the *Massachusetts Gazette; and the Boston Post-Boy and Advertiser*, "The effect this
must have had upon the minds of the people in general is obvious; they must
have formed their opinion upon a partial view of the subject." Imploring

the people of Massachusetts to "be calm," Leonard drew parallels between the "unaccountable phrenzy" of the present and the "Witchcraft" of New England's past. One must not follow the "madness" and "growing distemper" caused by "the bad policy of a popular party in this province," Leonard protested. He cited the tarring, feathering, beating, and whipping of loyalist John Malcolm as an instance of the "despotism" of the patriot party, which was "more incompatible with the rights of mankind, than the enormous monarchies of the East."[57]

Leonard's "Massachusettensis" series was a tour de force. He refuted patriot political theories, he countered whig interpretations of English history and how colonies were planted in America, and he continually argued that what the "patriots"—those "disappointed, ambitious, and envious men"—were really hatching was "rebellion," the "most atrocious offence that can be perpetrated by man." Never before in "the annals of the world," he concluded, had there been "so unnatural, so causeless, so wanton, so wicked, a rebellion."[58]

One of Leonard's keynotes, sounded from letter to letter, was another prediction about the improbability of intercolonial unity. The perceptive reasons that undergirded Leonard's disbelief were difficult to deny, as we have seen:

> There is perhaps as great a diversity between the tempers and habits of the inhabitants of this province, and the tempers and habits of the Carolinians, as there subsist between some different nations; nor need we travel so far, the Rhode-Islanders are as diverse from the people of the adjoining colony of Connecticut, as those mentioned before. Most of the colonies are rivals to each other in trade. Between others there subsist deep animosities, respecting their boundaries, which have heretofore produced violent altercations, and the sword of civil war has been more than once unsheathed, without bringing these disputes to a decision. It is apparent that so many discordant, heterogenius particles could not suddenly unite and consolidate into one body: It is most probable, that, if they were ever united, the union would be effected by some aspiring genius, putting himself at the head of the colonists army ... and taking advantage of the enfeebled, bleeding, and distracted state of the colonies, [would] subjugate the whole to the yoke of despotism.[59]

Unity would mean an American Cromwell or Caesar—or worse. Leonard could not conceive that, given all these countervailing factors, the "common cause" could possibly withstand war against the world's greatest military power. Without unity, what would happen to Massachusetts if the patriots had their way? Leonard, like Seabury and other loyalist writers during that season, predicted dark days ahead: "With the British navy in the front, Canadians and savages in the rear, a regular army in the midst, we must be certain that when ever the sword of civil war is unsheathed, desolation will pass through our land like a whirlwind, our houses be burnt to ashes, our fair possessions laid waste, and he that falls by the sword will be happy in escaping a more ignominious death."[60]

As loyalists raised their voices like never before, people were noticing. In early March 1775, one of Rivington's subscribers wrote from North Carolina, "The loyalists are lifting up their heads, and the saints, from their present appearance, will miss their dear commonwealth at last; A. W[estchester] Farmer, deserves the endless gratitude of every faithful subject." Putting his finger on another fault line, Rivington's Carolina informant boasted, "The western inhabitants will, in large numbers, address our worthy Governor, declaring their loyalty to the King and his laws, and their abhorrence of the colonies opposition." His thirst not yet slaked, the correspondent waited "with impatience" for shipments of Thomas Bradbury Chandler's advertised pamphlet, *What Think Ye of the Congress Now?* In that very publication, Chandler also acknowledged the shifting winds, celebrating that "the eyes of my countrymen and fellow-citizens begin, at last, to be opened to their true interest and happiness," and the "pretended *Sons of Liberty* . . . have already passed the meridian of their power and importance."[61]

These arguments, gone unchecked, could imperil the legitimacy of the common cause. If the patriots were to achieve victory, it was of vital importance that the public ignore the frightful loyalist warnings and reject them wholesale. This battle was reaching a crisis. On the first day of 1775, patriot leader James Warren lamented to Sam Adams, "The publications of Massachusettensis are read [by loyalists] with more devotion and Esteem than Holy writt." John Adams later admitted the real problem with "Massachusettensis": he was good. Leonard attacked the patriots, but he also reassured "the whole people" that "you are loyal at heart, friends to good order, and do violence to yourselves in harbouring one moment, disrespectful sentiments towards Great Britain, the land of our forefathers' nativity, the sacred repository of their bones." "These Papers were well written, abounded with Wit, discovered good Information, and were conducted with a Subtlety of Art and Address," Adams would confess in his autobiography. They were "wonderfully calculated to keep Up the Spirits of their Party, to depress ours, to spread intimidation and to make Proselytes among those, whose Principles and Judgment give Way to their fears, and these compose at least one third of Mankind." "Week after week passed away," he remembered, "and these Papers made a very visible impression on many Mind[s]." This was no hot-headed John Mein, someone who could be goaded into destroying himself. This situation was even more dangerous. Much later, Adams would think back on the "great exultation among the tories and gloomy apprehensions among the whigs" the "Massachusettensis" essays had produced during those critical winter weeks. Only one thing could be done, he recalled of his deci-sion: "I instantly resolved to enter the lists with him."[62]

Alexander Hamilton, but seventeen years of age, wrote two extended refutations of Seabury's Westchester letters — both published, interestingly, by James Rivington. A few anonymous letters appeared attacking "Massa-chusettensis." But it was John Adams's "Novanglus" letters, which appeared in Edes and Gill's *Boston Gazette* from January to April 1775, that sought to match Leonard point by point in an extended printed debate. The punch and counterpunch of "Massachusettensis" and "Novanglus" shed light on the often-misunderstood context of the years and months leading up to Lexington. It is too often discounted that there were two legitimate sides to this conflict, and it was not automatic, foreordained, or inevitable which one would gain overwhelming popularity when the bullets began to fly. That there were two sides to the issue or a yawning gulf in interpretation over the burgeoning crisis in 1775 should hardly surprise. What the Adams-Leonard print battle should tell us, however, is that no one at the time counted on his side's gaining widespread support. We know what would happen, but they did not. With thousands uncommitted, winning the battle of language and convincing enough of "the people" — on whose consent, opinion, and authority the patriot argument wholly rested — might be the secret to ulti-mate success. That such a campaign needed to be waged, however, is another example of the obstacles standing in the way of American unity in 1775.[63]

"Massachusettensis" argued that his series was meant to "penetrate the *arcana*" and "expose the wretched policy of the whigs." Adams could not let that stand, arguing in the first of twelve installments that he sought to "penetrate arcana too. — Shew the wicked policy of the Tories." Adams con-tested Leonard's plea to the senses of the people at large with his own call: "The cause of the whigs is not conducted by intrigues at a distant court, but by constant appeals to a sensible and virtuous people; it depends intirely on their good will, and cannot be pursued a single step without their concur-rence, to obtain which, all designs, measures, and means, are constantly pub-lished to the collective body." The Adams-Leonard debate also reminded that heroes and villains were up for grabs. For Leonard, John Malcolm was a martyr to despotic patriot mobs, but Adams flatly denied Malcolm's innocence — or even "torture." Malcolm was treated roughly, Adams allowed, but "the cruelty of his whipping, and danger of his life, are too highly coloured." A savage beating for Leonard was, for Adams, a "coincidence of circumstances." On the question of rebellion, Adams again rejected all claims that colonial resistance was mankind's most "atrocious offence." "We are not exciting a rebellion," said Adams. "Opposition, nay open, avowed resistance by arms, against usurpation and lawless violence, is not rebellion by the law of God, or the land." On whether New England was, in fact, seeking independence: "Nothing can be more wicked, or a greater slander on the whigs" than this accusation, Adams fumed. "There is not a man in the province among the whigs, nor ever was, who harbours a wish of that sort." "Novanglus" labeled those who were seduced by promises of financial and political promises, like Leonard, Sewell, Oliver, and Hutchinson, a "tribe of the *wicked.*" But added to that was the still-more-dangerous group of "the *weak,*" people "in every community" who rejected the boycotts and sapped the public's will to resist parliamentary tyranny just so they could satisfy "the present appetite, prejudice, or passion" and had "no consideration of the freedom of posterity!" Using exactly the same language Virginia planters would employ to warn rebellious slaves not to join the king's standard just ten months later, Adams implored neutral readers not to be "weak" or "wicked."[64]

Each of these themes — the appropriateness of rough justice, the definition of "rebel" and "rebellion," truth and ulterior motives, trust and honor — was essential for winning hearts and minds. But when it came to the critical issue of just how common the cause truly was, whoever convinced the public he could best predict the future might tip the balance. "Massachusettensis" envisioned only suffering and terror for New England once the rest of the colonies abandoned their northern neighbors upon the outbreak of war. Invoking the phantom of powerful enemies on all sides, Leonard tried his best to pull New Englanders back from the precipice. Adams offered the opposite: a positive, expectant, hopeful prediction of unity. The whole of the continent, he argued, "have been actuated by one great, wise, active and noble spirit, one masterly soul, animating one vigorous body." Of course, the colonies were diverse, but that led to strength, not weakness. Surveying the first Congress, he said that, despite the "variety of climates, soils, religions, civil governments, commercial interests . . . the harmony and unanimity which prevailed in it, can scarcely be paralleled in any assembly that ever met." There was no reason to doubt the "clearest demonstrations of the cordial, firm, radical, and indissoluble union of the colonies."[65]

But, as we have seen in this survey of the complications undermining the prospect of American unity, there were plenty of reasons to doubt the excessive confidence—perhaps hubris—of "Novanglus." In short order, when that confidence was tempered, the patriots would resort to fearmongering, too. But, for now, during the weeks and months before war, everyone was seemingly in the prediction business. Some forecasters were better than others. Many optimistic predictions forwarded by the patriots would seem fabulous, such as Benjamin Rush's prophecy that slavery would very soon be extinct in America after 1774. From the vantage point of that critical year, the smartest money, the safest bet would be against unity. Given the myriad problems—deep-seated cultural, religious, economic, and social jealousies between North and South or East and West; heated jurisdictional disputes; internal strife; the controversy over slavery; the large percentage of colonists who still supported Parliament and the crown—England's assumption that the thirteen colonies would fly apart appeared more credible than ever on the eve of war. We have given short shrift to the idea that things could have turned out differently and that many events might have transpired just the way King George, Lord North, Thomas Gage, Daniel Leonard, Samuel Seabury, Thomas Hutchinson, James Rivington, and scores of interested parties on both sides of the Atlantic expected them to: in a cascade of internal conflict, civil war, and bloody suffering.

So, when news reached Boston of the punitive actions Parliament had taken the previous March, based in part on predictions and expectations of American disunity, Samuel Adams gathered his colleagues together to draft a letter that would go across the American continent. Although the son of one patriot, followed by an entire nation, would seize upon and celebrate one phrase as "a continental watchword," we should not lose the desperate language of that letter, written on May 12, 1774, in response to the Coercive Acts: "Boston *must be regarded* as suffering in a common cause." That subsequent events would erase the memory of patriot anxiety, that things did not come to pass in the way the loyalists expected, and that enough Americans (whether in the Wyoming Valley, in settlements west of the Appalachians, on Carolina plantations, or in the Green Mountains) did respond to Adams's plea and agreed that "the cause" was common enough to support war against the British on a continental scale—all of these factors took a tremendous amount of work on many borders, fronts, and issues.[66]

CHAPTER 3

The "SHOT HEARD *round the* World"

REVISITED

The American Revolution entered a new phase on April 19, 1775. The instant the imperial crisis became a shooting war, colonists' views about their controversy with Britain — and about one another — changed, too.

Sixty years later, Ralph Waldo Emerson would write a hymn about the "embattled farmers" who made their stand at the Concord Bridge and "fired the shot heard round the world." He said they had a "Spirit, that made those heroes dare / To die, and leave their children free." Emerson helped construct a legend of Lexington, one that persists to this day. He told us it was the defense of liberty that animated those farmers — who stood ready at a minute's notice — to grab their muskets and heed the call of history.[1]

The real reaction to the news of this shocking event complicates the Lexington myth, however. All over North America, the news of war led immediately to concerns about what the outbreak of hostilities would mean for enslaved and Native peoples. How would they decide to act — for themselves and their children? In the weeks after Lexington and Concord, many American farmers felt embattled by the threat of African Americans and Indians far more than soldiers in red coats. The shockwaves of the "shot heard round the world" were not solely about defending colonial households from British tyranny. They were also about defending them from enslaved and Native people. The "spirit" that made those "heroes dare" was, in part, about fear.

"The regulars are out! The regulars are out!" This was the cry that shattered the earliest hours of April 19, 1775. Paul Revere's ride through the night to alert the Massachusetts countryside that their lives were in danger lies at the core of the founding mythology of the United States. The town chronicler of Natick, Massachusetts, writing in the 1850s, provided the standard account of what happened next: "When the news came, early in the morning, the people rapidly assembled on the common, provided themselves with ammunition, and marched, full of zeal, to attack the British." He claimed, "Every man that morning was a minute-man."[2]

But there was much more to the story. Who, exactly, were those farmers? Natick had been one of the original Indian "praying towns" that the Bay Colony had founded in the middle of the seventeenth century to teach Christianity to Algonquian Indians. Several of those people who marched, "full of zeal," were their descendants, now known as Natick Indians. The minutemen who claimed they were defending the rights of Englishmen weren't all descended from England.

Furthermore, *was* everyone a minuteman? Apparently not in the town next door. In another town history, published in 1887 about Framingham, Massachusetts, the writer contended that, for more than a century, the local memory of the Lexington Alarm did not revolve around Thomas Gage. Or Paul Revere. Or John Hancock.

The inhabitants of Framingham, he wrote, were more afraid of a slave rebellion. As soon as the minutemen left, a "strange panic" gripped those left behind. A different call broke the Massachusetts night in Framingham: "The Negroes were coming to massacre them all!" After Framingham's militia started on the road to Lexington, some in the rest of the town allegedly "brought the axes and pitchforks and clubs into the house, and securely bolted doors, and passed the day and night in anxious suspense." As much as the inhabitants were startled, shaken awake in the middle of that April night, so should we be by their response. That can't be how Framingham reacted. Afraid of a slave uprising—in Massachusetts? The African American population (enslaved and free) at the start of the Revolutionary War was less than 2 percent of the whole in Massachusetts. There were fewer than three dozen enslaved people in Concord in the 1770s. With numbers this low, our impulse is to chalk this up to colonial folklore.[3]

We are inclined to doubt this even more so because Framingham was the hometown of Crispus Attucks, the mixed-race martyr of the Boston Massacre. Further, we know one of those minutemen marching to Lexington was Peter Salem, a free Black man from Framingham, who would earn enduring fame two months later at Bunker Hill for gunning down the British officer leading the charge. From the 1840s to emancipation, the town was a favorite spot for the Independence Day rallies sponsored by the Massachusetts Anti-Slavery Society, which featured illustrious speakers such as William Lloyd Garrison and Henry David Thoreau. The town historian himself had a hard time believing the story of a Framingham slave rebellion. He claimed, "All our own colored people were patriots," and the scare was "probably a lingering memory of the earlier Indian alarms, which took this indefinite shape."[4]

He was wrong, and so are our expectations. It is quite plausible that Framingham's popular memory—that of a rebellion instigated by free and enslaved Blacks (and perhaps with Native partners)—was a real possibility to be feared in the spring of 1775.

A month before the British regulars marched out of Boston toward Lexington, newspapers throughout the colonies printed stories about several potential slave plots in the mid-Atlantic. The *New-York Journal* reported that, in Esopus, a small town on the Hudson River, two suspects "have been detected and confessed that their design was to convey ammunition to the Indians, and to set fire to Esopus, Marble-town and other places." Details of this plan further revealed that Blacks from four different towns were involved, that they had collected a "large Quantity" of powder and ball, and that the number of Indians supporting them was rumored to have reached as high as five to six hundred. Giving their deposition to the county magistrate, the accused slaves revealed their modus operandi in words that must have sent shivers up readers' spines: "When once begun, we must go through with it. We are to set Fire to the Houses, and stand by the Doors and Windows, to receive the People as they come out." At the same moment, two different plots downriver in Perth Amboy, New Jersey, and on Long Island were also discovered, facts that often appeared in the same columns of print alongside the Esopus event. These stories heightened notions that rebels—slave rebels, that is—were all around just days before the start of what would be the Revolutionary War.[5]

But these events were too far away from Framingham to induce the "strange panic." A similar scene next door, however, would. On March 9, the same day that the *Boston Weekly News-Letter* printed news of the foiled plot in Esopus, the *Norwich Packet* reported that a free Black man was arrested in Natick, just four miles east of Framingham, under charges of conspiracy. "It appeared that said Fellow has for some Time past been employed in forming a Plot to destroy the white People; for that Purpose he had enlisted Numbers of his own Complexion, as Associates, and they only waited until some Disturbance should happen that might occasion the Militia to turn out, and in their Absence it was proposed to Murder the defenceless inhabitants." Apparently not everyone in Natick was a minuteman, either. The article in the *Packet* continued, "The same Gentleman also informs us, that, last Monday Evening, another African, in the Vicinity of Natick, was discovered to have been deeply concerned in the above-mentioned infernal Scheme; and that his Master had delivered him up to Justice." Where was that justice located? "After Examination," the suspect was "committed to Concord G[ao]l." Amazing as it may seem, it is possible that those left be-

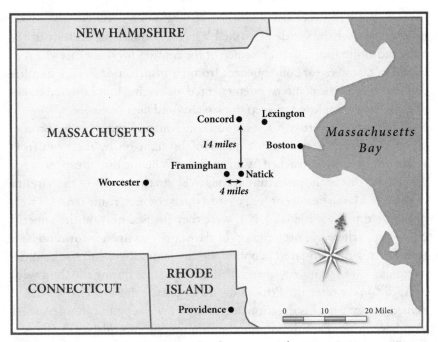

MAP 4. *Massachusetts, April 1775. Drawn by Gerry Krieg*

hind in Framingham were truly petrified that a very different sort of rebellion might break out in Massachusetts on April 19, 1775. It is also possible that man was still locked in the Concord jail when the townspeople clashed with British redcoats just over the hill at the "rude bridge that arched the flood," as Emerson would later put it.[6]

The news of war sped down the Atlantic coast. Before the Wednesday morning of April 19 was over, an express rider took up his mount armed with a report the Boston committee of safety had hastily drafted. Two days after the battles, the first newspaper appeared in the *New-Hampshire Gazette* under the heading "Bloody News." By Monday, printers in Connecticut, Rhode Island, and New York published various accounts taken from express riders, committee members, and witnesses. Within a week, notices of Lexington and Concord had traveled nearly one thousand miles.[7]

Once reports reached areas with denser slave populations, similar scenes of confusion and anxiety gripped the countryside from the Chesapeake to Carolina. Within hours of the announcement of the news in Annapolis, Maryland, Governor Robert Eden wrote that he "was waited on by six gentlemen of respectable characters, requesting me, that as, in consequence of this news, they were under great apprehensions of some attempt being made by the servants or slaves for their liberty." Eden related to his brother in England that the gentlemen asked him to "commit the custody of the arms and ammunition to the freemen of the country for that otherwise they would not answer for consequences from an insurrection." Although less concerned than the planters, Eden relented, delivering four hundred stands of arms "to be employed to keep the servants and negroes in order."[8]

Hours after Governor Eden sat down in Annapolis to write his brother about the "state of thorough confusion" brought on by the news from Lexington, the wave reached Williamsburg. When it did, it capped what was already one of the most tumultuous weeks in the history of the Virginia capital. As Massachusetts drifted toward open conflict, rising tensions were not limited to New England. Nor were they focused only on the imperial crisis. Just as there had been rumors of slave uprisings in New York and New Jersey that spring, enslaved people along the James River — in five counties stretching over 150 miles — threatened insurrections during the third week of April. On the fifteenth, Prince Edward County authorities charged a slave named Toney with insurrection and conspiracy to commit murder. Three days later, while Paul Revere watched the steeple at Old North Church, the Chesterfield County slave patrol galloped over the roads to prevent a different form of rebellion. Then, on April 21, Norfolk, Surry County, and Williamsburg all reported slave disturbances. In Norfolk, a court found two slaves, Emanuel and Emanuel de Antonio, guilty of conspiracy and sentenced them to hang.[9]

The night of the Williamsburg scare, as the news of Lexington dashed south, Virginia governor Lord Dunmore ordered the gunpowder stored in the town's public magazine removed to the nearby warship HMS *Magdalen*. His decision had nothing to do with the outbreak of violence in Massachusetts; Dunmore took this step because he feared slave rebellions were about to break out all across Virginia, and he could not afford for slave rebels to get their hands on the barrels of powder. Local authorities in Williamsburg were anxious, too, about facing a large-scale slave uprising, but without the gunpowder, they worried that they would be defenseless. The next day, the city government issued a strong public statement in the *Virginia Gazette*, arguing that the "magazine was erected at the public expence of this colony," whereby the munitions were kept "for the protection and security of the country, by arming thereout such of the militia as might be necessary in cases of invasions and insurrections." The governor must return the hijacked powder immediately. The news of Lexington would not arrive for another six days. Williamsburg's residents were not yet concerned about a British government that had moved into open conflict with the colonies. Instead, they saw the removal as leaving them without the ability to counteract the "various reports at present prevailing in different parts of the country . . . that some wicked and designing persons have instilled the most diabolical notions into the minds of our slaves, and that therefore the utmost attention to our internal security is become the more necessary." As in Esopus, Perth Amboy, and Natick, this threat was likely connected to the Revolution: enslaved people in Virginia, too, were watching how far relations with the empire had dissolved by early 1775. These rumors were the whispers of their preparations to take advantage of the "Disturbance" that seemed imminent.[10]

Many Virginians, like some in New England, reacted to the opening of the Revolutionary War as an episode of potential violence by an agitated enslaved population and a royal government that, at best, undermined their security. To make matters worse, Dunmore played his trump card. Through an intermediary, the governor sent a message to Burgesses Speaker Peyton Randolph: unless they acquiesced in his removal of the powder, he would "declare freedom to the slaves and reduce the City of Wmsburg to ashes." Sensing a far greater threat than the loss of fifteen barrels of gunpowder, city officials gave up their public bashing of Dunmore and quietly resorted to doubling the number of nightly slave patrols. In part of his own volition and also because of the independent actions of the enslaved themselves, Governor Dunmore rattled a sword in late April that would prove to be a very powerful and intimidating weapon throughout the southern colonies. Although not a direct result of the outbreak of war in Massachusetts, the timing and connections made by the powder removal incident in Williamsburg illustrated, for Virginians, the potential destructiveness of a combined force of Britain and the enslaved.[11]

One week later, Virginians began to learn about General Gage's attempt to seize gunpowder in Concord. Once this news arrived, the coincidence seemed too much, throwing Dunmore's action into a very different light. Now, his order for British marines to "secure" the public gunpowder on board the HMS *Magdalen* appeared to be part of a larger move against the colonies. The next day, six hundred "well armed and disciplined men, friends of constitutional liberty and America," gathered in a public space near Fredericksburg to decide whether they should march on Williamsburg to demand the truth. They decided not to go yet, but volunteers in Albemarle, Orange, and Hanover Counties did take to the roads as soon as they heard the news from Massachusetts. Dunmore called for reinforcements and issued a proclamation reminding Virginians about the problems facing "this distracted country," which not only included "intestine insurgents" but also "the dangers . . . [of] a savage enemy . . . ready to renew their hostilities" of the previous year.[12]

This was how Virginia's Revolution began: more agitated than it might have because of rising tensions from slave quarters throughout the colony. It was bad enough that Dunmore issued the same orders as Gage in Massachusetts. That coincidence smacked of conspiracy. But Dunmore compounded that mistake by threatening Virginians with one of their greatest fears.

A similar panic gripped Charleston, South Carolina, one week later. Again, a coincidence shaped how the capital received the news of Lexington, and it went straight to the heart of their worst nightmare. According to John Stuart, the British Superintendent for Indian Affairs, "Upon the news of the affair at Lexington . . . the people of [South] Carolina were thrown into a great Ferment." Edward Allen's ship, *Industry,* fresh from Salem with copies of the *Essex Gazette* containing the news of war, arrived in Charleston on Monday, May 8. But, as in Virginia, the "great Ferment" was not strictly because of the Lexington report. Allen's ship pulled up at the wharf alongside another vessel that had completed its transatlantic voyage only a couple of days before. That ship had carried a letter from Arthur Lee, South Carolina's agent in London, addressed to the president of Charleston's committee of safety, Henry Laurens. Lee's information was explosive. In the event of armed conflict with Britain, he wrote, the administration was exploring granting "freedom to such Slaves as should desert their Masters and join the King's troops." Laurens and his patriot friends must have looked at one another with wide eyes as they read these lines, for that event had already happened.[13]

Wasting no time on that memorable Monday, the committee immediately gathered to send this news to the Second Continental Congress that was scheduled to convene two days hence. They forwarded Lee's letter to their delegates who had already departed for Philadelphia. There was gossip in that city, too, concerning another letter from London that "arms [are] to be given to all the Negroes to act against the Colonies." In both Carolina and Virginia, this was the charged atmosphere into which the newspaper notices of Lexington and Concord would be read, read aloud, posted, passed back and forth, and discussed.[14]

One individual, a man named "black David," would amplify the fear that gripped Charleston that day. David, an African American preacher, had "shown some impudent Airs" in the city. This was dangerous on any day, but on May 8, 1775, it almost ended his life. "The Gentlemen of this Town are so possessed with an opinion that his Designs are bad," a man wrote from the Carolina capital, "that they are determined to pursue, and hang him, if they can lay hold of him, . . . I wou'd indeed be very sorry that the poor fellow should lose his Life." David's crime had been his exhortation, delivered in front of "several white People and Negroes, who had collected together to hear him," that God "send Deliverance to the Negroes, from the power of their Masters, as He freed the Children of Israel from Egyptian Bondage." This was no time to discuss that topic; so, for his own protection, David's friends quietly ushered him onto a ship bound for England.[15]

Although this quick action saved David's life, it did not calm the city's nerves. Four days later, the Charleston committee of safety issued a proclamation that again connected the two issues: "The actual Commencement of Hostilities against this Continent, the threats of arbitrary impositions from abroad, and the dread of instigated Insurrections at home, are causes sufficient to drive an oppressed People to the use of Arms . . . [and] we do solemnly promise that . . . we will go forth and be ready to sacrifice our Lives and fortunes in attempting to secure her Freedom and Safety." Neither rights nor principles were sufficient causes to take up arms, according to this proclamation. But "instigated Insurrections" were. In mid-May, a Charleston merchant maintained, "Our Province at present is in a ticklish Situation, on account of our numerous Domesticks, who have been unhappily deluded by some villainous Persons into the notion of being all set free." From the first hours of the Revolution, patriots in Charleston framed the conflict in relation to the enslaved.[16]

David could well have been the first casualty of South Carolina's Revolutionary War. The "great Ferment" produced by a remarkable double front of news from Boston and London nearly cost him his life. As it was, his exile would be the first of thousands over the next eight years of conflict. Nor would David be the last person whose life would be changed by news— real or not—forwarded in personal correspondence or newspaper columns. Moreover, the immediate intervention of David's friends to escort him out of an unsettled Charleston reveals how the news of Lexington was received: in towns and capitals from New England to Carolina, many colonists were worried about their slaves during the opening hours of the Revolutionary War. Imperial conflict was the new filter through which colonists interpreted social conflict that might have had little to do with the bloodshed in Massachusetts.

Take an encounter in Dorchester County, on Maryland's Eastern Shore, on Saturday, May 6. Less than a week after the news of Lexington made Maryland planters beg Governor Eden for security, a passerby asked John Simmons, a Dorchester wheelwright, whether he was going to town on Monday to report to the militia assembly—the same day Black David had put on "impudent Airs." Simmons returned, "Damn them (meaning the gentle-men), if I had a few more White People to join me I could get all the Negroes in the county to back us, and they would do more Good in the Night than the White people could in the day." Angry at his economic betters, Simmons swore that if he "had one of Colonel William Ennall's [money] bags, I would put it to a better use than he does." But, when the local patriot commit-tee reported the incident a few weeks later, Simmons's venting of class frus-trations was transformed into political agitation. The committee informed their friends in Baltimore, "The insolence of the Negroes in this county is come to such a Height that we are under a necessity of disarming them." "The malicious and imprudent speeches of some of the lower class of Whites have induced them to believe that their Freedom depended on the success of the King's Troops," the committee declared. "We cannot therefore be too vigilant nor too rigorous with those who promote and encourage this dispo-sition in our slaves." Simmons was tarred and feathered, and because of "his intimacy and connection with the negroes . . . we did not think it prudent to let him remain in the Province."[17]

All over North America, as the American Revolution became the Revo-lutionary War, colonists immediately began to think about how this new phase would affect enslaved people. For their part, African Americans in Massachusetts, New York, New Jersey, Virginia, and South Carolina had mulled this question even before Gage's redcoats fanned out across Lexing-ton Green. For weeks, they had been whispering plans and making arrange-ments, waiting to see what opportunities the "disturbance" might bring. They were not the only ones doing so.

Decades later, one of America's first historians helped to create the myth of the Lexington Alarm. Like Emerson, he rejoiced that "with one impulse the colonies sprung to arms" all across the continent and that the news of war had miraculous effects even deep into the American interior. The "voice" of Lexington "breathed its inspiring word to the first settlers of Kentucky; so that hunters who made their halt in the matchless valley of the Elkhorn, commemorated the nineteenth day of April by naming their encampment LEXINGTON." Writing from the safe distance of the mid-nineteenth cen-tury, this historian deepened the Lexington legend, complete with a neat ori-gin story for what would become the first capital of Kentucky. That legend endures—but it masks the fear that the "voice" actually produced.[18]

What about the people who lived all around the campsite of those Ken-tucky hunters? Like free and enslaved African Americans, Native people from Canada to the Gulf of Mexico paid attention to the new realities of war between Britain and its colonies. The "voice" inspired them, too. And, in turn, what critical role they might play was one of the most pressing issues facing both sides in the conflict's first days. How would they react to the news of a civil war between England and New England?

The issue of what to do about Indians was an immediate problem—for both sides. General Thomas Gage was already worried about this a month before he gave the order to march on Concord. He wrote to the new Northern Superintendent for Indian Affairs, Guy Johnson, who had just replaced his revered uncle, the late Sir William Johnson, a few months earlier. Gage told Johnson to reassure the Iroquois that "they will never be molested by the King's troops, while they chuse to be his friends, but on the Contrary, that they may expect from him every assistance and Justice he can give them." Soon after the battles of Lexington and Concord, Gage considered activating this contingency. "I would have you immediately cultivate the friendship of the Indians as much as possible, have them ready to detach on the first notice," he wrote to the commander at Fort Niagara on May 10. He sent similar messages to other outposts, ordering them to "cultivate the Friendships of the Indians on All Occasions, as they may be wanted for His Majesty's Service."[19]

Gage justified his actions to his superiors in Britain by saying he wasn't the first to take this step. "You may be tender of using Indians," he wrote back to London in mid-June, "but the Rebels have shewn us the Example, and brought all they could down upon us here." He was right: while Gage secretly ordered his officers to keep up good relations with Natives all over the American backcountry, the patriots sent out their own messages in an effort to convince Natives that Boston's cause was theirs, as well.[20]

Almost three weeks before Lexington, the Massachusetts patriots invited the Stockbridge Indians to join them in becoming minutemen. "This is a common cause," they proclaimed. "We are all brothers; and if the Parliament of *Great Britain* takes from us our property and our lands, without our consent, they will do the same by you." The outbreak of war produced many other ambassadors sent out to talk to Natives across the northern frontier. A correspondent in western Massachusetts wrote a militia officer outside Boston that Solomon, the *"Indian* King of *Stockbridge,"* said "that the *Mohawks* had not only given liberty to the *Stockbridge Indians* to join us" but promised "they would hold five hundred men in readiness to join us immediately on the first notice." "Those *Indians* would be of great service to you should the King's Troops march out of *Boston,"* he added.[21]

It was just this problem of Native participation that greeted the delegates to the Second Continental Congress as they first took their seats on May

10, 1775. When they had agreed to reconvene the following spring, the First Continental Congress anticipated they would be doing so to check on the effectiveness of the sweeping boycott they had passed. Instead, they were organizing the colonies for war. And that meant coming to some understanding about Indians, especially the Six Nations, who were most loyal to British Superintendent Guy Johnson.

During the same days that Virginians traded threats with their royal governor, South Carolina patriots stepped up their slave patrols, and New Englanders streamed toward Cambridge to make sure Gage's regulars remained inside Boston, the news from northern New York began to demand increasing attention. When Ethan Allen and his Green Mountain Boys sneaked across Lake Champlain and surprised the commander at Fort Ticonderoga on the evening of May 9, allegedly claiming the fort "in the name of the great Jehovah and the Continental Congress," they turned the northern frontier into the Revolutionary War's second theater. One hundred miles from the fort, Guy Johnson had not yet heard the news of its capitulation, but he was restless nonetheless. The Indian Superintendent was hearing threatening whispers in his neighborhood. On May 18, he sent a letter to patriot leaders in nearby Schenectady, denouncing the "gross and notorious falsehood, uttered by some worthless scoundrels, respecting my intentions." Two days later, Johnson sent off another message flatly denying "a ridiculous and malicious report that I intend to make the *Indians* destroy the inhabitants." Still, Johnson warned the patriots not to provoke him: "But should I neglect myself, and be tamely made prisoner, it is clear to all who know any thing of *Indians,* they will not sit still and see their Council fire extinguished, and Superintendent driven from his duty, but will come upon the frontiers, in revenge, with a power sufficient to commit horrid devastation." Johnson's threat that any attempts to capture him would be met with a "hot and disagreeable reception" only aggravated colonists already on the watch for any sign that the British and Indians were about to attack them. Soon, these letters would land on colonial printers' tables. On the same day Johnson sent his first threat to Schenectady, one such report began to appear in newspapers across the northern colonies.[22]

Benjamin Towne's *Pennsylvania Evening Post* reported a suspicious hunting trip conducted by a small party of Canadian officers and northern Indians on May 18. Stopped along the way by some curious colonists who wanted to know their "real intention," the Natives admitted they were reconnoitering the woods "to find a passage for an army to march to the assistance of the King's friends in Boston." Worse, the report went on to expose the identities of the suspicious officers, including one infamous name from the last

war that surely raised the hairs on the necks of colonial readers: "The conductors of this grand expedition are to be Monsieur St. Luke le Corne, the
villain who let loose the Indians on the prisoners at Fort William Henry."
That, all colonists knew, was the 1757 "massacre" in which Natives attacked
about two hundred English soldiers and camp followers as they filed out of
the surrendered fort. In case anyone missed the point of this name dropping,
Towne added a comment to the end of the report: *"Oh George, what tools art
thou obliged to make use of!"* Printers in cities up and down the continent exchanged both the story and its stinging remark.[23]

Reportage of this type of suspicious behavior did not ease tensions.
Rumors had reached Johnson that a band of New England militia was in
fact on its way to capture him, a report that disturbed the Six Nations. "He
is our property," a party of Mohawks warned the Albany committee of safety
on May 25, "and we shall not part with him." The New York frontier stood
on edge; any movement might widen the war. In early June, the New York
Provincial Congress requested that the Continental Congress intervene.
Worried that "our publick peace is more endangered by the situation of the
barbarians to the westward of us, than it can be by any inroads made upon
the sea-coast," they asked their delegates in Philadelphia for help. "We do not
presume to dictate any measure to you," they wrote, yet "at the same time we
submit it to your consideration whether it is proper to leave the management
of the numerous tribes of *Indians* entirely in the hands of persons appointed
and paid by the Crown."[24]

Those delegates in Philadelphia were already considering what to do
about the northern frontier. Richard Henry Lee wrote his brother on May
21, "We know the plan of Ministry is to bring the *Canadians* and *Indians*
down upon us." The Second Continental Congress was not even two weeks
old when New Hampshire's delegates reached the conclusion that Johnson
had "really Endeavoured to persuade the Indians to Enter into a war with us
and that many other Steps have been Taken by a Bloody Minded and Cruel
Ministry to Induce those Hereditary Enemies of America to fall upon and
Butcher its Inhabitants." In his notes for a speech during those days, John
Dickinson listed "the Danger of Insurrection by Negroes in Southern Colonies — Incursions of Canadians and Indians upon the Northern Colonies —
Incidental Proposals to disunite Us — false Hopes [and] selfish designs" in
his catalog of "Considerations that deserve the Attention of Gentlemen."[25]

At that moment, while patriot authorities fumbled about, trying to develop a coherent way to deal with these growing threats, another tumult
swept through the capital of South Carolina that suggested Dickinson's
worries were, in fact, coming true. This one was attributable to a choice one

Charleston printer made. Upon entering the house of an acquaintance, James Dealey boasted he had "good news" from England. One wonders whether or not Dealey carried a copy of Peter Timothy's May 29 *South-Carolina Gazette* under his arm when he initiated what would be a near-fatal conversation. In that issue, Timothy had published a letter from London that referenced "seventy-eight thousand guns, and bayonets, to be sent to America, to put into the hands of N[egroe]s, the Roman Catholics, the Indians and Canadians; and all the wicked means on earth used to subdue the Colonies." Timothy, a staunch patriot, surely did not intend readers to greet this as "good news." But Dealey did. Dealey's acquaintance later testified that when he asked Dealey about the report, the latter responded "that a number of arms was sent over to be distributed amongst the *Negroes, Roman Catholicks,* and *Indians.*" Dealey's happy receipt of this startling information led to a violent exchange. The fight, complete with drawn swords, spilled outdoors, where Dealey and a friend, Laughlin Martin, threatened to chop off their opponent's head in the middle of King Street. After their potential victim begged for his life, they relented, ending the incident with raised glasses, toasting "*Damnation to the Committee and their proceedings.*" The committee retaliated by having Dealey and Martin tarred and feathered, carted through the streets, and put aboard ship for England.[26]

The following day, leading patriot Henry Laurens anxiously searched the minds of his brother's slaves in South Carolina for evidence as to whether they sympathized with Dealey and his friends. "I called in all your Negroes last Saturday Evening," Laurens wrote, "admonished them to behave with great circumspection in this dangerous times, [and] set before them the great risque of exposing themselves to the treachery of pretended friends and false witnesses." Laurens contented himself that his audience was "sensibly affected," but, after the near-beheading on King Street and what had just appeared in the local paper, he could not really feel secure. That very day, Laurens had presided over an agreement that free South Carolina men would "associate as a band in [the colony's] defence" and hold themselves "ready to sacrifice our lives and fortunes to secure her freedom and safety." This martial step was necessary, Charleston patriots argued, because of "the dread of instigated insurrections in the Colonies."[27]

What Laurens and his compatriots in South Carolina did not know when they helped establish an emerging patriot catchphrase — "instigated insurrections" — was that their neighbors in Williamsburg, Virginia, and Newbern, North Carolina, were dealing with the exact same issue. The latter sent out warnings during the last weekend in May that "there is much Reason to fear, in these Times of general Tumult and Confusion, that the Slaves may be instigated, encouraged by our inveterate Enemies to an Insurrection." Just as New Yorkers viewed Guy Johnson and St. Luc de la Corne that spring, many southerners viewed men like James Dealey or Black David as even more dangerous to America than General Gage.[28]

These were the real ripples of the "shot heard round the world." In the month that followed the news of Lexington, Thomas Gage and his troops in Boston dominated a surprisingly small part of patriots' attention. Colonists viewed the conflict in terms of who might aid their enemies. Often, the first response to the news of bloodshed produced a changed vision; it necessitated a new way of seeing the people who lived in the backcountry or on slave plantations. But, as the spring of 1775 turned into summer, for the most part those colonists did not know that they had reacted in strikingly similar ways to the news. To be sure, a fever had gripped the colonies. Patriots and loyalists alike noted the "Infection which is so generally diffused thro' the Continent" that May. But how long might it last? Given all the fractures, fissures, controversies, and suspicions that had divided the colonies for decades, that initial "astonishing" spirit of unity, which John Adams contended "arose all of a Sudden," might subside just as quickly.[29]

It would take newspapers to make the cause common. As the summer started, so did the stories. Beginning in late June, patriot newspapers began to inform colonists of the activities of British officials throughout North America. They began the process of connecting the dots. Readers across the continent learned about British negotiations with Indians on the frontier with Guy Johnson and Canadian governor Sir Guy Carleton in the North, and their colleagues John Stuart and Alexander Cameron in the southern backcountry. Stories flooded the colonies that Lord Dunmore was only one of several royal governors plotting to arm slaves. By season's end, rumors about the crown's hiring of Russian or German mercenaries to conquer America first surfaced in print.

Patriot political leaders and publicists reinforced the foundations of American unity with fear. By emphasizing the connections between the British government and a host of terrifying proxies, patriots began the difficult task of turning their cultural cousins into dangerous foreigners, aliens who were not to be trusted. They did so by adapting the "common cause" appeal. In the new, wartime argument, the notion of America's enemies expanded to include far more groups than just Englishmen in red coats. This was not a reflection or a memory fastened decades later by historians. This was a purposeful campaign fashioned from colonial anxiety and amplified by patriot political leaders and printers. And it began early in the summer of 1775.

CHAPTER 4

"Britain *has* Found Means

to Unite Us"

"All Parties are now extinguish'd here," Benjamin Franklin wrote almost one month after shots echoed across Lexington Green. "Britain has found means to unite us." Franklin meant that the shedding of colonial blood in Massachusetts collapsed all those divisions, petty disputes, and controversies that had erupted throughout the 1760s and 1770s. But he didn't understand what exactly those "means" were. He thought it was just the news of war. As we have seen, colonists across the continent interpreted the reports of Lexington and Concord in terms of what role Native and enslaved people might play in what was suddenly a shooting war with Britain. It was not just musket fire that bound the colonies to one another.[1]

Fear was another element that held great potential to make "the cause" common.

It presented patriot leaders with a unique opportunity. Because it was universal and visceral, fear could do considerable work for the patriots. It did not require taking sides in any of the troublesome colonial controversies. Northerners had the chance to sympathize with southerners living on dangerous slave plantations, and easterners could express solidarity with westerners who would experience the horrors of Indian raids. All were potential victims alike of British treachery. This threat trumped squabbles over which colony controlled the Forks of the Ohio, the Wyoming Valley, or the New Hampshire Grants. It threw cold water on antislavery arguments—how could anyone advocate freeing people who might then take up arms against them? It made loyalist protests seem irrelevant and petty. And it had the potential of turning backcountry men and women into superpatriots for battling British-sponsored Natives. It was magic. Ben Franklin and his patriot colleagues would learn very quickly that the means to unite the American colonies was through playing upon these fears.

Patriot publicists moved quickly to exploit this new line of attack. They rendered the British as instigators of insurrections and potential massa-

cres, an argument that would increasingly become one of the most prevalent themes of the evolving common cause appeal. By the middle of the first
summer of war, patriot leaders were already using it to justify the reasons
colonists should pick up arms and outside observers should view this rebellion as legitimate and righteous.

Colonial printing shops and assembly houses broadcast stories — whether
real, rumored, or embellished — about British officials who encouraged
Indians, enslaved people, and others to act as proxies on the king's behalf
throughout 1775. What had once been a call to rally all people who loved
liberty, consent, and the ancient rights of the sacred British constitution
now revolved around warning those people to defend their households from
Indian massacre and slave insurrection. These were the depths to which the
king's corrupt agents were willing to descend, they argued, and even worse
fates awaited if American men all over the continent did not take up arms to
stop them. The wartime appeal took on a darker edge: it wasn't about representation anymore. Now, it was about who was trying to kill them.

Patriot publicists used every avenue of communication to make this case
in 1775. In areas of lower literacy, like the Carolina backcountry, they made
oral arguments, dispatching political missionaries to urge rural folk to take
up arms against the king. But the most popular and effective medium for
convincing the public to support the rebellion was print, especially newspapers. Nearly every week, printers related events happening throughout
North America, from the Canadian frontier to the islands off the Georgia
coast, that reflected the role African Americans and Indians might play in
the expanding conflict.

Inside their weekly newspapers, printers inserted what seem like small
stories in small paragraphs. Most of these tiny incidents are lost to us; they
have not figured in our retelling of the events of 1775. That Ethan Allen's
cousin Remember Baker shot Indians in canoes on the Richelieu River no
longer merits our attention. But stories like those were reported all over the
thirteen colonies. Because patriot leaders wanted them to, people hundreds
of miles away from the Canadian frontier knew about those few seconds of
musket fire on the Richelieu. We expect colonial readers to be learning about
George Washington and the Continental army camp outside Boston in the
summer of 1775. In fact, they were more likely reading stories about royal
governors "tampering" on southern slave plantations or Indian Superintendents "instigating" Native peoples on the frontier. Together, these stories
created and reinforced a continental portrait of oppression — aided by ready
Native and enslaved proxies. Patriot newspapers were a patriot archive in the
making, a documentary record of British tyranny that deepened each week

as new places, new people, and new proxies featured in those interior bulletins. They are essential to understanding the common cause and, by extension, the American Revolution.

We should pay attention because the people who put those stories in those newspaper columns set much store in their importance. Local, provincial, and continental patriot leaders spent a great deal of time and resources managing what people knew about the conflict. They understood that just because the British had united the colonists in the spring of 1775, it didn't mean they would stay that way. Patriot leaders, including Benjamin Franklin, were going to have to do considerable work to keep the cause common in the face of a host of new challenges. The narrative of British officials' using Black and Indian proxies against America, then, was a gift to patriot publicists, a golden opportunity to castigate their enemies as evil. They leaped upon it with gusto.

British agents all over North America steered right into this storm. Once General Thomas Gage heard American forces led by Green Mountain Boy Ethan Allen had surprised the British garrison at Fort Ticonderoga, Gage wrote home, "Things are now come to that Crisis, that we must avail ourselves of every resource, even to raise the Negroes in our cause. . . . Nothing is to be neglected of which we can avail ourselves. Hanoverians, Hessians, perhaps Russians May be hired," the British commander opined, and he admitted he had already drafted orders to Canadian governor Guy Carleton to raise "all the Canadians and Indians in his power to Attack them in his turn."[2]

Gage was not the only one weighing the possibility of including Native, enslaved, and foreign soldiers in the effort to put down the American rebellion. Indian Superintendents John Stuart and Guy Johnson, royal governors Lord William Campbell, Guy Carleton, Josiah Martin, and Lord Dunmore, and an assortment of lower-level military officers were doing the same. With Britain nearly broke, glory awaited the person who could defeat this rebellion without incurring the staggering cost of sending an army across the Atlantic. And, if fame potentially awaited the triumphant imperial official, opportunity potentially awaited enslaved or Native peoples who helped them achieve such a victory. Aiding the British might translate into tangible rewards: the enslaved might be able to secure personal freedom; Native peoples might be able to use this service to better protect their territories and families. Here was a chance for them unlike any that had ever come before. The empire had descended into civil war. Public authority was in flux and might be thrown into chaos. The forces of bondage and dispossession that had circumscribed the lives of one's parents, grandparents, and great-grandparents might be indeed changing in profound ways right before one's eyes. Patriots boasted they were remaking the world. It made just as much sense that, when British officials raised possibilities of emancipation or land security, enslaved people and Natives paid close attention. Some acted; more waited and watched cautiously. Perhaps this would be a new beginning for them.

One of the imperial officials who sought Native assistance was John Stuart, the Indian Superintendent whose job it was to manage the Cherokees, Creeks, Choctaws, and Chickasaws in the southern backcountry. At the same time colonists began to learn that Stuart's colleague for the northern Indians, Guy Johnson, was meeting with Indians "1500 Miles back of [Quebec]" and had "made them great Offers to take Arms against the English colonies," patriot leaders began to publicize rumors and reports that Stuart and his deputy, Alexander Cameron, were doing the same thing with the Cherokee and Creek Indians in the South.[3]

A few days before British regulars threw themselves at Massachusetts's militia on Bunker Hill, a group of Indians visiting Charleston made a public reference to Stuart's entreating them and the Cherokees to take up arms against South Carolina. Stuart had already left town after the "fury of a merciless and ungovernable Mob" had encouraged him to flee to Savannah in late May. The Charleston committee of safety sent two representatives down to Georgia to question him. On June 15, they called on the ill superintendent, demanding that he "lay before us all his letters with respect to Indian affairs." "Unluckily for Mr. Stuart he produce[d] a number of his letters to his deputy, Mr. [Alexander] Cameron," which ordered Cameron to "use his influence to dispose those people to act in defense of his Majesty and Government, if found necessary."[4]

At the very moment that patriots rifled through Stuart's papers in Georgia, back in Charleston, a slave court tried harbor pilot and free African American Thomas Jeremiah and several other Blacks on the charge of "plotting an Insurrection." The star witness for the prosecution, a slave called Sambo, testified that Jeremiah had asked him whether he knew "anything of the war that is coming." When Sambo answered no and asked what that would mean for the enslaved, Jeremiah reportedly answered, "Jump on shore, and join the [British] soldiers," for "the war was come to help the poor Negroes." Another slave stated that Jeremiah had been distributing guns and ammunition to other slaves; that "he believed he had Powder enough already, but that he wanted more arms"; and that he was trying to "get as many as he could." As a result of this testimony, the court found Jeremiah guilty and sentenced him to hang in August.[5]

The Jeremiah case aggravated public opinion about the alleged connections between Britain and its potential proxies. Another victim of poor timing, South Carolina's newly appointed royal governor, Lord William Campbell, reached Charleston just two days after the court's ruling on Jeremiah. His welcome to town consisted of warnings about "instigated insurrections." The new governor sympathized with the condemned man, but those feelings were politically risky in the city's tense atmosphere. Even though "My blood ran cold when I read on what ground they had doomed a fellow creature to death," as Campbell reported back to his superiors in London, under such circumstances he decided to keep his compassion to himself.[6]

Not only did Carolinians believe that the British were attempting "to instigate, and encourage an insurrection amongst the Slaves," Campbell related, but they were also convinced that "the Ministry had in agitation . . . to bring down the Indians on the inhabitants of this Province." As quickly as they had moved against Black David, James Dealey, and Thomas Jeremiah, patriot authorities also initiated proceedings against John Stuart. The committee of safety swore out a warrant to demand that he appear before them, restricted the movements of his wife (whom he had left behind in Charleston), and confiscated his estate as, in the words of patriot leader Henry Laurens, "a Security for the good Behaviour of the Indians in the Southern Department." The circumstances surrounding Stuart, in the judgment of one historian, "were to the Revolution in the lower South what the Boston Tea Party was to the Revolution in New England." Coupled with the simultaneous rumors of slave plots that washed over Charleston early that summer, Stuart posed a dire threat to the Deep South if he and Alexander Cameron could indeed deliver the Cherokees and Creeks.[7]

On July 4, the South Carolina committee of safety sent copies of Stuart's confiscated letters to their colleagues in North Carolina, Georgia, and to the Continental Congress in Philadelphia. When printer Adam Boyd published the damning letters in his Wilmington *Cape-Fear Mercury,* he appended a commentary: "Thus we see every engine is set to work and every tool of a corrupt ministry employed, to subjugate this once happy land . . . forbid it Heaven, and rouse the old Roman virtue, found spontaneous in these regions, to repel the force of wicked tyrants, who would level the world with their own base principles."[8]

Near Boyd's Wilmington print shop, patriots in New Hanover County signed an association pledging faith to the common cause, stating "the In-

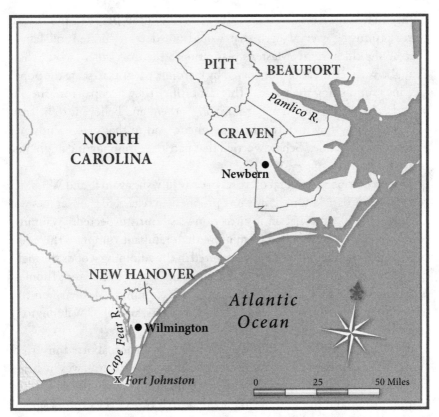

MAP 5. *North Carolina, 1775. Drawn by Gerry Krieg*

crease of Arbitrary Imposition from a Wicked and despotic Ministry and the dread of Instigated Insurrections in the Colonies are causes sufficient to drive an Oppress'd people to the Use of Arms." Immediately afterward, they resolved to prevent some people in their community from taking the same step. One of their first acts was to keep "the Negroes in order within the County of New Hanover" by appointing eight slave patrols.[9]

About seventy miles away, in Pitt County, just north of the capital of Newbern, nearly one hundred members of the committee of safety signed their own association, swearing they were "determined never to become slaves to any power upon earth." One of their next resolutions was to bolster surveillance and intimidation of people they actually enslaved: "If any Negro slave be *found with any fire arms* or ammunition," the patrollers were to seize it. For North Carolinians, like their anxious neighbors in South Carolina, the outbreak of war translated into renewed fears of slave violence.[10]

According to Janet Schaw, a Scottish lady visiting the Wilmington area, rumors of slaves taking advantage of war were as thick as Carolina's humidity that summer. The inhabitants of Wilmington believed the British were "promising every Negro that would murder his Master and family that he should have his Master's plantation." This particular twist, Schaw thought, was a fabrication concocted by Carolina patriots to scare the populace into supporting their side. "This last artifice they may pay for," she observed, "as the Negroes have got it amongst them and believe it to be true. 'Tis ten to one they may try the experiment, and in that case friends and foes would all be one." Schaw worried that patriot fearmongering might just prove successful.[11]

Her prediction was not far off base. In early July, she again found Wilmington "in an uproar." "I found my short prophesy in regard to the Negroes was already fulfilled, and that an insurrection was hourly expected." Wilmington's apprehension stemmed from more than rampant rumors. "There had been a great number of [Blacks] discovered in the adjoining woods the night before, most of them with arms, and a fellow belonging to Doctor [Thomas] Cobham was actually killed," Schaw reported. Committee leaders immediately dispatched patrols and searched slave quarters, and all of Wilmington's free white men who had arms carried them.[12]

The Wilmington scare was but one of several major, aborted insurrections in the Carolinas. On July 8, along the Pamlico River, slaves in Beaufort, Pitt, and Craven Counties were gathering for rebellion. Word reached Captain Thomas Respess of an "intended insurrection of the negroes against the whole people which was to be put into execution that night" in Beaufort County. The county committee went into action, arresting and jailing forty Black suspects. The next morning, the committee "proceeded to examine into the affair and [found] it a deep laid Horrid Tragick Plan laid for destroying the inhabitants of this province without respect of persons, age or sex."[13]

Local leaders, however, could hardly breathe easy. The following day, a new report arrived that 250 Blacks were in arms and under pursuit "on the line of Craven and Pitt" Counties about a dozen miles from Newbern. The Pitt committee of safety authorized slave patrollers to "shoot one or any number of Negroes who are armed and doth not willingly surrender their arms" and even to start blasting away at "any Number of Negroes above four, who are off their Masters Plantations, and will not submit." On Tuesday, July 11, four companies of Pitt militia went after the runaway mob. They uncovered more and more plots as they went. The arrested slaves

all confess nearly the same thing . . . that they were one and all on the night of the 8th inst to fall on and destroy the family where they lived, then to proceed from House to House (Burning as they went) until they arrived in the Back Country where they were to be received with open arms by a number of Persons there appointed and *armed by Government for their Protection,* and as a further reward they were to be settled in a free government of their own.

The last part of this confession was the most distressing for North Carolina patriots. The slave testimonies confirmed what provincial whites had suspected for at least a month: the British administration was aiding and abetting slave insurrections. This made the postscript even more chilling. "In disarming the negroes," a patriot leader confessed, "we found considerable ammunition."[14]

Just a few days before all this activity near the Pamlico River, Governor Josiah Martin wrote London about the omnipresent rumors that he was stirring poisonous pots. Martin had just fled from Newbern and took refuge in Fort Johnston, an outpost on the point of Cape Fear, ten miles south of Wilmington. Martin was sure patriot militias were about to take him hostage. A "most infamous report had lately been propagated among the People, that I had formed a design of Arming the Negroes, and proclaiming freedom to all such as should resort to the King's Standard," he reported to his superiors. Martin vehemently denied this "infamous report" and its "insinuations [of] abominable designs with pretended apprehensions of intestine insurrections."[15]

Martin's flight to Fort Johnston in mid-July turned the already-panicked colony upside down. In the midst of slave revolts the week before, the Wilmington committee of safety wrote on July 13 to Samuel Johnston, their representative in the Provincial Congress, "Our situation here is truly alarming, the Governor collecting men, provisions, warlike stores of every kind, spiriting up the back counties, and perhaps the Slaves." They accused Captain John Collet, Fort Johnston's commander, of severe infractions, the most serious being "his base encouragement of Slaves eloped from their Masters, feeding and employing them, and his atrocious and horrid declaration that he would excite them to an Insurrection." Rumors were one thing; now Collet was actually giving protection — and arms! — to escaped slaves.[16]

This would not stand. After nightfall on July 18, patriot forces set Fort Johnston ablaze. By threatening to incite slaves and harboring runaways in the fort, Martin and Collet had crossed a line. The tension of the past harrowing weeks had taken their toll. North Carolina's revolution in the summer of 1775 had little to do with taxes or rights, or even Thomas Gage and redcoats. It was a war over slavery.[17]

This power struggle between British authorities, patriot forces, and the

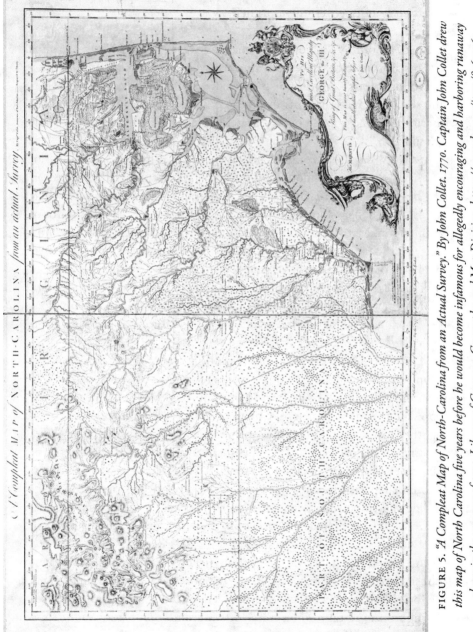

FIGURE 5. *"A Compleat Map of North-Carolina from an Actual Survey." By John Collet. 1770. Captain John Collet drew this map of North Carolina five years before he would become infamous for allegedly encouraging and harboring runaway slaves in the summer of 1775. Library of Congress, Geography and Map Division. https://www.loc.gov/item/83693769*

enslaved in coastal North Carolina was not simply a local matter. Its impact extended far outside the Carolinas. Probably aided by North Carolina's delegation to the Continental Congress, a letter from North Carolina appeared in the *Pennsylvania Ledger* on July 15. "We are much alarmed here with the intentions of Administration," an anonymous Carolinian wrote just before the Pitt-Craven uprising, admitting, "Unless affairs take a turn in our favor very shortly, we shall expect the worst effort of its villainy—that of spiriting up an enemy among ourselves, from whose barbarity, if roused, the most dreadful consequences must follow." Colonists in New York, Connecticut, and Massachusetts also read this letter. In addition, printer Alexander Purdie thought this news had local import for Virginians. When he copied this letter in his *Virginia Gazette,* Purdie italicized "an enemy amongst ourselves" and punctuated the article with the biting comment, "*Lord Dunmore and governour Martin have certainly compared notes.*" Despite these dangers, the thrust of this article was not that British agents were conspiring with slaves all over the mainland; it was that northern readers should be reassured that Carolinians would not abandon them. "Our brethren in the colonies may be assured that we never shall be bribed, by the benefit of an exclusive trade, to desert the common cause," the writer concluded. This letter offered a two-pronged message: the conspiracy from the king's men was real, but North Carolina's dedication to resist was undiminished. Such a representation was essential. Soon it would become a stock part of the patriot script.[18]

When historians tell the story of the beginning of the Revolutionary War, their narratives often feature George Washington's trip to Cambridge, Massachusetts, to take command of the new Continental army. Of course, Washington's assumption of the motley militia force on July 2, 1775, was critical; no one can deny his importance to the Revolution. But his journey, though celebrated, was not what many colonists were thinking and talking about at that moment. By the time Washington reached Cambridge, the continent was electric. It was full of movement, with emissaries fanning out in all directions across the frontier, "enemies" leaving their homes under duress, and slave patrols keeping watch day and night. Washington shared the road with dozens of express riders laden with letters and newspapers, galloping from station to station, carrying news of all these developments.

All summer, as the new commander surveyed his new army, the three dozen colonial newspapers featured an assortment of rumors of British involvement in slave and Indian hostilities. They drew readers' attention to another conspiracy in South Carolina, complete with frightening details that slaves "expected the King would send Troops here, on the Arrival of which they were to set the Town on fire, and fall on the Inhabitants" and that "the Insurrection was to have been general throughout the Province." They printed news that the "Cagnawaga Tribe have taken their Children from Dartmouth College, from which there is great Reason to fear some Attack upon our back Settlements will shortly be commenced." When a colonist was found murdered in a field not far from Iroquoia, anxious neighbors jumped to the conclusion that it had been "perpetrated by the *Oneida* Indians, and that this was only a commencement of Hostilities."[19]

A few weeks after these alarming stories appeared, more news of South Carolina's struggles with slave unrest began to circulate throughout the northern colonies. Having been imprisoned in the city workhouse all summer, Thomas Jeremiah waited as the South Carolina authorities made preparations to carry out his sentence. Governor Campbell did have the power to pardon Jeremiah and signaled he might intervene. The reaction quickly changed his mind. "My attempting to interfere in the matter raised such a Clamour amongst the People, as is incredible," he wrote to London. "They openly and loudly declared, if I granted the man a pardon they would hang him at my door." One prominent South Carolinian warned that a pardon "would raise a flame all the water in the Cooper River would not extinguish." On August 18, Jeremiah went to the gallows. His body was then cut down and burned to ashes.[20]

Patriot writers moved swiftly to document this news for their colleagues. A few days after Jeremiah's execution, a Philadelphia newspaper published a letter from Charleston. "Every thing here is suspended but warlike preparations," this bland but revealing letter began. "We are putting the town in a posture of defense, and are all determined to oppose whatever troops may come here. Yesterday a Negro was hanged and burnt, for intending sedition, and burning the town, etc." Another letter, dated September 12, began making its run through the papers. "We are not altogether without our fears from the Indian enemy," this correspondent wrote to the *Pennsylvania Packet,* "but our Negroes are quite quiet since the execution of one of the most sensible and daring of them, [Jeremiah], a free Negro, who was found guilty of having endeavoured to cause an insurrection."[21]

It is easy to pass over these small, matter-of-fact paragraphs without taking any notice. But we should pause and reconsider their importance. These notes from Carolina appeared all over the North. Patriot printers in almost two dozen shops decided they were important enough to exchange them. Why? What work were they doing?

These bulletins from South Carolina were essential to the common cause. The only place in America actually at war with British troops was outside

Boston. But security issues a thousand miles away mattered to all of them. The notes from Charleston reassured patriots everywhere that the South's biggest city had its business in order—and that meant keeping African Americans and Native peoples away from dangerous imperial officials. There weren't any British troops to fight in the Carolinas, but patriots there felt besieged all the same in the summer of 1775. Their revolution consisted of riding on slave patrols, monitoring the news from the backcountry, keeping a close eye on the governor, and letting their friends in the North know they were still staunch in the cause.

Policing and justifying were mutually reinforcing dynamics in the summer of 1775. Extralegal patriot bodies were improvising order during those confused months. Shoving imperial authority aside, they were taking the law into their own hands. This was a tricky business. It was essential they had enough of the people behind them. They had to have public recognition of their right to take drastic measures like executing Thomas Jeremiah. They needed permission. Getting and keeping permission required a continual campaign to justify and publicize their position. And publicity required print.

The actual fighting was confined to Massachusetts, but the battle over public opinion that had exploded in the winter of 1774–1775, as loyalists like Daniel Leonard picked up their pens to reject the First Continental Congress, raged on all across North America. Before Lexington, that battle roiled over Americans' and Britons' differing definitions of liberty, consent, and representation. After the news of war, however, the ways in which patriots highlighted the differences between them and their opponents changed. Now they consistently put before the public the argument that they alone were the true stewards of freedom because they alone protected American families from slave insurrection and Indian massacre. When the imperial crisis became a shooting war, it was only natural that the patriot argument for public support evolved, too. That transformation was increasingly framed in opposition to African Americans and Native people—and their British sponsors.

Making sense of all this bewildering news was the job of the Second Continental Congress. When the first Congress adjourned in November 1774, they made arrangements to reconvene in six months to check on the progress of the continental boycott. They didn't know then that they would be at war by May 10, 1775. So the Second Continental Congress had lots of unexpected business: organizing and equipping an army and navy, making initial diplomatic forays with other European powers, and keeping the peace between jealous colonies who might interpret this rupture as the perfect moment to settle old scores.

But there were more unexpected things to deal with. Just as they assembled in Philadelphia, all this news of British "tampering" began to dominate colonial newspapers. They were going to have to digest all that news, too — and react accordingly.

Even more than organizing a military response, Congress's most important job was to explain what was going on to the public. This was a supremely difficult task. They had to convince enough people in North America to be willing to put their homes, families, and bodies at risk to defend their own definition of liberty, not the one forwarded by their cultural cousins.

On the evening of July 5, John Adams described the work Congress had put in that Wednesday. "This day has been spent in debating a manifesto setting forth the causes of our taking arms," he wrote. "There is some spunk in it." Thomas Jefferson had arrived in Philadelphia to be added to Virginia's delegation to Congress only five days before. Even so, Congress immediately assigned him to join John Dickinson in a subcommittee to write "a declaration, to be published by General Washington, upon his arrival at the Camp before Boston."[22]

This, Adams's spunky proclamation, would be titled the Declaration of the Causes and Necessity of Taking up Arms. It began in typical Enlightenment fashion, invoking "a Reverence for our great Creator, Principles of Humanity, and the Dictates of Common Sense." But the bulk of the address, as Jefferson's more famous declaration would the following year, focused on fresh grievances. And, like the Declaration of Independence, this first official justification of the conflict reached its climax with war crimes. The last paragraphs of this declaration codified many of the swirling newspaper reports early that first wartime summer: "We have received certain Intelligence, that General Carleton, the Governor of Canada, is instigating the People of that Province and the Indians to fall upon us; and we have but too much reason to apprehend, that Schemes have been formed to excite domestic Enemies against us." Although they chose the formulation "to excite domestic enemies" instead of "instigated insurrections" as their friends in Carolina did, it undoubtedly meant rebellious slaves. Attempting to employ Indians and Blacks to help quell the rebellion: this was the crown's most serious crime now. From the very first days of the fighting, patriot leaders coupled Blacks and Indians with their British enemy. They moved quickly to craft this into an official theme, putting it at the center of the evolving common cause argument.[23]

True patriots would never stand for this type of behavior. Colonists faced

FIGURE 6. *General Sir Guy Carleton. Library and Archives Canada/Mabel Messer Collection/e011165560*

either "unconditional Submission to the tyranny of irritated Ministers, or resistance by force. The latter is our choice." "Our cause is just. Our union is perfect," the Declaration of the Causes and Necessity of Taking up Arms concluded. *"We will, in defiance of every Hazard, with unabating Firmness and Perseverance, employ for the preservation of our Liberties;* being with one Mind resolved to die Freemen rather than to live Slaves."[24]

John Adams went back to his Philadelphia lodgings triumphant, eager to tell his Boston pals what they had accomplished. "We have Spent this whole Day in debating Paragraph by Paragraph, a Manifesto [with] Some Mercury in it," he wrote to fellow patriot William Tudor. But something else had happened that afternoon. At some point late in the day's business, Adams related in a second letter to James Warren, "a curious Phenomenon appeared at the Door of our Congress." It was "a German Hussar, a veteran in the Wars of Germany, in his Uniform, and on Horse back . . . with a Deaths Head painted in Front . . . [i]n short the most warlike and formidable Figure, I ever saw." Here was an embodiment of the colonists' choice to fight. It was too perfect — the public needed to know about it.[25]

Adams recognized the potential of such a display and how the German veteran's spontaneous presentation might benefit the common cause. Adams concluded his letters with a suggestion that his friends go pay a visit to the *Boston Gazette*. This "Phenomenon," Adams knew, "would Set before our New England People, a fine Example for their Imitation: But what is of more Moment, it would engage the Affections of the Germans, of whom there are many in N[ew] York, Pennsylvania, Maryland, and other Colonies, more intensely in the Cause of America." One or both of Adams's correspondents followed his advice and carried this letter to the printer, for his description of the German soldier did indeed appear verbatim in Benjamin Edes's *Boston Gazette* — and in five subsequent papers under the heading from a "gentleman in Philadelphia to his Friend in this Town."[26]

This is another rare opportunity to see the curtain pulled back on how closely connected patriot political leaders were with their publicist counterparts in managing the common cause. We don't get many occasions to see the behind-the-scenes direction; it's worth pausing to investigate what was going on here. John Adams wasn't done "cooking up."[27]

Adams intended his private correspondence to work in tandem with the declaration Congress was about to order printers all over America to insert into their newspapers. That address was about "engaging the affections" of as many colonists as possible. Adams's letter — which he hoped would then be exchanged into places where there were lots of Germans — was explicitly intended to do the same.

This management had to be precise. If Edes were not careful, sections of Adams's letter to Warren might backfire; these were potentially explosive and could not see the light of day. Some of his colleagues from the middle and southern colonies had "a Secret Fear," Adams wrote, "a Jealousy, that New England will soon be full of Veteran Soldiers, and at length conceive Designs unfavourable to the other Colonies." Congress had just proclaimed that very day, "Our union is perfect," and such a sentiment could sink the whole program. Thanks to the surgical efforts of Boston patriots and printers, it didn't. They put forth only what they thought would further the cause.[28]

Then there was the matter of attribution. That was no ordinary friend in Philadelphia. Readers of the *Essex Journal, Connecticut Journal, Massachusetts Spy,* and *Newport Mercury* who saw this story probably thought it came from a casual eyewitness in Philadelphia—a friendly conversation between one gentleman in Philadelphia and another in Boston. But it came directly from the pen of the region's most important patriot leader, the head of Massachusetts's elected delegation to Congress. These productions of July 5, 1775—Congress's declaration and John Adams's letters—were twin examples of how the patriots understood the need to manage public opinion, one official and the other less so. Here is yet another instance of the extensive thought, time, and effort Adams and his friends put into developing strategies to propagate the common cause.

Another private letter written by a delegate to Congress that week also illustrates how the threat of African Americans and Indians had saturated patriots' perception of their enemies and justifications of the Revolution. Benjamin Franklin vented his frustrations to Jonathan Shipley, an Anglican bishop friendly to the patriots, just after Congress approved the final text of the Declaration of the Causes and Necessity. Franklin angrily detailed all the conspiracies he had read about since Lexington and Concord. Some people in Britain had "recommended" schemes to use the slaves and Indians against the colonists, he wrote, and now these plans were coming to fruition. "Lord Dunmore and Governor Martin have already, we are told, taken some steps towards carrying one part of the Project into Execution, by exciting an Insurrection among the Blacks," Franklin fumed in disbelief. "And Governor Carleton, we have certain Accounts, has been very industrious in engaging the Indians to begin their horrid Work. This is making War like Nations who had never been Friends, and never wish to be such while the World stands." At their separate writing tables that week, Adams, Franklin, Jefferson, and Dickinson all drew upon these multiplying stories of British sponsorship of proxies as a wedge to divide the two sides of the conflict.[29]

Newspapers were the key to making their case. The small stories inside the paper provided corroborating evidence to back up patriot claims. The middle pages were the proof, the affidavits that clinched the case made on the front. If colonial readers needed confirmation that British agents were indeed encouraging Indians to attack the backcountry, as Congress claimed they were in the declaration, all those skeptical readers needed to do was turn the page. During the same weeks in July that the Declaration of the Causes and Necessity ran through the prints, the other stories that those issues often shared featured news of John Stuart, Josiah Martin, and Indian agents in the North, Guy Johnson and Guy Carleton, making plans with enslaved and

Native peoples. John Stuart's confiscated letters arrived at the Pennsylvania State House a few days after the Congress sent the Declaration of the Causes and Necessity to the city's printers. The delegates whisked this packet of letters sent from Charleston into the arms of William Bradford and his *Pennsylvania Journal.* Bradford published the incriminating evidence, whereby Stuart instructed Cameron to "use your influence to dispose those people to act in defence of his Majesty," on July 12, the same issue that featured Congress's declaration across its front page. For the remainder of July, newspapers throughout New England and the mid-Atlantic exchanged the Stuart letters from the *Pennsylvania Journal.* It was from this source that Adam Boyd exchanged the letters in his *Cape-Fear Mercury* just as Wilmington, North Carolina, teetered on the edge of serious internal conflict.[30]

As would happen throughout the Revolutionary War, a circular process was at work here. Events would occur, the newspapers would report them, and then people reacted to those stories, bringing about new events and new stories, restarting the cycle. Sometimes the people who reacted were colonists singly or in groups who responded to news by taking sudden, vigilante action, such as attacking Black David or starting a fight with James Dealey. Sometimes those people were political leaders who drafted new official policies in response to the news.

This circular process is what happened in North Carolina that summer. At the very same moment the Stuart letters were in the local papers, North Carolina patriots took more radical steps against their governor, Josiah Martin. It is probable that the news of other British officials' stirring up conspiracies in the Deep South encouraged Carolina patriots to attack Fort Johnston. Then the process started over again, as news that Martin and Captain John Collet were trying to "spirit up an enemy among ourselves" made its way through patriot networks. These perpetual circles reinforced one another in 1775, securing Congress's case that the British were doing everything they could to destroy the rebellion.[31]

Together, patriot political leaders and publicists forwarded an emerging narrative that the king's representatives, from Carolina to Canada, were attempting to use all means to slaughter them. Of course, these were far from the only complaints patriots lodged against the British government that summer. But these accusations welled up from the darkest parts of the colonial imagination. Insurrectionist slaves and hostile Indians destroying their houses and families were the most terrifying of colonists' fears. These nightmares seemed more likely than ever in 1775 to be coming true. Thomas Jeremiah, hundreds of slaves along the Pamlico River in North Carolina, and leaders of the Caughnawaga and Cherokee Indians *were* all trying to take advantage of the conflict.

The Continental Congress persisted in converting these worries into political capital. In addition to publishing the Declaration of the Causes and Necessity for domestic consumption, Congress issued several other proclamations, aimed at distant audiences, that played upon these fears. On July 8, they approved an address to the inhabitants of Great Britain, begging them to intercede on the Americans' behalf. Fewer than two weeks later, they debated two more proclamations, one addressed to the Irish people, the other to the Jamaican Assembly. The message to Jamaica was particularly emotional, suggesting, "Ministerial insolence is lost in ministerial barbarity," which had "plunged us in all the horrors and calamities of civil war." The Irish address laid the rhetoric of destruction thickly on: "When we perceive our friends and kinsmen massacred, our habitations plundered, our house in flames, and their once happy inhabitants fed only by the hand of charity. . . . Who can censure our repeling the attacks of such a barbarous band?" Worse, "the wild and barbarous savages of the wilderness have been solicited, by gifts, to take up the hatchet against us; and instigated to deludge our settlements with the blood of innocent and defenceless women and children." Barbarous Indians, barbarous British. Congress broadcast these addresses in all directions — and not just to their intended audiences. Since a majority of colonial printers in America published the Irish address, it was not just for remote readers; it targeted the affections of people living in New York or Baltimore as much as those in Dublin or Belfast.[32]

By the end of that unprecedented summer, colonists were reading about unrest or potential unrest all over America. They did so because enslaved and Native peoples greeted the news of civil war with Britain in various ways. Some individuals took advantage of the disturbance to try to improve their future. Others chose a more cautious approach, waiting to see how things developed. British officials — especially royal governors, army and navy officers, and superintendents out in the backcountry — also made plans. They considered what role enslaved and Native peoples might play in bringing an end to this worrisome colonial rebellion, which seemed to be spreading all around them.

In so doing, Britain found means to accomplish what seemed impossible just a few years earlier: unite the American colonies. This was not, however, an organic act of cohesion. The colonists did not naturally forget all their jealousies, conflicts, and mistrust that had pitted them against one another for more than a century. Patriot political and communications leaders amplified these stories. They arranged for these particular reports to appear in colonial newspapers.

Further, they relied on them in their first justifications of the Revolutionary War. In their earliest proclamations and declarations, the Continental Congress consistently highlighted what they heard British officials were doing on slave plantations and in Indian country. Once the shooting started, the official justifications for taking up arms stopped being about rights, representation, or consent. Now it was about survival—and fear. British officials hoped that encouraging words to enslaved and Native peoples might bring a quick end to this nettlesome rebellion. Doing so played right into the patriots' hands. Nightmares about slave insurrections and Native massacres were what colonists really had in common in 1775. "Our union is perfect," Congress proclaimed in July 1775. The glue that held them together was a shared fear of British agents working in tandem with enslaved and Native peoples to destroy them. This was the new appeal that patriot leaders, from the Continental Congress down to the local level, broadcast as loudly as they could. This was the new common cause.

Patriot leaders would continue to add to their list of British villains for the remainder of 1775. Chief among the wicked, they argued, was the royal governor of Virginia, Lord Dunmore. Starting in September, as George Washington continued to organize his Continental army outside Boston, the continent's attention turned to—and remained fixed on—the growing battle between Virginia patriots and their dangerous governor; for Dunmore, more than any other British official, urged enslaved and Native peoples to rally around his and the crown's authority.

CHAPTER 5

A ROLLING SNOWBALL

As the Revolutionary War's first summer faded into autumn, patriot leaders increasingly justified their actions around British agents' use of proxies. A clergyman in Maryland recited lines from the emerging patriot script in early August. "The ministerial agents are endeavouring to rouse the *Indians* against us," he wrote to a correspondent in England, but "to complete the horrid scene, the Governour of *Virginia,* the Captains of the men-of-war, and mariners, have been tampering with our negroes; and have held nightly meetings with them; and all for the glorious purpose of enticing them to cut their master's throats while they are asleep." "Gracious *God!,*" he exclaimed, "that men, noble by birth and fortune, should descend to such ignoble base servility!"[1]

John Adams, Thomas Jefferson, and Benjamin Franklin agreed whole-heartedly. But those men shared more with this minister than his exasperation: it was in his mind and on his stationery because of them. Patriot political leaders and publicists had taken advantage of the opportunity the king's agents had presented them in the months after Lexington. They had broadcast these efforts in colonial newspapers as loudly as they could, in both official addresses and news stories. Proclamations asserting the British were trying to use slaves and Indians to kill colonists would run on the front page, and the proof would be inside the fold, in the form of affidavits, intercepted correspondence, or committee resolutions. None of it was there by accident. Because of the nature of the newspaper business in the late eighteenth century, printers depended on men like John Adams and his friends to provide those details. Once they got into the communication exchange networks, those stories and images about who were the friends and enemies of liberty reached colonial readers all over North America.

Patriot newspapers had reported details of two southern governors' dealings with the enslaved over that first summer of war. Josiah Martin had roiled North Carolina by being connected to the freeing and arming of slaves, and South Carolina governor Lord William Campbell had also sparred with local patriot leaders on this topic. Late in the summer, as the clergyman's letter noted with bitter disdain, there was a third southern governor who would begin to earn for himself a featured spot in the patriots' rogues' gallery: Virginia's royal governor, Lord Dunmore. Stories soon began to emerge from the Chesapeake, too, that local royal officials had decided to use all available resources to quell the rebellion.

Lord Dunmore had been at sea since early June. As we have seen, his reaction to rumors of slave unrest across Virginia in April was to confiscate the gunpowder from the public magazine, a move that, when coupled with the news of Lexington galloping south during those same hours, exacerbated outrage in Williamsburg and beyond. When anxious, vulnerable planters pressed the governor to restore their weapons, Dunmore doubled down, threatening to "declare freedom to the slaves and reduce the City of W[illia]msburg to ashes" if they continued to buck his authority. Warnings like those made a bad situation much worse. Within a few weeks, Dunmore would join the gunpowder barrels on board a Royal Navy ship in Chesapeake Bay. For most of 1775, he would attempt to administer his colony from the cabin of the HMS *Otter* instead of from his plush office in the governor's palace.[2]

By year's end, it would have been difficult for colonial readers all over North America to have missed the volatile controversy in Virginia over British officials' harboring runaway slaves. The theater of operations shifted north from Cape Fear to the Chesapeake, but the story remained the same: royal governors, aided by naval officers, were encouraging slaves to rebel against their masters. In June and July, the news had been about Josiah Martin and Captain John Collet; in August and September, it was Lord Dunmore and Captain Matthew Squire. The differences mattered little, but the aggregate effect was powerful.

This chapter narrates the outsize presence Lord Dunmore occupied in the patriots' wartime common cause appeal—and in the colonial imagination. The news from Virginia, which would merge together colonial concerns about attacks from Native and enslaved peoples, dominated the continent's news for the remainder of 1775. George Washington consistently described the threat Dunmore posed as a snowball rolling downhill, gaining size and speed as it plummeted out of control. Dunmore's schemes were more complicated, however. Washington was right in that the governor's willingness to embrace Native and enslaved allies was very dangerous to patriot prospects in the Chesapeake. At the same time, because Dunmore's emancipation proclamation to enslaved Virginians and machinations with Native groups in the Ohio country occurred in a broad and deep discourse about British officials all over America plotting to take these same steps, it further contributed to and helped sustain the new wartime common cause

FIGURE 7. *John Murray, Fourth Earl of Dunmore. By Sir Joshua Reynolds. 1765.*
National Galleries of Scotland. Purchased 1992 with contributions from the
Art Fund and the National Heritage Memorial Fund

MAP 6. *Virginia, 1775–1776. Drawn by Gerry Krieg*

appeal. Dunmore's actions brought the thirteen colonial clocks closer into harmony.

Tensions were rising in the lower Chesapeake Bay over the last weeks of summer. In early August, on the same day the Maryland minister sat down to write his friend in England, Norfolk printer John Hunter Holt published a report that "this town and neighbourhood have been much disturbed lately with the elopement of their negroes." There was a "mistaken notion," Holt wrote in his *Virginia Gazette, or the Norfolk Intelligencer,* "which has unhappily spread amongst them, of finding shelter on board the men of war in this harbor." This notice, which fourteen other printers exchanged in their own papers, was just the start of what would be a storm of news concerning Royal Navy officers' and Dunmore's harboring, and possibly arming, of enslaved Virginians.[3]

Then, when an actual storm—a hurricane—swept over the mouths of the James and York Rivers on the afternoon of Saturday, September 2, those tensions exploded into violence. The storm drove a tender attached to Captain Squire's Royal Navy squadron aground near Hampton. Local residents were growing angry at Squire's "most unfriendly disposition to the liberties of this continent, in promoting a disaffection among the slaves, and concealing some of them for a considerable time on board their vessels," according to the Norfolk committee. The hurricane brought those frustrations to the surface. A group of nearby inhabitants set fire to the foundered ship early Sunday morning. A few days later, John Hunter Holt published a short gloss on the torching in his *Virginia Gazette*. That September 6 issue was already chock-full of exchanged stories about British efforts to secure proxy allies, including an account whereby Canadian Indians "cannot be persuaded by governor Carleton," a letter from London that the government had given four men £40,000 each "for the barbarous purpose of hiring the Indians to . . . attack the colonies," and a report of Captain Collet's being "dislodged" from Fort Johnston. Then Holt inserted his own story about the crew of the *Otter:* "Is it not a melancholy reflection that men, who affect on all occasions to stile themselves 'his Majesty['s] servants' should think the service of their Sovereign consists in plundering his subjects, and in committing such pitiful acts of rapine as would entitle other people to the character of robbers?" Squire did not appreciate this characterization. Incensed, he fired off a warning to Holt, published in the next week's issue, that he had noticed the printer had "lately taken the freedom to mention MY NAME" in such a context, and if Holt ever did so again, "I will most assuredly seize your person and take you on board the *Otter*."[4]

The charred tender and the exchange between Squire and Holt quickly became major news stories throughout America. A few papers in Pennsylvania and South Carolina simply reprinted Squire's threat. More copied Alexander Purdie's confirmation in his Williamsburg *Virginia Gazette* that the crowd had indeed burned Squire's ship "in return for his harbouring gentlemen's negroes." Perhaps in defiance of Squire's attempt to intimidate his colleague, Purdie the following week condemned the captain in similar language to Holt's. "Squire," he sneered, "has seized three passage boats, with the Negroes in them, by way of reprisal" for the burnt tender, "which boats and Negroes, it is likely he intends taking into the *King's service,* to send out a pirating for hogs, fowls, etc. — A very pretty occupation for the Captain of one of his Majesty's ships of war." Thirteen other papers exchanged this comment, as well.[5]

The charge of "instigating" slaves had powerful effects in 1775. Less than a year before the hurricane, twenty-four-year-old James Madison had discussed the looming problem of slave insurrections with his friend William

Bradford, Jr., son of the *Pennsylvania Journal* printer. Madison was already worried in November 1774 that "an Insurrection among the slaves may and will be promoted" if war broke out with Britain. "In one of our Counties lately a few of those unhappy wretches met together and chose a leader who was to conduct them when the English Troops should arrive." These "Intentions were soon discovered" and the "Infection" prevented, Madison related with relief, but he cautioned: "It is prudent such attempts should be concealed as well as suppressed."[6]

Correspondence between the two college friends often turned on publishing and changing printing values, especially on the eve of Revolution. As noted above, earlier in 1774, Madison related to Bradford that loyalist printer James Rivington had better never show his face in Virginia. This letter, however, is extraordinary. It highlights just how apprehensive patriot leaders were about the effects civil war with Britain might have on the enslaved and how African Americans mulled these potential opportunities themselves. It also insists that silence is the best way to deal with these threats.[7]

The events of 1775 proved Madison right: the onset of war did involve a great deal of thinking and worrying about how it would involve the enslaved. But, just ten months on, Madison would not have given the same advice on suppression. In fact, with royal officials actually making plans to carry out the colonists' worst nightmares, censorship was the last thing on patriots' minds. Now that they could link British agents to these acts, patriot leaders did just the opposite: they rushed to tell as many colonists about it as they could reach. Printers like William Bradford, Sr., went out of their way to feature, not suppress, these stories. Publicity of British-inspired slave unrest was the best way to bolster the common cause among free American colonists.

In this context, seemingly insignificant actions—like the burning of a ship run aground on the shore of Chesapeake Bay—took on a great significance because patriot printers now broadcast them as widely as possible. Patriots hurled accusations and threats at British agents who they thought were dealing with runaway slaves, and colonial publicists rushed to amplify those exchanges all through North America.

John Hunter Holt found out the hard way how explosive the accusation of encouraging runaways could be. First calling Captain Squire a plunderer and a pirate, he then turned to the matter of Joseph Harris. Like Thomas Jeremiah in Charleston, Harris was a pilot and therefore extremely valuable. Sometime in July, Harris had run to the HMS *Fowey,* and his master, Henry King, wanted him back. When Squire demanded that the people of Hampton who had burned his ship return the stores they had plundered from it, they responded they would do so when the captain returned Harris to King. Squire balked, and Holt jumped at this chance to attack "the honest Captain." "After damning the IMPUDENCE of these people in demanding his Ethiopian director," Holt reported that Squire "swore he would make them no other reply than what his cannon could give them; accordingly he has taken his station between the two bars to be more convenient for the business." Perhaps it was the intimation behind the phrase "his Ethiopian director"—that maybe Harris was more commander than pilot—which set Squire off, but something in that issue certainly did.[8]

Ten days later, with Dunmore's permission, Squire made good on his threat. On September 30, a squad of twelve marines from the *Otter* landed at Norfolk, broke into Holt's printing office, confiscated his press and types, took two apprentices hostage, gave "three huzzas, in which they were joined by a crowd of negroes," and left town without any resistance, all in front of two or three hundred surprised onlookers. Squire was allegedly "very angry they did not get Mr. *Holt,*" but that was not Dunmore's main concern. The governor approved of the raid, not to settle a score, but to get his hands on a printing press. A few days later, all three *Virginia Gazettes* in Williamsburg reported news of what had happened to Holt. From there, printers throughout the colonies took up the cause, and over the next few weeks, stories about the raid surfaced in a total of twenty-three of thirty-one active newspapers.[9]

The news of the confiscation was as yet in Williamsburg newspapers traveling north toward Philadelphia when the aggrieved Norfolk printer took out an advertisement swearing that he, for one, would not be cowed by Dunmore's "arbitrary power." Holt informed the public in tidewater Virginia that he was "procuring a new set of materials, which, if he should be so fortunate to succeed in, will enable him once more to apprize his countrymen of the danger they may be in from the machinations and black designs of their common enemy." For more than two months, that public had been agitated by constant stories of slaves' "eloping," being "stolen" off plantations, or being "instigated" by sinister brokers. What they did not yet know was that Dunmore had other agents operating in other theaters, attempting to extinguish the common cause. The "machinations and black designs" were more extensive than they knew—yet.[10]

On the same day Holt pledged his defiance to the Virginia reading public, a servant (who, ironically, was also running away from his master) asked to speak with George Washington at his headquarters in the Continental army camp in Cambridge, Massachusetts. His testimony to the commander re-

vealed that, throughout the Squire squabble, Dunmore had also been approving plans to include Ohio Indians in the panoply of proxies to fight the
patriots in Virginia.

For much of the summer, Virginia militia captain James Wood had been
trekking through the Ohio River valley, calling the Shawnee, Delaware,
Wyandot, and Mingo Indians to a meeting at Fort Pitt in early September.
The Ohio Indians, Wood noted, were well aware of what had occurred in
Boston that past spring. The Wyandots were "Much Surprized" to hear about
war with Britain and about "several Engagements at Boston in which a great
Number of Men were killed on both sides." Far down the Ohio, Wood lis-
tened while Shawnee leaders informed him they knew all about Dunmore's
flight to the Royal Navy for protection. And, Wood learned to his dismay,
British agents at Detroit had told the Delawares that "the Virginians were
determined to drive us off and to take [their] Lands." Wood sent reports of
his tour back east, and three different reports found their way to printers in
Baltimore, Philadelphia, and Williamsburg (and, from there, across North
America) early in the autumn of 1775.[11]

One of the whisperers who undermined Wood's effort to evangelize the
patriot cause to the Ohio Indians was Dr. John Connolly. As we have seen,
Connolly had been Dunmore's agent in the border controversy that sparked
war with the Shawnees in 1774. When word reached Pittsburgh of war in
Massachusetts, Connolly, ever the governor's man, began to hatch a plan for
himself and the Ohio Indians. His vocal loyalism almost got him thrown in
prison at several points during that tumultuous summer. For his own safety,
Connolly had decided it was best to leave Pittsburgh and headed east to
pitch his idea to his patron. In mid-August, he had an audience with Dunmore aboard the *Otter*. His plan was this: he would get the Ohio Indians "to
act in concert with me against his Majesty's enemies . . . to penetrate through
Virginia and join his Excellency, Lord Dunmore, at Alexandria early next
spring." Connolly's plot was bold — and frightening. If the pair could pull it
off, an army of hostile Indians, aggrieved loyalists, emancipated slaves, and
British regulars would link up on the Potomac and, in Connolly's words,
cut off "the communication between the southern and northern governments," giving "a favourable turn indisputably . . . to his Majesty's affairs in
the southern Provinces." Dunmore liked the plan enough that he sent this
"active, spirited officer" north to get permission from commanding general
Thomas Gage.[12]

Connolly had an audience with Gage while Squire's tender still smoldered
at Hampton. Not having much military capital to lose by approving the plan,
and having just written to Carleton that the Canadian governor must "strain

every nerve to rouse both Canadians and Indians," the commander signed off on Connolly's plan. Over the following three days, Gage spun off a series of notes to all interested British agents across the frontier, alerting them that Connolly was en route with the commander's blessing. Even though letters flew out of Boston in all directions, Gage understood the proposal's combustibility. He concluded his approval letter to Dunmore with a prescient warning: "The greatest care ought to be taken, that the inclosed letters do not fall into the Rebels' hands."[13]

Across the lines in Boston, Gage's opponents did find out about Connolly's plan, but not because a British courier was stopped and searched. William Cowley, Connolly's personal servant, began writing a letter to Washington on the same Saturday that royal marines packed up Holt's printing press in Norfolk, but he could not find the means to get the letter to Cambridge. A few days later, when Connolly's southbound ship stopped in Newport, Cowley "left all my Cloaths and all that I had" and escaped. It would all be worthwhile if he "could be of any Service to [his] Country," he later affirmed. Cowley approached Washington's headquarters carefully, explaining to the sentries that he "could not be at Rest 'till [he] had disclosed [a] Matter" to the commander. He told Washington of Connolly's plans to meet Dunmore at Alexandria and "sweep all the Country before him." "A Person who has lately been a Servant to Major Conolly, a tool of Lord Dunmore's," Washington wrote to Congress, "has given an Account of a Scheme to distress the Southern Provinces, which appeared to me of sufficient Consequence to be immediately transmitted." Washington also that day forwarded Cowley's letter to his cousin and plantation manager, Lund Washington, at Mount Vernon to alert his neighbors in Fairfax County, who stood to be in immediate danger.[14]

From these notices, the patriot leadership put out what passed for an all-points bulletin in 1775. Having received Washington's letter on Saturday, October 21, the Virginia delegates to Congress turned around on Monday and (despite a schedule burdened with the preparations for the funeral of their president, Peyton Randolph) drafted instructions to the Virginia committee of safety. Informing them of the plot, the delegates ordered the committee to forward a copy to their peers in North Carolina. For his part, Lund Washington forwarded the letter to Fairfax leader George Mason, who sent it to the Maryland committee of safety. Through both official and unofficial channels, news was getting out that Dr. Connolly was a dangerous enemy.

As Connolly made plans to head west and the news of his plot fanned out, Virginia militia forces began to ready themselves for a clash with his benefactor. When Dunmore learned of men and matériel gathering east of

Norfolk, he ordered Captain Samuel Leslie and about 130 men — including a significant number of slaves who had already joined him — to attack a force of Virginia militia at least twice their size near Kemp's Landing on November 14. Leslie's greatly outnumbered men still routed the Virginians, killing seven and capturing eighteen while suffering only a single flesh wound in return. Two of the captured men were colonels, including Joseph Hutchings, apprehended by his own slave who had escaped to the governor. This victory at Kemp's Landing delighted Dunmore and raised his expectations for success. The performance of runaway slaves also confirmed Dunmore's suspicions that enslaved people might make effective counterrevolutionary soldiers. A week before, Dunmore had already drafted and printed his proclamation. With the success at Kemp's Landing, he decided to distribute it far and wide throughout the colony. Together, they would send white Virginians, and then colonists throughout North America, reeling.[15]

Dunmore thought his fortunes were promising enough to send word out that he was "raising the king's standard," an action that officially proclaimed Virginia in a state of rebellion and ordered all loyal subjects to assist in its restoration or suffer the penalty of law. But the governor had decided to make the king's standard a beacon for more than loyalists. Dunmore's newfound confidence encouraged him to unsheathe the sword he had rattled in Williamsburg back in April. As soon as word of Kemp's Landing reached him on board his flagship, he ordered Holt's printing press into action to make copies of his fateful proclamation: "I do hereby further declare all indented Servants, Negroes, or others, (appertaining to Rebels) free that are able and willing to bear Arms, they joining His Majesty's Troops as soon as may be, for the more speedy reducing this Colony to a proper Sense of their Duty, to his Majesty's Crown and Dignity." Hundreds, if not thousands, of enslaved people from Virginia, Maryland, and North Carolina would do their best to get to Norfolk.[16]

As word spread that Dunmore had followed through on his threat, Virginians did not suddenly realize that the rebellion was doomed and rally around the governor. From what the patriots have told us, they did just the opposite. For contemporaries then and historians since, alarm followed by backlash has been the standard interpretation that described Virginia's reaction to Dunmore's proclamation. Traveling through the Shenandoah Valley in late November, one diarist noted that Dunmore's "infernal Scheme . . . seems to quicken all in Revolution to overpower him however at every Risk." Richard Henry Lee wrote from Philadelphia on November 29, "Lord Dunmore's unparalleled conduct in Virginia has . . . united every Man in that large Colony. If Administration had searched thro' the world for a person the best fitted to ruin their cause, and procure union and success for these Colonies, they could not have found a more complete Agent than Lord Dunmore." Jefferson wrote the same day that the governor's actions had "raised our country into perfect phrensy." Fifteen years later, patriot political leader turned historian David Ramsay deepened the backlash thesis: "The injury done the royal cause by the bare proposal of the scheme, far outweighed any advantage that resulted from it. The colonists were struck with horror, and filled with detestation of a government which was exercised in loosening the bands of society." Modern historians have followed this lead, suggesting, "Whatever loyalty there was in Virginia pretty much flickered out with Dunmore's call." That backlash, however, was not an accidental or organic reaction. Although the proclamation was indeed "every white Virginian's nightmare" that sent "shock waves throughout the colony," by the middle of November, it was hardly an innovation. To be sure, Dunmore had taken the unprecedented step of printing the words "free" and "Negroes" in the same sentence, but accusations that royal officials across the South had been whispering such notions to the enslaved were months old by then.[17]

In other words, the backlash was managed. The threatening seeds of slave emancipation that Dunmore tossed at the end of 1775 fell upon already-fertile soil. Stories about British agents making similar promises had been in the news since the middle of summer. Patriot political leaders and publicists had already made the colonial reading public aware of just such possibilities.

Still, Dunmore's proclamation handed the patriots a fantastic opportunity to propagate the common cause. For his part, Dunmore hoped the news would spread all through the upper South. He ordered Holt's printing press to make broadsides to be disseminated all around the Chesapeake. But he also counted on the news crossing over from print-based information networks into the orally based slave quarter. The potential for the news to be carried across vast distances through these networks was great, as John Adams had recently learned from two southern slaveowners. In September, Adams listened while two newly arrived delegates gave him a "melancholy account of the state of Georgia." "They say that if 1000 regular Troops should land in Georgia and their commander be provided with Arms and Cloaths enough and proclaim Freedom to all the Negroes who would join his Camp," he wrote in his diary, "20,000 Negroes would join it from the two Provinces in a fortnight. The Negroes have a wonderfull Art of communicating Intelligence among themselves. It will run severall hundreds of

Miles in a Week or Fortnight." This was what Dunmore was counting on, especially after the military prowess runaway slaves had displayed at Kemp's Landing.[18]

Patriots found themselves wielding this double-edged sword by November. Madison's fear of the previous year hadn't evaporated completely—publicizing Dunmore's emancipation proclamation could blow up right in their faces. It could increase the number of enslaved people running to hail the governor's ships. On the other hand, broadcasting the news of Dunmore's "diabolical Schemes" (as Washington would refer to the governor's actions), improved with the addition of their own comments on the scheme, could also solidify the union. Suppress or broadcast?[19]

They chose the latter. Patriot printers made Dunmore's proclamation and its aftermath infamous throughout North America. They amplified the address far more than the governor ever could have on his purloined press. The staunchest patriot newspapers *(Pennsylvania Journal, Massachusetts Spy, Boston Gazette, New-York Journal, Providence Gazette)* and even some of the less radical ones *(Pennsylvania Evening Post* and *Pennsylvania Mercury)* printed the document in full. Others referred to it without publishing the text. In every instance except one, patriot commentary encircled Dunmore's proclamation.[20]

The patriots used literature to malign Dunmore. Alexander Purdie prefaced his text of the proclamation with an updated version of one of Shakespeare's invectives from *Macbeth*:

> ———*Not in the legions*
> *Of horrid hell, can come a devil more damn'd*
> *In evils, to top D*****e.*

New-York Journal printer John Holt inserted a short paragraph signed by "Minos," the judge from Virgil's *Aeneid* and Dante's *Inferno*. Minos opined that since Dunmore was "guilty of at least seven capital crimes . . . it is hoped he will shortly be taken, publickly tried and hanged, as the most atrocious criminal that ever appeared in America."[21]

The most extraordinary editorial comment that was appended to the reprinting of Dunmore's proclamation appeared right away. When John Pinkney printed the emancipation proclamation in his November 23 issue of the *Virginia Gazette,* a unique counterstatement followed it. Slaves should not heed the call of Dunmore's "cruel declaration," the anonymous writer charged.

But should there be any amongst the slaves *weak* enough to believe that lord Dunmore intends to do them a kindness, and *wicked* enough to provoke the fury of the Americans against their defenceless fathers and mothers, their wives, their women and children, let them only consider the difficulty of effecting their escape, and what they must expect to suffer if they fall into the hands of the Americans.

Do not be weak and wicked: this was the striking admonition Virginia patriots gave to their slaves. Dropping the facade that slaves were mindless, dependent objects, this Virginian asked Blacks to "consider." In a rhetorical move akin to breaking the fourth wall in cinema, the author said directly to the enslaved, "Be not then, ye negroes, tempted by this proclamation to ruin yourselves. . . . I have considered your welfare, as well of that of the country. Whether you will profit by my advice I cannot tell, but this I know, that whether we suffer or not, if *you* desert us, *you* most certainly will."[22]

Consider, yourself, what this remarkable piece shows. It admitted enslaved people were rational, even literate beings who would—just like other colonists—assess the situation, make decisions, and select the right side. When he admonished them not to be weak and wicked, the author treated them as people who were capable of making such choices. He asked them to consider liberty and righteousness over tyranny and destruction—the same decision patriot leaders assumed all free people in North America had to make in 1775. The patriots were people "sincerely attached to the interests of their country," who "stand forth in opposition to the arbitrary and oppressive acts of any man, or set of men," and were "moved by compassion, and actuated by sound policy." These were the real Americans. The enslaved had these decisions to make, too. And choosing wrong, this author implied, might disqualify them from the benefits of Revolution—if not end their lives.[23]

Even if this patriot author was able to take the remarkable step of admitting slaves were rational beings, he could not bring himself to admit that he and his friends were the ones committing arbitrary and oppressive acts on their plantations. He did not consider the irony of pleading for slaves to choose to remain enslaved. When a thousand of them did respond to Dunmore's call, patriots did not view this as liberation but rather abandonment—and those who rejected those lofty principles were subject to suffering. So they damned them all in the press. "The publick, no doubt, will be exceedingly incensed on finding that lord Dunmore has taken into his service the *very scum* of the country to assist him in his diabolical schemes against the good people of this government," one widely reprinted letter read. A few months later, another Virginian would continue this line of thinking, cordoning off what he referred to as "domestic insurrectionists" who ran to Dunmore as separate and distinct from the "we" who held truths to be self-evident in the Declaration of Independence.[24]

Virginia patriot leader Edmund Pendleton anxiously surveyed the slaves' reaction to Dunmore's emancipation call. "Letters mention that slaves Flock to him in abundance," Pendleton wrote to Richard Henry Lee on November 27, "but I hope it is Magnified." Those who paid attention to patriot newspapers, however, learned that Pendleton's earnest wish was fantasy. Most printed Dunmore's proclamation alongside a series of articles taken from the *Virginia Gazette* that added meaning to the declaration. One often-reprinted (and italicized) selection reported, *"Since Lord Dunmore's proclamation made its appearance here, it is said he has recruited his army . . . to the amount of about 2000 men, including his black regiment, which is thought to be a considerable part, with this inscription on their breasts: — 'Liberty to Slaves.'"* This information was far from trifling in the uncertain context of 1775. How the enslaved responded to Dunmore was a development to which readers paid close attention — or, at least, patriot publicists hoped they would.[25]

Patriot leaders, usually militia officers, consistently highlighted the presence of runaway Blacks in every raid or skirmish they reported. When patriot units from Virginia and North Carolina clashed with Dunmore's troops, the groups were mostly classified by color — and Blacks nearly always outnumbered whites. Witnesses categorized Dunmore's forces, never forgetting to mention the large number of Blacks in the ranks, usually accompanied by a snide reference to his "Royal Regiment of Black Fusileers" or the "Queen's Own Black Regiment." "Last Tuesday night," Colonel William Woodford related, "a party of men, chiefly blacks, from a tender, came up to Mr. Benjamin Wells's . . . pillaged his house of everything valuable, such as bedding, wearing apparel, liquors, a watch, the stock of poultry, and carried off two Negro girls." Reportage of another fight used similar language. "Since my last, we have sent a party of 100 men . . . over the river, who fell in last night, about 12 o'clock, with a guard of about thirty men, chiefly negroes." Patriot newspapers also skewed casualty reports to exaggerate the number of fugitive slaves in Dunmore's ranks. They never failed to mention the presence of Black combatants. As such, the above skirmish ended with the comment, "We killed one, burnt another in the house, and took two prisoners (all blacks) with 4 exceeding[ly] fine musquets, and defeated the guard." "We have been well informed," Lt. Colonel Charles Scott wrote in a letter that appeared in the *Pennsylvania Gazette,* "that we killed 16 negroes and

5 white men the first day we got to this place." With all the incidental references to "all black" raiding parties, skirmishes with groups that were "chiefly negroes," and notices of open boats full of runaways, American readers probably took away from their newspapers a similar image that their commander in chief had privately expressed. Washington, monitoring the situation from Massachusetts, fretted, "If . . . that Man is not crushed before Spring, he will become the most formidable Enemy America has—his strength will Increase as a Snow ball by Rolling; and faster, if some expedient cannot be hit upon to convince the Slaves and Servants of the Impotency of His designs."[26]

The first notices about Dunmore's proclamation began to surface in print late in November, at the same time that forewarned patriot militiamen in western Maryland surrounded Dr. John Connolly. It had been a few weeks since Washington had dispatched riders to Congress armed with William Cowley's intelligence that Connolly was planning to lead a Native force east from the Ohio Valley to meet up with Dunmore's (now mostly Black) men in Alexandria.

Connolly had set off from Virginia the day before the engagement at Kemp's Landing, traveling with Allen Cameron and Dr. John Smyth, two loyalists who were to lead his proposed Indian and tory regiment. A week later, as the party rested outside Hagerstown, Maryland, one man who had served under Connolly in Pittsburgh recognized him. In the middle of the night on November 19, a group of Maryland militia broke into their rooms and, according to Smyth, "without the least provocation abused us perpetually with every opprobrious epithet language can afford."[27]

The captives were carried to Frederick to appear before the local committee. Even though Connolly had taken pains to hide the incriminating papers in his saddle, thorough searches turned up part of a piece of paper containing his proposal to Gage, a damning bit of evidence that bound them over for further incarceration. After a month in town, a grateful Congress wrote to the Frederick committee requesting they send the three prisoners to Philadelphia. Arriving on New Year's Day, 1776, Connolly observed that they were greeted in the city by a "drum beating the rogue's march." Chances are, had he entered any city in America that day, Connolly would have met with a similar reception, for during the month the three loyalists sat in the Frederick jail, news of their arrest had spread across the continent.[28]

Williamsburg printer John Pinkney broke the story only three days after the fact. By the first days of December, all but one of the six Philadelphia papers had published it. Within a week, New York and Maryland prints had picked it up, followed by New England prints the next week. By the time

Connolly was settling into his new accommodations in the Philadelphia jail, nearly two-thirds of active papers in nearly every American province had featured at least one account about Connolly, Dunmore, and the plot to involve the Ohio Indians. "Thus you see," the most widely exchanged account concluded, "a part of the diabolical scheme is defeated."[29]

Indeed, the timing of Connolly's capture only multiplied public outrage at Dunmore's "diabolical scheme," which was now known to have several remarkable facets. The news from western Maryland merged with that of the Chesapeake in December. It seemed that Dunmore and his superiors would stop at nothing to destroy colonial liberty; at least, that was the conclusion patriots wanted the public to reach. Some audiences were very receptive to this message. During the late fall, another round of runaway slave scares had encouraged patriots in South Carolina to take preemptive actions at the same time that Virginians were battling Dunmore.[30]

The military success that Dunmore thought his proclamation would bring did not materialize. Two weeks after the governor's forces moved into Norfolk and fortified their position, a sizeable patriot militia under the command of Colonel Woodford gathered near Great Bridge on the Elizabeth River, twelve miles south of the town. Woodford's troops, numbering 700, engaged Dunmore's men on December 9, killing 17 and wounding 49. Five days later, Woodford and his victorious force, now swelled to 1,275, marched unopposed into Norfolk. Dunmore quickly evacuated onto his gubernatorial sloop and, rather than allow his enemies to use the town and its resources, bombarded Norfolk on January 1, 1776. His loyalist base of operations lost, Dunmore's remaining eight months of tenure in Virginia would be mainly at sea. Accompanied by as many loyalists and emancipated slaves as he could fit on board, the governor's swollen fleet—known derisively as the "floating town"—stayed out on Chesapeake Bay for the first half of 1776. Dunmore's proclamation did not result in the crushing victory its author imagined it would.[31]

By November, the men in the Cambridge camp in Massachusetts were nearing the end of their ropes. They were bored and restless. Except for a few small skirmishes between pickets and scouts across the lines, there had been no fighting in Massachusetts since Bunker Hill six long months ago. One observer of the Continental army concluded in early November, "The soldiers in general are most heartily sick of the service, and I believe it would be with the utmost difficulty that they could be prevailed upon to serve in another campaign." He was right: General Charles Lee pleaded with the Adams cousins later that month that it was "absolutely necessary" they should without delay repair to this Province, the affairs of which are really in a most alarming if not frightful situation. There seems to be a dearth or at least a total stagnation of all public virtue amongst your Countrymen. . . . If you therefore or some good Genius do not fly and anticipate the impending evil, God knows what may be the effects. I conjure You therefore. . . . You and your Friend Samuel have ever been their prime conductors — and unless they have from time to time a rub of their prime conductors no electrical fire can be struck out of 'em.

So much for patriotism. Even in Boston, even in 1775.[32]

Making matters worse, enlistments were starting to run out. Washington saw this as the first significant opportunity to achieve his goal of establishing the army on a more professional footing, to make the American army look and act like the English army. One way was to redistribute officers so they did not command men drawn solely from their own home colonies. This backfired almost immediately. Several thousand men from Connecticut regiments made plans to walk away from the Revolution when their enlistments expired on December 1. The problem of union reared its head again: they would never fight under officers from Rhode Island or Massachusetts! Washington reported to Congress of the "egregious want of publick Spirit which reigns here, instead of pressing to be engaged in the Cause of their Country which I vainly flattered myselfe would be the Case, I find we are likely to be deserted, at a Most Critical time."[33]

Washington and his officers did their best to keep Connecticut men in the ranks. According to General Nathanael Greene, all their appeals to Yankee patriotism were failing. "Where is that Enthusiastick Love of Liberty that has ever been the distinguish[ed] Characteristick of a New Englandman?" he wrote to a fellow patriot leader in Rhode Island. "If neither the Love of Liberty nor dread of Slavery will rouse from them the present stupid state they are in, and they obstinately persist in quitting the Service, they will deserve the curses of the present and future Generations to the lateest ages." This "infamous desertion" imperiled colonial unity and made New England appear a "laughing Stock" to the world: "We shall receive the curses of all the Southern Governments, [and] New England will be held in detestation and Abhorrence in every part of the Globe. We that have boasted so loud of our private Virtue and publick spirit, not to have the very Vital principles of Liberty. We have been considered a brave and spirited People, but without a great alteration we shall be as contemptible as we ever were honnorable." Essays in Samuel and Ebenezer Hall's *New-England Chronicle* made similar public calls for the soldiers to remember the cause. Those printers even

inserted a letter from "a mother to her only son, a soldier in the Connecticut troops at Roxbury." This Connecticut "mother" shamed her son into
rejecting "your country, when she stands most in need of your aid." "Your
sister Lucy bids you stay, and I conjure you not to return, you will meet with
nothing but scorn and ridicule if you attempt it," this Spartan mother — or,
more likely, the Hall brothers — wrote. These pleas all fell short. Six thousand
Connecticut soldiers did march home over the first ten days of December.
It is remarkable that the British command did not find out about this tur-
moil and discover a way to exploit the substantial gaps in the line. The emergency was so great that Washington was forced to call out the Massachusetts
minutemen again.[34]

This desertion of six thousand men should startle us. It is a reminder just
how fragile the common cause still was at the end of 1775. Charles Lee begged
Samuel and John Adams to come home and stir up dying Revolutionary em-
bers. He knew the need for constant reminders as to why American farmers
needed to put their fortunes and bodies in danger. New Englanders did not
want to take orders among one another, let alone from strangers far to the
south. Lee recognized that the union was not a natural, organic creation. It
was going to take lots of work to keep the colonies together.

It is difficult for the historian not to adopt the attitude of Greene, Lee,
and Washington. How could they walk away? True, there wasn't much to do
in the siege lines around Boston, but given that Dunmore was, in Washington's words, "like a snow Ball in rolling" in the Chesapeake, what made them
think they could abandon the Revolution?[35]

The problem was that they did not yet know about what was going on in
the South. From their perspective, the war was going well, so well that Providence was surely on their side. So far, the frontiers and plantations had not
been gruesome theaters of bloodshed. Patriots had foiled plots everywhere.
Many of those who had been away from their Connecticut farms since late
April probably would agree with one South Carolina patriot leader that the
events of 1775 were a "great reason to bless God, for all his abundant mer-
cies." Even with all the various British agents had tried — including "call[ing]
in Savages to ravage our frontiers, to massacre our defenceless women and
children, offer[ing] every incitement to our Slaves to rebel and murder their
masters" — not only did the rebellion survive, but the union held. "The
people so earnestly pressed to attack us, refusing every act, every force; our
Indians keeping up peace, against all acts to detach them from us, by lies,
calumnies, and interest. Our Slaves remaining faithful — against the promise even of liberty, dearest-best-of all rewards. . . . Could our most sanguine

hopes, have gone so far last spring?" The writer did not know what Dunmore had proclaimed five days earlier, and that might have curbed his zeal.[36]

It might have made a difference in the Continental army camp, too. Samuel Ward, for one, thought so. Ward, one of Rhode Island's delegates to the Continental Congress, wrote that the "news from Virginia . . . is alarming and if it had arrived before" the Connecticut troops started to leave, it "would I think have helped us in that question." The dire news might have convinced some among them to reconsider. Reports that verified Dunmore's proclamation reached Philadelphia at the height of the Connecticut controversy, but they had not yet reached Massachusetts. The last accounts from points south that literate soldiers in the camp read about the conflict were that things were under control. A calming letter from Charleston — which concluded that Carolinians were under "no apprehensions from their negroes" and that the backcountry was stable — might have stoked their desires to go home. It would not be until the last days of December that the reports of significant numbers of slaves flocking to Dunmore were published in New England. If the enlistments had been up a month later, on January 1, perhaps things would have been different. By then, the "dangerous Storm . . . gathering in the South," as the embarrassed delegation to Congress from Connecticut labeled it, would have been common knowledge in the camp. It might have given some rank-and-file patriots pause. It certainly did for their leaders. The assurances that all was well, born out of an anxious need to project confidence, almost ended the Revolution. Their bravado nearly cost them everything.[37]

In the last weeks of 1775, the effects of Dunmore's proclamation, aided by patriot printers who broadcast it as loudly as they could, were difficult to deny. In the private letters and newspaper accounts that express riders carried over wet December roads, the phrase "slaves flock" to Dunmore recurred again and again. Scores and scores of African Americans seemed to be — or were portrayed to be — in motion. Uncertainty was the rule. Lund Washington identified another reason free colonists were worried. Sending word that one of his cousin George's slaves had run to the governor, he allowed himself the ultimate confession: "Liberty is sweet."[38]

Patriot authorities far from the Chesapeake witnessed the effects of this wave. On December 14, as the text of Dunmore's proclamation was making its way through patriot print networks, the Maryland Convention resolved to post a guard on the estate of a suspected Worcester County loyalist so as "to prevent the Negroes on the said Estate being carried out of this Province" and into Dunmore's ranks. On that same day, the South Carolina committee of safety approved a militia raid on Sullivan's Island, a remote sandbar on the edge of Charleston Harbor. In previous years, captains of incoming slave ships would quarantine their cargo there before bringing them into the city for sale, but it had become a "den for runaway slaves, who were encouraged and protected by the people belonging to the [British] ships." Approximately sixty soldiers attacked the maroon camp on Sullivan's, killing four Blacks and capturing three British sailors. The committee justified the attack on the "alarming evil" posted by the "villains," "banditti," and "wretches" on Sullivan's as the best way "to humble our Negroes in general and perhaps to mortify his Lordship [Governor Campbell] not a little."[39]

At that same moment, David Owen, "a person suspected of inlisting *Negroes,*" was sent to the workhouse after the Pennsylvania committee of safety found his explanations wanting. In New York, too, a Long Island man had just finished testifying before the Provincial Congress about the "disaffection of sundry people in *Queen's* County, and of a suspicion that they had about inlisting *Negroes.*" A dozen residences along the Narragansett Bay were still smoldering after another African American pilot had, earlier that week, "pointed out" to Royal Navy raiders—including two hundred "Marines, Sailors, and Negroes"—which patriot "Houses to burn." Finally, the most revealing episode of that singular moment occurred in Philadelphia. Benjamin Towne's issue of the *Pennsylvania Evening Post* from that same Thursday, December 14, reported an encounter between a white woman and a Black man on a city street. When she reprimanded him for getting in her way, his impassioned reply laid bare the raw tension that was in the air across North America. "Stay, you damned white bitch, till Lord Dunmore and his black regiment come," he allegedly responded, "and then we will see who is to take the wall." It is impossible to know whether this exchange actually occurred or was invented by Towne or one of his contributors. It seemed plausible, given the uneasy moment, but more important, it appeared in print—in Pennsylvania, Connecticut, and Virginia—as fact.[40]

The impact of Dunmore's proclamation was significant and immediate. People were paying attention all over America. Leading New England minister Ezra Stiles, for example, closely followed Dunmore's actions from Newport, Rhode Island, copying long summaries into his diary from the newspaper reports about Blacks fighting with the governor. Samuel Hopkins, the Newport minister and delegate to Congress, saw Dunmore's campaign as a powerful opportunity for the patriots. "Does not the conduct of Lord Dunmore, and the ministerialists, in taking advantage of the slavery practised among us, and encouraging all slaves to join them, by promising their liberty," he wrote at year's end, "point out the best, if not the only way to defeat them in this, viz. granting freedom to them ourselves, so as no longer to use our neighbour's service without wages, but give them for their labours what is equal and just?" As consistent as Hopkins's logic was, few others wished to follow it.[41]

Hopkins was out of step with the ways in which the ground had shifted over the past few months. In the early 1770s, as we have seen above, pressure had been building against slavery. Only a year before, Jefferson had referred to the abolition of the slave trade as the "great object of desire" in America. Benjamin Rush had predicted that slavery would soon be extinct. But that was before the shooting—and the stories of British instigation—started. The stories about Lord Dunmore, Matthew Squire, John Collet, Josiah Martin, and Thomas Jeremiah, extensively publicized by patriot leaders, edged antislavery arguments, like those forwarded by Hopkins, to the margins of colonial opinion. In 1776, the Newport minister would write *A Dialogue concerning the Slavery of the Africans,* a pamphlet addressed to the Continental Congress and published in Norwich, but this treatise would be the only major publication about emancipating slaves produced for the entirety of the Revolutionary War.[42]

The stories detailing "liberty to slaves" shifted colonial attitudes toward Britain and each other. They galvanized opinion against the crown. As one exasperated Congressman wondered, Did the English people "really imagine . . . that after . . . our Liberties repeatedly invaded—our women and children, driven from their Habitations—our nearest Relatives sacrificed at the Altar of Tyranny, our Slaves emancipated for the express purpose of massacreing their Masters—can they . . . expect that we shall return to our former connection with a forgiving, and cordial Disposition[?]" The last of these, the threat of sponsored slave revolt, was the most terrifying because it had grounded, measurable effects. Patriot leaders had to react to African Americans in their neighborhoods taking similar actions. And, at the camp outside Boston, again, the news from Virginia shaped Washington's construction of the Continental army.[43]

Throughout the several months since Washington had taken command, he had convened multiple conferences to determine the present and future makeup of the army ranks. At every turn, Washington and his generals had voted unanimously to reject free and enslaved African Americans from the new Continental army. Some patriots were uncomfortable with the number of Blacks already in the camp and did not wish to see them remain there, in spite of the courage they had shown, especially at Bunker Hill. When the dust settled after the Connecticut emergency in early December, Washington decided not to allow those Black veterans to continue fighting for the patriots—even some of the more renowned fighters in camp, such as Salem Poor and Framingham's Peter Salem. The latter had killed the lead British officer at Bunker Hill, but his cause could not be Washington's, too. Dunmore changed the commander's mind. More precisely, the threat of seasoned Black troops deserting his ranks to take up arms for the crown had changed it for him.[44]

Washington again used his favorite metaphor of a rolling snowball to describe to Richard Henry Lee what might happen "if some expedient cannot be hit upon to convince the Slaves and Servants of the Impotency" of Dunmore's "designs." But, as Washington was about to experience in his first New England winter, snowballs could form in places other than Virginia. Four days after writing to Lee, Washington suddenly amended his decision about excluding all Blacks from army service, allowing reenlistments to those who had already served. The following day, he wrote to Congress to explain why. Washington informed Hancock that a group of veteran free Blacks had complained to his headquarters that they were "very much disatisfied at being discarded." In an atmosphere charged with Dunmore's actions, the last thing Washington needed was for the British to benefit from the intelligence that could be gained from Peter Salem, Salem Poor, and other spurned veteran troops. "As it is to be apprehended *that they may Seek employ in the ministerial Army*—I have presumed to depart from the Resolution respecting them, and have given Licence for their being enlisted." Washington knew he had ventured an unauthorized policy shift: "If this is disapproved of by Congress, I will put a Stop to it." Congress did support the decision, approving the reenlistment of those free Blacks "who have served faithfully in the army at Cambridge . . . but no others." Without their threat of going over to the other side of the siege lines, it is unlikely the free African Americans would have had enough leverage to change Washington's mind.[45]

Seventeen-seventy-five was quite a year for Peter Salem. When he marched out of Framingham in the middle of the night on April 19, his neighbors whispered that there was a slave revolt, not an imperial one, afoot in Middlesex County. Soon Salem was a hero for his actions at Bunker Hill, but this did not earn him a welcome place in the American army. Many patriot political and military leaders, from Washington on down, did not want Salem and scores of other free African Americans who manned the siege lines outside Boston that year as part of their Grand Continental army. Wave after wave of stories about the British rousing slaves throughout North America added to long-standing colonial prejudices to solidify suspicions of their loyalty and value. At the same time, however, Dunmore's emancipation proclamation gave Salem and other African American veterans just enough clout to force the patriots to begrudgingly accept them.

Back in May, Benjamin Franklin had informed Jonathan Shipley that Britain had found means to unite the American colonies. By September, when he sat down to write Shipley again, he showed the strains of four months of wild rumors and harried speculation. Shipley must have thought he had come unglued. Franklin made a list of what had happened all summer, including:

> The encouraging our Blacks to rise and murder their Masters. But above all,
> The Exciting the Savages to fall upon our innocent Outsettlers, Farmers, (who have no Concern in, and from their Situation can scarce have any Knowledge of this Dispute) especially when it is considered that the Indian Manner of making War, is by surprizing Families in the Night, and killing all, without Distinction of Age or Sex!*
> These Proceedings of Officers of the Crown, who it is presumed either act by *Instruction,* or know they shall *please* by such Conduct, give People here a horrid Idea of the *Spirit* of your Government.

Franklin added one last comment to his list, a catalog that foreshadowed the Declaration of Independence. His asterisk at the end of "exciting the savages" offered a clarification. "What would be thought of it," he thundered, "if the Congress should hire an Italian Bravo to break into the House of one of your Ministers, and murder him in his Bed? All his Friends would open in full Cry against us as *Assassins, Murderers,* and *Villains,* and the Walls of your Parliament House would resound with their Execrations! Of these two damnable Crimes which is the greatest?" Franklin's writing ability makes these letters singular in their expression, but not the content or the emotions conveyed. Although the patriots, too, considered how best to use Indians and African Americans in their armed forces, leaders like Franklin treated British use of proxies as a monstrous crime perpetrated by devious enemy agents.[46]

Franklin and his colleagues dedicated prodigious efforts to make sure as many people in America as possible agreed with them, and the issue of British officers "exciting" and "encouraging" was the issue that could deliver results. Or so they thought.

That the patriots sponsored these messages in order to shape attitudes in direct and instrumental ways is evident in the genealogy of the final news story of 1775. At the same time that colonial printers exchanged columns of reports from militia officers about groups of "chiefly negroes" wearing uniforms emblazoned with "liberty to slaves" in the Chesapeake, Congress ordered them to insert another story from the New York frontier. On December 22, Congress received two packets of intelligence that they wanted the public to be aware of. The first was the cache of letters found on John Connolly, along with his interrogation by patriot authorities in Maryland. The second was a shocking letter from General Philip Schuyler in Albany. They wasted no time in ordering both sets published in the Philadelphia newspapers — especially the second paragraph of Schuyler's correspondence.[47]

The day after Christmas, *Pennsylvania Evening Post* printer Benjamin Towne obeyed Congress's order. He had received their resolution asking him to publish the key section of Schuyler's letter "to perpetuate the *humanity* of the Ministers of George the Third and their Agents":

> The Indians delivered us a speech on the 12th, in which they related the substance of all the conferences Col. [Guy] Johnson had with them the last summer, concluding with that at Montreal, where he delivered to each of the Canadian tribes a war belt and a hatchet, who accepted it. After which they were invited to FEAST ON A BOSTONIAN AND DRINK HIS BLOOD.
>
> An ox being roasted for the purpose, and a pipe of wine given to drink, the war song was sung. One of the Chiefs of the Six Nations, that attended the conference, accepted a very large black war belt with a hatchet depictured in it; but would neither eat nor drink, nor sing the war song. This famous belt they have delivered up, and we now have a full proof that the ministerial servants have attempted to engage the savages against us.

Over the next few weeks, seventeen other publications throughout the colonies followed Congress's order, many of which were published in parallel columns alongside Connolly's papers, which compounded the phrase "now we have a full proof."[48]

Schuyler and the Congress made sure that word of purported cannibalism reached as wide an audience as possible. The ubiquity of these war stories — and the role that political leaders like Franklin, Adams, or Schuyler had in their production — was a critical factor in solidifying the common cause, fragile as it appeared to be. The desertion of thousands of Connecticut soldiers just that month was evidence enough that they had to keep explaining what the colonists were fighting for. They redoubled their efforts to

FIGURE 8. *Colonel Guy Johnson and Karonghyontye (Captain David Hill).*
By Benjamin West. Ca. 1775–1776. National Gallery of Art,
Andrew W. Mellon Collection, Accession No. 1940.1.10

publicize these particular stories to castigate their enemies. Both their perva-
siveness and their importance have disappeared from our understanding of
the Revolutionary experience. We need to recover their centrality.

Reports that the ministry was "putting Arms into the Hands of all that
would receive them, English, Scotch, Irish, Roman Catholics, Hessians,
Hanoverians, etc." — not to mention the enslaved, Indians, and maybe even
Russians, as one account guessed — were almost weekly affairs in colonial
newspapers by the end of 1775. When printer Alexander Purdie published an
essay by "An American" in his first issue of *Virginia Gazette* of 1776, his audience would be hard-pressed to miss the references. "An American" summed
up the shift in attitude that the pile of "instigation" stories had produced:

> How sunk is Britain! Could not Britons venture to wage war with
> America till they were told that Americans were cowards, till they
> had disarmed them, or had, as they thought, put it out of their power
> to procure arms, nor even then without the assistance of Roman
> Catholics and Indians, and endeavouring to raise amongst us a
> domestick enemy? Was this like a brave and generous nation! . . . Why
> make use of every base and inhuman stratagem, and wage a savage
> war unknown amongst civilized nations? Surely whoever has heard of
> Carleton's, Connolly's and Dunmore's plots against us, cannot but allow
> that they must have been authorised by a higher power; and whoever
> believes this cannot but wish to be instantly and for ever removed from
> under such a power, and to be guarded most effectually against it. Most
> freely would I *cut the Gordian knot.*

This essayist meant "higher power" as the sordid man in Britain who approved the plots, be it Lord North or even the king himself. But for many
readers of this essay, which would be reproduced in five other colonies, the
protection afforded Americans by the "higher power" in defusing these
schemes was the other key component to the patriots' depiction of the common cause in 1775. Thanks to Providence or virtuous colonists, they had
been saved thus far from destruction at the hands of Stuart's Cherokees,
Carleton's Iroquois, or Dunmore's emancipated slaves.[49]

Even though they were shooting stars that captured the public's atten-
tion for only a brief moment, the panoply of Revolutionary celebrities in
the war's first seasons was vast, far more so than traditional narratives of the
Revolution reflect. Public outrage focused on the king's officers in North
America, especially John Stuart, Guy Carleton, Josiah Martin, William
Campbell, and, of course, Lord Dunmore. Names of lesser British agents

were also renowned throughout the colonies: Matthew Squire, John Collet, Alexander Cameron, Guy Johnson, and John Connolly. For each, the source of their infamy was their alleged connections with insurrectionist slaves and bloodthirsty Indians. Those groups were largely an anonymous, amorphous mass of latent danger, but colonial newspaper readers knew some of their names, too, such as Joseph Harris and Thomas Jeremiah.

Each of these stars in the Revolutionary sky shone in some respect because the patriots took hypothetical suggestions or actual efforts to recruit slaves and Indians and broadcast them extensively, through official Congressional proclamations, intentional political leaks, and the newspaper exchange system. That all this occurred in just six columns of print in a weekly newspaper underscores how prevalent these stories were throughout 1775. Few weeks went by that year without the local paper featuring some account at British attempts at "instigation." Often, multiple stories from multiple sources would collide in those columns, reinforcing the sense that this threat was universal. These accounts appeared, in large part, because they were excellent transmitters of political and cultural messages about the common cause. They did not randomly appear there; they had sources and sponsors. The stories had a circular motion to them, influencing how people thought about their enemies, themselves, and the Revolution itself, which spurred new actions that lengthened the patriots' list of British crimes.

Amid all this commotion, colonists read about one another as they never had before. When they were not marching or listening or talking about how the war might touch their lives and families, they read about others who were doing the same things. The months that followed Lexington and Concord offered little opportunity for somber reflection. There were few major essays published on abstract issues, whether the imperial controversy or the African slave trade. Rights were not what dominated discussion at colonial dinner tables or tavern bars in 1775.

John Stuart knew exactly what the public was really talking about. "The news papers were full of Publications calculated to excite the fears of the People," the exiled Indian Superintendent reflected bitterly from the safety of Florida. "Massacres and Instigated Insurrections," he wrote, "were Words in the mouth of every Child." Those words — and how they got there — were the central story of 1775. The following year, that story would become a cornerstone for the new republic itself.[50]

CHAPTER 6

MERCILESS SAVAGES, DOMESTIC INSURRECTIONISTS, *and* FOREIGN MERCENARIES

In March 1776, Abigail Adams wrote to her husband asking how the Virginians were doing in their fight against British tyranny. Like so many other colonists from Carolina to Canada, Abigail didn't know much about them. "Are not the Gent[ry] Lords and the common people vassals, are they not like the uncivilized Natives Brittain represents us to be?" she asked. "I hope their Riffel Men who have shewen themselves very savage and even Blood thirsty; are not a specimen of the Generality of the people." Abigail was uneasy about the prospect of sharing a nation with such unsavory folk. Two paragraphs later, after prodding John to get Congress to declare independence, she made a simple request that would become famous. "In the new Code of Laws which I suppose it will be necessary for you to make," she wrote, "I desire you would Remember the Ladies and be more generous and favourable to them than your ancestors."[1]

John's reaction was insulting. "As to your extraordinary Code of Laws," he joked, "I cannot but laugh." "We have been told that our Struggle has loosened the bands of Government everywhere," he began. "That Children and Apprentices were disobedient—that schools and Colledges had grown turbulent—that Indians slighted their Guardians and Negroes grew insolent to their Masters," and now, John teased, his own wife hinted that "another Tribe" was following suit. We may judge John's reticence to acknowledge Abigail's request as petty, especially his choice to call her "saucy" for suggesting that women should be included in new American concepts of political participation. But there is more to unpack about John's banter than patriarchy.[2]

John responded as if Abigail had made a veiled military threat. Writing just five days before the anniversary of Lexington and Concord, his response reflected both the unsettling events that had engulfed the patriots throughout the first year of war and the near-reflexive ways in which they represented those events. John and his colleagues had spent the year figuring out who, exactly, their enemies were. By the spring of 1776, that list was long. Now John hinted that he needed to add women to it: "I begin to think the Ministry as deep as they are wicked," he continued. "After stirring up Tories, Landjobbers, Trimmers, Bigots, Canadians, Indians, Negroes, Hanoverians, Hessians, Russians, Irish Roman Catholicks, Scotch Renegadoes, at last they have stimulated the [women] to demand new Priviledges and threaten to rebell." After a full year of hearing story after story that British agents had tried to recruit these assorted groups, it was only natural for John to joke that perhaps now they had turned their attention to "another Tribe more numerous and powerfull than all the rest."[3]

This renowned exchange of letters is about women's rights, to be sure. But it is also an arresting, illuminating conversation about unity, the common cause, and the people who might be included in a new, independent America. Though Abigail was worried about the problems of including "savage" Virginians and not virtuous colonial ladies, John interpreted her letter in terms of the undertaking that his patriot colleagues faced throughout 1775–1776: cataloging, explaining, and dealing with all the Revolution's potential enemies.

Adams's list of proxy enemies was hardly a laughing matter, but it was laughable. Most of those groups had not actually taken up arms against the patriots. For the past year, patriot publicists had exchanged reports in their weekly papers accusing Natives of threatening to take up the king's hatchet, but, in truth, they had not done so. Though patriot leaders had screamed at the British for trying to instigate them, Indians had rejected all entreaties thus far. No Bostonians had been feasted upon. Likewise, there was, as yet, no general rising of slaves against their masters, although many African Americans across the Atlantic seaboard had seized on the outbreak of war as a way to better their situation. As for the various foreigners John listed, their participation was just a hazy rumor.

Nevertheless, the power of the images John cataloged was a vital force, nourished in both assembly houses and print shops. By the first anniversary of the Revolutionary War, those images of America's enemies had crystallized into an irresistible reason for declaring American independence. Ever since Lexington and Concord, patriot political leaders and their publicist friends had been constructing the keystone of that narrative arch: that liberty-loving Americans were all fighting for one common cause and that their cultural cousins were really their bitter enemies. The proof? British officials were plotting with Indian, enslaved, and foreign proxies to destroy them all.

The standard narrative of the run-up to independence is normally a straight line from Thomas Paine to Thomas Jefferson. It begins with *Common Sense*'s emphasis on the abuse of monarchy and hereditary privilege in January and ends in the Declaration's laying blame directly at King George's feet in July. The lived experience of those significant six months was a bit different. The millions of people living in America in 1776 would have millions of ways of telling their stories of that critical year, mixing together the big events with personal or local ones. Everyone would have his or her own story of how American independence came about. But John Adams and his peers in the patriot leadership had an official version they wanted colonists to believe and act upon.

Nearly two hundred fifty years later, we have forgotten much of what the American public knew in 1776. Instead, a few operatic episodes, telescoped into a triumphant narrative, have served as the myth of American independence. There is more to the story of how Americans came to declare independence in July 1776 than can be explained by one popular pamphlet.

Declaring independence was a radical act, one that satisfied some, such as Abigail Adams, but shocked many others. Why did it become imperative to leave the British Empire? Why then? Why July? These simple questions have complicated answers. They are full of contingency and chance. The timing is a critical issue — why did thirteen clocks strike that summer? — but the same events that determined timing also dictated the terms by which patriot leaders justified their actions. The *when* of independence was inextricably tied to patriots' claim of *why* such a step was essential.

The answers to both of those questions involved many of the people on John Adams's enemies list.

Common Sense appeared in Philadelphia on Tuesday, January 9, 1776. Over the next several weeks, as copies were being "greedily bought up and read by all ranks of people," many prominent patriot leaders talked to one another about its influence. Paine's forty-six-page pamphlet was indeed a remarkable political statement. Thousands read it, thousands more heard it read, and even more listened in on conversations about it in public and private places. According to one correspondent from Maryland, the pamphlet "has done wonders and miracles, made TORIES WHIGS, and washed Blackamores white."[4]

But who wrote it? Since Paine had published the pamphlet with a pseudonym ("Common Sense"), no one really knew. One writer in the *Pennsylvania Evening Post* asked, "Who is the author of COMMON SENSE? I can scarce refrain from adoring him. He deserves a statue of gold." Some suspected John Adams, others Benjamin Franklin. Nearly all guesses, however, involved someone very high up in the patriot ranks. That people assumed it to be a delegate to the Continental Congress further suggests just how blurred the line between political bodies and print shops was in the early years of the Revolutionary War.[5]

In later years, Paine would boast that *Common Sense* had sold an incredible number of copies, numbering in the hundreds of thousands. Starting with the author himself, a "cult of *Common Sense*" has grown up over the years that has turned it into a mythological phenomenon. It didn't sell as many as Paine bragged, but it was transformative in part because patriot leaders played a key role in its dissemination. They didn't write it, but they did help distribute it. Some in Congress sent bundles of copies home; at least one delegate suggested using public monies to print more. As with war stories, they wanted to propagate any print that would further the common cause.[6]

Paine did not spend much time in *Common Sense* talking about how British agents had tried to get Native people and the enslaved to fight against America. He had stated, "There are thousands, and tens of thousands, who would think it glorious to expel from the continent, that barbarous and hellish power, which hath stirred up the Indians and Negroes to destroy us, the cruelty hath a double guilt it is dealing brutally by us, and treacherously by them." In the main, though, *Common Sense* focused on the potential of American commerce and republican government to justify why colonists should embrace independence immediately.[7]

Perhaps that was why Samuel Adams took up his pen. Three weeks after *Common Sense* appeared in Philadelphia bookstores, Adams began sending essays to printer Benjamin Towne under the pseudonyms "Candidus" and "Sincerus." They began appearing in the *Pennsylvania Evening Post* over the course of February. Paine might not have spent much time talking about British plots, but Adams did. "Sincerus" ridiculed those who held out for reconciliation with Britain by reminding colonists that, although their enemies had tried their best, Americans had survived all the terrible conspiracies. The "great hopes" of British officials to incite the Indians on the New York frontier had failed. "Dunmore, with all his wanton rage, has done little more than exasperate the Virginians," Adams argued, "and convinced that brave colony that they can be formidable to savages on the east as well as west side of their dominion."[8]

Adams believed the well-established narrative of the king's agents forcing America out of the empire was an argument that complemented Paine's. Soon these essays began to appear together. A week after "Sincerus" appeared in the *Pennsylvania Evening Post,* Paine's publisher, Robert Bell, folded Adams's essays into a new, enlarged edition of *Common Sense.* In New York, bookseller William Green advertised that expanded edition in the Manhattan papers. Thus, *Common Sense* became more than just the work of Thomas Paine. By the end of February, readers were thumbing through a patriot anthology. For those confused about who the real author of "Common Sense" was, this new edition featured Sam Adams along with Paine. Any line between elected officials advocating independence in the assembly houses and writers calling for it from the printing houses was obliterated. Just as in Boston during the late 1760s, distinguishing between political leaders and publicists was becoming impossible.

Moreover, the inclusion of Adams's essays in the enlarged edition of *Common Sense,* with its detailing of British conspirators, also illustrates that there were alternative pro-independence arguments to Paine's in the late winter and early spring of 1776. We have focused on Paine's political and constitutional arguments, but they were not the only points being discussed in conversations all over America. They were, rather, part of a larger chorus against reconciliation.

Other publicists followed Adams's lead attacking Britain via Indians and slaves that season. "What stone have they left unmoved?" asked a so-called "honest, sensible, and spirited farmer" in a speech "addressed to an assembly of his neighbours, on his engaging in the continental service," which appeared in the *Pennsylvania Journal* in late February. "What device to ruin us, tho' never so mean, barbarous and bloody, such as no heart, but that of a Devil and a tyrant can refrain shuddering at, have they not pursued?"

> Have they not attempted to spirit up the Indian savages to ravage our frontiers, and murder, after inhuman manner, our defenceless wives and children? Have not our Negro slaves been enticed to rebel against their masters, and arms put into their hands to murder them? Have not the King of England's own slaves, the Hanoverians, been employed? And were not the poor Canadians made slaves, that they might be made fit instruments, with other slaves and savages, to make slaves and more wretched beings than savages of us?

All that was left, the "farmer" concluded, was to "fight or die." Another Philadelphia paper, the *Pennsylvania Packet,* added to the growing chorus of those late winter days. Printer John Dunlap published an essay that featured the ghost of Richard Montgomery, the patriot general slain at Montreal a few months before, visiting a timid delegate to the Continental Congress. Britain had "done their worst," Montgomery's ghost lectured. "They have called upon Russians—Hanoverians—Hessians—Canadians—Savages—and Negroes to assist them in burning your towns—desolating your country—and in butchering your wives and children." The apparition implored the Congressman, "You have nothing further to fear from them. Go, then, and awaken the Congress to a sense of their importance; you have no time to lose." Although this sounds like something an Adams would write (the list is almost exactly the same as the one John made for Abigail), the conjurer of Montgomery's ghost was none other than "Common Sense" himself, Thomas Paine.[9]

In short, although the vernacular language, reassuring arguments, and frontal assault on monarchy that Paine employed in *Common Sense* has dominated scholarly understandings for why colonial support for reconciliation and compromise flagged in early 1776, many patriots contended that America should declare independence simply because of British treachery. Whereas *Common Sense* laid out the positive reasons colonists should embrace American independence, other writers, publishers, and political leaders—and Thomas Paine—remained focused on attacking the crown for embracing Indians, slaves, and foreign mercenaries. No wonder they made that argument: look what else was in the news! During the days that Robert Bell set the type for *Common Sense,* all these items crowded into the middle pages of colonial newspapers all over America between late December and mid-January: Schuyler's letter about Indians' being asked to "feast on a Bostonian," the news of John Connolly's arrest, Dunmore's proclamation, and reports of Virginia runaways wearing "Liberty to Slaves" emblazoned on their new uniforms. This was the context for *Common Sense.*

In March, the *Pennsylvania Gazette* made its own list of the things Americans should not forget about British tyranny. "Remember their hiring Savages to murder your Farmers with their Families. Remember the Bribing Negroe Slaves to assassinate their Masters." When printer Samuel Loudoun exchanged this item in his *New York Packet,* it ran in the same issue next to a more formal request from the Continental Congress ordering Americans to remember British sins. New Jersey delegate William Livingston drafted a call for colonists to set aside May 17, 1776, as a day of fasting and thanksgiving. Congress, "considering the warlike preparations of the British Ministry to . . . reduce us by fire and sword, by the savages of the wilderness, and our own domestics to the most abject and ignominious bondage," told the

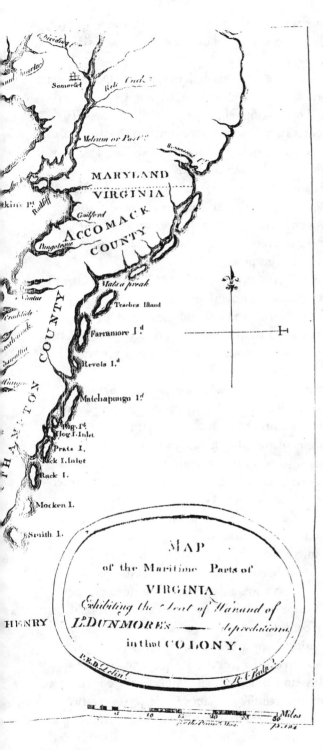

FIGURE 9. *"Map of the Maritime Parts of Virginia, Exhibiting the Seat of War and of Lord Dunmore's Depredations in That Colony."* From Pennsylvania Magazine *(April 1776), 184–185. By the spring of 1776, so many war stories had emanated out of the Chesapeake that Thomas Paine, editor of the* Pennsylvania Magazine, *inserted this map to help readers visualize all the inlets, islands, and creeks that had come to prominence over the past year.*

thirteen colonies to dedicate that day to "humiliation, fasting, and prayer; that we may, with united hearts, confess, and bewail our manifold sins and transgressions."[10]

Months before Thomas Jefferson sat at his desk to write the Declaration of Independence, many writers honed their skills in justifying the common cause. They did so especially by making reference to British proxies. These arguments, as much as Thomas Paine's, were the ones patriots forwarded to suggest America might be better off independent. "Is the King a legal Sovereign?" another writer asked "all the sound Heads and honest Hearts in America." Clearly not, this anonymous contributor to Bradford's *Pennsylvania Journal* opined, "when he endeavours to engage even savages to assassinate them and their wives and children in their dwellings" or when "he orders even slaves to be encouraged to rise and murder their masters, and furnishes them with arms for that purpose."[11]

There was a third reason the Americans should break with the crown: "He hires foreign troops, to enable him the more effectually to destroy his people." As spring bloomed in North America and the first anniversary of the war came and went, stories about another group of proxies — soldiers purchased from the German states — was about to sweep across the continent.[12]

Gossip had consistently cropped up in colonial newspapers throughout 1775 about British efforts to employ Russian or German soldiers. British commanders in Boston initially fueled that fire. Back in August 1775, General Thomas Gage warned Bostonians that they had better stay put in the city because "30,000 Hanoverians, 30,000 Hessians, and as many Russians, are shortly expected, when they shall destroy all the rebels at once." An intercepted message from one of Gage's aides to General John Burgoyne, published in Philadelphia, New York, and New Haven, boasted the British would have "early next Spring 20,000 Russians."[13]

In early 1776, more accounts about Russians circulated through the colonial press. The House of Lords' debates on the propriety of George's request to Catherine the Great for 20,000 soldiers ran in a few northern newspapers. In April, seven newspapers informed their readers that the crown had begged Catherine to reconsider her initial refusal. For months, while they worried about slaves rising from within and Indians sweeping down from Canada, a possible invasion of Russians also hung over patriot heads.[14]

With the prospect of Russian aid increasingly unlikely, the crown next called on the small German principalities of Hanover, Hesse-Cassel, Brunswick, and Waldeck for troops. By November 1775, William Faucitt, a colonel in the British army, was already drumming up recruits in Hanover and

Hesse; by mid-December, the princes had drawn up a draft treaty and sent it to England for confirmation. They finalized an official agreement in February 1776.[15]

Hesse-Cassell sent the largest contingent of troops, 12,000 infantrymen, while the other provinces sent various amounts: 3,964 infantry and cavalry from Brunswick, 668 soldiers from Hanau, and 500 from Waldeck. A fifth state, the Electorate of Hanover, also agreed to send troops. According to the treaties, Britain was to be responsible for transporting, paying, and caring for the German soldiers, who were to receive the same wages as regular British troops. In return, each prince was to receive a fee for every soldier enlisted, along with large bonuses paid annually for every year they were in America. Some of the treaties also made another financial demand of King George: blood money. The contracts with Brunswick, Waldeck, and Hanau guaranteed that the crown would reimburse the German princes for troops lost, with three wounded soldiers equaling one dead man and thus another fee. Even though these rather chilling calculations may seem distasteful to say the least (and patriots would loudly criticize them during the war and after), this practice was commonplace among European powers and sanctioned by international law.[16]

Word that Britain was negotiating with the princes of Germany rapidly reached America. Again, as in the case of Russia, verifiable information was hard to come by; in the absence of hard facts, unconfirmed reports flourished. Hearsay about German mercenaries began as early as the fall of 1775, but the reports were hazy.

That all changed in the first few days of May.

As soon as his ship touched the dock in Newburyport, Massachusetts, Captain John Lee rushed down the wharf to find the nearest patriot leader he could find. He had news. Lee had just completed a month-long voyage from Bilboa, Spain. Along the way, he fell in with a convoy of sixty transport ships, part of the incoming British invasion fleet headed for New York City. On board were two dozen commissioners sent to conduct negotiations, for whom many colonial moderates were holding their breath. But with them were twelve thousand Hessian troops.

The speed with which Captain Lee's eyewitness information sprinted through the chain of command was astounding. Lee arrived in port just after noon on May 2. That same day, he briefed the Salem committee of safety about the British fleet. The Salem committee immediately scribbled a letter to Thomas Cushing in the Massachusetts General Court. The following day, Continental army general Artemas Ward wrote Washington, who was already in New York making plans to defend the city. Cushing dashed off letters to Congress and other army commanders. Cushing's express arrived at Washington's headquarters first, after seven o'clock on the evening of May 7. With no time to lose, Washington composed his own letter to Congress that very night. Ward's rider galloped up in the dark, verifying the information from Salem before he sealed his letter to Congress, which Washington confirmed in a postscript. By May 10, just a week after the news touched dry land in Massachusetts, all the key patriot authorities—the Massachusetts provincial government, the Continental army in New York, and the Continental Congress in Philadelphia—had strong, corroborated testimony that an invasion fleet was headed their way.[17]

The remainder of the populace found out with commensurate speed. Just as the political and military network had transmitted Lee's message to Washington in the span of a few days, so, too, the continental communication system spread the word quickly. In fact, New England newspaper readers knew about the Hessian transports before George Washington did.

John Carter's *Providence Gazette* was the first to publish Lee's testimony on May 4, just two days after Lee's ship arrived. This report came directly from the Salem committee to the Massachusetts government—and was immediately sent over to the print shop. This statement shot through American papers. Two days later—still before Washington knew about it—Norwich, Connecticut, learned of the Lee report. New York papers picked it up a couple of days after that, then Philadelphia and Williamsburg. In all, thirteen prints in the month of May copied the Salem statement. Part of the reason for the electric response to Lee's intelligence was that it came as a shock. There had been no news on the European mercenary front for some time. Americans were largely aware that the king's efforts to gain Russian troops had failed, but they knew little else. Of course, this secrecy was part of Britain's plan, and they had successfully negotiated these deals without colonists' knowing.[18]

Lee's testimony broke the silence, and during those spring weeks, Americans would be deluged with news about foreign mercenaries. An exchanged account from a Dublin newspaper was also making its run through the newspaper network at that very moment, heading north from Philadelphia as Lee's report came south. Alarmingly, it put the number of German troops en route at 45,000. A few days later, another verification appeared. This one had real proof—the text of the treaties themselves—and the story of how the man carrying them had made it to Philadelphia was amazing.[19]

The day after Washington's letter about Captain Lee and the fleet reached Congress in Philadelphia, news from another informant arrived at Continental army headquarters. On May 10, just three days after he had forwarded

Captain Lee's report to President John Hancock, New Hampshire patriot John Langdon sent General Washington information about an escaped prisoner of war who was on his way south with an exciting story—and even more exciting documents. A rifleman in Captain Daniel Morgan's company, George Merchant, was captured in November while he stood guard at a post outside Quebec. The Virginia backwoodsman fascinated his captors, and they sent him across the Atlantic to London for interrogation. He wouldn't stay there long. According to one Congressman who later recounted the tale to his brother, "a number [of] Gentn" visited Merchant in jail and "procured [him] a passage to Hallifax," Nova Scotia; soon, he was headed back to America. "Tho[ugh] Searched at Hallifax two or three times, [he] brought undiscovered a Number of Letters and Newspapers to the Congress, by which we are possessed of all their plans for the destruction of America." Merchant had hidden the papers in the lining of his clothes.[20]

Among the secreted documents were copies he had made of the treaties between Britain and the German principalities and letters from colonial agent Arthur Lee that further detailed the imminent invasion force. Merchant arrived in New Hampshire and presented his papers to John Langdon, who took one look and went straight to his writing table. He sent Merchant on to Washington's headquarters. The commander had the same reaction. He took no chances risking this momentous news to express riders but sent Horatio Gates to lay the treaties in front of Congress personally. Merchant went along, turning up in a Philadelphia coffeehouse on the evening of May 20, where, ironically, he ran into Josiah Bartlett, Langdon's friend and New Hampshire delegate, to whom he again recounted his story.[21]

Like Lee's report, which was currently in the Philadelphia papers, Congress immediately sent Merchant's copies of the German treaties to the *Pennsylvania Journal* and *Pennsylvania Gazette,* where they quickly found space in more than half of all colonial papers in operation at that time. Reprinting the lengthy text required more than a small commitment; often printers would dedicate two or even three weeks to getting all the information to their readers, as Congress ordered them to do.[22]

The May news stories acted like turbulent weather fronts coming into contact with one another. One eye moved south from Massachusetts while the other two blew in all directions out from Pennsylvania. The news coverage that resulted from these storms, moreover, was extensive. Except for one print in Williamsburg, every colonial newspaper then in operation exchanged at least one of the three major news stories on the German mercenaries. It would have been difficult not to know that the Hessians were coming. Whether colonists read about them in their local prints, heard them being talked about in taverns or other social spaces, or learned of them from personal letters, Americans in May 1776 were well aware the king had purchased thousands of troops to cross the Atlantic to kill them. In fact, the news of the Hessians would be the last big news event of America's colonial history.

"This," one Philadelphia writer concluded in a letter published in several newspapers, "gives the *Coup de Grace* to the British and American connection." Landon Carter, a Virginia planter who had little love for the patriots, commented in his diary about how the news of foreign mercenaries affected people in his neighborhood. He didn't believe the story—they were baseless rumors invented by patriot printers "to alarm the people to promote the precipitate declaration of Independence." Carter concluded it was a "pure contrivance for weak minds to bring about Independency, and it has done it in Virginia, God help us all."[23]

Carter was more right than he knew. As he jotted those sour words down in his diary on May 18, patriot leaders in the Continental Congress had already set in motion the severing of all imperial ties with Great Britain. Even though the constitutional procedure of American independence was hardly finished by that date, the debate over independence had opened. It was the news brought by a ship captain and an escaped rifleman that signaled its beginning.

Before Captain Lee's ship docked at Newburyport, no one had permission to talk about independence in Congress. Rhode Island and the Carolinas had recently given their delegates liberty to vote *yea* on the question, but none of them were allowed to introduce the motion on the floor. Only the recently revised instructions for North Carolina's delegation even used the word "independence."

Then news of the fleet, with all those thousands of German soldiers on board, arrived. That information made it to Philadelphia the start of the second week in May; by the end of that week, Congress passed a resolution instructing all colonies to start drafting their own constitutions, a move that John Adams believed was all but a declaration of independency. The news of foreign mercenaries wasn't the only cause of this critical decision—as several historians have argued, some in Congress were searching for a way to outmaneuver moderates in Maryland and Pennsylvania—but this development was, nonetheless, a critical catalyst for action. In their explanations for why they were taking this step, they consistently invoked the news of German troops.[24]

On May 15, Virginia's representatives approved, in a nearly unanimous vote, a resolution instructing their delegates to the Continental Congress to bring forward a motion of independence. For the first time, a colony wanted to discuss the question. How did Virginia's representatives justify this step? The colonies had no choice but to sever ties, argued Edmund Pendleton, author of the Virginia resolution:

> Fleets and Armies are raised, and the aid of foreign troops engaged to assist these destructive purposes: The king's representative in this colony hath not only withheld all the powers of government from operating for our safety, but, having retired on board an armed ship, is carrying on a piratical and savage war against us, tempting our slaves, by every artifice, to resort to him, and training and employing them against their masters.

"In this state of extreme danger, we have no alternative left," Pendleton asserted on behalf of the Virginia Assembly. Only "a total separation from the crown and government of Great Britain" could "unit[e] and exer[t] the strength of all America."[25]

It had begun. Pendleton and the Virginia Convention initiated the process that, in six weeks, would produce the Declaration of Independence. The thirteen clocks were now wound tight. The combination of thousands of German mercenaries, the long-standing ordeal Virginians had endured with Dunmore, and the constant threat of potential Indian attacks across the frontier convinced them they needed to separate. The time for reconciliation had passed. "We are driven from that inclination by . . . wicked councils, and the eternal laws of self-preservation."[26]

Virginia's resolution took a week to reach Congress. It arrived on Monday, May 27, but they did not introduce it right away. Given what was about to happen, it is easy for us to think that independence consumed all their focus and energy as soon as the packet arrived from Williamsburg. But a deep focus on the context for independence and the Declaration reveals that the delegates to the Continental Congress had very full agendas — and they were thinking about proxy enemies quite a bit in the days and weeks leading up to July 4, 1776.

On that Monday, May 27, Benjamin Franklin wrote with signature grace, "The German Auxiliaries are certainly coming. It is our Business to prevent their Returning." During the same hours Franklin penned this quip, Lord Dunmore landed his ships on a small island in the Chesapeake Bay trying to fight the smallpox that was ripping through his Black regiment. And, in the Philadelphia newspapers, there were fresh stories relating Britain's true plans for the upcoming campaign. "Charles Town, South Carolina, is to be the first sacrifice, and then he is to go northward," an anonymous letter from

London reported in the *Pennsylvania Journal*. "I withhold any comments on this scheme, or those of setting the Indians and slaves to murder defenceless women and children; but surely the God who presides over the universe, with justice and mercy will shower down destruction on the advisers as well as executors of such horrid deeds." "There is no alternative but an instant declaration of independence," this London correspondent concluded.[27]

This was the information delegates carried with them to open the day's business on that Monday morning. But this was no normal day, certainly not for the momentous resolution that awaited them. At 9:00 that morning, they had already gathered to supervise a military review in the city to impress a delegation of Iroquois Indians who had come to town. They watched "between 2 and 3 thousand men parading on the Common," Richard Henry Lee reported, to the Natives' "great astonishment and delight. We hope effectually to secure to the friendship of their people." With that over, John Hancock gaveled the Congress to order, and they opened newly received letters. The first was from George Morgan, the patriots' Indian agent stationed at Fort Pitt. Morgan corroborated patriot concerns that the Ohio Indians were starting to fall away from the pledges of neutrality they had promised the previous autumn. "This is a critical time," and he feared that, unless something drastic was done, "you will hear of things going very wrong." To make matters worse, Morgan had heard "things are not right with the Northern Indians, particularly with the Senecas." One wonders what the delegates, having just come from a performance done exclusively to impress the Iroquois, made of Morgan's worrisome letter. At some point that day, a rider carrying Virginia's independence resolution arrived and placed the packet on Richard Henry Lee's desk. With all this hectic activity, it's no wonder he decided to hold off for a better moment to stand and introduce his motion.[28]

The next forty days would continue to center around how to deal with the king's proxies. First, Congress grappled with what to do about the German mercenaries. After Horatio Gates laid George Merchant's well-traveled copies of the German treaties in front of Congress, they formed a committee to "prepare an address to the foreign mercenaries who are coming to invade America." There were ideas floating about in colonial newspapers that Congress should craft "offers of settlement . . . to fling into the camp in German," which might have "a great effect." Another writer also suggested Congress grant German soldiers huge amounts of free land if they deserted. A third plan was a bit darker: John Holt's *New-York Journal* printed a letter that advised Congress to execute any captured Germans instantly. "They are invaders of the worst kind and should be treated accordingly. . . . Desperate situations require desperate exertions."[29]

Congress's formation of a committee to draft an address to the foreign mercenaries, then, took place in the middle of an energetic conversation in the press. That committee would consist of Richard Henry Lee, William Livingston, John Adams, Roger Sherman, and Thomas Jefferson; the last three would also be tapped to draft the Declaration two weeks later. The committee never completed the first task, but another delegate from Virginia, George Wythe, did, most likely at the behest of his former law student, Jefferson.[30]

In late May or early June (he left the final product undated), Wythe completed his draft address to the foreign mercenaries. "It is no small pleasure, when in this first address we ever made to you we must call you enemies, that we can affirm you to be unprovoked enemies," Wythe began, searching for a reason the Germans had agreed to participate in their Revolution. "We have not," he continued, "invaded your country, slaughtered wounded or captivated your parents children or kinsfolk, burned plundered or desolated your towns and villages, wasted your farms and cottages, spoiled you of your goods, or annoyed your trade." Why then, he asked rhetorically, did they interfere? Was it because of principles ("Do you think the cause you are engaged in just on your side?"), monarchical oppression ("Were you compelled by your sovereigns to undertake the bloody work of butchering your unoffending fellow-creatures?"), bloodlust ("Did lust of conquest prompt you?"), or perhaps opportunity ("Were you tempted by the prospect of exchanging the land you left for happier regions — for a land of plenty and abhorrent of despotism?") that the Hessians volunteered to "join in this quarrel with our foes"? "We wish," Wythe confessed, that opportunity

> might be your motive; because we have the means, and want not inclination, to gratify your desires, if they be not hostile, without loss to ourselves, perhaps with less expense, certainly with more honour and with more advantage to you than victory can promise. Numberless germans and other foreigners settled in this country will testify this truth.

He then left space for Congress to append a resolution granting land to mercenaries who deserted to American lines.[31]

They were too busy to get around to filling in the details that June. Other concerns pressed in. Incoming news from the northern frontier was not good. Congress — in the depths of the independence debate — would have to turn its attention to dealing with disaster in Canada.

In the middle of April, smallpox and desertion had so wracked the American army that had invaded Canada in the fall of 1775, it began to collapse. American soldiers gave up their siege of Quebec and retreated back across the St. Lawrence River. Benedict Arnold, the commander of the American-occupied city of Montreal, worried that this fleeing force was at risk of anni-hilation. He sent 400 men under New Hampshire colonel Timothy Bedel to build an outpost to protect them at a place called the Cedars. As construction was getting under way, Bedel rode out to negotiate with the Caughnawaga Indians, leaving Major Isaac Butterfield in charge. In mid-May, around the same time that Virginians were taking up their vote to propose independence, rumors began to swirl across the Canadian border that a force of Indians, numbering anywhere from 400 to a terrifying 1,300, was approaching the Cedars. When British captain George Foster did attack on May 18, with 36 regulars, 11 Canadian volunteers, and 160 Indians, the Americans panicked. According to one of the defenders, the Indians came "skipping and running out of the woods" with "nothing but a sort of wildgrass to secret or hide them from us." Unaware that reinforcements were on the way, Butterfield immedi-ately surrendered. His relief, consisting of Major Henry Sherburne and 120 Continental soldiers, were also ambushed and surrendered. In all, nearly one-quarter of Arnold's force in Canada was captured in the debacle.[32]

What happened to those prisoners clinched, in many colonists' minds, the accusation that the Indians were indeed merciless savages — even though, to be honest, at this point in the war, they could only be described as utterly merciful. Since the Americans had surrendered to the Natives and not to Foster, they were under their control. The Indians, allegedly, "fell to work" on the prisoners and "stripped them stark naked" as they took the soldiers' clothing as spoils of victory. After they "dispatched the wounded by knock-ing them in the head," one impassioned account detailed, "the dead [were] stripped naked, and thrown by the side of the road, the remaining troops was drove like cattle by them, it was a horrible sight . . . to see the Indians brandishing their knives and tomahawks over their heads and hollering and screaming and likewise dancing like so many mad men or devils."[33]

Knowing Arnold would come after him, Foster warned the American commander that, if attacked, he would allow the Indians to kill the pris-oners. Foster did offer to exchange them if they pledged never again to take up arms against the king. Outraged, Arnold refused all offers and made plans to rescue the captives, who were now being kept on an island in the St. Law-rence River. Foster convinced Butterfield and Sherburne to agree to the deal, and, against his wishes, Arnold signed it. The prisoners were set free on May 27, the same Monday Philadelphians were doing their best to impress the Iroquois.[34]

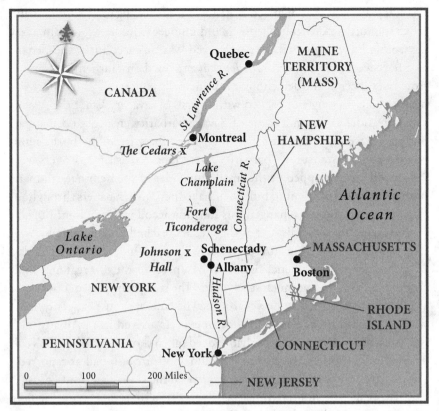

MAP 7. *Canada and New York, 1776. Drawn by Gerry Krieg*

The American leadership was incensed. Washington condemned the "Cowardly and disgraceful Behaviour" of Bedel and Butterfield (who were later court-martialed); John Adams lamented that the Cedars was "the first stain upon American Arms" and thought Butterfield deserved "the most infamous Death."[35]

News of this surrender and the Indians' rough treatment of American prisoners stormed through colonial newspapers. The first few months of 1776 had been quiet in the backcountry, compared to the intensity of the previous year's rumors. Still, rumblings about British plots persisted, reminding many colonial readers that the Indians still posed a threat.

The story of the Cedars, however, was a different matter. Here was the first instance of Indians' acting on the king's behalf. The first report from the St. Lawrence had the situation exactly wrong. A militia captain stated in the New York papers that the "whole body of the enemy" had been attacked and "killed and taken prisoners." *Connecticut Courant* printer Ebenezer Watson related the accurate, terrible news on June 10, a few columns over from a London account that divulged British plans of "setting on the Indians and slaves to murder defenceless women and innocent children." Within a few days, other New England papers exchanged Watson's account of the Cedars. The next week, Holt's *New-York Journal* provided an "authentic account" from "an officer of the detachment it principally concerns." This report was nearly a column long and packed with images of savagery. Once the Americans surrendered, "then a scene of Savage barbarity ensued; and many of our people were sacrificed to their fury," the officer from Sherburne's unit related. These instances of "barbarity" were repeated as the prisoners were "again and again stripped of the small remainder of their clothes, till many of them had not sufficient to hide their nakedness." Most papers throughout the northern colonies exchanged this startling account throughout June.[36]

The earliest news of disaster at the Cedars reached Philadelphia by Sunday, June 2. New Hampshire delegate William Whipple wrote that day, "Here is a report" that Bedel "is cut off by a party of the 8th regt and Indians," but he did not put much stock in it. "The story comes in so loose a way . . . that I do not credit it; however it may be true; we must expect to meet with some hard rubs." The next day, an express arrived from Albany with confirmation that patriot forces had indeed taken those rubs. Whipple's colleague Josiah Bartlett also hoped it would "not prove so bad as reported," but Congress took steps to improve security on the Canadian frontier just in case. They called up militia to create a "flying camp" to protect New England from invasion and resolved that General Philip Schuyler "be empowered to employ in Canada a number of Indians, not exceeding two thousand." Samuel Adams, for one, prayed that this step — which was exactly what they had screamed at the British for trying — would rescue patriot fortunes on the northern frontier. "Measures," he wrote to Massachusetts patriot James Warren, "have been adopted which I trust will repair Misfortunes and set Matters right in that Quarter."[37]

Warren would soon receive another letter from Philadelphia, this time from Sam's cousin. John Adams, ever the pessimist, was in a panic. He believed the loss of Canada could mean the concession of all northern Indians to Britain, a blow that would probably prove fatal to the common cause. Not only would the British have control of the St. Lawrence and Great Lakes and uninterrupted communication between Niagara, Detroit, and Michilimackinac, but

> they will have a free Communication with all the numerous Tribes of Indians, extending along the Frontiers of all the Colonies, and by their Trinkets and Bribes will induce them to take up the Hatchett, and

Spread Blood and Fire among the Inhabitants by which Means, all the Frontier Inhabitants will be driven in upon the middle settlements, at a Time when the Inhabitants of the Seaports and Coasts will be driven back by the British Navy.

"Is this Picture too highly coloured?" he asked, recovering his nerve. "Perhaps it is."[38]

The news from Canada shook others in Congress, too. On Tuesday, June 4, Congress issued a new round of proclamations in President Hancock's name, imploring patriot authorities from Maryland north to remain steadfast in the cause, despite the bad news. This address, probably written by Jefferson, Edmund Rutledge, George Wythe, and Sam Adams, rehearsed several of the themes the Declaration would make famous just one month later.

The "Tyrant of Britain and his Parliament" had such an "unrelenting Spirit," they argued, "that they have left no Measure unessayed." Although the cause had survived thus far, British "measures" were beginning to bear fruit. In Canada, this proclamation admitted, "it appears, that our Affairs in that Quarter wear a melancholy Aspect. Should the Canadians and Indians take up Arms agt. us (which there is too much Reason to fear) we shall then have the whole Force of that Country to contend with, joined to that of Great Britain, and all her foreign auxiliaries." What now? Congress asked: "In this Situation what Steps must we pursue?" If the Revolution was to survive, only "superior Exertions" would decide whether colonists would "live Slaves, or die Freemen." Instructing the various provincial governing bodies to call up their militia forces, Congress implored that now was the time for men to "step forth in Defence of their Wives, their Children, their Liberty, and every Thing they hold dear." This June 4 address invoked the patriot "spirit" as the polar opposite of the king's tyrannical measures — despite the fact that they, too, had secretly called on proxies to take up arms the day before. "The Cause is certainly a most glorious one and I trust every Man [in the northern colonies] is determined to see it gloriously ended, or to perish in the Ruins of it. In short, on your Exertions at this Critical Period, together with those of the other Colonies, in the Common Cause, the Salvation of America now evidently depends." The first of what would be several calls for colonists to remain dedicated to the cause that year, Congress handed those beseeching messages to express riders, who galloped off in all directions. Then they opened an investigation to find out what had gone wrong in Canada.[39]

Foreign mercenaries or Indians, both in person and hundreds of miles away, dominated Congress's attention from the middle of May through the first days of June. This absorption matched the newspapers during those weeks: papers in many locales published accounts from the Cedars together with — or closely behind — the news of Hessians on their way. During the weeks of 1776 in which Jefferson, Adams, Franklin, and their colleagues are usually depicted as weighing the heavy question of independence, they were, in fact, doing other things: working hard on addresses to convince the people to keep faith, meeting with Indians to impress upon them the power of unified patriot arms, quietly issuing orders to recruit northern Indians to defend New England, and concocting plans to convince German mercenaries to desert as soon as they arrived in America. All this explains why Virginia's resolution sat on Richard Henry Lee's desk for ten hectic days. Concerns about Indians threatening from the St. Lawrence or German troops en route across the Atlantic prevailed.

Or, more likely, these were exactly the reasons why Lee rose to introduce a motion on the floor of Congress on Friday, June 7, to consider "that these United Colonies are, and of right ought to be, free and independent States, that they are absolved from all allegiance to the British Crown, and that all political connection between them and the State of Great Britain is, and ought to be, totally dissolved." Debate opened the next day, June 8, and continued the following Monday. Given what came next, it would be easy to assume that this two-day debate was the most monumental discussion Congress had ever undertaken. It was — but what is most surprising about the debate over independence was that it lasted only two days. By the end of Monday's session, the delegates decided that they had other pressing things to take care of and tabled further discussion until the first of July.[40]

In the meantime, they appointed five members to draft a declaration of independence: John Adams, Benjamin Franklin, Thomas Jefferson, Robert Livingston, and Roger Sherman. They had eighteen days to craft a polished statement of purpose for the American Revolution that would be seen as legitimate and acceptable for foreign and domestic audiences alike. Despite all the practice the delegates had had in justifying the rebellion, this was a difficult assignment. American mythology lingers here, following the committee members as they filed out of the State House and listening in for Adams's insistence that Jefferson possessed the "peculiar felicity of expression" that made him the only suitable author. But, in reality, they all had too much work to do to spend any more time squabbling over who would write it.[41]

Indian affairs overshadowed everything. The secret journals of Congress reveal that, on the same day Lee introduced the fateful motion, Congress elaborated on their orders to Washington to employ Indians, allowing him to decide "where he shall judge they will be most useful," and they created a bounty for any British soldiers captured by Indian allies. The day after Congress sent Jefferson and the drafting committee off to compose the Declaration, they received the delegation from the Iroquois again, handing out presents and pledging a firm friendship that would "continue as long as the sun shall shine." Three days later, they instructed General Schuyler to solidify that relationship, authorizing him to organize a new treaty conference with the Iroquois "to engage them in our interest upon the best terms that can be procured."[42]

Frontier affairs continued to monopolize Congress's attention throughout June. On Saturday, June 15, they took Jefferson away from the Declaration so he could act as secretary for the committee to investigate the Cedars prisoner debacle. The four-man committee interviewed Major Sherburne and presented a report — in Jefferson's handwriting — two days later, a paper containing language that invoked prisoners' being delivered into the "hands of the Savages," a "horrid act," a "cruel and inhuman death," and a "gross and barbarous violation of the laws of nature and nations." Next, news arrived that British agents in the southern backcountry were conspiring with Cherokee and Creek Indians. Exiled Indian Superintendent John Stuart had sent his brother Henry to talk to the southern Indians, and on May 18, he issued a public letter warning all frontier inhabitants across the South that, if they fought against the crown, "five hundred warriors" from the Creeks, Chickasaws, and Cherokees were about to "take possession of the frontiers of North-Carolina and Virginia." This letter found its way to Williamsburg, where it was first handed to *Virginia Gazette* printer Alexander Purdie, and then sent on to the Virginia delegation in Philadelphia, where it arrived on June 18. If the situation on the northern frontier seemed teetering on collapse, during those same days it seemed that the South might not be any better.[43]

Then there was Lord Dunmore. On that portentous day of May 27, as Arnold begrudgingly signed the Cedars cartel, bad news arrived from Fort Pitt, and Congress did their best to impress the Iroquois, Dunmore landed his sickly fleet on Gwynn's Island, a move that sparked yet another round of newspaper reports. Just a few yards off the Virginia mainland, Gwynn's Island was a small sandbar in the Chesapeake between the mouths of the York and Rappahannock Rivers. As it turned out, this was the last piece of solid ground in Virginia Dunmore would occupy for the king.

Dunmore unloaded his ships there in the hopes of stopping the smallpox that was rampaging through the soldiers and loyalist refugees — Black and white — on board the "floating town." He quarantined them as far away as he could, on the bay side of the island. According to one published letter, this raging epidemic cost Dunmore "nine or ten of his black regiment every day." Nevertheless, a Royal Navy captain estimated on June 10 that the governor still gained "Six or eight fresh Men every day" to take their places. Even though many of these new recruits would die as soon as they reached the governor's lines, the sustained stream of runaways even in the face of smallpox testifies to the attraction of Dunmore's proclamation. Eight of Landon Carter's slaves thought the risk worthwhile. In late June, he noted in his diary that they had gone "to be sure, to Ld. Dunmore," taking guns, ammunition, silver buckles, and new sets of clothes with them.[44]

Virginia Gazette printers John Dixon and William Hunter first published a report on June 15 that Dunmore had taken this opportunity to initiate a new stage of germ warfare. Employing the most vague, least corroborated method of introducing a story, they wrote, "We learn from Gloucester, that Lord Dunmore has erected hospitals upon Gwyn's-island . . . and that they are inoculating the blacks for the small-pox." "Two of those wretches," they continued, were "inoculated and sent ashore, in order to spread the infection, but it was happily prevented." Nine patriot newspapers would exchange this accusation, in some cases in the same column of Williamsburg news with Henry Stuart's warning about southern Indians going to war for the king.[45]

Patriot leaders in Virginia, while they were supposed to be writing their first state constitution, had to pay attention to threats from both East and West. Jefferson, whom we would expect to be pouring all of his energy and concentration into what would become a world-historical statement of human rights, was also preoccupied with these dangers. At some point during the seven summer weeks Dunmore was camped there, Jefferson sketched an intricate map of Gwynn's Island. Although it is not certain when he received the information incorporated into this map or even who supplied the intelligence, his detailed sketches of the besieging American fleet and surrounding fortifications suggested that Jefferson had more than a passing interest in the actions on Gwynn's Island — even as he was helping George Wythe craft an address to the German mercenaries, investigating Indian attacks in Canada, and drafting the Declaration of Independence. Further, Jefferson sent several drafts of potential frames of government for the Virginia Convention to consider as they composed their state constitution. These drafts contained a preamble that rehearsed the essential grievances against the king, which Jefferson was also assembling on Congress's behalf. These accusations reached their highest pitch with the following assertions: George III attempted a "detestable and insupportable tyranny . . ."

by prompting our negroes to rise in arms among us; those very negroes whom [he hath from time to time] by an inhuman use of his negative he hath refused us permission to exclude by law;

by endeavouring to bring on the inhabitants of our frontiers the merciless Indian savages, whose known rule of warfare is an undistinguished destruction of all ages, sexes, and conditions of existence;

by transporting at this time a large army of foreign mercenaries to compleat the works of death, desolation, and tyranny already begun with circumstances of cruelty and perfidy so unworthy the head of a civilized nation.

When the Virginia Convention approved the constitution on June 29, they added only a couple of commas to these charges; with the exception of a final accusation that the king had answered "our repeated Petitions for Redress with a Repetition of injuries," the indictment of attempting to use proxy fighters was the most damning crime the crown had committed against Virginia.[46]

Jefferson was not the only person to argue that encouraging slaves, Indians, and foreigners to interfere in this civil dispute constituted a point of no return. In fact, the grievances of slave instigation, Indian tampering, and foreign invaders were so well known by the public that many local and provincial proclamations of independence cited British plots as a main justification for nationhood. Termed "little declarations of independence" by one historian, these often overlooked statements by counties, towns, and provincial associations also reflected the centrality of British proxies in building a consensus for independence.[47]

In New England, statements by provincial assemblies in Connecticut and New Hampshire as well as instructions from Boston and other Massachusetts towns, including Scituate and Wrentham, listed the incitement of proxies as a signal reason for independence. From Pennsylvania, groups at several levels, including militia units in Chester County, the Deputies of Philadelphia, and the provincial assembly, also featured British proxies in their lists of grievances. Charles and Talbot Counties in Maryland drafted their own declarations, stating, "Slaves, savages, and foreign mercenaries, have been meanly hired to rob a people of their property, liberties, and lives." Some of these found space in colonial newspapers. The June 24 declaration by Philadelphia's city deputies was especially popular. Appearing in more than a dozen papers, this justification for independence concluded with, "Whereas [the king] hath paid no regard to any of our remonstrances and

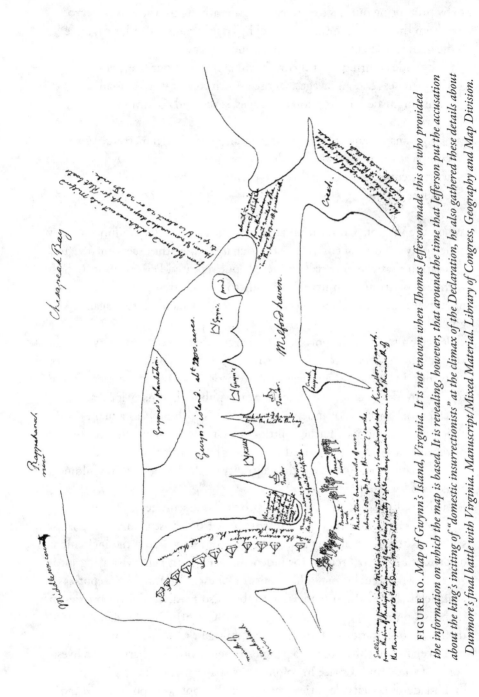

FIGURE 10. Map of Gwynn's Island, Virginia. It is not known when Thomas Jefferson made this or who provided the information on which the map is based. It is revealing, however, that around the time that Jefferson put the accusation about the king's inciting of "domestic insurrectionists" at the climax of the Declaration, he also gathered these details about Dunmore's final battle with Virginia. Manuscript/Mixed Material. Library of Congress, Geography and Map Division. https://www.loc.gov/item/mtjbib001518

dutiful petitions for redress of our complicated grievances, but hath lately purchased foreign troops to assist in enslaving us, and hath excited the Savages of this country to carry on a war against us, as also the Negroes to embrue their hands in the blood of their masters, in a manner unpracticed by civilized nations."[48]

It should be remembered: none of these things had actually occurred. There had been precious little "enslaving," "exciting," or "embruing." It didn't matter. Blaming the king for undertaking these terrible acts—whether they happened or not—was by now an article of faith among patriots. "Armatus" put it even more gruesomely (and falsely) in a widely exchanged screed in late June: "The [King] of England delights in blood: yea, thirsteth for the blood of America. Hessians, Hanoverians, Brunswickers, Canadians, Indians, Negroes, Regulars and Tories are invited to the carnage. This is no fiction, but an awful reality, not the production of a delirium, but substantial matter of fact." Here was the rhetoric of feasting, again. It truly was fiction, if not delirium. Yes, slaves had rebelled all over the South, but they spent their energy securing freedom rather than seeking vengeance. Nearly all Natives had remained neutral to this point. There wasn't a single German boot on American soil yet. But, because patriot leaders at all levels—from local to provincial to continental—had given these fantasies their stamp of approval, they were not only mainstream; they were at the heart of the common cause appeal. Little would separate Armatus's bloodthirsty imagery from the Declaration of Independence.[49]

Thomas Jefferson thought he was missing out on the real show. He believed that drafting new constitutions was not only the "most interesting" work of the Revolution at that point but "the whole object of the present controversy"—and, he had lamented to a friend in May, it was going on in Williamsburg without him. But those charters depended on justifications. A constitution's articles were essential for securing liberty in the future; that document's preamble was essential for making that future possible. If the people were going to recognize and abide by the provisions of a new constitution, first they had to accept the reasons those laws needed to exist in the first place.[50]

Congress's declaration of independence was meant as an extended preamble. Its purpose was to legitimize this decision, unprecedented in the history of New World colonies, and garner support from audiences foreign and domestic for the patriot cause. If the Continental Congress expected thousands of colonists to continue voluntarily placing their lives at risk, the delegates had to write a convincing manifesto.[51]

For the CONNECTICUT COURANT.

THE whole strength of Britain and her allies is now employed in the destruction of America. Fleets and armies, and every engine of fraud and violence, that the sophistry of hell can invent, are prepared to execute the horrid plan. The work is already begun, and a few days will unfold the infernal design, to the weakest sight. The ------- of England delights in blood, yea, thirsteth for the blood of America. Hessians, Hanoverians, Brunswickers, Canadians, Indians, Negroes, Regulars and Tories are invited to the carnage. This is no fiction, but an awful reality, not the production of a delirium, but substantial matter of fact. The tyrant of Britain hath sold himself to work wickedness, and the blood of Naboth must be shed that the vineyard may be peaceably possessed. The plan is ripe for execution and begins to operate.---Lift up your eyes, my countrymen, and see destruction, like a flood, pouring in upon you from every quarter, even from the north and the south, and from the east and the west. The decree is gone forth, and as sure as you now exist, death is the portion of all that the power of Britain can overcome. Rouse up, therefore, and arm yourselves for the encounter, gird on the harness, and let him that hath no sword sell his garment and buy one. Remember that the salvation of your country depends on your present exertion; and that this summer will decide the fate of America. Don't boggle at the expence when your all is at stake, if we conquer the vacant lands and confiscations will abundantly repay the expence of the war, and if we are overcome, our all is gone, and it matters not how much we expend in the contest. Let us therefore give every encouragement to those who go forth to battle, and jeopard their lives in the high places of the field, being assured, that if the ardor of the soldiery is suppressed the cause will inevitably sink, and that he who, at this season, cavils at the charge, and wastes the precious time in idle harangues, on trivial matters, betrays a very weak or wicked mind, and like Nero, would have fiddled while Rome was burning.

ARMATUS.

FIGURE 11. *Letter from "Armatus." From* Connecticut Courant, *June 17, 1776. "Armatus" implored readers of the* Connecticut Courant *to resist because of the king's proxies just as Thomas Jefferson drafted very nearly the same grievances in the Declaration of Independence. "Armatus" also reached audiences in Massachusetts, New York, and Maryland.*

The grievances, then, were essential to the document's success. They had to be ironclad and compelling to contemporary readers or listeners. Long before generations would revere it as a sacred text, in its time, the Declaration of Independence was simply a political document with pressing work to do: it had to clarify a very confusing conflict, distinguish "friends" from "enemies," inspire military resistance, and earn sympathy (and hopefully money) from Europeans. The pressure on the Declaration to rouse the people to a spirited defense increased exponentially on July 2, when the lead ships carrying the largest invasion fleet ever assembled arrived in New York Harbor and began unloading what would eventually be thirty thousand British and German troops on Staten Island. John Adams referred to that Tuesday as America's "Day of Deliverance" because of the vote for independence, but many loyalists hoped that that day's appearance of the fleet would be remembered as the first day of their salvation. What if the Declaration failed to inspire? What if the cause turned out to be not common enough — in the face of thousands upon thousands of enemy bayonets?

The nearly thirty charges Jefferson leveled at George III were the core of the matter. They were not assembled at random. Instead of presenting the evidence chronologically, Jefferson grouped them for maximum effect. They began slowly and gained emotional speed. The first dozen detailed the king's abuses of executive power, the next ten protested "pretended legislation," and the final five documented acts of war and cruelty.

The twelve grievances that began the Declaration's presentations of "facts [to] be submitted to a candid world" reached back a decade or more into the imperial crisis. They centered on perceived abuses of executive authority, accusing the king of many misdeeds, especially concerning the legitimacy of colonial assemblies and the authority of the laws they passed. But, again, Jefferson was starting softly, building to a dramatic crescendo. Many of these first charges — although they were broadly accepted in the colonies as violations of constitutional authority — were in and of themselves hardly inspiring enough to encourage farmers to rush for their muskets. Often they referred to disagreements certain provinces had with crown authorities, and although Congress wanted to include everyone's issues in this continental declaration, local controversies didn't motivate the people as a whole. Furthermore, the tone of the first dozen accusations is rather modest; the king is indicted with mild verbs such as "obstructed," "refused," and "affected."

The second group of grievances focused on specific acts of Parliament and the king's willingness to enforce them, including each of the Coercive Acts, various mercantile regulations governing imperial trade, and the Quebec Act. To heighten the sense of these acts as an unceasing attack on American liberties, Jefferson abandoned his device of beginning each accusation with "he has," placing personal blame on the king. Charges fourteen through twenty-two are, instead, a list separated by colons. Rhetorically, they act as one single sentence that dramatizes the sheer volume of oppression the colonies had endured over the decade.

The real drama was yet to come, though. The final five charges highlighted the past year's violence. The verbs in the last grievances are more evocative and stirring than the previous ones. In these indictments, George's crimes are deeper than moving the seat of government or discouraging immigration. In the concluding charges, Jefferson and Congress submitted accusations that the king had "plundered," "ravaged," "destroyed," forced Americans to become "executioners of their friends and brethren," and recruited foreign mercenaries "to complete the Works of Death, Desolation, and Tyranny, already begun with circumstances of Cruelty and Perfidy, scarcely paralleled in the most barbarous Ages, and totally unworthy the Head of a civilized Nation." These charges carried a great deal of weight; their acceptance by the "candid world," both at home and abroad, could determine whether American independence was deemed righteous and defensible.

Or not.

The delegates understood this. They tinkered with this last group of war accusations more than all the other grievances during their editing sessions on July 2–3. Other than a few touches to rearrange words or slice extraneous phrases, for the most part, Jefferson's first twenty grievances entered the final Declaration intact. But as the stakes increased, so did Congress's attention, much to Jefferson's discomfort. Often, they deepened the king's crimes, inserting stirring phrases such as "waging war against us" and the stinging comment that his hiring of German troops was "scarcely paralleled in the most barbarous ages."

They also struck out two of Jefferson's accusations almost entirely. The first charged George with inciting loyalists to fight for the promise of gaining confiscated patriot property. This was, on its face, a problematic charge, awkwardly condemning the king for encouraging his subjects to stay loyal. Moreover, it made practical political sense to leave the tories out of the Declaration: condemning the loyalists might breed antipathy toward the common cause among those on the fence, and, worse, prove an obstacle for incorporating those people into the nation in the future. Not knowing just how common it truly was, they wanted to welcome any and all disaffected people to the cause.

The second grievance Congress eliminated was Jefferson's long, moving passage censuring the king for "wag[ing] cruel war against human nature itself" by promoting the slave trade, then doubly damning him for manipulating "those very people to rise in arms among us, and to purchase that liberty of which *he* has deprived them, by murdering the people upon whom *he* also obtruded them; thus paying off former crimes committed against the *liberties* of one people, with crimes which he urges them to commit against the *lives* of another." Blaming the king wholesale for the slave trade was too tenuous to stand as the final accusation, so Congress tragically eliminated nearly all of it. Generations later, when abolitionists would seize upon "all men are created equal" as a testimony that slavery betrayed the principles of the Revolution, one wonders what they could have done with the stirring phrases that Jefferson's rough draft originally contained. In what would have been the Declaration's final charge, Jefferson denounced the slave trade as "an assemblage of horrors," "piratical warfare," and "cruel war against human nature." These were powerful words. Congress sliced them all out.

Almost all. They removed the part that accused the king of foisting slavery upon the colonists, yet they retained the second half of the charge, inserting the words "excited domestic insurrections amongst us" in what would now be the twenty-seventh and final grievance against George III. They cut all reference to slavery as a war against human nature but retained the evil of slave insurrections. They struck what in 1774 had been the "great object of desire" — antislavery — and kept Dunmore's proclamation of 1775. In essence, they made a trade. They edited out Jefferson's impassioned attack on slavery in order to bolster the union. They avoided offending slaveholders for participating in cruel wars against human nature but still benefited from blaming the king for trying to use slaves to kill them. The Declaration's last grievance would be formidable: "He has excited domestic insurrections among us and has endeavoured to bring on the inhabitants of our frontiers the merciless Indian savages, whose known rule of warfare is an undistinguished destruction of all ages, sexes, and conditions."[52]

This was the ultimate deal breaker with the British. The language Congress put forward in this final accusation would have powerful consequences. Its inclusion at the heart of the founding document would cast a long shadow over the definition of who was a part of the new republic and who was not.

At the moment of its approval, the Declaration of Independence was a political document, not a philosophical one. The most important two words in it, therefore, have nothing to do with equality or happiness. They are actually its shortest words: "he" and "we." The Declaration was an effort to draw a line between friends and enemies, between "us" and "them" — or, in this case, between "he" and "we." These pronouns are mighty weapons, rhetorically and conceptually. They are independence. The interpretation signified by "he" and "we" is the central premise of the Declaration. It is a formal announcement of the separation of one people ("we") from another ("he"). In this distinction lay the American assertion of self-determination, of casting off monarchical subjecthood and a claim of popular sovereignty. It contained the first assertion of an "American people."

As soon as Congress approved the Declaration's final text, they sent the manuscript to *Pennsylvania Packet* printer John Dunlap for publication as a broadside, even though the news was already spreading through the city. Dunlap completed his work over that Thursday night. The next day, copies of that broadside were disseminated to assembly halls, brigade headquarters, and printing shops throughout North America. Twenty-nine newspapers followed Congress's orders to print the text, starting with Benjamin Towne's *Pennsylvania Evening Post* on July 6 and ending with the *Boston Gazette* two weeks later. Patriot political organizations at the provincial and local level staged public readings over the next few July weeks. Army officers assembled troops in formation to hear why they were fighting.[53]

One group listening to the Declaration grasped the document's performative aspects immediately. At the already war-weary Fort Ticonderoga, after Colonel Arthur St. Clair read the text to a cheering crowd, an observer commented, "It was remarkably pleasing to see the spirits of the soldiers so raised after all their calamities; the language of every man's countenance was, Now we are a people!" The packet of values attributed to that "free people" undoubtedly contributed to their collective happiness. If they had paid even casual attention, the crowd at Ticonderoga and similar venues throughout the mainland would have been reminded of what comprised that abstract "we": "humble," "patient" sufferers who placed a "firm reliance on the protection of Divine Providence," displayed a "manly firmness," believed that everyone was "created equal," respected "the rights of the people," "the consent of the governed," and the "pursuit of happiness," and broadcast the "voice of justice and consanguinity" even when no one was listening. The king opposed these virtuous people and therefore was an enemy of freedom. The "long train of abuses"—especially the last few items on the list—only threw the Americans' heroic qualities into greater relief. The ecstatic garrison apparently grasped the point: without even having to say anything, they became Americans. It was written on their faces. But, as much as the patriot officers at Ticonderoga might have wanted this expression to be sufficient, it was more complicated than that. What did that phrase mean? Who, exactly, were "the American people"?[54]

The crucial division in the Declaration, denoted by "he" and "we," did

In CONGRESS, July 4, 1776.

A DECLARATION

By the REPRESENTATIVES of the

UNITED STATES OF AMERICA,

In GENERAL CONGRESS Assembled.

WHEN in the Course of human Events, it becomes necessary for one People to dissolve the Political Bands which have connected them with another, and to assume among the Powers of the Earth, the separate and equal Station to which the Laws of Nature and of Nature's God entitle them, a decent Respect to the Opinions of Mankind requires that they should declare the causes which impel them to the Separation.

We hold these Truths to be self-evident, that all Men are created equal, that they are endowed by their Creator with certain unalienable Rights, that among these are Life, Liberty, and the Pursuit of Happiness--That to secure these Rights, Governments are instituted among Men, deriving their just Powers from the Consent of the Governed, that whenever any Form of Government becomes destructive of these Ends, it is the Right of the People to alter or to abolish it, and to institute new Government, laying its Foundation on such Principles, and organizing its Powers in such Form, as to them shall seem most likely to effect their Safety and Happiness. Prudence, indeed, will dictate that Governments long established should not be changed for light and transient Causes; and accordingly all Experience hath shewn, that Mankind are more disposed to suffer, while Evils are sufferable, than to right themselves by abolishing the Forms to which they are accustomed. But when a long Train of Abuses and Usurpations, pursuing invariably the same Object, evinces a Design to reduce them under absolute Despotism, it is their Right, it is their Duty, to throw off such Government, and to provide new Guards for their future Security. Such has been the patient Sufferance of these Colonies; and such is now the Necessity which constrains them to alter their former Systems of Government. The History of the present King of Great-Britain is a History of repeated Injuries and Usurpations, all having in direct Object the Establishment of an absolute Tyranny over these States. To prove this, let Facts be submitted to a candid World.

He has refused his Assent to Laws, the most wholesome and necessary for the public Good.

He has forbidden his Governors to pass Laws of immediate and pressing Importance, unless suspended in their Operation till his Assent should be obtained; and when so suspended, he has utterly neglected to attend to them.

He has refused to pass other Laws for the Accommodation of large Districts of People, unless those People would relinquish the Right of Representation in the Legislature, a Right inestimable to them, and formidable to Tyrants only.

He has called together Legislative Bodies at Places unusual, uncomfortable, and distant from the Depository of their public Records, for the sole Purpose of fatiguing them into Compliance with his Measures.

He has dissolved Representative Houses repeatedly, for opposing with manly Firmness his Invasions on the Rights of the People.

He has refused for a long Time, after such Dissolutions, to cause others to be elected; whereby the Legislative Powers, incapable of Annihilation, have returned to the People at large for their exercise; the State remaining in the mean time exposed to all the Dangers of Invasion from without, and Convulsions within.

He has endeavoured to prevent the Population of these States; for that Purpose obstructing the Laws for Naturalization of Foreigners; refusing to pass others to encourage their Migrations hither, and raising the Conditions of new Appropriations of Lands.

He has obstructed the Administration of Justice, by refusing his Assent to Laws for establishing Judiciary Powers.

He has made Judges dependent on his Will alone, for the Tenure of their Offices, and the Amount and Payment of their Salaries.

He has erected a Multitude of new Offices, and sent hither Swarms of Officers to harrass our People, and eat out their Substance.

He has kept among us, in Times of Peace, Standing Armies, without the consent of our Legislatures.

He has affected to render the Military independent of and superior to the Civil Power.

He has combined with others to subject us to a Jurisdiction foreign to our Constitution, and unacknowledged by our Laws; giving his Assent to their Acts of pretended Legislation:

For quartering large Bodies of Armed Troops among us:

For protecting them, by a mock Trial, from Punishment for any Murders which they should commit on the Inhabitants of these States:

For cutting off our Trade with all Parts of the World:

For imposing Taxes on us without our Consent:

For depriving us, in many Cases, of the Benefits of Trial by Jury:

For transporting us beyond Seas to be tried for pretended Offences:

For abolishing the free System of English Laws in a neighbouring Province, establishing therein an arbitrary Government, and enlarging its Boundaries, so as to render it at once an Example and fit Instrument for introducing the same absolute Rule into these Colonies:

For taking away our Charters, abolishing our most valuable Laws, and altering fundamentally the Forms of our Governments:

For suspending our own Legislatures, and declaring themselves invested with Power to legislate for us in all Cases whatsoever.

He has abdicated Government here, by declaring us out of his Protection and waging War against us.

He has plundered our Seas, ravaged our Coasts, burnt our Towns, and destroyed the Lives of our People.

He is, at this Time, transporting large Armies of foreign Mercenaries to compleat the Works of Death, Desolation, and Tyranny, already begun with circumstances of Cruelty and Perfidy, scarcely paralleled in the most barbarous Ages, and totally unworthy the Head of a civilized Nation.

He has constrained our fellow Citizens taken Captive on the high Seas to bear Arms against their Country, to become the Executioners of their Friends and Brethren, or to fall themselves by their Hands.

He has excited domestic Insurrections amongst us, and has endeavoured to bring on the Inhabitants of our Frontiers, the merciless Indian Savages, whose known Rule of Warfare, is an undistinguished Destruction, of all Ages, Sexes and Conditions.

In every stage of these Oppressions we have Petitioned for Redress in the most humble Terms: Our repeated Petitions have been answered only by repeated Injury. A Prince, whose Character is thus marked by every act which may define a Tyrant, is unfit to be the Ruler of a free People.

Nor have we been wanting in Attentions to our British Brethren. We have warned them from Time to Time of Attempts by their Legislature to extend an unwarrantable Jurisdiction over us. We have reminded them of the Circumstances of our Emigration and Settlement here. We have appealed to their native Justice and Magnanimity, and we have conjured them by the Ties of our common Kindred to disavow these Usurpations, which, would inevitably interrupt our Connections and Correspondence. They too have been deaf to the Voice of Justice and of Consanguinity. We must, therefore, acquiesce in the Necessity, which denounces our Separation, and hold them, as we hold the rest of Mankind, Enemies in War, in Peace, Friends.

We, therefore, the Representatives of the UNITED STATES OF AMERICA, in GENERAL CONGRESS, Assembled, appealing to the Supreme Judge of the World for the Rectitude of our Intentions, do, in the Name, and by Authority of the good People of these Colonies, solemnly Publish and Declare, That these United Colonies are, and of Right ought to be, FREE AND INDEPENDENT STATES; that they are absolved from all Allegiance to the British Crown, and that all political Connection between them and the State of Great-Britain, is and ought to be totally dissolved; and that as FREE AND INDEPENDENT STATES, they have full Power to levy War, conclude Peace, contract Alliances, establish Commerce, and to do all other Acts and Things which INDEPENDENT STATES may of right do. And for the support of this Declaration, with a firm Reliance on the Protection of divine Providence, we mutually pledge to each other our Lives, our Fortunes, and our sacred Honor.

Signed by ORDER and in BEHALF of the CONGRESS,

JOHN HANCOCK, President.

ATTEST.
CHARLES THOMSON, Secretary.

PHILADELPHIA: PRINTED BY JOHN DUNLAP.

FIGURE 12. *John Dunlap's broadside of the Declaration of Independence. 1776. Unlike the engrossed copy (with a single block of script lines) that has become the iconic image, the printed version of the Declaration features the list of twenty-seven grievances prominently. Americans in 1776 would have seen the Declaration exclusively in this broadside form or as printed in newspaper columns. Library of Congress, Printed Ephemera Collection. https://www.loc.gov/item/2003576546*

provide some answers to this puzzle. Jefferson's Declaration cordoned off far more than just Americans from Britons, republicanism from monarchy. As is well documented, the transfer of blame from Parliament to King George himself was an innovation of 1776, a shift usually ascribed to the influence of *Common Sense*. Jefferson addressed the king directly in the grievances; George was America's enemy.

But, again, it wasn't that simple. Others fought on his behalf. When the Declaration connected these proxy fighters with "he," they also enlarged the definition of America's "enemy" to include those groups. Leaving no room for the thousands of African Americans or Native peoples who supported the patriot cause, the Declaration portrayed them all as mindless, blood-thirsty barbarians too naive to realize they were being duped by a tyrant.

There was, moreover, a subtle difference between these proxies listed at the end of the grievances, a tiny shift that helps explain how many viewed the distinctions between them. The so-called "merciless savages" would take the war into their own hands and devastate the frontiers, Congress argued. "In-surrections" also connoted a hostile activity initiated by "domestics." But the "foreign mercenaries" charge is messier. In fact, it pulls a switch on the reader. The grievances argue these men were going to do deadly things once they stopped being "transported," but on closer inspection, the final clause turns back to the king for deciding to include them. It wasn't their fault; it was his. His was an action "totally unworthy the Head of a civilized Nation." It seems the "Works of Death, Desolation, and Tyranny, already begun with circumstances of Cruelty and Perfidy, scarcely paralleled in the most barba-rous Ages" were, not the anticipated works of Hessians, but rather the prod-uct of George's decisions. This is a brilliant sleight of hand: with the Hes-sians rendered as passive—empty vessels of the king standing on transport ships like robots waiting to carry out the tyrant's evil schemes—the blame did not center on them personally, very unlike slaves and Indians. The Decla-ration withholds judgment on the German troops, making a future redemp-tion possible. African Americans and Indians were not so lucky.

These war grievances help clarify the problems inherent in drawing a line between "us" and "them." According to Congress, the king's proxies were unable to discern liberty from slavery, an interpretation that drips with irony. "We" would never fall victim to such crimes. The "we" of "we hold these truths to be self-evident" is the most important word in the Declara-tion. Who are "we"? The twenty-seventh grievance addresses that definition: *we* are those patriotic, liberty-loving people who had the foresight and moral courage to resist the "repeated injuries and usurpations" of the "Present King of Great Britain." "We"—the American people—would not include "he" nor his helpers, the "merciless savages," "domestic insurrectionists," and (at least for now) "foreign mercenaries."

At the key founding moment, then, the definition of what it meant to be "an American" was a negative one: "not British." But the heated language of the Declaration's final grievances gave it other shapes: "not slave," "not savage," and "not mercenary." Those constructions reinforced the patriots' positive assessment of themselves as holding the moral, philosophical, and political high ground in this conflict. Because those tropes plugged into embedded colonial prejudices about Africans and Indians, however, they were about more than merely not behaving in manners that were slavish or savage. They had the effect of casting out real Indians and African Americans.

For another group of New Yorkers listening to the Declaration, they were enemies just like King George. While soldiers at Fort Ticonderoga cheered, "Now we are a people," a crowd on Long Island's north shore celebrated the same announcement. In a less cheerful mood, this crowd "from all the distant quarters of the district" of Huntington showed their approval for independence by constructing a visual representation of the multiple enemies of the new United States of America. A newspaper report detailed the actions of that July afternoon: "An effigy of [George III] being hastily fabricated out of base materials, with its face black, like *Dunmore's* Virginia regiment, its head adorned with a wooden crown, and its head stuck full of feathers, like *Carleton* and *Johnson's* Savages, and its body wrapped in the Union [Jack], instead of a blanket or robe of state, and lined with *gun-powder,* which the original seems to be fond of." "The whole," the article concluded, "was hung on a gallows, exploded, and burnt to ashes." In essence, the crowd of Long Islanders gave their own performance of the Declaration, using fire instead of ink to kill the king and his various helpers. The crowd defended "life, liberty, and the pursuit of happiness" by animating and then destroying both His Majesty and his proxies simultaneously. The New Yorkers consigned all their enemies — the king, the merciless savages, and the domestic insurrectionists — to the flames, leaving "Americans" to stand outside and watch the blaze.[55]

Without the benefit of a patriot observer to interpret the faces of the onlookers in this crowd, we must consider what might have been on their minds. At least a few of them must have greeted with trepidation the news of independence, the Declaration's accusations, and the specific behavior it literally sparked. Since this was Long Island, there had to be some in the crowd who doubted whether independence was the best course. People in Huntington and Suffolk County showed much more support for the common cause than their western neighbors in King's or Queen's County — where the popular perception was that "Tories are 3 to 1 against the Whiggs"—but quite a few disaffected folk lived in the area. Considering the strong possibility that there were many in places like Long Island (and lots of other locales throughout the continent) who were apprehensive of independence, it was wise of Congress not to alienate them in the Declaration. The decision to omit Jefferson's loyalist grievance might have paid considerable dividends in a place like Huntington, which, in a matter of weeks, would be fewer than twenty miles away from the right flank of a massive British army. At the same time, since nearly one in ten residents of Suffolk County was African American, there was also a decent chance more than a few watched their neighbors spread black powder all over the effigy to prepare the king for execution. That fastening could only have raised doubts in their minds as to the patriots' true interest in making the cause common to everyone.[56]

From the patriot perspective, however, this exclusion could not be helped, especially at this moment, with more ships from the British invasion fleet appearing on the horizon each day. Like the Declaration itself, the exploding proxy effigy in Huntington was a production that patriots believed would inspire political and military mobilization in a strategic area. If capitalizing on that rhetorical opportunity meant the sacrifice of "good" Blacks or Indians who supported the Revolution, so be it. Once the historical moment passed—after the Long Islanders had dispersed and the king's ashes were cast to the winds—that powerful accusation casting out "domestics" and "merciless savages" would remain, indelible.

These were the peals those thirteen clocks made when they all struck together on that first Fourth of July. Their striking as one was, indeed, a "singular example in the history of mankind," as Adams would remember it more than four decades later. But this "perfection of mechanism" was not the simple consequence of a previous revolution of the American mind. Nor was it the product of an omniscient "artist." It was a highly contingent event, one that depended on the actions of thousands of African Americans and Indians. They animated the proxy stories that patriot leaders howled about almost incessantly in the fifteen months between April 19, 1775, and July 4, 1776. Proxy stories that patriot leaders told about "merciless savages," "domestic insurrectionists," and "foreign mercenaries" were what made those clocks strike on that particular date. Nothing else fully explains that timing.[57]

Why now? The opening paragraphs of the Declaration certainly do not explain why the colonies had to become independent when they did so. The final, climactic grievance does. It explains what brought those clocks to strike in July 1776. This was no mystery: the stories that lay behind that grievance dominated the newspapers over those fifteen months. Some of those stories were real, some were rumored, and others were invented. But patriot leaders had put them there. They spent their efforts telling the American people that evil British agents, led by the king, were trying to destroy their liberty with the willing assistance of enslaved and Native peoples. These were the stories that convinced a majority of Americans to support the idea that "all political connection between them and the State of Great Britain is, and ought to be, totally dissolved."

CONCLUSION
FOUNDING STORIES

Human beings crave origin stories. They are an essential aspect of our existence; it is an inescapable way we try to make sense of our society, our planet, our lives, and our afterlives. Hollywood producers know this all too well: how many movies have been or will be made about how superheroes got their powers?

So it is with nations, none more so than the United States. Washington's triumph with the sword and Jefferson's achievement with the pen give America's founding a singular drama that other nations lack — or so we have boasted for more than two centuries. The events of 1776 are the cornerstone of American exceptionalism: from its very birth, the United States has been unlike anywhere else in the world.

But our heroic recounting of the events of 1775–1776 has missed much of the story. We have underestimated how much African Americans and Indians were on the minds of patriot political leaders (including but not limited to the so-called "founding fathers") at the moment of independence. Patriots were talking about these groups constantly in assembly houses and army councils, reading or writing letters and declaring about them. Very often, those writings would find their way into print. This underestimation has also translated into our not truly comprehending the stories that patriot leaders told the American people at the founding of the United States. American independence was justified, explained, realized, and made possible because of stories patriots told and retold about proxy enemies working with the king to destroy the Revolution. They submitted these reasons for why the thirteen colonies needed to be independent of King George. We cannot read the opening lines of the Declaration without including the twenty-seventh and climactic grievance. The words "all men are created equal," "pursuit of happiness," and "we hold these truths to be self-evident" can't be understood without "merciless Indian savages" and "domestic insurrectionists." Don't take my word for it: John Adams, Benjamin Franklin, and Thomas Jefferson said so.

Fusing these ideas about African Americans and Indians into the heart of the Declaration and the American founding was powerful enough. There was far more damage, though. This conclusion sketches the continued, compounded importance of these founding stories after July 4, 1776.

First, the stories did not go away after 1776. They were not fleeting. They did not expire, thrown out in the trash as last week's news. Whenever patriot publicists felt especially threatened, they embraced images of British officials using proxy enemies to destroy them. At the lowest points of the Revolutionary War — when the invading British force crushed them on Long Island, conquered New York City, and chased Washington all the way across New Jersey late in 1776; when General Burgoyne's army marched south from Canada in the summer of 1777 to sever New England; when the British captured Charleston and threatened to control the entire South in 1780; when Benedict Arnold committed his treason; and in the dark days just before the breakthrough at Yorktown — patriots returned again and again to these stories, believing they stood the best chance of mobilizing the populace to defend the Revolution.

One of the more famous examples occurred in the summer of 1777, when Natives attached to Burgoyne's invading army killed a young woman named Jane McCrea, who might or might not have been dressed in her wedding gown. McCrea's being "scalped and mangled in the most shocking manner," as General Horatio Gates eulogized her, featured in every single active newspaper in America. Only three events earned total coverage during the Revolution: Lexington, independence — and Jane McCrea. Patriot military and political leaders ensured that McCrea's name found its way to as much of the public as possible.[1]

Throughout the long war, patriot leaders pleaded with the American public to keep faith with the Revolution by never forgetting who their enemies really were. The best example of how patriot publicists made these stories durable and permanent is a curious assignment Congress gave their ambassador to France, Benjamin Franklin. They ordered Franklin to contract an artist in Paris to create thirty-five engravings for a child's schoolbook. As he described the job to a correspondent, Ambassador Franklin was to produce a book "to impress the minds of Children and Posterity with a deep sense of [Britain's] bloody and insatiable Malice and Wickedness." Those illustrations were to document — and preserve — British cruelties; the book itself was to be a catalog of suffering for future generations of American children to absorb from a very young age.[2]

Franklin enlisted the help of the marquis de Lafayette to help him craft what the two of them referred to as their "little book." Franklin and Lafayette

FIGURE 13. *"The Murder of Jane McCrea." By John Vanderlyn. 1804. Born in Kingston, New York, just as the Revolutionary War started, Vanderlyn grew up with the story of McCrea's death. His painting kept ideas about British-sponsored "merciless savages" murdering vulnerable white women at the heart of the romance surrounding the Revolution in the early years of the nineteenth century. Wadsworth Atheneum Museum of Art, Hartford, Conn. Purchased by Subscription, 1855.4*

drafted twenty-six detailed descriptions of proposed illustrations. The first eighteen are in Franklin's handwriting, Lafayette added six of his own, and Franklin then came up with the final two.[3]

Franklin's list started with fire. The first seven pictures were to depict various New England towns being blasted and set afire by the Royal Navy. Then, after two pictures about the mistreatment of prisoners, Franklin began a run of prints that centered on British proxies. The tenth illustration was to depict the following:

> Dunmore's hiring the Negroes to murder their Master's Families.
> A large House
> Blacks arm'd with Guns and Hangers
> Master and his Sons on the Ground dead,
> Wife and Daughters lifted up in the Arms of the Negroes as they are
> carrying off.

The next portrayed a similar scene, also meant to terrify young children. The Parisian engraver was to show "Savages killing and scalping the Frontier Farmers and their Families, Women and Children, English Officers mix'd with the Savages, and giving them Orders and encouraging them." Prints 13, 14, and 15 further developed this theme of British pleasure at the sight of American scalps. Print 13 focused on the governor of East Florida sitting at a table receiving the "Scalps of the Georgia People." Print 14 was the same scene, only with the commander at Fort Niagara in New York. Then it was the king's turn. Print 15 was to depict the secretary at war presenting George III with an "Acct. of Scalps. which he receives very graciously."[4]

Lafayette continued this bloody theme. His first contribution to the list recaptured one of the more infamous images of 1775: Philip Schuyler relating to Congress that the British had asked Natives to "feast on a Bostonian and drink his blood." Lafayette instructed the engraver to show American prisoners being "Roasted for a great festival where the Canadian indians are eating American flesh, Colonel [John] Buttler, an english officer Setting at table." Lafayette added more images involving proxy actions. Illustration 19 was another shocking scene: "British officers who being prisoners on parole are well Receiv'd in the Best American families, and take that opportunity of corrupting Negroes and Engaging them to desert from the house, to Robb, and even to Murder they Masters."[5]

The list of prints is a fascinating document of patriots' attempts to mobilize emotions in support of the war effort. Congress wanted Americans to remember British crimes, and these were the impressions Franklin and Lafayette decided upon. Both believed that British instigation of Blacks and Indians was essential to understanding the conflict. They sought to transform stories about "domestic insurrectionists" and "merciless savages" into indelible pictures that would instruct future generations about who tried to destroy liberty at the founding of the United States.

Although the "little book" never materialized, Franklin and Lafayette worked diligently on it for nearly two years. Franklin hired an engraver and had at least one image created by April 1780. He, especially, had high hopes for it. He envisioned these illustrations, "expressing every abominable Circumstance of [British] Cruelty and Inhumanity," to be the basis for the first coinage of the United States.[6]

You read that right: if Ben Franklin had his way, pictures of runaway slaves killing their masters and Native people eating Americans would have been on the United States' first nickels and dimes. Think about how you might call those coin tosses.

Long after independence, American political leaders and publicists returned again and again to the theme of British instigation of Natives and the enslaved. After his "little book" project fizzled, Franklin tried again in 1782. With the war seemingly over after Yorktown but no official peace treaty signed, Franklin was worried that Americans might forget all that had occurred and be lulled into offering the British easy terms. He had heard the word "reconciliation" in the air and was determined to stoke American fury. So, on a printing press that he had installed in his house in the Paris suburbs, Franklin made up a hoax. This was most certainly what we would call "fake news" today. He created an entirely fictional newspaper issue, called "Supplement to the Boston *Independent Chronicle*," which featured letters documenting the grisly discovery of bags upon bags of American scalps—boys', girls', women's, infants'—taken from the New York frontier, and how they were laid before George III with well-wishes from a Seneca chief that the king "may regard them and be refreshed." None of it was true, but it appeared in English newspapers and, soon, crossed the Atlantic and surfaced in several American prints.[7]

Other productions joined Franklin's hoax in the postwar years. Many of the earliest cultural productions of the new American republic, like John Trumbull's enormously popular epic poem *M'Fingal* and pieces by Philip Freneau, featured scenes of British officers instigating Indians and the enslaved. The first histories of the Revolution began to appear in the 1780s. These initial volumes were written by patriot leaders, many of whom were deeply invested in the broadcasting of these stories of proxy enemies, including David Ramsay, William Gordon, Jedidiah Morse, and Mercy Otis Warren.

Moreover, because of the ongoing rivalry between the new United States and Great Britain, these stories stayed relevant for decades. Because the British refused to leave their forts along the Great Lakes after the Treaty of Paris, Americans commonly believed that they were still instigating the continued Native unrest of the 1780s and 1790s. They were. American leaders on the frontier in the first years of the nineteenth century, like William Henry Harrison and Andrew Jackson, conceived of their battles with Native people as a continuation of the Revolutionary struggle. Harrison saw the British behind Tecumseh's growing resistance in the North in 1807, and Jackson saw their influence among the Creeks in the South. "There can remain no doubt," Jackson wrote to President Thomas Jefferson in 1808, that there were "agents of a foreign nation; exciting the creeks, to hostilities against the United States." "These horrid scenes bring fresh to our recollections, the influence, during the revolutionary war," Jackson continued. "That raised the scalping knife and Tomhawk, against our defenceless weoman and children—I have but little doubt but the present savage cruelty is excited from the same source."[8]

A second war with Britain, starting in 1812, brought many of these Revolution stories and images into American newspapers all over again. In asking Congress for a declaration of war against Britain, President James Madison all but plagiarized his friend Jefferson in the Declaration: "In reviewing the conduct of Great Britain towards the United States, our attention is necessarily drawn to the warfare just renewed by the Savages . . . a warfare which is known to spare neither age nor sex, and to be distinguished by features peculiarly shocking to humanity." In January 1813, along the Raisin River, a scene replayed that was very much like what had occurred four decades earlier at the Cedars. After they had defeated an American force in battle, British-allied Wyandot Indians plundered those who had suffered severe wounds and set fire to their shelters. Dozens of soldiers from Kentucky died in what would quickly be named the "River Raisin Massacre." In order to get their readers to understand the deep roots of British and Native treatment of suffering American frontiersmen, newspaper printers pulled out Benjamin Franklin's 1782 hoax, the "Supplement to the Boston *Independent Chronicle.*" Franklin's fake bags of scalps appeared again as "proof" of the treachery of the "Savage Allies of England."[9]

Just as newspaper printers resurrected Franklin's hoax, a British fleet under the command of Admiral George Cockburn sailed into the Chesapeake Bay, and history repeated itself for slaveholders in the tidewater, too. The British presence in the Chesapeake meant another possibility of escape

FIGURE 14. *"A Scene on the Frontiers as Practiced by the* Humane *British and Their*
Worthy *Allies." By William Charles. 1812. The connection between the British and*
Indians was a constant theme of the early American republic for decades after
the Revolution. Library of Congress Prints and Photographs Division.
https://www.loc.gov/item/2002708987

for enslaved people. "A considerable number of negroes belonging to Princess Ann[e] County, have at different times eloped from their owners and
gone on board the British men of war," reported the *Daily National Intelli-*
gencer in May 1813. "One would have thought from the treatment which the
fathers of these deluded wretches met with, by deserting the British last war,
that they would have been deterred from such a course," opined a correspondent from Norfolk, "but it seems they have forgot how the great Lord Dunmore enticed the Princess Ann[e] negroes away from their masters, with fine
promises, and afterwards shipped them off to Jamaica."[10]

Reports were nearly identical to those in 1775 with just the names
changed. Dunmore stalked Virginia again. A few papers even resurrected
primary sources here, too, including a letter to Colonel William Woodford,
dated November 28, 1775, which provided details for how Americans could
battle British predators. When thousands of enslaved people in the Chesapeake ran to British lines again, they featured in the forgotten third verse of
Francis Scott Key's "Star Spangled Banner":

No refuge could save the hireling and slave
From the terror of flight or the gloom of the grave.
And the star-spangled banner — O! Long may it wave,
O'er the land of the free and the home of the brave.

As one historian has noted, "Key regarded the land of the free and the home of the brave as properly a white man's republic. In this sentiment, he expressed the consensus of his contemporaries." This made "The Star Spangled Banner" a truly national anthem, one not born out of battling the British in 1814 but arising from the founding itself. Key's reference to hirelings and slaves as having no place in America was an idea already four decades old.[11]

"Hireling" for Key meant the lowly British private soldier who donned the red coat for a paycheck. This was, of course, in contrast to the mythological American citizen-soldier who, ever since the minutemen at Concord and Bunker Hill, put his life at risk for principles. No one could call these men "hirelings." But, in 1776, the term "hireling" referred to the thousands of German mercenaries whose services King George purchased to put down the American rebellion. The news of their coming touched off the process for independence. What happened to them, the original hirelings?

In the summer and fall of 1776, as British and German troops swept Washington's men out of New York City and knocked them clear across New Jersey, they seemed a terrifying, unstoppable force that would quickly extinguish the Revolution. Patriot leader James Wilson wrote about their "great Inhumanity" in New York, while another of his colleagues in Congress screeched about the "ungovernable Brutality" of "those Men monsters the Hessians." Patriot newspapers especially publicized any evidence of their sexual assaults on innocent American women. "The Hessians" were a chief reason why the end of 1776 was what Thomas Paine labeled the "times that try men's souls."[12]

Then they disappeared. Once George Washington surprised them in the famous Christmas raid on Trenton and captured nearly one thousand Hessians, they stopped being so fearsome. Mary Katherine Goddard, printer of the *Maryland Journal*, summed it up in a poem:

The man who submits, without striking a blow,
May be said, in a sense, no danger to know:
I pray then, what harm, by the humble submission,
At Trenton was done to the standard of Hessian?

This was the universal sentiment after 1776. After Trenton, they ceased being effective, fearsome British proxies, and patriot leaders all but stopped talking about them. For the remainder of the war, whenever patriot newspapers mentioned Hessian soldiers, it was almost exclusively about how they, too, were the dupes of monarchical tyranny, fellow sufferers who could (and would) be incorporated into the American republic if they threw down their weapons.[13]

The silence that held on the Hessians after 1776 is astounding. In their list of illustrations for British atrocities, Franklin and Lafayette did not consider including German mercenaries. There were no Hessians in their "little book." This silence mattered: once they stopped telling frightening stories about the German mercenaries, a pathway for their redemption opened. The Hessians were now portrayed as sympathetic creatures in their own right — something enslaved and Native peoples did not receive in print during the war — and therefore deserving of a place in the United States. When between five and six thousand of them chose to remain in America after the war, they did not have much trouble settling down in communities, becoming, as one historian put it, "welcome members of the American fold," able to "wager their futures on the new republic."[14]

Over the eighteenth century, as thousands of German-speaking immigrants had arrived in America, a dislike and distrust of them had grown apace. Benjamin Franklin famously worried in a 1751 pamphlet that Pennsylvania was rapidly becoming a "Colony of *Aliens,* who will shortly be so numerous as to Germanize us instead of our Anglifying them, and will never adopt our Language or Customs, any more than they can acquire our Complexion." Franklin's reference to Germans as an alien force that resisted assimilation illustrates this distrust. But what did he mean by "acquire our Complexion"?[15]

Franklin went on to talk about whiteness in the next paragraph of the pamphlet. "The Number of purely white People in the World is proportionably very small," he continued.

> All Africa is black or tawny. Asia chiefly tawny. America (exclusive of the new Comers) wholly so. And in Europe, the Spaniards, Italians, French, Russians and Swedes, are generally of what we call a swarthy Complexion; as are the Germans also, the Saxons only excepted, who with the English, make the principal Body of White People on the Face of the Earth. I could wish their Numbers were increased.

Franklin did not consider Germans as "white." That this statement may surprise is a function of how concepts and definitions of race developed in

America over the nineteenth and twentieth centuries. But part of the reason the Germans soon joined the English among the United States' "principal Body of White People" is a result of the American Revolution. Independence and the creation of a new republic based on citizenship refigured and reshaped what race meant in the polity and opened a door for Germans to stop being seen as unwelcome aliens.[16]

How this happened is important. Part of the reason Germans were readily accepted was because they had shed the label of "men Monsters." It would be nearly half a century until American readers would be terrified by a Hessian soldier again: the ghostly horseman who stalked Ichabod Crane in Washington Irving's horror story "The Legend of Sleepy Hollow" (1820) was a Hessian soldier who had lost his head to a patriot cannonball. By then, the "man Monsters" had become nostalgic legends of the American past.

Second, these stories guided policy during the Revolution. Another reason stories told and not told during the early years of the Revolutionary War mattered was because they affected the shape and outcome of that conflict itself. Patriot leaders continued to tell the stories we've examined here long after 1776, adding new characters (villains, really) and scenes. The repetition of these stories had an effect of closing off possibilities during the war, limiting the radical scope of the Revolution.

This happened almost immediately, as we have seen, in the tussle late in 1775 over whether free Black veterans would be allowed to stay in Washington's army. Stories would continue to shape political and military policy after 1776.

Take, for example, Pennsylvania's gradual abolition law of 1780. Long considered the high point of patriots' actually living up to their rhetoric of liberty and freedom, the Pennsylvania abolition bill must be seen in its wartime context. Quakers began pressuring the Pennsylvania legislature late in 1778 to write a gradual emancipation law, and a draft came up for readings once in the spring and again in the autumn of 1779. But between those moments, British commander Henry Clinton had issued a proclamation promising freedom to any rebel slaves who reached the king's lines as the British moved to carry the war to the Deep South; nearby, African American partisans led by a notorious runaway slave named "Colonel Tye" had wreaked havoc on patriot militia in New Jersey. Patriot publicists had, of course, broadcast widely the news of Clinton's proclamation—instantly recalling Dunmore's and joining the two together—and roared that Tye needed to be eliminated.[17]

Luckily for the seven thousand enslaved men, women, and children in

Pennsylvania who stood to become free after 1808, these stories did not carry enough political weight to stop the gradual abolition bill from becoming law on March 1, 1780. But the bill did have its critics (nearly 40 percent of the assembly voted against), and they invoked proxy stories as evidence that abolishing slavery was a terrible idea while the British yet menaced America. Twenty-three concerned members of that legislature filed a petition protesting that the law's "pernicious consequences," which might have an effect on "any state or states in the union . . . tend to weaken that body." They were just as worried about what might happen if all of Pennsylvania's men marched south to fight British redcoats: this law might "lead the negroes of these states, to a demand of an immediate and intire freedom, or to other disorders that may end in the greatest cruelties, which an ignorant, and perhaps desperate people, *stimulated by the enemies of their masters,* can be capable of committing."[18]

The enslaved in New Jersey would not be as fortunate. Having had success in Pennsylvania, Quakers in New Jersey began sending petitions to the assembly in the spring of 1780 to take up their own gradual emancipation bill. When that body refused to touch them, proponents of the bill, especially Quaker John Cooper, kept up the pressure by sending essays to the two New Jersey newspapers. Cooper said that Americans must follow the ideals of the Declaration of Independence or else "our words must rise up in judgment against us." But opponents quickly countered, and throughout the fall and winter of 1780–1781, a lively debate ensued. Essayists using pseudonyms like "A Whig," "A Lover of true Justice," and "A Friend to Justice" argued for what they thought the Revolution was about: the meaning of equality, property rights, human nature, and the threat emancipated slaves posed to the public. On this final point, writers against emancipation forwarded the examples of Colonel Tye and other Black partisans as compelling evidence for postponing any talk of emancipation until after the war. One writer asked where Quakers thought freed people would go next. Emancipated slaves would immediately revert to savagery, he figured, and *"O horrida bella"*—they would join forces with other proxies. If "200,000 Negroes" joined Indians, they would "sweep our land by outsallies of murder and rapine. Then will the shrieks of murdered children, and the lamentations of assassinated friends . . . force conviction upon us of the evils we have brought upon ourselves, our friends and country." These arguments won: the cause of abolition in New Jersey—as it would in New York—had to wait until long after the emergencies of the Revolutionary War had ended.[19]

Starting in 1775, proxy stories had become a foundational narrative for the United States. Only a few months before Lexington, Thomas Jefferson had written that abolition of the slave trade was the "great object of desire" throughout the American colonies. That "desire" matched up with the Revolutionaries' rhetoric of universal rights, or at least John Cooper thought so. But the wartime common cause appeal also provided arguments that undermined and diluted that radical universalist impulse. It cut against the grain, giving opponents of emancipation critical ammunition: stories, narratives, and images that connected emancipated slaves with the nation's enemies. As of 1780, the scorecard was mixed: "all men are created equal" had worked in Pennsylvania, but "domestic insurrectionists" had aided in the continuation of slavery in New Jersey.[20]

For another example of how stories told—or not told—shaped policy during the Revolution, we have to take up the issue of the "good Indians" who assisted the United States. When the Declaration said that Native peoples were "merciless savages whose known rule of warfare is an undistinguished destruction of all ages, sexes, and conditions," there wasn't an asterisk that said: except the ones who are helping us. Patriot publicists created the notion that all Native peoples helped the British at the moment, but they did not talk very much (or loudly) about Delaware leaders like Captain White Eyes, John Killbuck, and Captain Pipe, or about Shawnee leaders like Cornstalk, who were the Americans' best friends in the Ohio country. Nor did they talk very much (or loudly) about the sacrifices the Stockbridge or Oneidas made while serving in the Continental army. Unless you were in that army or watched it march by your house, you would have precious little idea how many Native peoples fought for the United States.

Of course, they were there, but American newspapers very rarely mentioned them. Notice of Oneida and Tuscarora scouts helping American forces did appear in some patriot newspapers, but when a party of fifty Stockbridge attached to the Continental army ran into a British ambush near Kingsbridge, New York, and thirty-seven of them were killed (a horrendous death rate of 74 percent!), notice of the tragedy appeared only in a few loyalist newspapers. No patriot papers mentioned their sacrifice. When compared to the oceans of ink they *did* feature about Indians helping the British, these were tiny drops.[21]

The notion that all Indians were enemies nurtured military decisions, most notoriously the 1779 invasion of Iroquois country led by General John Sullivan. "The immediate object" of Sullivan's campaign, as Washington's orders went, was the "total destruction and devastation of their settlements and the capture of as many prisoners of every age and sex as possible. It will be essential to ruin their crops now in the ground and prevent their planting more." As they gathered together before setting off in pursuit of these ghastly orders, Sullivan's officer corps celebrated the nation's third anniversary of independence. After raising toasts to Congress, the French alliance, and George Washington, the staff officers proclaimed, "Civilization or Death to all American Savages!" They soon would begin to attempt the latter, wreaking havoc throughout Iroquoia, burning hundreds of houses in seven towns and destroying thousands of acres of ripening fields.[22]

At the same time, the drastic underreporting of the service of Natives allied to the United States not only contributed to policy moves like Sullivan's campaign; it also closed down potential avenues for alternative decisions. The chances of "civilization" rather than death were foreclosed by stories not told.

One such example is this missed opportunity: in 1778, a delegation of "friendly" Delaware Indians met with U.S. officials at Fort Pitt to work out a treaty of alliance. The commissioners, sent by the Continental Congress, reached an accord that included a stunning provision. To counteract growing concerns about British intrigues in the Ohio Valley, patriot leaders at Fort Pitt extended an offer of statehood. They invited the Delaware leaders, including White Eyes, Killbuck, and Pipe, "to join the present confederation, and to form a state whereof the Delaware nation shall be the head, and have a representation in Congress." This was a striking, radical option, a new way to make a place for Native people inside the new republic: a pathway to citizenship.[23]

It would be an illusion. Patriot leaders outside Fort Pitt did not share the commissioners' inclusive vision. When the treaty reached Congress a few weeks later, it was assigned to a committee and never heard from again. One would assume that patriot leaders would broadcast such important news: that a crucial group of Ohio Indians had reached amicable terms with the United States. But they did not. The Delaware treaty conference left no traces in patriot newspapers. For all that Americans far from the backcountry knew, it had never happened.

Perhaps patriot leaders didn't want to publish details about pro-American Native leaders because they kept getting murdered. Both Cornstalk and White Eyes were killed in suspicious circumstances in 1778. This was another legacy of not telling those stories: because they didn't talk much at all about Natives allied to the United States, Americans in the backcountry felt not only allowed but encouraged to kill them.

That construction armed settlers with a lethal new weapon: American patriotism.

In the 1860s, American politicians and military officers began to say out loud, "The only good Indian is a dead one." This brutal notion, however, had its origins in the Revolution. Patriot leaders looked the other way when people killed Natives—even "good ones"—in the backcountry during and after the Revolution. They did not investigate or prosecute what they knew were crimes. When Pennsylvania militia officers voted to murder more than ninety Native men, women, and children by bludgeoning each one on the head with mallets at Gnadenhutten in 1782, patriot leaders—including Benjamin Franklin—expressed outrage and disgust. But they didn't do anything about it. In fact, 1782 would become the bloodiest year of the Revolutionary War, in no small part because Ohio Indians, themselves outraged by what had happened at Gnadenhutten, did take action, carrying horrendous violence across the Kentucky frontier, mostly in revenge for those brutal murders.[24]

Those 1782 attacks would serve to deepen the legend of one of those Kentuckians: Daniel Boone. When schoolteacher John Filson published his book *The Discovery, Settlement, and Present State of Kentucke* in 1784, an appendix featured a thirty-three-page narrative entitled "The Adventures of Col. Daniel Boon." Thus was born an American folktale. What happened in those pages that so resonated with the American public? Throughout Filson's rendering, Natives all appear as British proxies whose "savage minds were inflamed to mischief" by the king's Indian agents. They act the role of merciless savages perfectly. Boone documents their treachery in battle and "savage treatment" of the "tender women, and helpless children, [who] fell victims to their cruelty." The heroic Kentucky frontiersmen, however, stand above the fray. Boone is the opposite of the British instigators and Indian proxies. As Filson presents him, Boone possesses what the Indians cannot: civic responsibility, restraint, and humanity in war.[25]

Before the Revolution, few people viewed Daniel Boone this way. American frontiersmen were seen as troublemakers. They caused problems all over the place, destabilizing jurisdictions in the New Hampshire Grants, the Wyoming Valley, and the Ohio country. Newspaper articles referred to them as worse than savages. The Revolution transformed men like Boone: when they killed Indians, they were helping secure the United States, protecting it from British-allied Indians. As far as most Americans had understood during the Revolution, *all* Indians had been the king's allies. Patriot leaders had chosen not to publish stories about Cornstalk or White Eyes, so men who killed Indians, whether it was Daniel Boone at the battle of Blue Licks or the Pennsylvanians at Gnadenhutten, were helping the common cause. Banditti no longer, Boone and his fellow Kentuckians were now pioneers. As such, they had moved to the center of America's emerging myth about its manifest continental destiny.

Third, the proxy stories foreclosed alternatives after the war was over. We need to keep the contingency, the arbitrariness of these stories, in the front of our minds. Patriot leaders *chose* to broadcast stories about "merciless savages." They *chose* not to broadcast stories about "good" Indians. They *chose* not to tell stories about German mercenaries after Trenton. These decisions nourished a particular interpretation about who deserved to be "an American" and who did not.

The consequences and aftereffects of these proxy stories gripped the second session of the first Federal Congress as they gathered in New York City in February 1790. The first U.S. Congress took up the task of giving life to one of its constitutionally enumerated powers: establishing a uniform rule of naturalization. This issue of adding new members to the republic was a critical and controversial one. It went to the heart of what it meant to be an American citizen.

The assumptions that framed their debate over naturalization are revealing. The members of the House of Representatives spent a great deal of time discussing some issues, such as appropriate residency requirements, stipulations for purchasing land, barriers for officeholding, and the constitutional question of whether the Federal government could dictate these rules to the states. They said anyone who would be added to "the American people" had to be "person[s] of good character." What they did not question, however, was the key phrase that led to the eventual Naturalization Act of 1790: "that any Alien being a free white person" would be eligible to become an American citizen.[26]

People who were "free" and "white"—the only people Congress deemed worthy of enjoying the full fruits of citizenship—were the only ones with such character. Thanks to their rescue of the common cause, the French qualified; in fact, one Congressman made this plain, arguing on the floor that even Frenchmen, "brought up under an absolute monarchy, evinced their love of liberty in the late arduous struggle." "Many of them are now worthy citizens, who esteem and venerate the principles of our revolution."[27]

Former German mercenaries—people whom Ben Franklin did not see as "white" in 1751—qualified, too. A perfect example of the "man monsters" redemption is the story of Philip Phile (Pfeil). Phile was one of the near-one thousand Hessians captured at Trenton. He was a corporal, but he was also a violinist. After the war, he decided to stay in America and composed a tune entitled "President's March" to celebrate the election of President

George Washington. Choruses of singers had serenaded the new chief executive with Phile's song *in Trenton* on his way from Mount Vernon to his 1789 inauguration in New York City. Later, another former patriot publicist and political leader, Francis Hopkinson, would attach lyrics to Phile's tune, and it became better known as "Hail Columbia," America's unofficial national anthem until 1931, when Congress bestowed official honors on Francis Scott Key's hymn about hirelings and slaves' inability to defeat the land of the free. They chose a song about proxies over one written by another proxy, a man sent to America to stop the Revolution. Thanks to patriot leaders like Washington, who heard this new song written for and about him, Phile became a comfortable, welcome, naturalized American citizen.[28]

Who did not qualify is, of course, apparent. The Naturalization Act did not address the chances for free, nonwhite people who already met the residency requirements to become citizens. Alternative paths during the Revolution that might have led to Indian citizenship, such as the idea of Indian statehood floated in 1778, were not followed. At bottom, Natives suffered from the interpretation that they had, as a whole, fought against the United States and therefore would not want to join it, even if invited.

What about free African Americans? Either through their own efforts to press for emancipation via freedom suits or through state legislatures or courts passing gradual abolition laws, thousands of enslaved people were now free in the 1770s–1780s. But what that freedom meant was difficult for many in the United States to imagine. In the 1780s, writers forwarded more plans for emancipation, but only if accompanied by wholesale removal. As one Virginia planter opined in the spring of 1790, "It would never do to allow them *all* the privileges of citizens" because they would form a "separate interest from the rest of the community." Jefferson raised these issues in his *Notes on the State of Virginia,* too, believing the wrongs of the colonial past and "new provocations"—i.e., the Revolutionary War—had poisoned the chances of peace and community. Emancipated slaves could never be loyal, the thinking went; they would be perpetual threats to the safety of the union. They did not have the right character.[29]

On March 22, 1790, all discussion in the Senate about the Naturalization Bill ended, and the draft went to President Washington's desk for his signature. That afternoon, Pennsylvania Senator William Maclay wondered what all the noise emanating from the House of Representatives was about. Upon entering their chamber, he recorded the scene with wide eyes:

> The house have certainly greatly debased their dignity. Using base
> invective indecorous language 3 or 4 up at a time. manifest signs of

passion. the most disorderly Wandering, in their Speeches, telling Stories, private anecdotes etc etc. I know not What may come of it. but there seems a General discontent among the Members. and many of them do not Hesitate to declare, that the Union Must fall to pieces, at the rate we go on.

It seems something had lit a fire under the Congressmen on that March afternoon. What had caused such a shocking disturbance?[30]

The ruckus in the House was a debate over three petitions that demanded the Federal government close the twenty-year window mandated by the Constitution allowing the international slave trade to continue to the United States. That several members of the petitions' Quaker sponsors were sitting in the gallery to apply pressure made things more intense. Worse, one of the petitions came under the signature of the president of the Pennsylvania Abolition Society: Benjamin Franklin. It was exceedingly difficult to ignore this issue with that person's name attached to it. No wonder things got bitter, personal, and passionate very fast.

Southern congressmen wondered aloud whether the eighty-four-year-old Franklin had gone insane. As he was a member of the convention that drafted that document, one of them suggested Franklin "ought to have known the Constitution better." It was "astonishing," one South Carolina delegate sneered, "to see Dr. Franklin taking the lead in a business which looked so much like a persecution of the southern inhabitants."[31]

Southerners attacked the Quakers as supporters of the British during the late war. "Are [these Quakers] not the very men who, a few short years ago were the avowed friends and supporters of the most abject slavery?" queried South Carolina's Aedanus Burke. "They, in the needful hour," Burke continued, "were the enemies of America, but now assume another mask, that of enemies to slavery." A Virginia representative stated that he hoped his colleagues would not "gratify people who never had been friendly to the independence of America." A Georgian Congressman stressed that lots of people shared these anti-Quaker attitudes: "Public opinion has declared them, throughout America, to have been enemies to our cause and constitution." Finally, another deepened this accusation: "In time of war they would not defend their country from the enemy, and in time of peace they were interfering in the concerns of others, and doing every thing in their power to excite the slaves in the southern states to insurrection."[32]

Here was the vital linkage. The southerners' line of attack was significant. Unlike the elderly John Adams, these southerners wanted their colleagues and constituents to remember the Revolutionary War. The war was proof that the new republic must remain committed to slavery. What made the recent, terrible memories of the war so important was that former tories were now taking on many aspects of their British enemy: namely, exciting "tumults, seditions, and insurrections" throughout the South. Emancipation, Burke testified, would bring the "greatest cruelty" to the Africans; "Of this we have had experience in South Carolina in 1780." He reminded his listeners that Lord Cornwallis, "A very intimate old friend of the Quakers," had issued a proclamation giving freedom

> to all the Africans who should join his army. After plundering the country, they crowded to him from all quarters, but the invitation in a short time proved one of the greatest calamities to them. Thousands perished miserably by hunger and disease, exhibiting a melancholy example, to sh[o]w, how totally incapable *he* is of making a proper use of his new gained liberty, who has been brought up in the habits of slavery.

The British had already attempted these "cruel" emancipation schemes during the war, and now, the southern Congressmen argued, Quakers were following in their footsteps.[33]

Franklin's prominent signature on the petition did not deter Burke and his colleagues from smearing the Quakers who surrounded them in the galleries as British sympathizers. The aged Franklin, only a few weeks from death, took umbrage with these men questioning his sanity and fired back in a typically Franklinian way. Soon, he would turn these southern proslavery arguments against them, ventriloquizing their words into the voice of an imaginary African Muslim slaveholder, "Sidi Mehemet Ibrahim." "Ibrahim" then defended his keeping of white Christian slaves with Burke's own thoughts. This would be Franklin's final satire, and it is a pointed, brilliant attack on the southern congressmen.[34]

But Burke and his allies could never have made those arguments in the first place if it hadn't been for Franklin — who, as we have seen, worked harder than any other patriot leader to put before the American public the accusation that evil British agents were working with proxy enemies to stop the Revolution. Franklin was the most creative publicist of the proxy image. For the last fifteen years, he had labored to connect British tyranny and Black resistance. When Aedanus Burke invoked those images in the spring of 1790 to keep the United States in the international slave trade, he had Franklin to thank for their discursive resonance.

All the screaming and name-calling convinced House Speaker James

Madison to table the Quakers' petitions. There would be no closing of the twenty-year window written into the Constitution that allowed the United States to participate in the Atlantic slave trade. The common cause argument had armed slaveholders with a new rhetorical weapon: attack any abolitionists as pro-British enemies of the Revolution. American patriotism led men on the frontier to believe violence against British-allied Natives was an act in support of their country. It also provided slavery's defenders with a way to justify a continued commitment to holding millions of men, women, and children in bondage. The persistence of those war stories a decade after Yorktown helped foreclose policy alternatives for the early republic that might have been more inclusive.

What lay at the bottom of this argument? Senator Maclay summed it up: "Many [Congressmen] do not Hesitate to declare, that the Union Must fall to pieces, at the rate we go on." The need for the states to remain united did not abate with the Treaty of Paris. Throughout the so-called "critical period" of the 1780s, political leaders were more convinced than ever that peace in North America depended on the sustenance of a strong union. If the states were disunited, the men who eventually framed the Constitution argued, the continent would devolve into Europe: the states would make alliances with one another (or, worse, with foreign powers), and soon they would be at war again. The union had always been the most important thing. Patriot leaders, starting in 1775, prioritized it over any other considerations. This had not changed by 1790, and it remained the case throughout the years of the early republic. Contentious issues, like antislavery, threatened this fragile consensus, and even fifteen years after the start of the Revolutionary War, political leaders were just as terrified that even the slightest disagreement might make the union "fall to pieces." Abolition could very well disrupt the sweet sound of thirteen clocks chiming as one.[35]

Finally, these war stories mattered because patriot leaders decided to create a new republic based on citizenship. Of course, these things had happened before. This book does not argue that Adams, Jefferson, Franklin, and their colleagues invented racial stereotypes or prejudices about enslaved and Native peoples. As far back as the earliest encounters between Africans, Indians, and Europeans, there were cultural conceptions of difference.

Episodes of violence, moreover, intensified these prejudices. Historians have pointed to a variety of moments to explain when colonists' fears about violent Indians and Africans hardened into a racial ideology. They have suggested a host of different times and places: the 1622 massacre in Virginia, King Philip's War, Bacon's Rebellion, the 1741 New York City slave insurrection, the Seven Years' War, Pontiac's Rebellion, and the Paxton Boys massacre.

They are not wrong; all of those events did sharpen ideas of difference and provided more images to stoke colonial fears. By 1775, when patriot leaders reached into the toolbox of colonial ideology to shore up what *was* something new under the sun—the union of thirteen suspicious, jealous colonies—those stereotypes, expectations, and nightmares were lying right on top, in plain sight and ready to go. They were what colonists had in common long before the British tried to reform their empire.

But the Revolution was unlike any of those previous events.

The Revolution was not just any colonial episode of violence—it created the United States of America. Never before had those moments been accompanied by the creation of a new political regime. Here, again, is the contingent nature of 1775–1776: we take for granted the incredible decisions that patriot leaders made during those chaotic months. Patriot leaders did not have to do so, but they transformed their entire theory of government. When they roundly rejected monarchy and instead chose to create independent republics, they also rejected the theory of subjecthood in favor of citizenship.

Those political choices are what made the Revolution different. They were not part of the experience of the Seven Years' War or King Philip's War, or Bacon's Rebellion. The nation-making, constitution-making side of the Revolution cannot be overlooked in our histories of race-making in the eighteenth century.

Jurists early in the seventeenth century defined what an English subject is. They ruled that all subjects are theoretically equal under the king's authority. Only the monarch can make distinctions between the statuses of his or her subjects: kings or queens can raise people up (by making them a duke or earl), but only they have that power. Citizenship, on the other hand, allows for people to decide who belongs to the community and who does not. Inclusion confers certain privileges, including participation in the political process, the ability to buy and sell property, and pathways of seeking justice. In short, citizenship is a club. Members can choose whom they let in and whom they exclude.

But no one really understood what this looked like in 1776. It would take decades for politicians, lawyers, and judges to determine what it meant to be an American citizen, who qualified, and what they got for it. The Naturalization Act of 1790 was an important signpost, but that road has been a long and twisting one, and we have not reached its terminus yet.

This is why the stories patriot leaders decided to tell and not tell still matter to us today. I am not saying that Jefferson, Adams, Franklin, and Washington created these ideas about race. Rather, they weaponized them. When they reached into that ideological toolbox to find some ways of getting Americans to see one another in common and solidify a union, these were the ideas they selected. But, because they were doing so at a time of political regime change, at a revolutionary moment of nation making, they not only sharpened those tools; they refurbished and updated them for the new republic, then cemented them in the cornerstone of the United States.

Another of those signposts for the definition of an American citizen came in 1858 with *Dred Scott v. Sanford*. In that landmark Supreme Court decision, Chief Justice Roger B. Taney declared that African Americans were never included in the American republic. For Taney, as one historian put it, African Americans "had never been citizens of the United States . . . because they did not belong to the sovereign people for whom the Declaration of Independence was written." The *Dred Scott* decision rings like a thunderclap in our ears. Taney's statement seems a deliberate provocation, a proslavery innovation, a southern gauntlet thrown down that would soon spark civil war. It was—and it wasn't. In some ways it was a codification, a formalization of that notion of exclusion, first raised in 1775–1776.[36]

Just like Aedanus Burke in the 1790 firestorm over closing the slave trade loophole, Taney could not have made those arguments if it hadn't been for patriot leaders who put those stories at the heart of the American founding. In 1775–1776, stories of violence on slave plantations or on the frontier were no longer tales from the colonial past. Instead, they were Revolution stories—founding stories—freighted with theories of self-government, American patriotism, and the ongoing construction of a republican regime based on the hazy principles of citizenship. Although they sprang from those older sources and retained much of the same, terrifying power that they held in 1676 or 1741, these founding stories of Indian massacres and slave insurrections would take on a permanence, unlike those that came before.

The Naturalization Act of 1790 stipulated that a "person of good character" who would "support the Constitution of the United States" could become an American citizen. After all the proclamations, newspaper reports, children's books of atrocities, and declarations of independence that connected "black," "Indian," and "enemy," Congress did not need to include the words "free" and "white" when defining who constituted "we the people." Those words were well understood at the founding and a quarter century before Dred Scott was born. The thousands of free Blacks created by liberalized manumission statutes and gradual emancipation schemes in the Revolutionary era would struggle to find a place in the new United States. They joined

Native peoples, even those who served with honor in the Continental army, as outsiders inside the American republic.

Republicanism and exclusion are inseparable. Not only is white supremacy an ideology; it is intertwined with and dependent upon the republicanism that was born in 1776. It would gain speed and power over the next century, as slavery spread across North America and Native peoples suffered continental dispossession, and more voices came to clarify what it meant to be — and not to be — an American citizen. But that future, and our past, couldn't have happened without the stories that brought those thirteen clocks to ring out on July 4, 1776.

When we celebrate the good things about America, we often say the best parts of us come from those opening statements in the Declaration. There is a concreteness to that, a piece of parchment that we can point to as proof that Americans stand for life, liberty, and the pursuit of happiness. Yet, when we realize there are difficult, tragic, and uncomfortable parts to our history, we often struggle to find concrete things. We have been reticent to suggest that perhaps those things all stem from the very same sources and involve the very same people.

When the war was won, the so-called "founding fathers" wanted the "candid world" to believe that only the first paragraphs of the Declaration — with the lofty sentiments of self-evident truths and inalienable rights — animated the colonists' fight for liberty and was the foundation of the United States. They wanted Americans to remember only a certain segment of the fight for independence: the heroic, the liberating, and the creative. As John Adams put it in 1818, *"This radical change in the principles, opinions, sentiments, and affections of the people, was the real American Revolution."* We have, for too long, taken Adams and his colleagues at their word. What they wanted us to forget — and we largely have — was that the drive to have thirteen colonial clocks strike as one was also a campaign stamped by the vicious, the confining, and the destructive. That, too, was the real Revolution for many Americans, then and since. Our founding story is a complicated one. We have the capacity to understand that. We just have to look.[37]

NOTES

INTRODUCTION

1. John Adams to Hezekiah Niles, Quincy, Mass., Feb. 13, 1818, in Charles Francis Adams, ed., *The Works of John Adams, Second President of the United States . . .* , X (Boston, 1856), 282–286, esp. 282.

2. JA to Thomas Jefferson, Quincy, Aug. 24, 1815, ibid., 172–174, esp. 172, 283.

3. JA to Niles, Quincy, Feb. 13, 1818, ibid., 283 (emphasis added).

4. Adams's original expression to Jefferson that the real revolution occurred long before 1775 appears on page 1 of what is, arguably, the most influential book ever written on the Revolution: Bernard Bailyn's landmark *Ideological Origins of the American Revolution* (Cambridge, Mass., 1967). Bailyn was so enamored with Adams's interpretation that he prefaced chapters 1 and 5 with his thoughts. Adams's 1815 letter to Jefferson appears before chapter 1, and his 1818 letter to Niles (which expresses the same thoughts nearly verbatim), before chapter 5. See *Ideological Origins*, 1, 160.

5. Gordon S. Wood, *The Radicalism of the American Revolution* (New York, 1991), 4, 169–171; Robert A. Gross, *The Minutemen and Their World* (New York, 1976), 153.

6. David Ramsay, *The History of the American Revolution,* ed. Lester H. Cohen, 2 vols. ([1789]; rpt. Indianapolis, 1990), II, 633. Ramsay's quotation has become so universal, in fact, that Joseph M. Adelman has noted its use by more than 150 books about the Revolution; see Adelman, *Revolutionary Networks: The Business and Politics of Printing the News, 1763–1789* (Baltimore, 2019), 2.

7. Benjamin Franklin to Richard Price, Passy, June 13, 1782, *PBF,* XXXVII, 472–473.

8. BF to Jonathan Shipley, Philadelphia, May 15, 1775, *LDC,* I, 350.

CHAPTER 1

1. "Americus," *Boston Gazette,* Jan. 18, 1768.

2. Edes wrote up his account of the confrontation in the *Boston Gazette,* Jan. 25, 1768. Adams's letter appeared as "Populus," ibid., Feb. 1, 1768. For more on Mein's battles with Boston patriots, see Arthur M. Schlesinger, *Prelude to Independence: The Newspaper War on Britain, 1764–1776* (New York, 1958), 104–107; Hiller B. Zobel, *The Boston Massacre* (New York, 1970), 66–67, 156–163; and Richard Archer, *As if an Enemy's Country: The British Occupation of Boston and the Origins of Revolution* (New York, 2010), 144–165.

3. *Gill v. Mein,* in L. Kinvin Wroth and Hiller B. Zobel, eds., *Legal Papers of John Adams,* series 3 of *The Adams Papers* (Cambridge, Mass., 1965), I, 151–157.

4. Archer, *As if an Enemy's Country,* 162–163.

5. Zobel, *Boston Massacre,* 154; entry for Sept. 3, 1769, in L. H. Butterfield, ed., *Diary and Autobiography of John Adams,* series 1 of *The Adams Papers* (Cambridge, Mass., 1961), I, 343.

6. Zobel, *Boston Massacre,* 154.

7. *Boston Gazette,* Sept. 4, 1769.

8. James Madison to William Bradford, [Jr.], March 1775, in *PJM,* I, 141–142.

9. Peter Timothy to Benjamin Franklin, [Charleston, S.C.], June 12, 1777, *PBF,* XXIV, 155.

10. In Boston: *Boston Gazette,* Sept. 4, 1769; *Boston Chronicle,* Sept. 11, 1769; *Boston News-Letter,* Sept. 14, 1769. Outside Boston: *Essex Gazette,* Sept. 12, 1769; *Connecticut Gazette,* Sept. 15, 1769; *Connecticut Journal,* Sept. 15, 1769; *New-Hampshire Gazette,* Sept. 15, 22, 1769; *Providence Gazette,* Sept. 16, 1769; *New-York Gazette,* Sept. 18, 1769; *Newport Mercury,* Sept. 18, 1769; *Pennsylvania Chronicle,* Sept. 18, 1769; *Pennsylvania Journal,* Sept. 21, 1769; *New-York Journal,* Sept. 21, 1769; *Georgia Gazette,* Sept. 27, 1769; *Virginia Gazette* (Purdie & Dixon), Sept. 28, 1769.

11. Benedict Anderson, *Imagined Communities: Reflections on the Origins and Spread of Nationalism* ([1983]; rpt. London, 2016), 35–36.

12. For much more analysis of the Bradfords' book and what was in the *Pennsylvania Journal* issues they published in 1775, see Robert G. Parkinson, *The Common Cause: Creating Race and Nation in the American Revolution* (Williamsburg, Va., and Chapel Hill, N.C., 2016), 44–77, 704–729.

13. E. Jennifer Monaghan, *Learning to Read and Write in Colonial America* (Amherst, Mass., 2005), 3, 384–385; "Publication," in David D. Hall, *Cultures of Print: Essays in the History of the Book* (Amherst, Mass., 1996), 16. For an argument about the staying power of oral and other dramaturgic communication modes, see Rhys Isaac, "Dramatizing the Ideology of the Revolution: Popular Mobilization in Virginia, 1774–1776," *WMQ,* 3d Ser., XXXIII (1976), 357–385.

CHAPTER 2

1. R. C. Simmons and P. D. G. Thomas, eds., *Proceedings and Debates of the British Parliaments respecting North America, 1754–1783* (White Plains, N.Y., 1982–), IV, 31 (king's message), 55–82 (Mar. 14 debate). See also [William Cobbett], ed., *Parliamentary History of England: From the Earliest Period to the Year 1803,* XVII, *A.D. 1771–1774* (London, 1813), 1159, 1163–1184, esp. 1183.

2. [Cobbett], ed., *Parliamentary History of England,* XVII, 1181. British notions of American disunity and subsequent effects on imperial policy are explored in Julie Flavell, "British Perceptions of New England and the Decision for a Coercive Colonial Policy, 1774–1775," in Flavell and Stephen Conway, eds., *Britain and America Go to War: The Impact of War and Warfare in Anglo-America, 1754–1815* (Gainesville, Fla., 2004), 95–115.

3. Josiah Quincy III, *Memoir of the Life of Josiah Quincy, Jun. of Massachusetts,* 2d ed. (Boston, 1825), 143.

4. Benjamin Franklin, *The Interest of Great Britain Considered . . .* (London, 1760), in *PBF,* IX, 90. For the career of Franklin's snake cartoon, see Lester C. Olson, *Emblems of American Community in the Revolutionary Era* (Washington, D.C., 1991), 24–74; Timothy J. Shannon, *Indians and Colonists at the Crossroads of Empire: The Albany Congress of 1754* (Ithaca, N.Y., 2000), 83–89.

5. Jonathan Boucher, *Reminiscences of an American Loyalist, 1738–1789* (Boston, 1925), 130–136, esp. 133, 134; Merrill Jensen, "The Sovereign States: Their Antagonisms and Rivalries and Some Consequences," in Ronald Hoffman and Peter J. Albert, eds., *Sovereign States*

in an Age of Uncertainty (Charlottesville, Va., 1981), 226–250; Flavell, "British Perceptions of New England," in Flavell and Conway, eds., *Britain and America Go to War,* 100–101.

6. For colonial perceptions and misperceptions of the backcountry, see Gregory H. Nobles, "Breaking into the Backcountry: New Approaches to the Early American Frontier, 1750–1800," *WMQ,* 3d Ser., XLVI (1989), 641–670; the excellent essays in Andrew R. L. Cayton and Fredrika J. Teute, eds., *Contact Points: American Frontiers from the Mohawk Valley to the Mississippi, 1750–1830* (Williamsburg, Va., and Chapel Hill, N.C., 1998); and Eric Hinderaker and Peter C. Mancall, *At the Edge of Empire: The Backcountry in British North America* (Baltimore, 2003). Colonial fears of "going native" are found in John Demos, *The Unredeemed Captive: A Family Story from Early America* (New York, 1995); and Philip J. Deloria, *Playing Indian* (New Haven, Conn., 1998).

7. Richard J. Hooker, ed., *The Carolina Backcountry on the Eve of the Revolution: The Journal and Other Writings of Charles Woodmason, Anglican Itinerant* (Williamsburg, Va., and Chapel Hill, N.C., 1953), 54, 56. For colonial attitudes about the Paxton Boys, see Alden T. Vaughan, "Frontier Banditti and the Indians: The Paxton Boys' Legacy, 1763–1775," *Pennsylvania History,* LI (1984), 1–29.

8. "The Apology of the Paxton Volunteers Addressed to the Candid and Impartial World," in John R. Dunbar, ed., *The Paxton Papers* (The Hague, 1957), 185–204, esp. 186, "The Quaker Unmask'd; or, Plain Truth . . . ," 207–215, esp. 208; Franklin, *A Narrative of the Late Massacres, in Lancaster County* ([Philadelphia], 1764), *PBF,* XI, 42–69, esp. 66.

9. Charles E. Clark, *The Public Prints: The Newspaper in Anglo-American Culture, 1665–1740* (New York, 1994), 215–266.

10. Daniel R. Coquillette and Neil Longley York, eds., *Portrait of a Patriot: The Major Political and Legal Papers of Josiah Quincy Junior,* III, *The Southern Journal (1773)* (Boston, 2007), 142 ("traversing the town"), 165 ("renounce"), 167 ("very great respect," "to the test").

11. Ibid., 190 ("about 20 or 30"), 211–212 ("whole body"), 215 ("Cards, dice").

12. Ibid., 219.

13. Ibid., 240 ("Samuel Adams," "highly relished"), 252 ("very apparent"), 256 ("very little").

14. Ibid., 277 ("very bitter"), 306 ("ever believed"). Quincy went back and corrected this page in January 1775, stating that Franklin had been "grossly calumniated" and that he, himself, should have been more cautious in believing the "slander of envious or malevolent tongues." Franklin, he now judged, was "one of the wisest and best of men upon Earth: — One, of whom it may be said that this world is not worthy." See ibid., 308 ("first proposer"), 325 ("industrious, sensible, and wealthy").

Massachusetts Bay's outlawing and executing dissenters in the mid-seventeenth century was certainly not forgiven. Pennsylvania Quakers and Baptists verbalized these old scars to John Adams, too. On October 14, 1774, during the First Continental Congress, Adams was summoned to Carpenters' Hall, which, to his "great surprise," was "almost full of people," for an interview with the city's leading Quakers and Baptists. Adams wrote in his autobiography that Israel Pemberton, the chief of this "self-created tribunal," wanted the Massachusetts delegation to know that "there were difficulties in the way" of creating a "Union of the Colonies . . . and none of more importance than Liberty of Concience." Adams noted in his diary that Pemberton was "quite rude," but the prominent merchant was not the only one who raised the century-old specter of executed Quakers. A few weeks before the Carpenters' Hall examination, Adams wrote that New York delegate Philip Livingston "seems to dread N. England — the Levelling Spirit etc. Hints were thrown out of the Goths and Vandalls — mention was made of our hanging the Quakers etc." See entries for Aug. 22, Oct. 14, 1774, in *Diary and Autobiography of John Adams,* II, 107, 152; autobiography, ibid., III, 311.

15. The friends he made along the way shared his concern. One new connection, George Clymer, wrote to Quincy a few months after his trip. Although Quincy's journal did not delve into the nest of New York politics, Clymer related that New York's "political principles are truly as unfixed as the wind. One year sees the New-Yorkers champions for Liberty, and the next hugging their chains." See George Clymer to Josiah Quincy, Jr., Philadelphia, July 29, 1773, in Quincy, *Memoir of Josiah Quincy, Jun.,* 145.

16. Jon Butler, *Becoming America: The Revolution before 1776* (Cambridge, Mass., 2000); T. H. Breen, *The Marketplace of Revolution: How Consumer Politics Shaped American Independence* (New York, 2004).

17. For a synthesis of the burgeoning literature on this topic, see Gary B. Nash, *The Unknown American Revolution: The Unruly Birth of Democracy and the Struggle to Create America* (New York, 2005), esp. 88–149. Religious dissent: Rhys Isaac, *The Transformation of Virginia, 1740–1790* (Williamsburg, Va., and Chapel Hill, N.C., 1982), 161–177. Urban dissent: Nash, *The Urban Crucible: The Northern Seaports and the Origins of the American Revolution* (Cambridge, Mass., 1979); and Paul A. Gilje, *The Road to Mobocracy: Popular Disorder in New York City, 1763–1834* (Williamsburg, Va., and Chapel Hill, N.C., 1987), 37–68. New Jersey: Brendan McConville, *These Daring Disturbers of the Public Peace: The Struggle for Property and Power in Early New Jersey* (Ithaca, N.Y., 1999), 239–245.

18. Black Boys: Patrick Spero, *Frontier Rebels: The Fight for Independence in the American West, 1765–1776* (New York, 2018). South Carolina Regulators: Rachel N. Klein, *Unification of a Slave State: The Rise of a Planter Class in the South Carolina Backcountry, 1760–1808* (Williamsburg, Va., and Chapel Hill, N.C., 1990), 47–77; and Richard Maxwell Brown, *The South Carolina Regulators* (Cambridge, Mass., 1963). North Carolina Regulators: Marjoleine Kars, *Breaking Loose Together: The Regulator Rebellion in Pre-Revolutionary North Carolina* (Chapel Hill, N.C., 2002); Wayne E. Lee, *Crowds and Soldiers in Revolutionary North Carolina: The Culture of Violence in Riot and War* (Gainesville, Fla., 2001); and A. Roger Ekirch, *"Poor Carolina": Politics and Society in Colonial North Carolina, 1729–1776* (Chapel Hill, N.C., 1981), 157–161.

19. Several leaders of the Revolution in New Jersey came from families who were targets of the Liberty Boys, including Richard Stockton, Elias Boudinot, Frederick Frelinghuysen, and Lord Stirling. See McConville, *Daring Disturbers,* 253.

20. "Lawless desperadoes": *North-Carolina Gazette,* May 24, 1771; *Virginia Gazette* (Purdie & Dixon), June 13, 1771; *Boston News-Letter,* June 13, 1771; *Connecticut Journal,* June 14, 1771; *Providence Gazette,* June 15, 1771; *Boston Gazette,* June 17, 1771; *Massachusetts Spy,* June 20, 1771; *Pennsylvania Gazette,* June 20, 1771; *Pennsylvania Journal,* June 20, 1771; *Maryland Gazette,* June 22, 1771; *New-York Gazette,* June 24, 1771. "Dangerous and daring conspiracy": *Virginia Gazette* (Purdie & Dixon), July 4, 1771; *Pennsylvania Journal,* July 11, 1771; *Pennsylvania Journal,* July 11, 1771; *Connecticut Journal,* July 12, 1771; *Providence Gazette,* July 13, 1771; *Boston Gazette,* July 15, 1771; *Essex Gazette,* July

16, 1771; *Maryland Gazette,* July 18, 1771; *Boston News-Letter,* July 25, 1771. "What shall we in future think": Leonidas, *"To Gouvernour Tryon," Massachusetts Spy,* June 27, 1771. *"Posse Commitatus":* Mucius Scaevola, "To the Writers of the Resolves and Letter from Newbern, in North-Carolina," ibid., Sept. 5, 1771.

21. *North-Carolina Gazette,* July 29, 1771.

22. Coquillette and York, eds., *Portrait of a Patriot,* III, 227 ("change my opinion"), 246–247 ("most celebrated lawyers").

23. Josiah Tucker, *The True Interest of Great Britain* (Philadelphia, 1776), 61, *Early American Imprints,* no. 15199.

24. See David C. Hendrickson, *Peace Pact: The Lost World of the American Founding* (Lawrence, Kans., 2003); and Peter S. Onuf, *The Origins of the Federal Republic: Jurisdictional Controversies in the United States, 1775–1787* (Philadelphia, 1983).

25. Julian P. Boyd, ed., *The Susquehanna Company Papers,* 11 vols. (Wilkes-Barre, Pa., 1930), I, xv, lxiv–lxv.

26. *Pennsylvania Gazette,* Dec. 21, 1769.

27. Michael A. Bellesiles, *Revolutionary Outlaws: Ethan Allen and the Struggle for Independence on the Early American Frontier* (Charlottesville, Va., 1993), 25–32, 105.

28. Tryon's Mar. 9, 1774, proclamation in E. B. O'Callaghan, ed., *The Documentary History of the State of New York,* 4 vols. (Albany, N.Y., 1851), IV, 871–873. Tryon also referred to them as the "New Hampshire Rioters" in his official correspondence. See Tryon to Major General Haldimand, Sept. 1, 1773, in John Romeyn Brodhead, ed., *Documents relative to the Colonial History of the State of New York,* 15 vols. (Albany, N.Y., 1853–1887), VIII, 394. For the "Bloody Act" and its consequences for the common cause, see Edward Countryman, *A People in Revolution: The American Revolution and Political Society in New York, 1760–1790* (1981; rpt. New York, 1989), 70, 156.

29. Eric Hinderaker, *Elusive Empires: Constructing Colonialism in the Ohio Valley, 1673–1800* (Cambridge, 1997), 170–183; Woody Holton, *Forced Founders: Indians, Debtors, Slaves, and the Making of the American Revolution in Virginia* (Williamsburg, Va., and Chapel Hill, N.C., 1999), 3–38; Patrick Griffin, *American Leviathan: Empire, Nation, and Revolutionary Frontier* (New York, 2007), 72–123; Rob Harper, *Unsettling the West: Violence and State Building in the Ohio Valley* (Philadelphia, 2018).

30. Griffin, *American Leviathan,* 102–105; Jack M. Sosin, *Whitehall and the Wilderness: The Middle West in British Colonial Policy, 1760–1775* (Lincoln, Neb., 1961), 181–210.

31. See Dunmore's proclamation of Apr. 25, 1774, *Whereas I Have Reason to Apprehend . . .* ([Williamsburg, Va.], 1774), *Early American Imprints,* no. 42742; and a response by Penn of Oct. 12, 1774, *By the Honourable John Penn, Esquire . . . a Proclamation . . .* ([Philadelphia], 1774), *Early American Imprints,* no. 13521; Robert G. Parkinson, "From Indian Killer to Worthy Citizen: The Revolutionary Transformation of Michael Cresap," *WMQ,* 3d Ser., LXIII (2006), 97–122, esp. 99–100; Griffin, *American Leviathan,* 109–113.

32. "John Adams' Diary," Oct. 10, 1774, *LDC,* I, 167–168.

33. *Pennsylvania Gazette,* July 6, 1774; *Pennsylvania Journal,* July 6, 1774; *Pennsylvania Packet,* July 11, 1774; *New-York Journal,* July 14, 1774; *Connecticut Courant,* July 26, 1774; *South-Carolina and American General Gazette,* July 29, 1774.

34. Christopher Leslie Brown, *Moral Capital: Foundations of British Abolitionism* (Williamsburg, Va., and Chapel Hill, N.C., 2006).

35. Ibid., 91; Marcus Rediker, *The Fearless Benjamin Lay: The Quaker Dwarf Who Became the First Revolutionary Abolitionist* (Boston, 2017). For the religious influences that led to criticism of slavery by the late eighteenth century, see David Brion Davis, *The Problem of Slavery in Western Culture* (Ithaca, N.Y., 1966), 219–364; Winthrop D. Jordan, *White over Black: American Attitudes toward the Negro, 1550–1812* (Williamsburg, Va., and Chapel Hill, N.C., 1968), 179–214. Benezet's pamphlets included *Observations on the Enslaving, Importing, and Purchasing of Negroes* . . . (Germantown, Pa., 1759), *A Short Account of That Part of Africa, Inhabited by the Negroes* (Philadelphia, 1762), and *Some Historical Account of Guinea* . . . (Philadelphia, 1771).

36. Brown, *Moral Capital,* 33–101.

37. For the slavery metaphor, see Bernard Bailyn, *The Ideological Origins of the American Revolution* (Cambridge, Mass., 1967), 232–245; David Brion Davis, *The Problem of Slavery in the Age of Revolution, 1770–1823* (Ithaca, N.Y., 1975), 273–284; F. Nwabueze Okoye, "Chattel Slavery as the Nightmare of the American Revolutionaries," *WMQ,* 3d Ser., XXXVII (1980), 3–28; Patricia Bradley, *Slavery, Propaganda, and the American Revolution* (Oxford, Miss., 1998); John Dickinson, "Letters from a Farmer in Pennsylvania" (1768), in Forrest McDonald, ed., *Empire and Nation* (Englewood Cliffs, N.J., 1962), 44. Dickinson, who was himself a former chattel slaveholder, revealed his blindness when he asked, "Is it possible to form an idea of a slavery more *complete,* more *miserable,* more *disgraceful,* than that of a people, where *justice is administered, government exercised,* and a *standing army maintained,* AT THE EXPENSE OF THE PEOPLE, and yet WITHOUT THE LEAST DEPENDENCE UPON THEM?" (ibid., 57). Slave population: Duncan J. MacLeod, *Slavery, Race, and the American Revolution* (Cambridge, 1974), 62.

38. James Otis, *The Rights of British Colonies Asserted and Proved,* in Bernard Bailyn, ed., *Pamphlets of the American Revolution* (1764) (Cambridge, Mass., 1965), 409–482, esp. 439. See also Gary B. Nash, *Race and Revolution* (Madison, Wis., 1990), 8–9; Benjamin Rush, *An Address to the Inhabitants of the British Settlements, on the Slavery of the Negroes in America* (Philadelphia, 1773), 25–26; Rush, *A Vindication of the Address to the Inhabitants of the British Settlements, on the Slavery of the Negroes in America, in Answer to a Pamphlet Entitled, "Slavery Not Forbidden by Scripture"* (Philadelphia, 1773), 30; [John Allen], *The Watchman's Alarm to Lord N—h; or, The British Parliamentary Boston Port-Bill Unwrapped* . . . (Salem, Mass., 1774), 27, *Early American Imprints,* no. 13757.

39. Colonists' "discovery" of slavery was first discussed by Jordan in *White over Black,* 269–311. For how the American Revolution also lifted the veil for Britons, see Brown, *Moral Capital,* 105–153. On *Somerset,* see William R. Cotter, "The Somerset Case and the Abolition of Slavery in England," *History,* LXXIX (1994), 31–56; Mark S. Weiner, "New Biographical Evidence on *Somerset's Case," Slavery and Abolition,* XXIII, no. 1 (2002), 121–136; George Van Cleve, "*Somerset's Case* and Its Antecedents in Imperial Perspective," *Law and History Review,* XXIV (2006), 601–645, esp. 631–632. For the response to *Somerset,* see Jerome Nadelhaft, "The Somerset Case and Slavery: Myth, Reality, and Repercussions," *Journal of Negro History,* LI (1966), 193–208; Bradley, *Slavery, Propaganda, and the American Revolution,* 66–80; Eliga H. Gould, "Zones of Law, Zones of Violence: The Legal Geography of the British Atlantic, circa 1772," *WMQ,* 3d Ser., LX (2003), 471–510.

40. "Pregnant": *Boston News-Letter,* July 23, 1772; *Boston Post-Boy,* July 27, 1772; *Con-*

necticut Journal, July 31, 1772; *Newport Mercury,* Aug. 3, 1772; *Essex Gazette,* Aug. 4, 1772; *Massachusetts Spy,* Aug. 20, 1772. One report that circulated in America referred to the case only as the "great negro cause": *Pennsylvania Packet,* Aug. 24, 1772; *Pennsylvania Gazette,* Aug. 26, 1772; *Essex Gazette,* Sept. 1, 1772; *New-York Journal,* Sept. 3, 1772; *Connecticut Journal,* Sept. 4, 1772. On October 10, 1772, John Carter's *Providence Gazette* featured an English essay on the case entitled "Reflections on the Negro Cause." "Much talked of cause": *Virginia Gazette* (Purdie & Dixon), July 23, 1772; *Providence Gazette,* July 25, 1772. "Concerns the whole nation": *Pennsylvania Gazette,* Aug. 12, 1772. Final pleadings: *Essex Gazette,* Aug. 25, 1772; *Boston News-Letter,* Aug. 27, 1772. Mansfield decision: *Essex Gazette,* Aug. 25, 1772; *Virginia Gazette* (Purdie & Dixon), Aug. 27, 1772; *Connecticut Journal,* Aug. 28, 1772; *Providence Gazette,* Sept. 5, 1772. "Greater ferment": *New-York Journal,* Aug. 27, 1772; *Boston Post-Boy,* Aug. 29, 1772; *Providence Gazette,* Sept. 12, 1772; *Newport Mercury,* Sept. 14, 1772. "On account of colour": *Pennsylvania Packet,* Aug. 3, 1772; *Virginia Gazette* (Purdie & Dixon), Aug. 20, 1772.

41. "Unique asylum": Brown, *Moral Capital,* 101. Hutchinson: Arthur Zilversmit, *The First Emancipation: The Abolition of Slavery in the North* (Chicago, 1967), 101. For the changes in Virginia's tobacco economy and its relationship to the slave trade, see Allan Kulikoff, *Tobacco and Slaves: The Development of Southern Cultures in the Chesapeake, 1680–1800* (Williamsburg, Va., and Chapel Hill, N.C., 1986), 118–161; for the planters' efforts to secure a slave duty in the mid-eighteenth century, see Bruce A. Ragsdale, *A Planters' Republic: The Search for Economic Independence in Revolutionary Virginia* (Madison, Wis., 1996), 66–73, 115–136. Townshend Duties in Virginia: Holton, *Forced Founders,* 83–92. "Trade of great Inhumanity": *Rev. Va.,* I, 85–88, esp. 87.

42. New York and New Jersey: Zilversmit, *First Emancipation,* 91–93; petition by Peter Bestes, Sambo Freeman, Felix Holbrook, and Chester Joie to Boston committee of correspondence, Apr. 20, 1773, *Early American Imprints,* no. 42416. When the 1773 petition failed, the following May, "a Grate number of Blackes of the Province" filed another memorial, and when that was tabled, as well, they submitted another one in June. See Stanley Kaplan and Emma Nogrady Kaplan, *The Black Presence in the Era of the American Revolution,* rev. ed. (Amherst, Mass., 1989), 13–14. Massachusetts towns: Richard D. Brown, *Revolutionary Politics in Massachusetts: The Boston Committee of Correspondence and the Towns, 1772–1774* (New York, 1970), 173–174. These included Leicester, Salem, and Sandwich. See also Zilversmit, *First Emancipation,* 100. The preamble of the 1774 Rhode Island law prohibiting slave imports is quoted in Jordan, *White over Black,* 291. Connecticut: Zilversmit, *First Emancipation,* 107–108.

43. "Thursday, October 20, 1774," in *JCC,* I, 75–80, esp. 77.

44. Thomas Jefferson, *A Summary View of the Rights of British America* (1774), in *PTJ,* I, 121–137, esp. 130; Darien (Georgia) Resolutions, Jan. 12, 1775, in 4 *Am. Archives,* I, 1135–1136, esp. 1136.

45. Benjamin Rush to Granville Sharp, Nov. 1, 1774, in John A. Woods, ed., "The Correspondence of Benjamin Rush and Granville Sharp, 1773–1809," *Journal of American Studies,* I (1967), 1–38, esp. 13, 14.

46. Pamphlets: Winthrop D. Jordan, "An Antislavery Proslavery Document?" *Journal of Negro History,* XLVII (1962), 54–56; Patrick Henry, speech to Virginia House of Burgesses, Jan. 18, 1773, in Granville Sharp Collection, New-York Historical Society, reel 1,

quoted in Christa Dierksheide, "'The Great Improvement and Civilization of That Race': Jefferson and the 'Amelioration' of Slavery, c. 1770–1826," *Early American Studies,* VI (2008), 165–197, esp. 167; Samuel Allinson to Patrick Henry, Burlington, N.J., Oct. 10, 1774, in Larry R. Gerlach, ed., *New Jersey in the American Revolution, 1763–1783: A Documentary History* (Trenton, N.J., 1975), 88–89.

47. Samuel Hopkins, *A Dialogue concerning the Slavery of the Africans: Shewing It to Be the Duty and Interest of the American Colonies to Emancipate All Their African Slaves* (Norwich, Conn., 1776), *Early American Imprints,* no. 14804. Rising Sun Tavern: Gary B. Nash and Jean R. Soderlund, *Freedom by Degrees: Emancipation in Pennsylvania and Its Aftermath* (New York, 1991), 80.

48. Zilversmit, *First Emancipation,* 228–229; Jordan, *White over Black,* 310–311. There has been a resurgence of early abolitionist studies with Manisha Sinha, *The Slaves' Cause: A History of Abolition* (New Haven, Conn., 2016); and Paul J. Polgar, *Standard-Bearers of Equality: America's First Abolition Movement* (Williamsburg, Va., and Chapel Hill, N.C., 2019). The argument that the Revolutionaries let the moment slip away is most identified with Nash. He made this claim in *Race and Revolution* (1990) and updated it in *The Forgotten Fifth: African Americans in the Age of Revolution* (Cambridge, Mass., 2006), 69–122. Practical elements: Davis, *Problem of Slavery in Western Culture,* 440.

49. Samuel Johnson, *Taxation No Tyranny: An Answer to the Resolutions and Address of the American Congress* (1775), in Donald J. Greene, ed., *Works of Samuel Johnson,* X, *Political Writings,* 12 vols. (New Haven, Conn., 1977), 454. New Jersey: Zilversmit, *First Emancipation,* 91–92. "Pandemonium": Coquillette and York, eds., *Portrait of a Patriot,* III, 221.

50. Johnson, *Taxation No Tyranny,* in Greene, ed., *Works of Johnson,* X, 452.

51. Samuel Seabury, "A View of the Controversy between Great Britain and Her Colonies . . ." (1774), in Clarence H. Vance, ed., *Letters of a Westchester Farmer, 1774–1775* (White Plains, N.Y., 1930), 109.

52. *Rivington's New-York Gazetteer,* Jan. 26, 1775; "To the People of New-Jersey" from "Z," ibid., Dec. 1, 1774; "Massachusettensis" [Daniel Leonard], *Boston News-Letter,* Mar. 6, 1775.

53. *Rivington's New-York Gazetteer,* Jan. 12, 1775; and see Brad Jones, *Resisting Independence: Popular Loyalism in the Revolutionary British Atlantic* (forthcoming), esp. chap. 4.

54. "A. W[estchester] Farmer" [Seabury], "Free Thoughts on the Proceedings of the Continental Congress . . . In a Letter to the Farmers," in Vance, ed., *Letters of a Westchester Farmer,* 41–68, esp. 58, 65. Rivington published some excerpts of Seabury's "Farmer" letters and also advertised them in pamphlet form throughout December 1774 to April 1775. See "A. W[estchester] Farmer" [Seabury], "The Congress Canvassed; or, An Examination into the Conduct of the Delegates at Their Grand Convention," ibid., 69–100, esp. 81, 99; "A. W[estchester] Farmer" [Seabury], "A View of the Controversy between Great-Britain and Her Colonies . . . ," ibid., 101–148, esp. 107.

55. [Jonathan Boucher], *Letter from a Virginian to the Members of the Congress to Be Held at Philadelphia, on the First of September 1774* (Boston, 1774), *Early American Imprints,* no. 42565; "A North American" [Thomas Bradbury Chandler], *The American Querist; or, Some Questions Proposed relative to the Present Disputes between Great Britain and America Her Colonies* (Boston, 1774), *Early American Imprints,* no. 13222; [Chandler],

What Think Ye of the Congress Now? or, An Enquiry How Far the Americans Are Bound to Abide by and Execute the Decisions of the Late Congress (New York, 1775), *Early American Imprints,* no. 13866; [Myles Cooper and John Vardill], *The Patriots of North-America: A Sketch* (New York, 1775); "Phileirene" [Jonathan Sewell], *Boston News-Letter,* Jan. 26, Mar. 9, Apr. 6, 1775; [Richard Wells], *A Few Political Reflections Submitted to the Consideration of the British Colonies, by a Citizen of Philadelphia* (Philadelphia, 1774), *Early American Imprints,* no. 13760. "British common cause" and "Loyalist moment": Jones, *Resisting Independence,* chap. 4.

56. John Adams to William Tudor, Quincy, Nov. 16, 1816, in Charles Francis Adams, ed., *The Works of John Adams, Second President of the United States: With a Life of the Author, Notes, and Illustrations,* X, *General Correspondence, 1811–1825* (Boston, 1856), 231.

57. "Little has been published," "unaccountable phrenzy," "Witchcraft": "Massachusettensis," Letter I, *Boston Post-Boy,* Dec. 5, 1774. "Madness," "growing distemper": "Massachusettensis," Letter II, ibid., Dec. 12, 1774. "Despotism": "Massachusettensis," Letter III, ibid., Dec. 19, 1774. Several of Leonard's essays would be reprinted in other papers, including the *New-Hampshire Gazette* (Mar. 31, Apr. 7, Apr. 14, 1775), and *Rivington's New-York Gazetteer* (Jan. 19, 26, 1775).

58. "Envious men": "Massachusettensis," Letter X, *Boston Post-Boy,* Feb. 13, 1775. "Rebellion": "Massachusettensis," Letter IX, ibid., Feb. 6, 1775. "Annals of the world": "Massachusettensis," Letter XV, ibid., Mar. 20, 1775.

59. "Massachusettensis," Letter VIII, ibid., Jan. 23, 1775. In an earlier installment, Leonard argued that, cultural jealousies aside, New England would stand alone for the sheer fact that "the colonies south of Pennsylvania would be unable to furnish any men; they have not more than is necessary to govern their numerous slaves, and to defend themselves against the Indians." See Letter I, ibid., Dec. 12, 1774.

60. Ibid. Chandler expressed a similar worry about civil wars in his 1775 pamphlet, *What Think Ye of the Congress Now?* 25.

61. *Rivington's New-York Gazetteer,* Mar. 2, 1775; Chandler, *What Think Ye of the Congress Now?* 4–5.

62. James Warren to Samuel Adams, Jan. 1, 1775, in Samuel Adams Papers, quoted in *PJA,* II, 221. "Loyal at heart": "Massachusettensis," Letter IV, *Boston Post-Boy,* Jan. 2, 1775. "These Papers": *PJA,* III, 313. "Great exultation": John Adams and William Tudor, *Novanglus and Massachusettensis* (Boston, 1819), vi.

63. [Alexander Hamilton], *A Full Vindication of the Measures of Congress . . .* (New York, 1774), *Early American Imprints,* no. 13313; [Hamilton], *The Farmer Refuted . . .* (New York, 1775), *Early American Imprints,* no. 14096. Anonymous letters: *Massachusetts Spy,* Mar. 2, 1775; *Connecticut Courant,* June 19, 1775.

64. "Wretched policy of the whigs": "Massachusettensis," Letter III, *Boston Post-Boy,* Dec. 26, 1774. "Wicked policy of the Tories": "Novanglus," Letter I, *Boston Gazette,* Jan. 23, 1775. "Coincidence of circumstances" and "not exciting a rebellion": "Novanglus," Letter V, ibid., Feb. 20, 1775. "Harbours a wish": "Novanglus," Letter IV, ibid., Feb. 13, 1775. Adams returned to this theme in Letter VIII, ibid., Mar. 13, 1775. "Tribe of the *wicked*": "Novanglus," Letter VI, ibid., Feb. 27, 1775.

65. "Novanglus," Letter III, ibid., Feb. 6, 1775.

66. Quincy, *Memoir of Josiah Quincy,* 128 (emphasis added).

CHAPTER 3

1. Ralph Waldo Emerson, "Hymn: Sung at the Completion of the Concord Monument," in [John Hollander, ed.], *American Poetry: The Nineteenth Century,* I, *Philip Freneau to Walt Whitman* (New York, 1993), 318–319.

2. Oliver N. Bacon, *A History of Natick from Its Settlement in 1651 to the Present Time with Notices of the First White Families* . . . (Boston, 1856), 41; Emerson, "Hymn," in [Hollander, ed.], *American Poetry,* I, 318–319.

3. J[osiah] H. Temple, *History of Framingham, Massachusetts, Early Known as Danforth's Farms, 1640–1880; with a Genealogical Register* (Framingham, Mass., 1887), 275; Lorenzo Johnston Greene, *The Negro in Colonial New England* (1942; rpt. New York, 1969), 74; Elise Lemire, *Black Walden: Slavery and Its Aftermath in Concord, Massachusetts* (Philadelphia, 2009), 9.

4. Elaine Brooks, "Massachusetts Anti-Slavery Society," *Journal of Negro History,* XXX (1945), 311–330; Eric J. Chaput, "Republicans and Abolitionists on the Road to 'Jubilee': Recent Scholarship and Primary Sources on the Destruction of American Slavery, 1861–1865," *Common-Place,* XIV (2014), http://commonplace.online/article/republicans-and-abolitionists-on-the-road-to-jubilee/.

5. Esopus: *New-York Journal,* Mar. 2, 1775; *Rivington's New-York Gazetteer,* Mar. 2, 1775; *Pennsylvania Evening Post,* Mar. 4, 1775; *New-York Gazette,* Mar. 6, 1775; *Connecticut Courant,* Mar. 6, 1775; *Connecticut Journal,* Mar. 8, 1775; *Pennsylvania Gazette,* Mar. 8, 1775; *Boston News-Letter,* Mar. 9, 1775; *Connecticut Gazette,* Mar. 10, 1775; *Providence Gazette,* Mar. 11, 1775; *Maryland Journal,* Mar. 13, 1775; *Virginia Gazette* (Pinkney), Mar. 16, 1775; *Virginia Gazette* (Purdie), Mar. 17, 1775; *Virginia Gazette* (Dixon & Hunter), Mar. 18, 1775. For Long Island, see *Rivington's New-York Gazetteer,* Feb. 9, 1775; *New-York Gazette,* Mar. 6, 1775; *Pennsylvania Gazette,* Mar. 8, 1775; *Virginia Gazette, or the Norfolk Intelligencer,* Mar. 9, 1775; *Maryland Journal,* Mar. 29, 1775. For Perth Amboy, see *Pennsylvania Evening Post,* Mar. 4, 1775; *New-York Gazette,* Mar. 6, 1775; *Pennsylvania Gazette,* Mar. 22, 1775; *Maryland Journal,* Mar. 29, 1775.

6. *Norwich Packet,* Mar. 9, 1775; Emerson, "Hymn," in [Hollander, ed.], *American Poetry,* I, 318–319.

7. Frank Luther Mott, "The Newspaper Coverage of Lexington and Concord," *New England Quarterly,* XVII (1944), 489–505; Richard D. Brown, *Knowledge Is Power: The Diffusion of Information in Early America, 1700–1865* (New York, 1989), 247–253; David Hackett Fischer, *Paul Revere's Ride* (New York, 1994), 269–275; "The Following Interesting Advices Were This Day Received Here, by Two Vessels from Newport, and by an Express by Land," New York, Apr. 23, 1775, *Early American Imprints,* no. 14337. "Bloody News": *New-Hampshire Gazette,* Apr. 21, 1775; *Salem Gazette,* Apr. 21, 1775; *Norwich Packet,* Apr. 22, 1775 (supplement); *Providence Gazette,* Apr. 22, 1775; *New-York Gazette,* Apr. 24, 1775.

8. Robert Eden to William Eden, Apr. 28, 1775, quoted in Ronald Hoffman, *A Spirit of Dissension: Economics, Politics, and the Revolution in Maryland* (Baltimore, 1973), 146–147.

9. Woody Holton, *Forced Founders: Indians, Debtors, Slaves, and the Making of the American Revolution in Virginia* (Williamsburg, Va., and Chapel Hill, N.C., 1999), 140–148; Gerald W. Mullin, *Flight and Rebellion: Slave Resistance in Eighteenth-Century Vir-*

ginia (New York, 1972), 131; Philip Schwarz, *Twice Condemned: Slaves and the Criminal Laws of Virginia, 1705–1865* (Baton Rouge, La., 1988), 182–183; John E. Selby, *The Revolution in Virginia, 1775–1783* (Williamsburg, Va., 1988), 1–7.

10. *Virginia Gazette* (Dixon & Hunter), Apr. 22, 1775.

11. "Deposition of Dr. William Pasteur, in regard to the Removal of Powder from the Williamsburg Magazine," 1775, *VMHB,* XIII (1905), 49.

12. "Pledge of Readiness at a Moment's Warning," *Rev. Va.,* III, 70–72; Governor Dunmore to his council, Williamsburg, Va., May 2, 1775, ibid., 77–78, esp. 77, also published in *Virginia Gazette* (Pinkney), May 4, 1775.

13. John Richard Alden, "John Stuart Accuses William Bull," *WMQ,* 3d Ser., II (1945), 318; D. D. Wallace, "Gage's Threat — or Warning?" *South Carolina Historical and Genealogical Magazine,* XLVII (1946), 191; Alexander Innes to [Lord Dartmouth], May 16, 1775, in B. D. Bargar, ed., "Charles Town Loyalism in 1775: The Secret Reports of Alexander Innes," *South Carolina Historical Magazine,* LXIII (1962), 125–136, esp. 128.

14. James Kenny to Humphry Marshall, Philadelphia, Apr. 25, 1775, in Humphry and Moses Marshall Papers, William L. Clements Library, University of Michigan, Ann Arbor.

15. James Habersham to Robert Keen, Savannah, May 11, 1775, *Collections of the Georgia Historical Society,* VI, *The Letters of Hon. James Habersham, 1756–1775* (Savannah, Ga., 1904), 243–244. Henry Laurens described the charged atmosphere in Carolina a few days later, telling a correspondent that a few patriots in Charleston had to work hard "to restrain the Zeal and ardour of the many from entering upon Acts which appear to us to be at present impolite and inexpedient" (Laurens to William Manning, Charleston, S.C., May 22, 1775, *PHL,* X, 128).

16. Josiah Smith, Jr., to James Poyas, Charleston, May 18, 1775, and Smith to George Appleby, Charleston, June 16, 1775, both quoted in Jeffrey J. Crow, "Slave Rebelliousness and Social Conflict in North Carolina, 1775–1802," *WMQ,* 3d Ser., XXXVII (1980), 79–102, esp. 84n–85n. Laurens included the proclamation in his letter to his son, John Laurens (Charleston, May 15, 1775, *PHL,* X, 118–119).

17. James Mullineaux, deposition, Dorchester County, Maryland Committee of Inspection to Baltimore Committee of Inspection, May 23, 1775, Robert Gilmor, Jr., Collection, 1774–1848, MS 387, III, Maryland Historical Society, Baltimore.

18. George Bancroft, *History of the United States from the Discovery of the American Continent,* 4th ed. (Boston, 1860), VII, 312.

19. Thomas Gage to Guy Johnson, Boston, Mar. 10, 1775, CXXVI, Gage to Captain DePeyster, Boston, May 20, 1775, and Gage to Captain Lernoult, Boston, May 20, 1775, both CXXIX, all in Thomas Gage Papers, William L. Clements Library, University of Michigan, Ann Arbor.

20. Gage to Lord Barrington, Boston, June 12, 1775, in Clarence Edwin Carter, ed., *The Correspondence of General Thomas Gage with the Secretaries of State, 1763–1775,* 2 vols. (New Haven, Conn., 1931), II, 684.

21. "To Johoiakin Mothksin, and the Rest of Our Brethren, the Indians, Natives of Stockbridge," Apr. 1, 1775, 4 *Am. Archives,* I, 1347, "A Gentleman at Pittsfield, in Berkshire County, to an Officer in Cambridge," May 9, 1775, II, 546.

22. Ethan Allen, *A Narrative of Colonel Ethan Allen's Captivity: Containing His Voyages and Travels* (1799; rpt. Mineola, N.Y., 2013), 8; Guy Johnson to Committee of Schenec-

tady, New York, Guy Park, May 18, 1775, 4 *Am. Archives*, II, 638, Johnson to the Magistrates of Schenectady and Albany, Guy Park, May [20?], 1775, 661–662.

23. *"Oh George"*: *Pennsylvania Evening Post*, May 18, 1775; *Pennsylvania Mercury*, May 19, 1775; *Pennsylvania Journal*, May 24, 1775; *Pennsylvania Gazette*, May 24, 1775; *New-York Gazette*, May 29, 1775; *Virginia Gazette* (Purdie), June 2, 1775; *New-England Chronicle*, June 8, 1775; *Essex Journal*, June 9, 1775; *Virginia Gazette, or the Norfolk Intelligencer*, June 21, 1775.

24. "Answer of the Mohawks to the Speech of the Magistrates, etc. of Albany and Schenectady," Guy Park, May 25, 1775, 4 *Am. Archives*, II, 842–843, esp. 843, New York Provincial Congress to New York Delegates of Continental Congress, June 7, 1775, 1281.

25. Richard Henry Lee to Francis Lightfoot Lee, Philadelphia, May 21, 1775, *LDC*, I, 367. Several paragraphs of this letter (but not the ones quoted above) appeared in the *Virginia Gazette* (Pinkney), June 1, 1775, under the vague — and misleading — description "Extract of Letter from Gentleman in Philadelphia to a Friend in Williamsburg." See New Hampshire Delegates to the Provincial Committee of New Hampshire, Philadelphia, May 22, 1775, *LDC*, I, 369–370, esp. 369, John Dickinson's Notes for a Speech in Congress, May 23–[25?], 1775, 371–383, esp. 377.

26. *South-Carolina Gazette*, May 29, 1775. Timothy had exchanged the Feb. 10, 1775, letter from a London correspondent in John Holt's *New-York Journal*, Apr. 27, 1775. Holt did not substitute "negroes" for "N*****s" as Timothy did for sensitive Charleston readers.

27. Henry Laurens to James Laurens, Charleston, June 7, 1775, *PHL*, X, 162–163; Provincial Congress of South Carolina, "Association," June 3, 1775, 4 *Am. Archives*, II, 897.

28. "In the Committee at Newbern, May 31, 1775," in Adelaide L. Fries et al., eds., *Records of the Moravians in North Carolina*, 11 vols. (Raleigh, N.C., 1922–1969), II, 929.

29. William Hooper to Samuel Johnston, Philadelphia, May 23, 1775, *LDC*, I, 398–400, esp. 399, John Adams to James Warren, Philadelphia, May 2, 1775, 364.

CHAPTER 4

1. Benjamin Franklin to Jonathan Shipley, Philadelphia, May 15, 1775, *LDC*, I, 350.

2. Thomas Gage to Lord Barrington, Boston, June 12, 1775, in Clarence Edwin Carter, ed., *Correspondence of General Thomas Gage with the Secretaries of State, and with the War Office and the Treasury, 1763–1775* (New Haven, Conn., 1933), II, 684.

3. *New-Hampshire Gazette*, July 11, 1775; *Pennsylvania Ledger*, July 22, 1775; *Pennsylvania Packet*, July 24, 1775; *Pennsylvania Journal*, July 26, 1775; *Virginia Gazette, or the Norfolk Intelligencer*, Aug. 2, 1775; *Virginia Gazette* (Pinkney), Aug. 3, 1775; *Virginia Gazette* (Purdie), Aug. 4, 1775. Norfolk printer John Hunter Holt made a telling slip of the type when he copied the story, mistakenly increasing the distance from 1,500 miles to a whopping 15,000. Other accusations that Johnson was "suspected of endeavouring to stir up Indians against the Colonies" appeared in *New-York Journal*, June 22, 1775; *Connecticut Journal*, June 28, 1775; *New-England Chronicle*, June 29, 1775; *Essex Journal*, June 30, 1775; *New-Hampshire Gazette*, July 4, 1775.

4. J. Russell Snapp, *John Stuart and the Struggle for Empire on the Southern Frontier* (Baton Rouge, La., 1996), 160. Stuart sent Thomas Gage two packets of letters on July 9 and 20, 1775, which explained the episode in great detail, including his disappointment that "any set of Gentlemen of Probity would pay attention to a Drunken Catawba." See

Thomas Gage Papers, CXXXI, CXXXII, William L. Clements Library, University of Michigan, Ann Arbor.

5. Peter H. Wood, "'Taking Care of Business' in Revolutionary South Carolina: Republicanism and the Slave Society," in Jeffrey J. Crow and Larry E. Tise, eds., *The Southern Experience in the American Revolution* (Chapel Hill, N.C., 1978), 268–293, esp. 284. See also Robert Olwell, *Masters, Slaves, and Subjects: The Culture of Power in the South Carolina Low Country, 1740–1790* (Ithaca, N.Y., 1998), 234–235.

6. South Carolina Provincial Congress to Lord William Campbell, June 20, 1775, 4 *Am. Archives,* II, 1043. Campbell sent this report to Lord Dartmouth on Aug. 31, 1775; see W. Noel Sainsbury, ed., *Records in the British Public Record Office Relating to South Carolina, 1663–1782* (Columbia, S.C., 1955), XXXV, 191.

7. Sainsbury, ed., *Records Relating to S.C.,* XXXV, 192. "Revolution in the lower South": Snapp, *John Stuart and the Struggle for Empire,* 162.

8. *Cape-Fear Mercury,* Aug. 7, 1775.

9. Leora H. McEachern and Isabel M. Williams, eds., *Wilmington–New Hanover Safety Committee Minutes, 1774–1776* (Wilmington, N.C., 1974), 30–31.

10. Minutes of Pitt County committee of safety, July 1, 1775, in William L. Saunders, ed., *Colonial Records of North Carolina* (Raleigh, N.C., 1890), X, 61, 63.

11. [Janet Schaw], *Journal of a Lady of Quality: Being the Narrative of a Journey from Scotland to the West Indies, North Carolina, and Portugal, in the Years 1774 to 1776,* ed. Evangeline Walker Andrews and Charles McLean Andrews (1921; rpt. New Haven, Conn., 1923), 199.

12. Ibid., 199–200.

13. John Simpson to Richard Cogdell, July 15, 1775, in Saunders, ed., *Col. Records of N.C.,* X, 94–95.

14. Minutes of Pitt County committee of safety, July 8, 1775, ibid., 87, Simpson to Cogdell, July 15, 1775, 94–95 (emphasis added).

15. Governor Martin to Dartmouth, June 30, 1775, ibid., 43, "A Proclamation by Governor Martin," June 16, 1775, 17.

16. "Letter from Safety Committee in Wilmington to Samuel Johnston, Esq.," July 13, 1775, ibid., 91, "Letter from 'the People' to Governor Martin," July 16, 1775, 102–103, esp. 104.

17. Martin to Dartmouth, July 20, 1775, ibid., 108–109, "Depositions about the Burning of Fort Johnston," 130–133.

18. *Pennsylvania Ledger,* July 15, 1775; *New-York Journal,* July 20, 1775; *Virginia Gazette* (Purdie), July 22, 1775; *Virginia Gazette, or the Norfolk Intelligencer,* July 26, 1775; *Connecticut Journal,* July 26, 1775; *Connecticut Gazette,* July 28, 1775; *Virginia Gazette* (Dixon & Hunter), July 29, 1775.

19. "Set the Town on fire": *Providence Gazette,* July 29, 1775; *Newport Mercury,* July 31, 1775; *New-York Gazette,* July 31, 1775; *Massachusetts Spy,* Aug. 9, 1775; *Essex Journal,* Aug. 11, 1775; *New-Hampshire Gazette,* Aug. 22, 1775. Dartmouth: *New-Hampshire Gazette,* July 11, 1775; *Pennsylvania Evening Post,* July 22, 1775; *Essex Journal,* July 22, 1775; *Pennsylvania Packet,* July 24, 1775; *Pennsylvania Journal,* July 26, 1775; *Maryland Gazette,* July 27, 1775; *Rivington's New-York Gazetteer,* July 27, 1775; *Virginia Gazette* (Pinkney), Aug. 3, 1775. "Only a Commencement": *New-York Journal,* July 27, 1775; *New-York Gazette,* July

31, 1775; *Connecticut Journal,* Aug. 2, 1775; *Connecticut Gazette,* Aug. 4, 1775; *Norwich Packet,* Aug. 7, 1775; *Massachusetts Spy,* Aug. 16, 1775; *New-Hampshire Gazette,* Aug. 22, 1775.

20. Campbell to Dartmouth, Charleston, Aug. 19, 1775, in Sainsbury, ed., *Records Relating to S.C.,* XXXV, 184–190; Campbell to Dartmouth, Charleston, Aug. 31, 1775, in K. G. Davies, ed., *Documents of the American Revolution, 1770–1783,* Colonial Office Series, XI, *Transcripts, 1776* (Dublin, 1976), 93–98, esp. 95. The Jeremiah execution controversy is also detailed in Peter H. Wood, "'Liberty Is Sweet': African-American Freedom Struggles in the Years before White Independence," in Alfred F. Young et al., eds., *Beyond the American Revolution: Explorations in the History of American Radicalism* (Dekalb, Ill., 1993), 166–167; Olwell, *Masters, Slaves, and Subjects,* 234–238; J. William Harris, *The Hanging of Thomas Jeremiah: A Free Black Man's Encounter with Liberty* (New Haven, Conn., 2009), 136–150.

21. "Posture of defense": *Pennsylvania Evening Post,* Aug. 31, 1775; *Pennsylvania Mercury,* Sept. 1, 1775; *Constitutional Gazette,* Sept. 2, 1775; *Pennsylvania Ledger,* Sept. 2, 1775; *Pennsylvania Packet,* Sept. 4, 1775; *Rivington's New-York Gazetteer,* Sept. 7, 1775; *Connecticut Courant,* Sept. 11, 1775; *Newport Mercury,* Sept. 11, 1775; *Connecticut Journal,* Sept. 13, 1775; *Virginia Gazette* (Purdie), Sept. 15, 1775; *New-Hampshire Gazette,* Sept. 19, 1775; *Essex Journal,* Sept. 22, 1775. "We are not altogether": *Pennsylvania Packet,* Oct. 16, 1775; *New-York Journal,* Oct. 19, 1775; *New-York Gazette,* Oct. 23, 1775; *Connecticut Journal,* Oct. 25, 1775; *Maryland Gazette,* Oct. 26, 1775; *Massachusetts Spy,* Oct. 27, 1775; *Providence Gazette,* Oct. 28, 1775.

22. John Adams to Joseph Palmer, Philadelphia, July 5, 1775, *LDC,* I, 584; *JCC,* II, 105–108.

23. *JCC,* II, 105–108. For the full details of the Declaration of the Causes and Necessity of Taking up Arms, see *PTJ,* I, 187–219, esp. 213, 217.

24. *PTJ,* I, 217. The ending sections of the declaration were Jefferson's; Dickinson did not amend the final four paragraphs from Jefferson's draft.

25. JA to William Tudor, Philadelphia, July 6, 1775, *LDC,* I, 587, JA to James Warren, Philadelphia, July 6, 1775, 590–591.

26. JA to Tudor, July 6, 1775, ibid., 586–588; *Boston Gazette,* July 24, 1775; *New-England Chronicle,* July 27, 1775; *Essex Journal,* July 28, 1775; *Newport Mercury,* July 31, 1775; *New-Hampshire Gazette,* Aug. 1, 1775; *Massachusetts Spy,* Aug. 2, 1775; *Connecticut Journal,* Aug. 2, 1775.

27. Entry for Sept. 3, 1769, in L. H. Butterfield, ed., *Diary and Autobiography of John Adams,* series 1 of *The Adams Papers* (Cambridge, Mass., 1961), I, 343.

28. JA to Warren, July 6, 1775, *LDC,* I, 591.

29. BF to Shipley, Philadelphia, July 7, 1775, *LDC,* I, 604–608, esp. 607.

30. Nearly every colonial paper published the Declaration of the Causes and Necessity. The publication run was as follows: *Pennsylvania Packet,* July 10, 1775; *Pennsylvania Evening Post,* July 11, 1775; *Dunlap's Maryland Gazette,* July 11, 1775; *Pennsylvania Journal,* July 12, 1775; *Pennsylvania Gazette,* July 12, 1775; *Connecticut Journal,* July 12, 1775; *Maryland Journal,* July 12, 1775; *Rivington's New-York Gazetteer,* July 13, 1775; *Pennsylvania Mercury,* July 14, 1775; *Pennsylvania Ledger,* July 15, 1775; *New-York Gazette,* July 17, 1775; *Connecticut Courant,* July 17, 1775; *Virginia Gazette, or the Norfolk Intelligencer,*

July 19, 1775; *Maryland Gazette,* July 20, 1775; *Virginia Gazette* (Pinkney), July 20, 1775; *Connecticut Gazette,* July 21, 1775; *Virginia Gazette* (Purdie), July 21, 1775; *Massachusetts Spy,* July 22, 1775; *South-Carolina Gazette; And Country Journal,* July 22, 1775; *Virginia Gazette* (Dixon & Hunter), July 22, 1775; *Boston Gazette,* July 24, 1775; *Norwich Packet,* July 24, 1775; *New-England Chronicle,* July 27, 1775; *Essex Journal,* July 28, 1775; *South-Carolina and American General Gazette,* July 28, 1775; *Providence Gazette,* July 29, 1775; *Georgia Gazette,* Aug. 2, 1775; *South-Carolina Gazette,* Sept. 19, 1775. Stuart letters: *Pennsylvania Journal,* July 12, 1775; *Pennsylvania Packet,* July 17, 1775; *New-York Gazette,* July 17, 24, 1775; *Connecticut Journal,* July 19, 26, 1775; *New-York Journal,* July 20, 1775; *Connecticut Gazette,* July 21, 28, 1775; *Providence Gazette,* July 22, 1775; *Virginia Gazette* (Dixon & Hunter), July 22, 1775; *Connecticut Courant,* July 24, 1775; *Newport Mercury,* July 24, 1775; *Norwich Packet,* July 24, 31, 1775; *Massachusetts Spy,* Aug. 2, 1775; *Cape-Fear Mercury,* Aug. 7, 1775. The *New-York Gazette, Connecticut Gazette, Connecticut Journal,* and *Norwich Packet* also published the declaration and Stuart's letters in the same issues. The *Essex Journal* and *New-England Chronicle* published it at the same time as Adams's letter on the German soldier at Congress.

31. "Letter from Safety Committee in Wilmington to Samuel Johnston, Esq.," July 13, 1775, in Saunders, ed., *Col. Records of N.C.,* X, 91.

32. Address to Inhabitants of Britain: *JCC,* II, 158–162. The addresses to Ireland and Jamaica were first considered on July 21. The Jamaica address was completed on July 25, for which see "Address to the Assembly of Jamaica," *JCC,* II, 204–207, esp. 206; and the Irish declaration was completed on July 28, for which see "To the People of Ireland," *JCC,* II, 212–218, esp. 215–217. The Irish address printed in *Pennsylvania Mercury,* Aug. 4, 1775; *Pennsylvania Ledger,* Aug. 5, 1775; *Pennsylvania Evening Post,* Aug. 5, 1775; *Pennsylvania Packet,* Aug. 7, 1775; *Dunlap's Maryland Gazette,* Aug. 8, 1775; *Pennsylvania Gazette,* Aug. 9, 1775; *New-York Journal,* Aug. 10, 1775; *Connecticut Journal,* Aug. 16, 1775; *Massachusetts Spy,* Aug. 16, 1775; *Virginia Gazette* (Pinkney), Aug. 17, 1775; *Virginia Gazette* (Dixon & Hunter), Aug. 19, 1775; *Boston Gazette,* Aug. 21, 1775; *Connecticut Courant,* Aug. 21, 1775; *New-England Chronicle,* Aug. 24, 1775; *Essex Journal,* Aug. 25, 1775; *Virginia Gazette, or the Norfolk Intelligencer,* Aug. 30, 1775; *Massachusetts Gazette,* Aug. 31, 1775; *Connecticut Gazette,* Sept. 1, 1775.

CHAPTER 5

1. "Letter from a Clergyman in Md. to His Friend in England, Aug. 2, 1775; Signed 'T.T.,'" 4 *Am. Archives,* III, 10.

2. "Deposition of Dr. William Pasteur, in regard to the Removal of Powder from the Williamsburg Magazine," 1775, *VMHB,* XIII (1905), 49.

3. "Mistaken notion": *Virginia Gazette, or the Norfolk Intelligencer,* Aug. 2, 1775; *Virginia Gazette* (Purdie), Aug. 4, 1775; *Virginia Gazette* (Dixon & Hunter), Aug. 5, 1775; *Pennsylvania Evening Post,* Aug. 15, 1775; *Pennsylvania Journal,* Aug. 16, 1775; *Pennsylvania Gazette,* Aug. 16, 1775; *Rivington's New-York Gazetteer,* Aug. 17, 1775; *Pennsylvania Mercury,* Aug. 18, 1775; *New-York Gazette,* Aug. 21, 1775; *Pennsylvania Packet,* Aug. 21, 1775; *Dunlap's Maryland Gazette,* Aug. 22, 1775; *New-York Journal,* Aug. 24, 1775; *Norwich Packet,* Aug. 28, 1775; *South-Carolina and American General Gazette,* Sept. 8, 1775; *Newport Mercury,* Oct. 2, 1775. This first story of the "elopement" of Norfolk Blacks ap-

peared in four of the above papers in the same issue as August 6 reports from Newbern that North Carolina militia forces had to burn down Fort Johnston because Collet was hiding slaves there. See *Pennsylvania Journal,* Aug. 16, 1775; *Pennsylvania Mercury,* Aug. 18, 1775; *Pennsylvania Packet,* Aug. 21, 1775; and *New-York Gazette,* Aug. 21, 1775.

    4. "Most unfriendly": *Rev. Va.,* III, 452–453. "Melancholy reflection": *Virginia Gazette, or the Norfolk Intelligencer,* Sept. 6, 1775. "I will most assuredly seize": ibid., Sept. 13, 1775.

    5. Squire / Holt exchanged in *Virginia Gazette* (Pinkney), Sept. 14, 1775; *Virginia Gazette* (Purdie), Sept. 15, 1775; *Pennsylvania Journal,* Sept. 27, 1775; *Pennsylvania Ledger,* Sept. 30, 1775; *Pennsylvania Packet,* Oct. 2, 1775; *South-Carolina Gazette,* Oct. 24, 1775. "In return for his harbouring": *Virginia Gazette* (Purdie), Sept. 8, 1775; *Virginia Gazette* (Dixon & Hunter), Sept. 9, 1775; *Pennsylvania Journal,* Sept. 20, 1775; *New-York Journal,* Sept. 21, 1775; *Pennsylvania Mercury,* Sept. 22, 1775; *New-York Gazette,* Sept. 25, 1775; *Pennsylvania Packet,* Sept. 25, 1775; *Connecticut Journal,* Sept. 27, 1775; *New-England Chronicle,* Sept. 28, 1775; *Essex Journal,* Sept. 29, 1775; *Connecticut Gazette,* Sept. 29, 1775; *Massachusetts Spy,* Sept. 29, 1775; *New-Hampshire Gazette,* Oct. 10, 1775. "A pirating": *Virginia Gazette* (Purdie), Sept. 15, 1775; *Virginia Gazette* (Dixon & Hunter), Sept. 16, 1775; *Pennsylvania Evening Post,* Sept. 26, 1775; *Pennsylvania Gazette,* Sept. 27, 1775; *Pennsylvania Journal,* Sept. 27, 1775; *Pennsylvania Mercury,* Sept. 29, 1775; *New-York Gazette,* Oct. 2, 1775; *Pennsylvania Packet,* Oct. 2, 1775; *Connecticut Journal,* Oct. 4, 1775; *Boston Gazette,* Oct. 9, 1775; *Norwich Packet,* Oct. 9, 1775; *Essex Journal,* Oct. 13, 1775; *Newport Mercury,* Oct. 16, 1775; *South-Carolina Gazette,* Oct. 24, 1775.

    6. James Madison to William Bradford, [Jr.], Virginia, Nov. 26, 1774, in *PJM,* I, 129–131, esp. 130.

    7. Ibid., 130.

    8. Patriots in mid-September published an intercepted July 20 letter from Captain George Montague, commander of the HMS *Fowey,* which discussed Harris. Montague told Squire that, since the *Fowey* would *"soon leave the province, I think him* too useful to his Majesty's service to take away," suggesting the pilot should be transferred to the HMS *Otter.* See *Virginia Gazette* (Purdie), Sept. 15, 1775; *Pennsylvania Evening Post,* Sept. 26, 1775; *Pennsylvania Packet,* Oct. 2, 1775. For the Elizabeth City County committee's September 16 resolution to Squire, which made its top priority getting the "restitution of a certain *Joseph Harris,*" see *Rev. Va.,* IV, 119–120. The resolutions were printed in *Virginia Gazette* (Purdie), Sept. 22, 1775; *Virginia Gazette* (Dixon & Hunter), Sept. 23, 1775; *Pennsylvania Evening Post,* Oct. 5, 1775; *Norwich Packet,* Oct. 23, 1775. "Ethiopian director": *Virginia Gazette, or the Norfolk Intelligencer,* Sept. 20, 1775. Also printed in *Pennsylvania Journal,* Oct. 4, 1775, and *Constitutional Gazette,* Oct. 11, 1775.

    9. *Virginia Gazette* (Purdie), Oct. 6, 1775; "Extract of a Letter Received in Williamsburgh, Dated Norfolk, Virginia, October 1, 1775," 4 *Am. Archives,* III, 923. The letter appeared at least in the *South-Carolina Gazette,* Nov. 14, 1775. Holt was apparently hidden in the printing house the entire time the soldiers were packing up his press. See also *Virginia Gazette* (Purdie), Oct. 6, 1775; *Virginia Gazette* (Pinkney), Oct. 7, 1775; *Virginia Gazette* (Dixon & Hunter), Oct. 7, 1775; *Pennsylvania Evening Post,* Oct. 17, 1775; *Pennsylvania Gazette,* Oct. 18, 1775; *Pennsylvania Journal,* Oct. 18, 1775; *Maryland Gazette,* Oct. 19, 1775; *Pennsylvania Mercury,* Oct. 20, 1775; *Pennsylvania Ledger,* Oct. 21, 1775; *Constitutional Gazette,* Oct. 21, 1775; *Pennsylvania Packet,* Oct. 23, 1775; *New-York*

Gazette, Oct. 23, 1775; *Connecticut Journal,* Oct. 25, 1775; *New-York Journal,* Oct. 26, 1775; *Rivington's New-York Gazetteer,* Oct. 26, 1775; *Connecticut Gazette,* Oct. 27, 1775; *Connecticut Courant,* Oct. 30, 1775; *Norwich Packet,* Oct. 30, 1775; *Newport Mercury,* Oct. 30, 1775; *Essex Journal,* Nov. 3, 1775; *Massachusetts Spy,* Nov. 3, 1775; *New-Hampshire Gazette,* Nov. 8, 1775; *South-Carolina and American General Gazette,* Dec. 8, 1775; *Pennsylvania Magazine,* I (1775), 485.

10. John Hunter Holt to the Public, Norfolk, Oct. 12, 1775, 4 *Am. Archives,* III, 1031; *Virginia Gazette* (Purdie), Oct. 13, 1775.

11. James Wood, journal, in Reuben Gold Thwaites and Louise Phelps Kellogg, eds., *The Revolution on the Upper Ohio, 1775–1777* (Madison, Wis., 1908), 36, 47, 51, 57. One report first ran in Dixon and Hunter's *Virginia Gazette,* stating that the Ohio Indians "appear to be friendly . . . but that many of the more western and south western tribes seem determined to take up the hatchet against us." See *Virginia Gazette* (Dixon & Hunter), Aug. 26, 1775; *Pennsylvania Journal,* Sept. 6, 1775; *Pennsylvania Gazette,* Sept. 6, 1775; *Rivington's New-York Gazetteer,* Sept. 7, 1775; *New-York Gazette,* Sept. 11, 1775; *Connecticut Journal,* Sept. 13, 1775; *Boston Gazette,* Sept. 18, 1775. A second, longer article originated in *Dunlap's Maryland Gazette,* Aug. 29, 1775. This one confessed that "diabolical artifices had been used by those tools of Government, to instigate these Savages to attack our frontiers" and was exchanged in fourteen papers. See *New-York Gazette,* Sept. 4, 1775; *Connecticut Journal,* Sept. 6, 1775; *New-York Journal,* Sept. 7, 1775; *Rivington's New-York Gazetteer,* Sept. 7, 1775; *Pennsylvania Mercury,* Sept. 8, 1775; *Pennsylvania Ledger,* Sept. 9, 1775; *Pennsylvania Packet,* Sept. 11, 1775; *New-England Chronicle,* Sept. 14, 1775; *Connecticut Gazette,* Sept. 15, 1775; *Virginia Gazette* (Dixon & Hunter), Sept. 16, 1775; *New-Hampshire Gazette,* Sept. 19, 1775; *Massachusetts Spy,* Sept. 20, 1775; *Essex Journal,* Sept. 22, 1775; *Providence Gazette,* Sept. 30, 1775. A third report, which took up an entire page, was Wood's August 10 testimony to the Pittsburgh committee of safety on his return. See *Pennsylvania Evening Post,* Sept. 8, 1775; *Dunlap's Maryland Gazette,* Sept. 11, 1775; *New-York Gazette,* Sept. 18, 1775; *Boston Gazette,* Oct. 2, 1775. Several of these papers printed more than one article from Wood.

12. Clarence Monroe Burton, "John Connolly, a Tory of the Revolution," *Proceedings of the American Antiquarian Society,* N.S., XX (1909), 17–18; "A Narrative of the Transactions, Imprisonment, and Sufferings of John Connolly, an American Loyalist and Lieut. Col. in His Majesty's Service," *PMHB,* XII (1888), 411; Lord Dunmore to Thomas Gage, August 1775, in Thomas Gage Papers, CXXXIV, William L. Clements Library, University of Michigan, Ann Arbor.

13. Gage to Carleton, Boston, Sept. 5, 1775, to Dunmore, Boston, Sept. 10, 1775, to Captain Lernoult, Detroit, Sept. 10, 1775, to Carleton, Sept. 10, 1775, to Guy Johnson, Sept. 11, 1775, to Captain Hugh Lord, Illinois, Sept. 12, 1775, to Alexander McKee, Sept. 12, 1775, and to John Stuart, Sept. 12, 1775, all in Gage Papers, CXXXV.

14. "Deposition of William Cowley," *Rev. Va.,* IV, 202–203, and 4 *Am. Archives,* III, 1047–1048; Cowley to George Washington, Sept. 30, 1775, *PGW: RW,* II, 67–69, GW to John Hancock, Cambridge, Oct. 12, 1775, 148.

15. Michael A. McDonnell, *The Politics of War: Race, Class and Conflict in Revolutionary Virginia* (Williamsburg, Va., and Chapel Hill, N.C., 2007), 131–132; John E. Selby, *The Revolution in Virginia, 1775–1783* (Williamsburg, Va., 1988), 64.

16. Dunmore's proclamation, *Rev. Va.,* IV, 334.

17. Entry for Nov. 28, 1775, in Robert Greenhalgh Albion and Leonidas Dodson, eds., *Philip Vickers Fithian: Journal, 1775–1776; Written on the Virginia-Pennsylvania Frontier and in the Army around New York* (Princeton, N.J., 1934), 135; Richard Henry Lee to Catherine Macauley, Philadelphia, Nov. 29, 1775, *LDC,* II, 406; Thomas Jefferson to John Randolph, Philadelphia, Nov. 29, 1775, *PTJ,* I, 269; David Ramsay, *History of the American Revolution,* ed. Lester H. Cohen (1789; rpt. Indianapolis, 1990), I, 233; Robert Middlekauff, *The Glorious Cause: The American Revolution, 1763–1789,* rev. ed. (1982; rpt. New York, 2005), 322. Nightmare: Cassandra Pybus, *Epic Journeys of Freedom: Runaway Slaves of the American Revolution and Their Global Quest for Liberty* (Boston, 2006), 9. "Shock waves": McDonnell, *Politics of War,* 135.

18. "John Adams' Diary," Sept. 24, 1775, *LDC,* II, 49–51.

19. GW to Richard Henry Lee, Cambridge, Dec. 26, 1775, *PGW: RW,* II, 611.

20. *Virginia Gazette* (Pinkney), Nov. 23, 1775; *Virginia Gazette* (Purdie), Nov. 24, 1775; *Virginia Gazette* (Dixon & Hunter), Nov. 25, 1775; *Pennsylvania Evening Post,* Dec. 5, 1775; *Pennsylvania Journal,* Dec. 6, 1775; *New-York Journal,* Dec. 7, 1775; *Pennsylvania Mercury,* Dec. 8, 1775; *Massachusetts Spy,* Dec. 15, 1775; *Providence Gazette,* Dec. 23, 1775; *Boston Gazette,* Dec. 25, 1775. References to proclamation without publishing text: *Pennsylvania Packet,* Dec. 4, 1775; *Connecticut Journal,* Dec. 13, 1775; *New-England Chronicle,* Dec. 14, 1775; *Essex Journal,* Dec. 15, 1775; *Norwich Packet,* Dec. 18, 1775. The only newspaper not to feature any patriot commentary at all was the loyalist-leaning *Pennsylvania Mercury.*

21. *"Not in the legions":* *Virginia Gazette* (Purdie), Nov. 24, 1775. The lines are Macduff's from *Macbeth,* 4.3. Others who exchanged the *Macbeth* lines were *Pennsylvania Journal,* Dec. 6, 1775; *New-York Journal,* Dec. 7, 1775; *Massachusetts Spy,* Dec. 15, 1775; *Providence Gazette,* Dec. 23, 1775; *Boston Gazette,* Dec. 25, 1775.

22. *Virginia Gazette* (Pinkney), Nov. 23, 1775. The address ran in the other Williamsburg papers over the next two days: *Virginia Gazette* (Purdie), Nov. 24, 1775; *Virginia Gazette* (Dixon & Hunter), Nov. 25, 1775.

23. *Virginia Gazette* (Pinkney), Nov. 23, 1775.

24. Printers did their professional best to emphasize the words "very scum" for their readers. Some used italics, others all capital letters. See *Virginia Gazette* (Purdie), Nov. 17, 1775; *Pennsylvania Evening Post,* Nov. 28, 1775; *Maryland Journal,* Nov. 29, 1775; *New-York Journal,* Nov. 30, 1775; *Pennsylvania Mercury,* Dec. 1, 1775; *Connecticut Courant,* Dec. 4, 1775; *New-York Gazette,* Dec. 4, 1775; *Connecticut Journal,* Dec. 6, 1775; *Boston Gazette,* Dec. 11, 1775; *Maryland Journal,* Dec. 13, 1775; *New-England Chronicle,* Dec. 7, 1775.

25. Pendleton's letter appended to Richard Henry Lee's letter to GW, Dec. 6, 1775, Philadelphia, *PGW: RW,* II, 501. "Liberty to Slaves" ran in twenty papers: *Virginia Gazette* (Dixon & Hunter), Dec. 2, 1775; *Pennsylvania Evening Post,* Dec. 12, 1775; *Pennsylvania Gazette,* Dec. 13, 1775; *Pennsylvania Journal,* Dec. 13, 1775; *Maryland Gazette,* Dec. 14, 1775; *Pennsylvania Mercury,* Dec. 15, 1775; *Pennsylvania Ledger,* Dec. 16, 1775; *Constitutional Gazette,* Dec. 16, 1775; *New-York Gazette,* Dec. 18, 1775; *Connecticut Journal,* Dec. 20, 1775; *New-York Journal,* Dec. 21, 1775; *North-Carolina Gazette,* Dec. 22, 1775; *Connecticut Gazette,* Dec. 22, 1775; *Providence Gazette,* Dec. 23, 1775; *Newport Mer-*

cury, Dec. 25, 1775; *Norwich Packet,* Dec. 25, 1775; *New-England Chronicle,* Dec. 28, 1775; *Essex Journal,* Dec. 29, 1775; *New-Hampshire Gazette,* Jan. 2, 1776; *Massachusetts Gazette,* Jan. 4, 1776; *New York Packet,* Jan. 4, 1776.

26. *Virginia Gazette* (Pinkney), Dec. 9, 1775; *Pennsylvania Gazette,* Dec. 13, 20, 1775; *Maryland Gazette,* Dec. 14, 1775; *Pennsylvania Mercury,* Dec. 15, 1775; *New-York Gazette,* Dec. 18, 1775; *Pennsylvania Evening Post,* Dec. 19, 1775; *Connecticut Journal,* Dec. 20, 1775, Jan. 3, 1776; *North-Carolina Gazette,* Dec. 22, 1775; *Pennsylvania Packet,* Dec. 25, 1775; *Newport Mercury,* Dec. 25, 1775; *New-York Journal,* Dec. 28, 1775; *Norwich Packet,* Jan. 1, 1776; *Connecticut Gazette,* Jan. 5, 1776; *Massachusetts Spy,* Jan. 5, 1776; *New-Hampshire Gazette,* Jan. 9, 1776; GW to Richard Henry Lee, Cambridge, Dec. 26, 1775, *PGW: RW,* II, 611.

27. Cowley deposition, *PGW: RW,* II, 67–68; "Narrative of Connolly," *PMHB,* XII (1888), 411; John Frederick Dalziel Smyth, *A Tour in the United States of America* (London, 1784), II, 252–253. Allen Cameron has often been confused with the aforementioned Alexander Cameron, Stuart's deputy in the Carolina backcountry. People at the time confused them (George Mason) and historians since have, also (Woody Holton). It is probable that Allen and Alexander were related. Connolly's "Narrative" does not help, either, referring to Allen Cameron as "having acted as agent under the honourable John Stuart" ("Narrative of Connolly," 412). See Mason ("Cameron I take to be the Deputy Indian agent to the Southward") to Maryland committee of safety, Nov. 29, 1775, *Rev. Va.,* IV, 491; Holton, *Forced Founders,* 163.

28. "Narrative of Connolly," *PMHB,* XII (1888), 415, 418; Smyth, *Tour in the U.S.,* II, 254–256.

29. Many papers ran multiple reports about the story. One of Connolly's letters to the West — written to Indian trader John Gibson and laying the groundwork for the expedition — had already surfaced in a few papers before the Hagerstown arrest, one factor Connolly himself attributed to his eventual fate. See *Virginia Gazette,* Nov. 10, 1775; *Maryland Journal,* Nov. 22, 1775; *Pennsylvania Evening Post,* Nov. 25, 1775. Reports of the arrest: *Virginia Gazette* (Pinkney), Nov. 23, Dec. 16, 1775; *Virginia Gazette* (Purdie), Dec. 1, 1775; *Pennsylvania Mercury,* Dec. 1, 1775; *Pennsylvania Evening Post,* Dec. 2, 12, 23, 1775; *Pennsylvania Ledger,* Dec. 2, 1775; *Pennsylvania Packet,* Dec. 4, 25, 1775; *Pennsylvania Gazette,* Dec. 6, 27, 1775; *Constitutional Gazette,* Dec. 6, 30, 1775; *Maryland Gazette,* Dec. 7, 1775; *New-York Journal,* Dec. 14, 1775; *Essex Journal,* Dec. 15, 1775; *Massachusetts Spy,* Dec. 15, 1775; *Virginia Gazette* (Dixon & Hunter), Dec. 16, 1775; *Connecticut Journal,* Dec. 20, 1775; *Maryland Journal,* Dec. 20, 1775; *Newport Mercury,* Dec. 25, 1775; *Pennsylvania Journal,* Dec. 27, 1775; *New-York Gazette,* Jan. 1, 1776; *South-Carolina and American General Gazette,* Jan. 5, 1776; *Norwich Packet,* Jan. 8, 15, 1776; *Pennsylvania Magazine,* I (1775), 583–584.

30. By November, enough slaves had run to the British naval squadron off Charleston Harbor that it touched off a confrontation between Captain Edward Thornbrough, commander of the HMS *Tamar,* and the Charleston council of safety. In a replay of the confrontation in Hampton over the fate of pilot Joseph Harris, the Charleston council informed Captain Thornbrough on October 28 that they had "received information that a Negro Man named Shadwell, a Mariner by profession, . . . is employed on board." "As the said Negro is a runaway," they commanded, "and as harbouring him is highly penal and

the carrying such a one off the Colony Felony by the laws of this Country . . . we think it necessary to give you this intimation, in order that the Negro be delivered to his lawful owner." The suggestion that the captain was a felon was a serious charge, and Thornbrough reacted accordingly. According to the messenger, the captain "appeared angry at the contents of the letter [and] declared his astonishment and concern that any Gentleman could Suspect that any runaway Negro could be on board his Sloop." Thornbrough threatened that, if Charleston leaders did not treat him or his men fairly, he would shut the port. See Council of Safety to Edward Thornbrough, Oct. 28, 1775, *PHL,* X, 504–505. See also William R. Ryan, *The World of Thomas Jeremiah: Charles Town on the Eve of the American Revolution* (New York, 2010), 98–99; Keith Krawczynski, *William Henry Drayton: South Carolina Revolutionary Patriot* (Baton Rouge, La., 2001), 198–205.

31. Adele Hast, *Loyalism in Revolutionary Virginia: The Norfolk Area and the Eastern Shore* (Ann Arbor, Mich., 1982), 55.

32. Benjamin Thompson, *Stopford-Sackville Manuscripts,* Great Britain Historical Manuscripts Commission, II, 15–18, quoted in Henry Steele Commager and Richard B. Morris, eds., *The Spirit of Seventy-Six: The Story of the American Revolution as Told by Its Participants* (New York, 1958), 153–154; Charles Lee to JA, Cambridge, Nov. 19, 1775, *PJA,* III, 311–312.

33. GW to Hancock, Cambridge, Nov. 28, 1775, *PGW: RW,* II, 446.

34. Nathanael Greene to Nicholas Cooke, Prospect Hill, Mass., Nov. 29, 1775, in *PNG,* I, 154–155; *New-England Chronicle,* Nov. 30, Dec. 14, 1775.

35. GW to Joseph Reed, Cambridge, Dec. 15, 1775, *PGW: RW,* II, 553. Washington also used the snowball metaphor in a Dec. 26 letter to Richard Henry Lee on 611.

36. Thomas Lynch to Ralph Izard, Philadelphia, Nov. 19, 1775, *LDC,* II, 363.

37. Samuel Ward to Henry Ward, Philadelphia, Dec. 2, 1775, ibid., 429. The extract of a letter from Charleston appeared in seven of the nine papers closest to the camp. See *Connecticut Courant,* Nov. 13, 1775; *Connecticut Gazette,* Nov. 17, 1775; *Massachusetts Spy,* Nov. 17, 1775; *Boston Gazette,* Nov. 20, 1775; *Newport Mercury,* Nov. 20, 1775; *Connecticut Journal,* Nov. 22, 1775; *Essex Journal,* Nov. 24, 1775. The last significant news from Williamsburg that reached New England by the end of November was the fight between Matthew Squire and the people of Hampton over Joseph Harris. "Dangerous Storm": Connecticut Delegates to Jonathan Trumbull, Sr., Philadelphia, Dec. 5, 1775, *LDC,* II, 440.

38. Lund Washington to GW, Mount Vernon, Dec. 17, 1775, *PGW: RW,* II, 570.

39. 4 *Am. Archives,* IV, 717, "Extract of a Letter to a Gentleman in Philadelphia," dated Charleston, Feb. 7, 1776, 950; "Minutes of the South Carolina Council of Safety," Dec. 14, 1775, in William Bell Clark, ed., *Naval Documents of the American Revolution* (Washington, D.C., 1968–), III, 105; Josiah Smith, Jr., to James Poyas, Jan. 10, 1776, Josiah Smith Letter Book, no. 3018, Southern Historical Collection, The Wilson Library, University of North Carolina at Chapel Hill; Council of Safety to Richard Richardson, Dec. 19, 1775, *PHL,* X, 576.

40. 4 *Am. Archives,* IV, 403, 498; Greene to Samuel Ward, Sr., Prospect Hill, Dec. 18, 1775, in *PNG,* I, 165; Dec. 11, 1775, in Franklin Bowditch Dexter, ed., *The Literary Diary of Ezra Stiles* (New York, 1901), I, 642. "Stay, you": *Pennsylvania Evening Post,* Dec. 14, 1775; *Norwich Packet,* Dec. 25, 1775; *Virginia Gazette* (Purdie), Dec. 29, 1775.

41. Dexter, ed., *Literary Diary of Ezra Stiles,* I, 644 (entry for Dec. 21, 23, 1775), 645

(Jan. 1, 1776), 648 (Jan. 23, 1776), 659 (Jan. 29, 1776). See also Jan. 2, 1776, Robert Honyman Diary, 1776–1782, no. 8417, University of Virginia Library, Charlottesville, 3–5; Samuel Hopkins to Thomas Cushing, Newport, Dec. 29, 1775, *PJA*, III, 389.

42. Samuel Hopkins, *A Dialogue concerning the Slavery of the Africans* (Norwich, Conn., 1776), *Early American Imprints*, no. 14804; Thomas Jefferson, *A Summary View of the Rights of British America* (1774), in *PTJ*, I, 121–137, esp. 130.

43. Edmund Rutledge to Ralph Izard, Philadelphia, Dec. 8, 1775, *LDC*, II, 462.

44. See "Instructions for the Officers of the Several Regiments of the Massachusetts Bay Forces," July 8, 1775, 4 *Am. Archives*, II, 1368; Proceedings of the Committee of Conference, Oct. 18–24, 1775, *PGW: RW*, II, 199, General Orders, Oct. 31, 1775, 268, General Orders, Nov. 12, 1775, 354. For more on Peter Salem and Salem Poor, see Benjamin Quarles, *The Negro in the American Revolution* (Williamsburg, Va., and Chapel Hill, N.C., 1961), 13–18; Sidney Kaplan and Emmy Nogrady Kaplan, *The Black Presence in the Era of the American Revolution*, rev. ed. (1973; rpt. Amherst, Mass., 1989), 20–24.

45. GW to Richard Henry Lee, Dec. 26, 1775, *PGW: RW*, II, 611, General Orders, Dec. 30, 1775, 620, GW to Hancock, Dec. 31, 1775, 623 (emphasis added). Congress's support of Washington came on Jan. 16, 1776, in *JCC*, IV, 60; "Richard Smith's Diary," *LDC*, III, 102.

46. Benjamin Franklin to Jonathan Shipley, Philadelphia, Sept. 13, 1775, *PBF*, XXII, 199–200.

47. Philip Schuyler to President of Congress, Albany, Dec. 14, 1775, 4 *Am. Archives*, IV, 260–261. Congress ordered Connolly's letter published on December 22; Schuyler's, on December 23. See "Richard Smith's Diary" for Connolly, *LDC*, II, 513, and also that day's official journal, in *JCC*, III, 443, 445. For Schuyler, see ibid., 456.

48. *Pennsylvania Evening Post*, Dec. 26, 1775. Schuyler's letter reprinted in the *Pennsylvania Gazette*, Dec. 27, 1775; *Pennsylvania Journal*, Dec. 27, 1775; *Pennsylvania Ledger*, Dec. 30, 1775; *Constitutional Gazette*, Dec. 30, 1775; *Pennsylvania Packet*, Jan. 1, 1776; *New-York Gazette*, Jan. 1, 1776; *Maryland Journal*, Jan. 3, 1776; *Maryland Gazette*, Jan. 4, 1776; *New-York Journal*, Jan. 4, 1776; *Virginia Gazette* (Purdie), Jan. 5, 1776; *Norwich Packet*, Jan. 8, 1776; *New-England Chronicle*, Jan. 11, 1776; *Massachusetts Spy*, Jan. 12, 1776; *Connecticut Gazette*, Jan. 12, 1776; *Providence Gazette*, Jan. 13, 1776; *Boston Gazette*, Jan. 15, 1776; *Pennsylvania Magazine*, I (1775), 581. Connolly's letters: *Pennsylvania Evening Post*, Dec. 23, 1775; *Pennsylvania Packet*, Dec. 25, 1775, Jan. 1, 1776; *Pennsylvania Journal*, Dec. 27, 1775; *Pennsylvania Gazette*, Dec. 27, 1775; *Maryland Journal*, Dec. 27, 1775; *Pennsylvania Ledger*, Dec. 30, 1775; *Constitutional Gazette*, Dec. 30, 1775; *New-York Gazette*, Jan. 1, 1776; *Maryland Gazette*, Jan. 4, 1776; *Norwich Packet*, Jan. 15, 1776. Four of these issues had the two stories on the same page (*New-York Gazette*, *Pennsylvania Journal*, *Maryland Gazette*, and *Constitutional Gazette*).

49. "Putting Arms": *Providence Gazette*, Nov. 18, 1775; *New-York Journal*, Nov. 23, 1775; *Connecticut Gazette*, Nov. 24, 1775; *Newport Mercury*, Nov. 27, 1775; *Constitutional Gazette*, Nov. 29, 1775; *New-England Chronicle*, Nov. 30, 1775; *New-Hampshire Gazette*, Dec. 5, 1775; *Maryland Journal*, Dec. 13, 1775. "An American": *Virginia Gazette* (Purdie), Jan. 5, 1776; *Pennsylvania Journal*, Jan. 17, 1776; *Constitutional Gazette*, Jan. 24, 1776; *New-York Journal*, Jan. 25, 1776; *Norwich Packet*, Jan. 29, 1776; *New-England Chronicle*, Feb. 1, 1776; *Providence Gazette*, Feb. 10, 1776.

50. John Richard Alden, "John Stuart Accuses William Bull," *WMQ,* 3d Ser., II (1945), 320.

CHAPTER 6

1. Abigail Adams to John Adams, Braintree, Mar. 31, 1776, in L. H. Butterfield, Marc Friedlaender, and Mary-Jo Kline, eds., *The Book of Abigail and John: Selected Letters of the Adams Family, 1762–1784* (Cambridge, Mass., 1975), 120–121.

2. JA to Abigail Adams, Apr. 14, 1776, ibid., 122–123.

3. Ibid.

4. "Greedily bought up": Josiah Bartlett to John Langdon, Philadelphia, Jan. 13, 1776, *LDC,* III, 88. "Has done wonders and miracles": *Pennsylvania Evening Post,* Feb. 13, 1776; *Constitutional Gazette,* Feb. 21, 1776.

5. "Who is the author": *Pennsylvania Evening Post,* Mar. 26, 1776. Adams as "Common Sense": the *Connecticut Gazette* exchanged a story from the *London Evening Post* from May 21, 1776, that noted, "This pamphlet, they say, has been ascribed to Mr. Adams, one of the Delegates in the Continental Congress." See *Connecticut Gazette,* Aug. 30, 1776; *Virginia Gazette* (Dixon & Hunter), Sept. 27, 1776. Franklin as "Common Sense": Horatio Gates to Charles Lee, Cambridge, Mass., Jan. 22, 1776, "The Lee Papers, Vol. I, 1754–1776," *Collections of the New-York Historical Society: For the Year 1871,* IV (New York, 1872), 252.

6. "Cult": Trish Loughran, *The Republic in Print: Print Culture in the Age of U.S. Nation Building, 1770–1870* (New York, 2007), 37–44. Sending copies home: Joseph Hewes to Samuel Johnston, Philadelphia, Feb. 20, 1776, *LDC,* III, 289–290. Public expense: Samuel Ward to Henry Ward, Philadelphia, Feb. 19, 1776, ibid., 285–286.

7. [Thomas Paine], *Common Sense: Addressed to the Inhabitants of America,* in Eric Foner, ed., *Thomas Paine: Collected Writings* (New York, 1995), 20, 35.

8. *Pennsylvania Evening Post,* Feb. 13, 1776; *Pennsylvania Packet,* Feb. 15, 1776; *Constitutional Gazette,* Feb. 21, 1776; and see William V. Wells, *The Life and Public Services of Samuel Adams: Being a Narrative of His Acts and Opinions . . .* (Boston, 1865), II, 349–352, 360–363.

9. "Honest farmer": *Pennsylvania Journal,* Feb. 28, 1776; *Boston Gazette,* Mar. 25, 1776; *Essex Gazette,* Apr. 5, 1776. "Done their worst": Thomas Paine, "A Dialogue between the Ghost of General Montgomery and a Delegate, in a Wood near Philadelphia," in Philip S. Foner, ed., *The Complete Writings of Thomas Paine,* 2 vols. (New York, 1945), II, 88–93; *Pennsylvania Packet,* Feb. 19, 1776; *Virginia Gazette* (Purdie), Mar. 8, 1776; *Continental Journal,* May 30, 1776.

10. "Remember": *Pennsylvania Gazette,* Mar. 13, 1776; *Maryland Journal,* Mar. 20, 1776; *Constitutional Gazette,* Mar. 20, 1776; *New York Packet,* Mar. 21, 1776; *Connecticut Gazette,* Apr. 5, 1776; *Newport Mercury,* Apr. 8, 1776; *Boston Gazette,* Apr. 8, 1776; *Massachusetts Spy,* Apr. 12, 1776. Livingston's call for thanksgiving: Mar. 16, 1776, *JCC,* IV, 208–209, published in *Pennsylvania Evening Post,* Mar. 19, 1776; *New York Packet,* Mar. 21, 1776; *New-York Gazette,* Mar. 25, 1776; *Connecticut Journal,* Mar. 27, 1776; *New-York Journal,* Apr. 4, 1776; *Virginia Gazette* (Purdie), Apr. 5, 1776; *Essex Journal,* Apr. 5, 1776; *Virginia Gazette* (Dixon & Hunter), May 11, 1776; *Providence Gazette,* May 11, 1776.

11. *Pennsylvania Journal,* Mar. 20, 1776; *Constitutional Gazette,* Mar. 30, 1776; *Con-*

necticut Gazette, Apr. 12, 1776; *Newport Mercury,* Apr. 29, 1776; *Virginia Gazette* (Dixon & Hunter), May 18, 1776.

12. *Pennsylvania Journal,* Mar. 20, 1776.

13. Gage: *Pennsylvania Gazette,* Aug. 23, 1775; *Maryland Journal,* Aug. 20, 1775. "20,000 Russians": *Pennsylvania Packet,* Nov. 27, 1775; *Pennsylvania Journal,* Nov. 29, 1775; *Pennsylvania Gazette,* Nov. 29, 1775; *Constitutional Gazette,* Dec. 2, 1775; *New-York Gazette,* Dec. 2, 1775; *Connecticut Courant,* Dec. 11, 1775.

14. House of Lords: *Boston Gazette,* Jan. 15, 1776; *Norwich Packet,* Jan. 22, 1776; *New-York Journal,* Jan. 25, 1776. British request to Russia: *Pennsylvania Journal,* Mar. 20, 1776; *New-England Chronicle,* Apr. 13, 1776; *Connecticut Gazette,* Apr. 19, 1776; *Connecticut Courant,* Apr. 22, 1776; *Newport Mercury,* Apr. 22, 1776; *Connecticut Journal,* Apr. 24, 1776; *Constitutional Gazette,* Apr. 24, 1776. For Catherine's refusal, see Catherine II to George III, Moscow, Sept. 23, [Oct. 4], 1775, in Nina N. Bashkina et al., eds., *The United States and Russia: The Beginning of Relations, 1765–1815* (Washington, D.C., 1980), 33–35.

15. Rodney Atwood, *The Hessians: Mercenaries from Hessen-Kassel in the American Revolution* (Cambridge, 1980), 25. For more on the professional soldier market the German states had perfected in the eighteenth century, see Charles W. Ingrao, *The Hessian Mercenary State: Ideas, Institutions, and Reform under Frederick II, 1760–1785* (Cambridge, 1987), 122–163.

16. Treaties: Frances Gardiner Davenport and Charles Oscar Paullin, eds., *European Treaties Bearing on the History of the United States and Its Dependencies* (Washington, D.C., 1937), IV, 118–122. Hiring practices: Atwood, *Hessians,* 1–2, 22–24; Ingrao, *Hessian Mercenary State,* 136–137.

17. Thomas Cushing to John Hancock, [Watertown, Mass.], May 3, 1776, in William Bell Clark et al., eds., *Naval Documents of the American Revolution,* 12 vols. (Washington, D.C., 1964–), IV, 1390–1391; Cushing to George Washington, Watertown, Mass., May 3, 1776, *PGW: RW,* IV, 190–191; Richard Derby, Jr., to Col. Artemas Ward, Ipswich, May 2, 1776, and Ward to GW, Boston, May 3, 1776, in 4 *Am. Archives,* V, 1183–1184; GW to Hancock, New York, May 7, 1776, *PGW: RW,* IV, 226. This was not the only channel that provided information about the Lee account. Isaac Smith wrote to John Adams from Salem on May 4 with some of the Lee information (*PJA,* IV, 165–167).

18. *Norwich Packet,* May 6, 1776; *New-England Chronicle,* May 9, 1776; *New-York Gazette,* May 9, 1776; *Pennsylvania Evening Post,* May 9, 1776; *Connecticut Gazette,* May 10, 1776; *Connecticut Journal,* May 15, 1776; *Pennsylvania Gazette,* May 15, 1776; *Pennsylvania Journal,* May 15, 1776; *Pennsylvania Ledger,* May 18, 1776; *Constitutional Gazette,* May 22, 1776; *Maryland Gazette,* May 23, 1776; *Virginia Gazette* (Purdie), May 24, 31, 1776.

19. Dublin account (published Mar. 2, 1776): *Pennsylvania Packet,* May 6, 1776 (supplement); *Pennsylvania Evening Post,* May 7, 1776; *Pennsylvania Journal,* May 8, 1776; *New-York Journal,* May 9, 1776; *New York Packet,* May 9, 1776; *Pennsylvania Ledger,* May 11, 1776; *Massachusetts Spy,* May 13, 1776; *Maryland Journal,* May 13, 1776; *Norwich Packet,* May 13, 1776; *Connecticut Courant,* May 13, 1776; *New-York Gazette,* May 13, 1776; *Constitutional Gazette,* May 15, 1776; *Maryland Gazette,* May 16, 1776; *New-England Chronicle,* May 16, 1776; *Connecticut Gazette,* May 16, 1776; *Virginia Gazette* (Purdie), May 17, 1776; *Providence Gazette,* May 18, 1776; *Newport Mercury,* May 20, 1776; *Boston Gazette,* May 20, 1776; *Freeman's Journal,* May 25, 1776.

20. Don Higginbotham, *Daniel Morgan: Revolutionary Rifleman* (Williamsburg, Va., and Chapel Hill, N.C., 1961), 38–39; Caesar Rodney to Thomas Rodney, Philadelphia, May 22, 1776, *LDC,* IV, 61–63, esp. 62.

21. Langdon to GW, Portsmouth, N.H., May 10, 1776, *PGW: RW,* IV, 255–257; Bartlett to Langdon, Philadelphia, May 21, [1776], *LDC,* IV, 55. See also May 30, 1776, *JCC,* IV, 405.

22. *Pennsylvania Gazette,* May 22, 1776; *Pennsylvania Journal,* May 22, 24, 1776; *Pennsylvania Packet,* May 27, 1776; *Constitutional Gazette,* May 29, June 1, 1776; *Connecticut Journal,* May 29, June 5, 1776; *New York Packet,* May 30, June 6, 1776; *Connecticut Gazette,* May 31, 1776; *New-York Gazette,* June 3, 1776; *Norwich Packet,* June 3, 10, 17, 1776; *Newport Mercury,* June 3, 6, 1776; *Connecticut Courant,* June 3, 10, 17, 1776; *Maryland Gazette,* June 6, 1776; *New-England Chronicle,* June 13, 1776; *Freeman's Journal,* June 15, 1776. The day after Merchant appeared before Congress, the delegates resolved to "extract and publish the treaties, and such parts of the intelligence as they think proper; also, to consider of an adequate reward for the person who brought the intelligence; and to prepare an address to the foreign mercenaries who are coming to invade America" (May 21, 1776, *JCC,* IV, 369).

23. *"Coup de Grace": New-York Journal,* May 9, 1776; *New-York Gazette,* May 13, 1776; *Connecticut Journal,* May 15, 1776; *Connecticut Gazette,* May 16, 1776. Virginia planter: diary entry for May 18, 1776, in Jack P. Greene, ed., *The Diary of Colonel Landon Carter of Sabine Hall, 1752–1778,* 2 vols. (Richmond, Va., 1987), II, 1041.

24. May 10, 1776, *JCC,* IV, 342. For the relationship between Congress, the Pennsylvania and Maryland Assemblies, and the May 10 resolution, see Richard Alan Ryerson, *The Revolution Is Now Begun: The Radical Committees of Philadelphia, 1765–1776* (Philadelphia, 1978), 208–216.

25. Fifth Virginia Convention, "Proceedings of Ninth Day of Session," May 15, 1776, *Rev. Va.,* VII, 141. Virginia motion for independence: *PTJ,* I, 290–291; see also *Rev. Va.,* VII, 4–6.

26. *PTJ,* I, 290–291.

27. Benjamin Franklin to the Commissioners of Canada, New York, May 27, 1776, *LDC,* IV, 85. London correspondent: *Pennsylvania Journal,* May 24, 1776.

28. Richard Henry Lee to Charles Lee, Philadelphia, May 27, 1776, *LDC,* IV, 87; George Morgan to Lewis Morris, Pittsburgh, May 16, 1776, 4 *Am. Archives,* VI, 474–475, read in Congress on May 27 (*JCC,* IV, 396). The Six Nations reciprocated with their own performance, putting on a "War-dance" on May 28. See Caesar Rodney to Thomas Rodney, Philadelphia, May 29, 1776, ibid., 99.

29. "Fling into the camp": *Providence Gazette,* May 18, 1776; *Norwich Packet,* May 20, 1776; *Freeman's Journal,* May 22, 1776; *Connecticut Journal,* May 22, 1776; *Pennsylvania Gazette,* May 22, 1776; *Pennsylvania Journal,* May 22, 1776; *New-York Journal,* May 23, 1776; *Pennsylvania Ledger,* May 25, 1776; *Virginia Gazette* (Purdie), June 14, 1776. Free land: *Pennsylvania Journal,* June 19, 1776; *Norwich Packet,* June 24, 1776; *Massachusetts Spy,* July 10, 1776. "Invaders of the worst kind": *New-York Journal,* May 30, 1776.

30. Lyman H. Butterfield suggests Jefferson probably asked Wythe to write the draft address in "Psychological Warfare in 1776: The Jefferson-Franklin Plan to Cause Hessian Desertions," *Proceedings of the American Philosophical Society,* XCIV (1950), 233–241.

31. "George Wythe's Draft Address to the Foreign Mercenaries," *LDC,* IV, 110–112, esp. 110–111.

32. John Greenwood journal, 33, William L. Clements Library, University of Michigan, Ann Arbor; Zaphaniah Shepardson, "Journal," 7, quoted in Robert McConnell Hatch, *Thrust for Canada: The American Attempt on Quebec in 1775–1776* (Boston, 1979), 198.

33. John Greenwood journal, 34, 36.

34. The May 26, 1776, Articles of Capitulation at the Cedars is in item 29, 251–256, in the *Papers of the Continental Congress, 1774–1789,* National Archives Microfilm Publication M247, roll 36.

35. GW to Philip Schuyler, New York, June 16, 1776, *PGW: RW,* V, 8; JA to John Sullivan, Philadelphia, June 23, 1776, *PJA,* IV, 330–331, esp. 330.

36. Wrong report: *Constitutional Gazette,* June 8, 1776; *New-York Gazette,* June 10, 1776; *Connecticut Journal,* June 12, 1776; *Continental Journal,* June 13, 1776; *New-England Chronicle,* June 13, 1776; *Freeman's Journal,* June 13, 1776; *Essex Journal,* June 14, 1776; *Pennsylvania Evening Post,* June 15, 1776; *Providence Gazette,* June 15, 1776; *American Gazette,* June 18, 1776; *Virginia Gazette* (Purdie), June 21, 1776; *Virginia Gazette* (Dixon & Hunter), June 22, 1776. British plans: *Connecticut Courant,* June 10, 1776. "Authentic account": *Connecticut Journal,* June 12, 1776; *New-England Chronicle,* June 13, 1776; *Continental Journal,* June 13, 1776; *Essex Journal,* June 14, 1776; *Pennsylvania Evening Post,* June 15, 1776; *Boston Gazette,* June 17, 1776; *Newport Mercury,* June 20, 1776. "Scene of Savage barbarity": *New-York Journal,* June 20, 1776; *Pennsylvania Evening Post,* June 22, 1776; *New-York Gazette,* June 24, 1776; *Pennsylvania Packet,* June 24, 1776; *Connecticut Courant,* June 24, 1776; *New-England Chronicle,* June 27, 1776; *Essex Journal,* June 28, 1776; *Newport Mercury,* July 1, 1776; *Norwich Packet,* July 1, 1776; *American Gazette,* July 2, 1776; *Maryland Gazette,* July 4, 1776; *Connecticut Gazette,* July 5, 1776; *Freeman's Journal,* July 6, 1776; *Virginia Gazette* (Dixon & Hunter), July 6, 1776.

37. William Whipple to Langdon, June 2, 1776, *LDC,* IV, 120, Bartlett to Langdon, Philadelphia, June 3, 1776, 126, Samuel Adams to James Warren, June 6, 1776, 150; June 3, 1776, *JCC,* IV, 412.

38. JA to Warren, Philadelphia, June 16, 1776, *LDC,* IV, 228–229.

39. In the secret journals of Congress, the May 29, 1776, entry stipulates Congress's order for those four members to produce "an animated address . . . to impress the minds of the people with Necessity of now stepping forward to save their country, their freedom, and property." See "Secret Journals of Congress," May 29, 1776, in Charles Thomson Papers, case 76, MSS, Historical Society of Pennsylvania, Philadelphia; "John Hancock to Certain Colonies," Philadelphia, June 4, 1776, *LDC,* IV, 136–137.

40. June 7, 1776, *JCC,* V, 425–426.

41. JA to Timothy Pickering, Aug. 6, 1822, in Charles Francis Adams, ed., *The Works of John Adams, Second President of the United States . . . ,* 10 vols. (Boston, 1856), II, 512n–514n. See also Pauline Maier, *American Scripture: Making the Declaration of Independence* (New York, 1997), 97–102.

42. June 7, 1776, "Secret Journals of Congress," in Thomson Papers, case 76; June 11, 14, 17, 1776, *JCC,* V, 430, 442, 452.

43. "Report of the Committee on the Cedars Cartel," June 17, 1776, *PTJ,* I, 400–404, esp. 401–402; Henry Stuart to John Stuart, Toquah, May 7, 1776, in K. G. Davies,

ed., *Documents of the American Revolution, 1770–1783,* Colonial Office Series, XII, *Transcripts, 1776* (Dublin, 1976), 130–133; "Letter Addressed to the Frontier Inhabitants by Mr. [Henry] Stuart . . . ," May 18, 1776, 4 *Am. Archives,* VI, 497. We know this had reached Philadelphia by June 18 because Elbridge Gerry gave particulars of this letter, including his hopes that Stuart's "Vile Designs will be frustrated" in his letter of that date to Joseph Trumbull, Philadelphia, June 18, 1776, *LDC,* IV, 263–264. Henry Stuart letter published in: *Virginia Gazette* (Purdie), June 7, 1776; *Maryland Journal,* June 17, 1776; *Dunlap's Maryland Gazette,* June 19, 1776; *Maryland Gazette,* June 20, 1776; *New-York Journal,* June 27, 1776; *New York Packet,* June 27, 1776; *Pennsylvania Ledger,* June 29, 1776; *Pennsylvania Packet,* July 1, 1776; *New-York Gazette,* July 1, 1776; *Norwich Packet,* July 8, 1776; *Connecticut Courant,* July 8, 1776; *Massachusetts Spy,* July 10, 1776; *Newport Mercury,* July 11, 1776.

44. "Nine or ten": *Constitutional Gazette,* June 22, 1776; *Providence Gazette,* June 29, 1776; *South-Carolina and American General Gazette,* Aug. 2, 1776. "Six or eight": "Narrative of Captain Andrew Snape Hamond," in Clark et al., eds., *Naval Documents,* V, 840. "To be sure": June 26, 1776, in Greene, ed., *Diary of Landon Carter,* II, 1051–1052, esp. 1051.

45. "Sent ashore": *Virginia Gazette* (Dixon & Hunter), June 15, 1776; *New-York Journal,* June 27, 1776; *New York Packet,* June 29, 1776; *Pennsylvania Ledger,* June 29, 1776; *New-York Gazette,* July 1, 1776; *Massachusetts Spy,* July 5, 1776; *Connecticut Courant,* July 8, 1776; *Boston Gazette,* July 8, 1776; *Freeman's Journal,* July 13, 1776; *American Gazette,* July 16, 1776. Three papers *(New-York Journal, New-York Gazette,* and *Connecticut Courant)* published this alongside the Henry Stuart letter.

46. Gwynn's Island map: *PTJ,* I, 566. Jefferson sent three drafts of a potential state constitution to Williamsburg. For the first draft, he wrote out this preamble; for the second, he did not copy it but left only blank space for it; and for the third, he copied a large part of it, making some editorial changes. See "The Virginia Constitution," [June 1776], *PTJ,* I, 329–386, esp. 356–357. For the final text of the preamble as adopted, see "The Constitution as Adopted by the Convention," [June 29, 1776], *PTJ,* I, 378.

47. Maier, *American Scripture,* 69–75. These "little" declarations are found throughout 4 *Am. Archives,* VI. Consult Appendix A of Maier's *American Scripture,* 217–223, for a full list.

48. Scituate town meeting, June 4: 4 *Am. Archives,* VI, 699. Wrentham town meeting, June 5: 699–700. Natick town meeting, June 20: 703. Connecticut Assembly, June 14: 867–868. New Hampshire Assembly: 1030. Elk Battalion, Chester County, June 10: 786. First Battalion, Chester County, June 6: 785. Pennsylvania Assembly instructions to Congress delegates, June 8: 755. Delegates of Charles County, Maryland: 1018. Talbot County, Maryland, June 21–22: 1019–1020. See also "A Declaration of the Delegates of Maryland," July 6, 1776, 1506. "Paid no regard": *Pennsylvania Gazette,* June 26, 1776; *Pennsylvania Ledger,* June 29, 1776; *Pennsylvania Packet,* July 1, 1776; *Maryland Journal,* July 2, 1776; *New-York Journal,* July 4, 1776; *New York Packet,* July 4, 1776; *Connecticut Gazette,* July 5, 1776; *Freeman's Journal,* July 6, 1776; *Norwich Packet,* July 8, 1776; *Connecticut Courant,* July 8, 1776; *Continental Journal,* July 11, 1776; *Boston Gazette,* July 15, 1776; *Massachusetts Spy,* July 17, 1776.

49. *Connecticut Courant,* June 17, 1776; *Boston Gazette,* June 24, 1776; *Maryland Jour-*

nal, June 26, 1776; *Massachusetts Spy,* June 28, 1776; *Constitutional Gazette,* July 3, 1776; *Essex Journal,* July 5, 1776.

50. Thomas Jefferson to Thomas Nelson, May 16, 1776, *PTJ,* I, 292.

51. For the argument that the Declaration was really just the first of a "suite of documents," including the Model Treaty and the Articles of Confederation, that established the United States as equal and legitimate participants in the international states system, see Leonard J. Sadosky, *Revolutionary Negotiations: Indians, Empires, and Diplomats in the Founding of America* (Charlottesville, Va., 2009), 82–89.

52. "Great object of desire": Thomas Jefferson, *A Summary View of the Rights of British America . . .* (Williamsburg, Va., 1774), 29; and see Chapter 2, above.

53. Massachusetts delegate Elbridge Gerry wrote on July 2 that, after the vote succeeded on independence, "the facts are as well known at the Coffee House of the City as in Congress" (Gerry to James Warren, Philadelphia, July 2, 1776, *LDC,* IV, 370). The first to publish notice of the Declaration was, interestingly, Henrich Miller, printer of the German-language *Wöchentliche Pennsylvanischer Staatsbote,* on July 5. A survey of the public readings is found in Maier, *American Scripture,* 155–160. For a list of the printings of the Declaration in the newspapers, see Clarence S. Brigham, *Journals and Journeymen* (Philadelphia, 1950), 58–59.

54. *Constitutional Gazette,* Aug. 12, 1776; *New York Packet,* Aug. 15, 1776; *Pennsylvania Evening Post,* Aug. 15, 1776; *New-York Gazette,* Aug. 19, 1776; *Connecticut Courant,* Aug. 19, 1776; *Pennsylvania Packet,* Aug. 20, 1776; *Continental Journal,* Aug. 22, 1776; *Providence Gazette,* Aug. 24, 1776; *New Hampshire Gazette* (Exeter), Aug. 24, 1776.

55. *New-York Journal,* Aug. 8, 1776.

56. Tories 3 to 1: William Tudor to JA, July 7, 1776, *PJA,* IV, 368. A census taken in July 1776 listed 821 Blacks and 7,523 whites in Suffolk County, or 9.8 percent of the population. See "Number of Inhabitants in the Several Towns of Suffolk County, New-York, July 1776," 4 *Am. Archives,* VI, 1236–1252.

57. JA to Hezekiah Niles, Quincy, Mass., Feb. 13, 1818, in Adams, ed., *Works of John Adams,* X, 283.

CONCLUSION

1. Horatio Gates in *Boston Gazette,* Sept. 15, 1777; *Pennsylvania Evening Post,* Sept. 16, 1777; *Continental Journal,* Sept. 18, 1777; *Massachusetts Spy,* Sept. 18, 1777; *Independent Chronicle,* Sept. 18, Oct. 2, 1777; *Connecticut Gazette,* Sept. 19, 1777; *Providence Gazette,* Sept. 20, 1777; *Freeman's Journal,* Sept. 20, 1777; *Norwich Packet,* Sept. 22, 29, 1777; *Maryland Journal,* Sept. 23, 1777; *Dunlap's Maryland Gazette,* Sept. 23, 1777; *Virginia Gazette* (Dixon & Hunter), Oct. 3, 1777; *New-York Gazette,* Oct. 6, 1777; *Connecticut Courant,* Oct. 7, 1777; *Connecticut Journal,* Oct. 15, 1777; *Gazette, of the State of South-Carolina,* Oct. 21, 1777; *South-Carolina and American General Gazette,* Oct. 23, 1777.

2. Benjamin Franklin to David Hartley, Passy, Feb. 2, 1780, *PBF,* XXXI, 436–439, esp. 439.

3. "Franklin and Lafayette's List of Prints to Illustrate British Cruelties," ibid., XXIX, 590–593.

4. Ibid., 591–592.

5. Ibid., 592.

6. BF to Edward Bridgen, Passy, Oct. 2, 1779, ibid., XXX, 430.

7. BF, "Supplement to the Boston Independent Chronicle," Passy, 1782, ibid., XXXVII, 187–190, esp. 189. Franklin's hoax appeared in *Parker's General Advertiser and Morning Intelligencer,* June 29, 1782; *Public Advertiser* (London), Sept. 27, 1782; *The Remembrancer; or, Impartial Repository of Public Events,* part 2 (London, 1782), 135–136; *New-Jersey Gazette,* Dec. 18, 1782; *Pennsylvania Packet,* Dec. 26, 1782; *Connecticut Courant,* Jan. 14, 1783; *New York Packet,* Jan. 16, 1783; *Providence Gazette,* Jan. 18, 1783; *Massachusetts Spy,* Jan. 23, 1783; *Continental Journal,* Jan. 23, 1783; *New-York Gazetteer,* Jan. 27, 1783.

8. William Henry Harrison to Secretary of War, Vincennes, Aug. 13, 1807, in Logan Esarey, ed., *Indiana Historical Collections,* VII, *Governor's Messages and Letters: Messages and Letters of William Henry Harrison,* I (Indianapolis, 1933), 229; Andrew Jackson to Thomas Jefferson, Apr. 20, 1808, in Sam B. Smith et al., eds., *Papers of Andrew Jackson,* 11 vols. to date (Knoxville, Tenn., 1980–), II, 191–193.

9. Franklin hoax: *Columbian Register* (New Haven, Conn.), Mar. 23, 1813; *Richmond Enquirer* (Va.), Mar. 26, 1813; *City Gazette* (Charleston, S.C.), Mar. 27, 1813; *Investigator* (Charleston, S.C.), Mar. 29, 1813; *Carolina Gazette* (Charleston, S.C.), Apr. 3, 1813; *National Advocate* (Washington, D.C.), Apr. 9, 1813; *Columbian* (New York), Apr. 16, 1813; *Bee* (Hudson, N.Y.), Apr. 20, 1813; *New-Hampshire Patriot* (Concord), Apr. 27, 1813; *Ontario Messenger* (Canandaigua, N.Y.), Apr. 27, 1813; *Long-Island Star* (Brooklyn), Apr. 28, 1813; *Washingtonian* (Windsor, Vt.), May 3, 1813; *Lexington Reporter* (Ky.), May 8, 1813; *Baltimore Patriot,* Apr. 28, 1813; *Daily National Intelligencer* (Washington, D.C.), Sept. 10, 1813; *Federal Republican* (Washington, D.C.), Sept. 17, 1813; *Universal Gazette* (Washington, D.C.), Sept. 17, 1813. "The Savage Allies of England": *Independent Chronicle,* Aug. 17, 1812; *Essex Register* (Salem, Mass.), Aug. 19, 1812; *National Aegis* (Worcester, Mass.), Sept. 2, 1812.

10. *Daily National Intelligencer,* May 12, 1813.

11. Alan Taylor, *The Internal Enemy: Slavery and War in Virginia, 1772–1832* (New York, 2013), 309–310, esp. 310.

12. James Wilson to John Montgomery and Jasper Yates, Woodstock, N.J., Sept. 14, 1776, *LDC,* V, 170, 171, William Hooper to Robert R. Livingston, Philadelphia, Sept. 25, 1776, 238; "The American Crisis: Number I," Dec. 19, 1776, in Eric Foner, ed., *Thomas Paine: Collected Writings . . .* (New York, 1995), 348, 352.

13. *Maryland Journal,* Jan. 8, 1777; *Continental Journal,* Jan. 30, 1777; *New Hampshire Gazette* (Exeter), Feb. 4, 1777; *South-Carolina and American General Gazette,* Feb. 6, 1777; *Essex Journal,* Feb. 6, 1777; *Norwich Packet,* Feb. 10, 1777; *Connecticut Journal,* Feb. 12, 1777.

14. Ken Miller, *Dangerous Guests: Enemy Captives and Revolutionary Communities during the War for Independence* (Ithaca, N.Y., 2014), 184–185, esp. 185.

15. Benjamin Franklin, "Observations concerning the Increase of Mankind, 1751," *PBF,* IV, 225–234, esp. 234.

16. Ibid., 234.

17. For more on "Colonel Tye," see Graham Russell Hodges, *Slavery and Freedom in the Rural North: African Americans in Monmouth County, New Jersey, 1665–1865* (Madison, Wis., 1997), 97–104; and Douglas R. Egerton, *Death or Liberty: African Americans and Revolutionary America* (New York, 2009), 65–70.

18. *Journals of the House of Representatives of the Commonwealth of Pennsylvania: Beginning the Twenty-Eighth Day of November, 1776 and Ending the Second Day of October, 1781* . . . (Philadelphia, 1782), 436 (emphasis added), *Early American Imprints*, no. 17658.

19. "Our words": *New-Jersey Gazette*, Sept. 20, 1780; *Pennsylvania Gazette*, Oct. 4, 1780. *"O horrida bella"*: *New-Jersey Journal*, Dec. 20, 1780. "A Whig": *New-Jersey Gazette*, Oct. 4, 1780. "A Friend to Justice": *New-Jersey Gazette*, Nov. 8, 1780. "A Lover of true Justice": *New-Jersey Gazette*, Feb. 14, 1781.

20. Thomas Jefferson, *A Summary View of the Rights of British America* (1774), in *PTJ*, I, 130.

21. Oneidas and Tuscaroras: *Continental Journal*, May 7, 1779; *American Journal*, May 7, 1779; *Independent Chronicle* (Boston), May 7, 1779; *Providence Gazette*, May 8, 1779; *Boston Gazette*, May 10, 1779; *Massachusetts Spy*, May 13, 1779. Stockbridge: Thomas F. DeVoe, "The Massacre of the Stockbridge Indians, 1778," *Magazine of American History*, V (1880), 187–195, esp. 193. Stockbridge deaths in loyalist papers in *Royal American Gazette* (New York), Sept. 3, 1778; *Royal Gazette*, Sept. 5, 1778; *New-York Gazette*, Sept. 7, 1778.

22. "Gen. Washington's Instructions to Gen. Sullivan, May 31, 1779," in Otis G. Hammond, ed., *Letters and Papers of Major-General John Sullivan, Continental Army*, III, *1771–1777* (Concord, N.H., 1939), 48–53, esp. 48–49. Toast: July 4, 1779, George Reid journal, Massachusetts Historical Society, Boston.

23. "Treaty with the Delawares, 1778," Sept. 17, 1778, in Charles J. Kappler, comp. and ed., *Indian Affairs: Laws and Treaties*, II, *Treaties* (Washington, D.C., 1904), 3–5, esp. 5.

24. Wolfgang Mieder, "'The Only Good Indian Is a Dead Indian': History and Meaning of a Proverbial Stereotype," *Journal of American Folklore*, CVI (1993), 38–60; Rob Harper, "Looking the Other Way: The Gnadenhutten Massacre and the Contextual Interpretation of Violence," *WMQ*, 3d Ser., LXIV (2007), 621–644.

25. John Filson, *The Discovery, Settlement, and Present State of Kentucke; and an Essay towards the Topography and Natural History of That Important Country* (1784; rpt. Bowie, Md., 1996), 49–82, esp. 72, 75.

26. *DHFFC*, VI, 1516 ("person[s] of good character").

27. Ibid., XII, 167.

28. Kenneth Silverman, *A Cultural History of the American Revolution: Painting, Music, Literature, and the Theatre in the Colonies and the United States from the Treaty of Paris to the Inauguration of George Washington, 1763–1789* (New York, 1976), 375, 605–606, 674.

29. Ferdinando Fairfax, "Plan for Liberating the Negroes within the United States," Richmond, Va., Mar. 6, 1790, *American Museum*, VIII (1790), 285–287; Thomas Jefferson, *Notes on the State of Virginia*, ed. William Peden (1954; rpt. Chapel Hill, N.C., 1982), 138.

30. *DHFFC*, IX, 226.

31. Ibid., XII, 813.

32. Ibid., 748 ("a few short years ago"), 754 ("in time of war"), 762 ("gratify people"), 800 ("public opinion").

33. Ibid., 648 ("tumults, seditions"), 747 ("intimate old friend").

34. "Ibrahim": *Federal Gazette* (Philadelphia), Mar. 25, 1790.

35. *DHFFC,* IX, 226; David C. Hendrickson, *Peace Pact: The Lost World of the American Founding* (Lawrence, Kans., 2003).

36. Don E. Fehrenbacher, *Slavery, Law, and Politics: The Dred Scott Case in Historical Perspective* (New York, 1981), 189.

37. John Adams to Hezekiah Niles, Quincy, Mass., Feb. 13, 1818, in Charles Francis Adams, ed., *The Works of John Adams, Second President of the United States* . . . , X (Boston, 1856), 282.

Guide to Further Reading

The depth of the historical literature on the Revolution and the American Founding is second only to that of the Civil War. Since the 1780s, the literature on what caused the Revolution, how it happened, and what consequences it had for America and the world has grown into a small library unto itself. What follows is a very brief guide for students to investigate further some of the topics and issues raised in *Thirteen Clocks*. This only scratches the surface, however, of the secondary sources about the Revolutionary era.

Students looking for a broad overview of the American Revolution should consult Robert Middlekauff, *The Glorious Cause: The American Revolution, 1763–1789,* rev. ed. (1982; rpt. New York, 2005). Another, more recent and revisionist overview is Alan Taylor, *American Revolutions: A Continental History, 1750–1804* (New York, 2016).

One of the biggest interpretative divides in early American historiography is who or what caused the American Revolution. For studies that stress ideas or ideology, see Bernard Bailyn, *Ideological Origins of the American Revolution,* expanded ed. (1967; rpt. Cambridge, Mass., 1992), Gordon S. Wood, *The Creation of the American Republic, 1776–1787* (Williamsburg, Va., and Chapel Hill, N.C., 1969), Pauline Maier, *From Resistance to Revolution: Colonial Radicals and the Development of American Opposition to Britain, 1765–1776* (New York, 1972), Richard L. Bushman, *King and People in Provincial Massachusetts* (Williamsburg, Va., and Chapel Hill, N.C., 1985), Edmund S. Morgan, *Inventing the People: The Rise of Popular Sovereignty in England and America* (New York, 1988), and the essays written by Joyce Appleby, collected in *Liberalism and Republicanism in the Historical Imagination* (Cambridge, Mass., 1992). For scholars who stress different sources of ideas, see T. H. Breen, *The Marketplace of Revolution: How Consumer Politics Shaped American Independence* (New York, 2004), and Sarah Knott, *Sensibility and the American Revolution* (Williamsburg, Va., and Chapel Hill, N.C., 2009).

Historians who emphasize the power of ideas have often put the Declaration of Independence at the center of their interpretation. Scholarship about the Declaration starts with Carl Becker, *The Declaration of Independence: A Study in the History of Political Ideas* (New York, 1922). Several excellent studies have dissected every phrase and clause in that text, and how they got to be there: Garry Wills, *Inventing America: Jefferson's Declaration of Independence* (Garden City, N.Y., 1978), Pauline Maier, *American Scripture: Making the Declaration of Independence* (New York, 1997), and Danielle Allen, *Our Declaration: A Reading of the Declaration of Independence in Defense of Equality* (New York, 2014). David Armitage has explored the Declaration's international influence in *The Declaration of Independence: A Global History* (Cambridge, Mass., 2007). Steve Pincus's *Heart of the Declaration: The Founders' Case for an Activist Government* (New Haven, Conn., 2016) suggests patriot leaders wanted more government, not less, and they declared independence to build a more activist administration.

Many historians put less stock in the power of ideas. Doubting that ideas or ideology alone could cause or sustain the American Revolution, they have searched for alternatives. Several generations of historians have, instead, emphasized unrest, discontent, and conflict bubbling up "from below" as the main factor that brought the thirteen colonies to revolution. For an overview to this approach, students should start with Edward Countryman, *The American Revolution,* rev. ed. (1985; rpt. New York, 2003). Another overview that shares this perspective is Gary B. Nash, *The Unknown American Revolution: The Unruly Birth of Democracy and the Struggle to Create America* (New York, 2005). Three classic studies are Staughton Lynd, *Class Conflict, Slavery, and the United States Constitution,* new ed. (1967; rpt. Cambridge, 2009), Jesse Lemisch, "Jack Tar in the Streets: Merchant Seamen in the Politics of Revolutionary America," *WMQ,* 3d Ser., XXV (1968), 371–407, and Gary B. Nash, *The Urban Crucible: The Northern Seaports and the Origins of the American Revolution* (Cambridge, Mass., 1979). More recently, see Woody Holton, *Forced Founders: Indians, Debtors, Slaves, and the Making of the American Revolution in Virginia* (Williamsburg, Va., and Chapel Hill, N.C., 1999), Terry Bouton, *Taming Democracy: "The People," the Founders, and the Troubled Ending of the American Revolution* (New York, 2007), Michael A. McDonnell, *The Politics of War: Race, Class, and Conflict in Revolutionary Virginia* (Williamsburg, Va., and Chapel Hill, N.C., 2007), Barbara Clark Smith, *The Freedoms We Lost: Consent and Resistance in Revolutionary America* (New York, 2010), and Gerald Horne, *The Counter-Revolution of 1776: Slave Resistance and the Origins of the United States of America* (New York, 2014). See also the essential essays in two collections edited by Alfred F. Young, *The American Revolution: Explorations in the History of American Radicalism* (Dekalb, Ill., 1976) and *Beyond the American Revolution: Explorations in the History of American Radicalism* (Dekalb, Ill., 1993).

This book emphasizes the importance of the Revolutionary War as more than just a sideshow or phase of the American Revolutionary experience. John Shy's scholarship is essential for approaches that interweave military, social, and political history. See especially his *People Numerous and Armed: Reflections on the Military Struggle for American Independence,* rev. ed. (1976; rpt. Ann Arbor, Mich., 1990). The burgeoning "new military history" that Shy helped pioneer is carried on in Charles Royster, *A Revolutionary People at War: The Continental Army and American Character, 1775–1783* (Williamsburg, Va., and Chapel Hill, N.C., 1979), James Kirby Martin and Mark Edward Lender, *"A Respectable Army": The Military Origins of the Republic, 1763–1789,* 3d ed. (1982; rpt. Hoboken, N.J., 2015), John Grenier, *The First Way of War: American War Making on the Frontier, 1607–1814* (Cambridge, 2005), and two books by Wayne E. Lee, *Crowds and Soldiers in Revolutionary North Carolina: The Culture of Violence in Riot and War* (Gainesville, Fla., 2001) and *Barbarians and Brothers: Anglo-American Warfare, 1500–1865* (New York, 2011). Not to be missed is the sweeping survey of warfare's significance to American history, Fred Anderson and Andrew Cayton's *Dominion of War: Empire and Liberty in North America, 1500–2000* (New York, 2005). Two modern collections of essays show how central the war experience has become for interpreters of the American Revolution: John Resch and Walter Sargent, eds., *War and Society in the American Revolution: Mobilization and Home Fronts* (Dekalb, Ill., 2007) and Patrick Spero and Michael Zuckerman, eds., *The American Revolution Reborn* (Philadelphia, 2016).

Another important line of inquiry has been to document the experience of Native peoples during the Revolutionary War. Colin G. Calloway's *American Revolution in*

Indian Country: Crisis and Diversity in Native American Communities (Cambridge, 1995) is the standard work. His *Indian World of George Washington: The First President, the First Americans, and the Birth of the Nation* (New York, 2018) is also essential. Another valuable overview is Gregory Evans Dowd, *A Spirited Resistance: The North American Indian Struggle for Unity, 1745–1815* (Baltimore, 1992). Other studies focus on smaller groups or regions. For the Iroquois, see Barbara Graymont, *The Iroquois in the American Revolution* (Syracuse, N.Y., 1972), Max M. Mintz, *Seeds of Empire: The American Revolutionary Conquest of the Iroquois* (New York, 1999), Joseph T. Glatthaar and James Kirby Martin, *Forgotten Allies: The Oneida Indians and the American Revolution* (New York, 2006), and Alan Taylor, *The Divided Ground: Indians, Settlers, and the Northern Borderland of the American Revolution* (New York, 2006). For Natives in the Great Lakes region, the key texts are Richard White, *The Middle Ground: Indians, Empires, and Republics in the Great Lakes Region, 1650–1815* (Cambridge, 1991) and Michael A. McDonnell, *Masters of Empire: Great Lakes Indians and the Making of America* (New York, 2015). For the Cherokees, Creeks, and other Natives in the South, see James H. O'Donnell, *Southern Indians in the American Revolution* (Knoxville, Tenn., 1973), Tom Hatley, *The Dividing Paths: Cherokees and South Carolinians through the Era of Revolution* (New York, 1995), James Piecuch, *Three Peoples, One King: Loyalists, Indians, and Slaves in the Revolutionary South, 1775–1782* (Columbia, S.C., 2008), and Kathleen DuVal, *Independence Lost: Lives on the Edge of the American Revolution* (New York, 2015).

This book also benefits from the scholarship that has highlighted African American participation in the Revolutionary War. The pioneering study is Benjamin Quarles, *The Negro in the American Revolution* (Williamsburg, Va., and Chapel Hill, N.C., 1961). Sylvia R. Frey's *Water from the Rock: Black Resistance in a Revolutionary Age* (Princeton, N.J., 1991) remains an essential study of the war's effect on enslaved African Americans. Cassandra Pybus made the Revolutionary diaspora for enslaved Americans global in *Epic Journeys of Freedom: Runaway Slaves of the American Revolution and Their Global Quest for Liberty* (Boston, 2006). Douglas R. Egerton synthesized what we now know about African Americans in the Revolutionary era in *Death or Liberty: African Americans and Revolutionary America* (New York, 2009). Judith L. Van Buskirk broke more ground, however, with *Standing in Their Own Light: African American Patriots in the American Revolution* (Norman, Okla., 2017). Two essays by Peter H. Wood were especially valuable for this book: "'Liberty Is Sweet': African-American Freedom Struggles in the Years before White Independence," in Young, ed., *Beyond the American Revolution* and "'Taking Care of Business' in Revolutionary South Carolina: Republicanism and the Slave Society," in Jeffrey J. Crow and Larry E. Tise, eds., *The Southern Experience in the American Revolution* (Chapel Hill, N.C., 1978).

These studies underscored the participation and experience of free and enslaved African Americans during the Revolutionary period. Another rich vein of scholarship that sits adjacent to these works addresses how the institution of slavery complicated American claims to liberty. The two most important books to study this question came out on the eve of the bicentennial of American independence: Edmund S. Morgan, *American Slavery, American Freedom: The Ordeal of Colonial Virginia* (New York, 1975) and David Brion Davis, *The Problem of Slavery in the Age of Revolution, 1770–1823* (Ithaca, N.Y., 1975). Since Morgan's and Davis's works, several important books have developed our understanding of the connections between slavery and freedom, either through examining the emancipatory promises the Revolutionaries kept or exploring how opportunities were squandered. For emancipation and abolition, see Arthur Zilversmit, *The First Emancipation: The Abolition of Slavery in the North* (Chicago, 1967), Gary B. Nash and Jean R. Soderlund, *Freedom by Degrees: Emancipation in Pennsylvania and Its Aftermath* (New York, 1991), David N. Gellman, *Emancipating New York: The Politics of Slavery and Freedom, 1777–1827* (Baton Rouge, La., 2006), Manisha Sinha, *The Slave's Cause: A History of Abolition* (New Haven, Conn., 2016), and Paul J. Polgar, *Standard-Bearers of Equality: America's First Abolition Movement* (Williamsburg, Va., and Chapel Hill, N.C., 2019). For Virginia's complicated history, see Eva Sheppard Wolf, *Race and Liberty in the New Nation: Emancipation in Virginia from the Revolution to Nat Turner's Rebellion* (Baton Rouge, La., 2006), Alan Taylor, *The Internal Enemy: Slavery and War in Virginia, 1772–1832* (New York, 2013), and, most of all, the magnificent *Hemingses of Monticello: An American Family* (New York, 2008) by Annette Gordon-Reed. A collection of essays, in which some of the material of *The Common Cause* appeared, is John Craig Hammond and Matthew Mason, eds., *Contesting Slavery: The Politics of Bondage and Freedom in the New American Nation* (Charlottesville, Va., 2011).

If the problem of enslaving people while claiming natural rights posed one dilemma about the Revolutionaries, another is how those inalienable declarations competed with the rights of Native peoples in the American backcountry. What about Natives' claims to their lives, liberties, and pursuits of happiness? For studies that analyze the problem of what the American Revolution meant to and for the trans-Appalachian west, see Stephen Aron, *How the West Was Lost: The Transformation of Kentucky from Daniel Boone to Henry Clay* (Baltimore, 1996), Eric Hinderaker, *Elusive Empires: Constructing Colonialism in the Ohio Valley, 1673–1800* (Cambridge, 1997), Patrick Griffin, *American Leviathan: Empire, Nation, and Revolutionary Frontier* (New York, 2007), Bethel Saler, *The Settlers' Empire: Colonialism and State Formation in America's Old Northwest* (Philadelphia, 2015), Honor Sachs, *Home Rule: Households, Manhood, and National Expansion on the Eighteenth-Century Kentucky Frontier* (New Haven, Conn., 2015), and Rob Harper, *Unsettling the West: Violence and State Building in the Ohio Valley* (Philadelphia, 2018). I have explored this in "From Indian Killer to Worthy Citizen: The Revolutionary Transformation of Michael Cresap," *WMQ*, 3d Ser., LXIII (2006), 97–122.

Both of these problems—enslavement and dispossession—also contributed to the development of racial thought and ideology in colonial and Revolutionary America. The classic text is Winthrop D. Jordan, *White over Black: American Attitudes toward the Negro, 1550–1812* (Williamsburg, Va., and Chapel Hill, N.C., 1968). After Jordan, students looking to explore how American racialism developed in the early republic should turn to Barbara Jeanne Fields, "Slavery, Race, and Ideology in the United States of America," *New Left Review,* no. 181 (1990), 95–118, and Duncan J. MacLeod, *Slavery, Race, and the American Revolution* (Cambridge, 1974). Ibram X. Kendi's *Stamped from the Beginning: The Definitive History of Racist Ideas in America* (New York, 2016) carries the story forward from the eighteenth century. See also Bruce Dain, *A Hideous Monster of the Mind: American Race Theory in the Early Republic* (Cambridge, Mass., 2002) and, especially, Nicholas Guyatt, *Bind Us Apart: How Enlightened Americans Invented Racial Segregation* (New York, 2016). For racial thinking about and by Native peoples, see Philip J. Deloria, *Playing Indian* (New Haven, Conn., 1998), Nancy Shoemaker, *A Strange Likeness: Becoming Red and White in Eighteenth-Century North America* (New York, 2004), and David J. Silverman, *Red Brethren: The Brothertown and Stockbridge Indians and the Problem of Race in Early America* (Ithaca, N.Y., 2010).

The news that thousands of German mercenaries were headed for America was one of the triggers for independence. Scholarship on the German troops who served in America (mistakenly lumped together as "the Hessians") includes Rodney Atwood, *The Hessians: Mercenaries from Hessen-Kassel in the American Revolution* (Cambridge, 1980), Charles W. Ingrao, *The Hessian Mercenary State: Ideas, Institutions, and Reform under Frederick II, 1760–1785* (Cambridge, 1987), and Brady J. Crytzer, *Hessians: Mercenaries, Rebels, and the War for British North America* (Yardley, Pa., 2015). David Hackett Fischer's *Washington's Crossing* (New York, 2004) also features analysis of the German troops.

The Hessians feature briefly in *Thirteen Clocks*, but in *The Common Cause*, they appear in more depth as a counterexample: after the capture of nearly one thousand German troops at Trenton and Princeton, they no longer garnered attention as fearful proxy enemies. Newspaper printers stopped telling stories about them, and they all but disappeared after the end of 1776. For more on the captivity of German troops, see Ken Miller, *Dangerous Guests: Enemy Captives and Revolutionary Communities during the War for Independence* (Ithaca, N.Y., 2014) and Daniel Krebs, *A Generous and Merciful Enemy: Life for German Prisoners of War during the American Revolution* (Norman, Okla., 2013).

There are a few theoretical fields of scholarship that underpin the argument of *Thirteen Clocks*. The first is print culture. The touchstone text for this is Michael Warner, *The Letters of the Republic: Publication and the Public Sphere in Eighteenth-Century America* (Cambridge, Mass., 1990). David D. Hall's scholarship in the history of the book has also been revelatory. See his *Cultures of Print: Essays in the History of the Book* (Amherst, Mass., 1996) and the essays in Hugh Amory and Hall, eds., *A History of the Book in America*, I, *The Colonial Book in the Atlantic World* (Cambridge, 2000). See also Richard D. Brown, *Knowledge Is Power: The Diffusion of Information in Early America, 1700–1865* (New York, 1989).

For more on the development of colonial newspaper culture, start with Stephen Botein's foundational essay, "'Meer Mechanics' and an Open Press: The Business and Political Strategies of Colonial American Printers," *Perspectives in American History,* IX (1975), 127–228. Next, see Charles E. Clark, *The Public Prints: The Newspaper in Anglo-American Culture, 1665–1740* (New York, 1994), David A. Copeland, *Colonial American Newspapers: Character and Content* (Newark, Del., 1997), and Ralph Frasca, *Benjamin Franklin's Printing Network: Disseminating Virtue in Early America* (Columbia, Mo., 2006).

For newspapers during the Revolution, see Arthur M. Schlesinger, *Prelude to Independence: The Newspaper War on Britain, 1764–1776* (New York, 1957), Bernard Bailyn and John B. Hench, eds., *The Press and the American Revolution* (Worcester, Mass., 1980), Carol Sue Humphrey, *"This Popular Engine": New England Newspapers during the American Revolution, 1775–1789* (Newark, Del., 1992), and Joseph M. Adelman, *Revolutionary Networks: The Business and Politics of Printing the News, 1763–1789* (Baltimore, 2019). Trish Loughran's iconoclastic study, *The Republic in Print: Print Culture in the Age of U.S. Nation Building, 1770–1870* (New York, 2007) casts doubt on the effectiveness and reach of print in the eighteenth century.

Revolution scholars over several generations have debated the issue of whether the patriots' activities constituted "propaganda." Early studies that viewed patriots as unabashed manipulators include John C. Miller, *Sam Adams: Pioneer in Propaganda* (Boston, 1936) and Philip Davidson, *Propaganda and the American Revolution, 1763–1783* (Chapel Hill, N.C., 1941). Two modern studies that reconsider this are William B. Warner, *Protocols of Liberty: Communication Innovation and the American Revolution* (Chicago, 2013) and Russ Castronovo, *Propaganda 1776: Secrets, Leaks, and Revolutionary Communications in Early America* (New York, 2014).

Theories of nation making and nationalism also laid the foundation for *Thirteen Clocks*. Modern studies of nationalism must start with Benedict Anderson, *Imagined Communities: Reflections on the Origin and Spread of Nationalism* ([1983]; rpt. London, 2016), Eric Hobsbawm and Terence Ranger, eds., *The Invention of Tradition* (Cambridge, 1983), Hobsbawm, *Nations and Nationalism since 1780: Programme, Myth, Reality* (Cambridge, 1990), and Ernest Gellner, *Nations and Nationalism* (Ithaca, N.Y., 1983). Essential studies of American nationalism are David Waldstreicher, *In the Midst of Perpetual Fetes: The Making of American Nationalism, 1776–1820* (Williamsburg, Va., and Chapel Hill, N.C., 1997) and Peter S. Onuf, *Jefferson's Empire: The Language of American Nationhood* (Charlottesville, Va., 2000).

The patriots' decision to reject monarchy in favor of republican government also meant they jettisoned the political theory of subjecthood. What replaced it — citizenship — was ill-defined and hazy at best in the Revolutionary era. See James H. Kettner's pathbreaking study, *The Development of American Citizenship, 1608–1870* (Williamsburg, Va., and Chapel Hill, N.C., 1978) and Douglas Bradburn's equally important *Citizenship Revolution: Politics and the Creation of the American Union, 1774–1804* (Charlottesville, Va., 2009). For theoretical examinations of early American conceptions of what it meant to be an American citizen, begin with Rogers M. Smith, *Civic Ideals: Conflicting Visions of Citizenship in U.S. History* (New Haven, Conn., 1997) and his *Stories of Peoplehood: The Politics and Morals of Political Membership* (Cambridge, 2003).

Finally, the power and uses of fear — especially as it relates to the development of racial prejudices — has emerged as one of the most important analytical threads for early American history. Both this book and *The Common Cause* contribute to this interpretation. For the best examples of how fear (as channeled through print) fostered exclusion in colonial America, see two books by Jill Lepore, *The Name of War: King Philip's War and the Origins of American Identity* (New York, 1998) and *New York Burning: Liberty, Slavery, and Conspiracy in Eighteenth Century Manhattan* (New York, 2005), as well as Peter Silver, *Our Savage Neighbors: How Indian War Transformed Early America* (New York, 2008) and Carroll Smith-Rosenberg, *This Violent Empire: The Birth of an American National Identity* (Williamsburg, Va., and Chapel Hill, N.C., 2010).

Despite the thousands of books on the American Revolution, there are more to be written. The importance of the United States' founding demands that we continue to return to the archives so that we may reinterpret and reexamine even what, at first glance, seem to be the most well-worn and exhausted sources, like the printed sources that John Adams told us to look at two centuries ago. With the shelves groaning under the weight of so many volumes, finding something new to say about the founding may seem a daunting task. But there is still much more to learn about the American Revolution. We just have to keep searching and asking questions.

Index

Page numbers in italics refer to illustrations.

Adams, Abigail, 128
Adams, John: on American Revolution, 1, 2, 4, 162; and discrediting of loyalists, 14, 16, 30, 62, 64–67; and "cooking up" of news, 15–17, 30; provincialism of, 40; as "Novanglus," 65–67; and British use of foreign mercenaries, 94–96; and Declaration of the Causes and Necessity of Taking up Arms, 94–99; and management of news, 96–99; and enslaved people's communication networks, 111–112; on potential for desertion, 116–117; on women's place in society, 128–130; and list of proxies, 129; on independence, 140; and committee on German mercenaries, 143; on the Cedars, 145–147; and Declaration of Independence, 148; on Massachusetts's religious intolerance, 189n14
Adams, Samuel: and *Boston Gazette,* 13; and discrediting of loyalists, 13, 16, 30; and "cooking up" of news, 16, 30; provincialism of, 40; response of, to Coercive Acts, 67; on potential for desertion, 116–117; as "Candidus," 131–132; contribution of, to *Common Sense,* 131–132; on use of Indians against British in Canada, 146; on the Cedars, 147
Address to the Inhabitants of the British Settlements, on the Slavery of the Negroes in America, An (Rush), 52–53
Alamance, battle of, 44–46
Albany (N.Y.) committee of safety, 79
Albany Congress (1754), 37–38
Algonquian Indians, 69
Allegheny Mountains, 49

Allen, Edward, 74
Allen, Ethan, 48–49, 78, 84
Allen, John, 53
Allen, William, 42
Allinson, Samuel, 57
"American, An," 126
"Americus," 13–14
Antislavery movement, 55, 173–175; emergence and growth of, 51–57; and abolitionism, 57, 180–182; decline of, 57–59, 121. *See also* Slave trade, Atlantic
"Armatus," 153, *154*
Arnold, Gen. Benedict, 144
Attucks, Crispus, 69

Baker, Remember, 48, 83
Baptists, 189n14
Barré, Col. Isaac, 47
Bartlett, Josiah, 139, 146
Beaters (print shop laborers), 26–27, *26*
Bedel, Col. Timothy, 144–145
Bell, Robert, 132
Benezet, Anthony, 51–52, 55, 57
Bernard, Francis, 17
Black Boys, 43
Boone, Daniel, 177–178
Boston: British occupation of, 14, 18; presses of, 18; Coercive Acts' singling out of, 36–37. *See also* Massachusetts
Boston Chronicle. See Mein, John
Boston committee of correspondence, 40, 46, 55
Boston Gazette: and Sons of Liberty, 13–14; and altercation with John Mein, 13–14, 16; and sneaking of printing press out of Boston, 18; and publication

of "Novanglus," 65; and news of German mercenaries, 96

Boston Massacre, 69

Boston Port Bill, 36

Boston Tea Party, 36–37

Boucher, Jonathan, 62

Boycotts, nonimportation, 13, 14

Boyd, Adam, 86, 98

Bradford, Thomas, 18. *See also* Bradford, William; *Pennsylvania Journal*

Bradford, William, 18; and London Coffee House, 27; as Philadelphia postmaster, 27. *See also* Bradford, William, Jr.; *Pennsylvania Journal*

Bradford, William, Jr., 18, 105–106

Bunker Hill, battle of, 69, 121–122

Burgoyne, Gen. John, 136

Burke, Aedanus, 180–182

Burke, Edmund, 36

Butler, Col. John, 167

Butler, Zebulon, 47

Butterfield, Maj. Isaac, 144–145

Cameron, Alexander, 85

Cameron, Allen, 115

Campbell, Lord William, 84, 86, 92, 101

"Candidus" (Samuel Adams), 131–132

Cape-Fear Mercury, 86, 98

Carheart, William, 32–34

Carleton, Sir Guy, *95,* 97–98, 108–109

Carter, John, 138

Carter, Landon, 140, 150

Catherine the Great, 136

Caughnawaga Indians, 92, 144–146

Chandler, Thomas Bradbury, 62; *What Think Ye of the Congress Now?* 64

Charleston (S.C.) committee of safety, 74, 75, 85, 86

Charleston (S.C.) council of safety, 205n30

Cherokee Indians, 85, 149

Chickasaw Indians, 149

Children, colonial: as purported victims of Indian attack, 99, 118, 142, 146, 165, 167–169, 174, 177; as purported victims

of slave rebellions, 113, 142, 146, 167, 174; schoolbook for, by Franklin and Lafayette, 165–168

Children, Indian: as victims of patriot attack, 177. *See also* Indians

Citizenship: in Declaration of Independence, 157–163; and inclusion of populations, 160–161, 172, 178–179; and exclusion of populations, 170–171, 176–178, 179; in comparison with subjecthood, 183; and United States, 183–185; defining of, 183–185

Clinton, George, 48–49

Clinton, Gen. Henry, 173

Clymer, George, 42

Cobham, Thomas, 88

Cockburn, Adm. George, 169–170

Coercive Acts, 36–37, 155–156; response to, 46, 56, 67

Collet, Capt. John, 89, 98, 105, 202n3

Committees of correspondence, 4, 30. *See also* Boston committee of correspondence

"Common Sense" (pseudonym). *See* Paine, Thomas

Common Sense (Paine), 130–132; expanded edition of, 132

Congress, Federal: and debate over naturalization, 178–179

Congress, First Continental, 18, 56, 61–62, 189n14

Congress, Second Continental: regional tensions at, 38; on British instigation of slave insurrections, 74; on relations with Indians, 77–79; and Declaration of the Causes and Necessity of Taking up Arms, 93–99; proclamations of, to distant audiences, 99, 201n32; and Connolly, 115; and orders to print news stories, 123–126, 139, 158; and German mercenaries, 137–140, 142–143; and debate over independence, 140–141, 148; Iroquois Indian delegation to, 142, 149; and the Cedars, 146–148; and Washington's employment of Indians, 148–

149; committee of, to draft Declaration of Independence, 148

Connecticut: and Wyoming Valley dispute with Pa., 46–48; soldier desertion in, 117–119

Connecticut Assembly, 55

Connecticut Courant, 145–146

Connolly, Dr. John, 49–51, 108–110, 115–116, 124

Continental army: desertion in, 117–119, 143–144; and free Black enlistment, 121–123; and the Cedars, 143–145; and smallpox, 143–144; Indians' serving in, 148–149, 175

Continental Association, 56, 61, 62

Cooper, John, 174

Cooper, Miles, 62

Cornstalk (Shawnee Indian leader), 175, 176

Cornwallis, Gen. Charles, 181

Cowley, William, 109, 115

Crane, Ichabod (character from "Legend of Sleepy Hollow"), 173

Creek Indians, 149

Cushing, Thomas, 137–138

David (African American preacher), 74–75

Dealey, James, 80

De Antonio, Emanuel (enslaved person), 72

Declaration of Independence, 8, *159;* and "domestic insurrectionists," 113–114, 157; themes of, in earlier documents, 147; as unprecedented, 153; grievances of, 153–158; and slave trade, 156–157; and exclusion vs. inclusion for citizenship, 157–163; printing and dissemination of, 158; response to, at Fort Ticonderoga, 158; response to, on Long Island, 161–162

Declaration of the Causes and Necessity of Taking up Arms, 94–99

Delaware Indians, 108, 142, 175, 176

Dialogue concerning the Slavery of the Africans, A (Hopkins), 57, 121

Dickinson, John, 42, 52, 79, 94–95

Discovery, Settlement, and Present State of Kentucke, The (Filson), 177

Dixon, John, 28–29, 150

Draper, Richard. See *Massachusetts Gazette*

Dred Scott v. Sanford, 184

Duane, James, 48

Dunlap, John, 133, 158

Dunmore, John Murray, 4th earl of, *103;* and Connolly, 49, 108; and Va. and Pa. border dispute, 49–51; and slave insurrections, 72–74, 167; and threat of slave emancipation, 73, 102; and use of Indians as proxies, 84; and patriot news of proxies, 97, 108–109; seizure of gunpowder by, 102; and attempts to govern from *Otter,* 102; and confiscation and use of press, 107, 110, 111; on Squire and Holt altercation, 107; and use of slave runaways in battle, 109–110; retreat of, to sloop, 116; and Black regiment, 141, 149–150; and smallpox outbreak on ship, 149–150; legacy of, 169–171

Dunmore's proclamation: issuance of, 110; reaction to, by patriot leaders, 110–115; enslaved people's response to, 111–113, 119–120, 150; spread of news about, 118–120; and end to antislavery movement, 121

Dunmore's War (1774), 50

Eden, Robert, 71–72

Edes, Benjamin, 13–14, 15, 18, 20, 96. See also *Boston Gazette*

Effigies, 45–46, 161–162

Emanuel (enslaved person), 72

Emerson, Ralph Waldo, 68

Ennall, William, 76

Enslaved people: and runaway ads, 29; population of, 52, 54–55, 69, 195n59; and freedom suits, 55, 184; British threats of arming, 58–59; awareness of and response to Revolution by, 73, 76, 88, 99; and rewards for British cause, 84–85; communication networks of,

111–112; response of, to Dunmore's proclamation, 113–115, 119–120, 150; patriot admissions of rationality in, 113; exclusion of, from citizenship, 160–163, 184–185. *See also* Antislavery movement; Slave insurrections; Slave patrols; Slavery; Slave trade, Atlantic

Faucitt, Col. William, 136–137
Filson, John, 177
Fleeming, John, 13, 16. *See also* Mein, John
Fort Johnston, 89, 98, 105, 202n3
Fort Niagara, 77
Fort Pitt, 49, 108, 142, 176
Fort Ticonderoga, 78, 84, 158
Fort William Henry, 79
Foster, George, 144
Fowey (ship), 106–107
Franklin, Benjamin: as official printer for Pennsylvania, 15; on colonial unity at Albany Congress, 37–38; on Paxton Boys, 39–40; view of, before Revolution, 42; on colonial unity after Lexington and Concord, 82; on proxies, 97, 123, 141; and Declaration of Independence, 148; and children's book, 165–168; in France, 165; and fabrication of Indian atrocities, 168–169; on threat of German immigrants, 172; on murder of Indians, 177; on Atlantic slave trade, 180–182; as "Sidi Mehemet Ibrahim," 181
Free African Americans: population of, in Mass., 39–40; and whites' fear of slave insurrections, 70–71, 85–86; and Continental army, 121–123; exclusion of, from citizenship, 179, 184–185
Freneau, Philip, 168
Frontier: and relationship to East, 38–40; and Indian attacks, 39; and Regulator movement, 43–46; changes to perceptions of, 177–178

Gage, Gen. Thomas, 73, 77, 84, 108–109, 136

Galloway, Joseph, 42
Gates, Gen. Horatio, 139, 142, 165
Georgia, 20, 85
German mercenaries: and treaties with Britain, 136–137; arrival of, in patriot news, 137–140; and patriot copies of treaties with Britain, 138–139, 210n22; and citizenship, 160–161, 172, 178–179; and occupation of New York City, 171; silence on, after Trenton, 171–173
Gerry, Elbridge, 213n53
Gill, John, 13–14, 18. See also *Boston Gazette*
Gill v. Mein, 14
Gnadenhutten massacre, 177
Goddard, Mary Katherine. See *Maryland Journal*
Goddard, William. See *Maryland Journal*
Green, William, 132
Greene, Gen. Nathanael, 117
Greenleaf, Joseph, 45–46
Green Mountain border dispute, 48–49
Green Mountain Boys, 48–49, 78, 84

"Hail Columbia" (Phile [Pfeil]), 178–179
Hall, David. See *Pennsylvania Gazette*
Hall, Ebenezer. See *New-England Chronicle*
Hall, Samuel. See *New-England Chronicle*
Hamilton, Alexander, 65
Harris, Joseph (enslaved pilot), 106–107, 127, 202n8
Harrison, William Henry, 169
Henry, Patrick, 57
Hessians. *See* German mercenaries
Holt, John. See *New-York Journal*
Holt, John Hunter. See *Virginia Gazette, or the Norfolk Intelligencer*
Hooper, William, 41, 45–46
Hopkins, Samuel, 51–52, 120–121; *A Dialogue concerning the Slavery of the Africans,* 57, 121
Hopkinson, Francis, 179
Howe, Robert, 41, 45–46
Hunter, William, 20, 150

Hutchings, Col. Joseph, 110
Hutchinson, Thomas, 14, 17, 54

"Ibrahim, Sidi Mehemet" (Benjamin Franklin), 181
Indentured servants, 29
Indian raids: on frontier, 39; at Fort William Henry (1757), 79; and patriot rumors of cannibalism, 124–126, 167; fear of, as unfounded, 129; and murder of Jane McCrea, 165; depictions of, in children's book, 167–168; before Revolution, 182–183
Indians: eastern sympathies for, 50–51; as threat to patriots, 76–79; courting of, 77, 84–85, 107–109; as purported British proxies, 92, *170;* response of, to Revolution, 99, 108; and rejections of British entreaties, 129; and the Cedars, 143–148; as allies to patriots, 148–149, 175–178; and exclusion from citizenship, 160–161, 179; nineteenth-century wars of, and legacy of proxies, 169; murder of, 176–178. *See also individual Indians and Indian nations*
Industry (ship), 74
Iroquois Indians, 47, 77, 175–176; delegation of, to Congress, 142, 149
Irving, Washington: "The Legend of Sleepy Hollow," 173

Jackson, Andrew, 169
Jefferson, Thomas: and colonial antislavery before 1775, 56–57, 121, 157, 175; *A Summary View of the Rights of British America,* 56; and Declaration of the Causes and Necessity of Taking up Arms, 94–95; on Dunmore's proclamation, 111; on slave trade, 121, 156–157, 175; and committee on German mercenaries, 143; and Congressional address after the Cedars, 147; and Declaration of Independence, 148, 153–158; and fascination with Dunmore at Gwynn's Island, 150, *152;* and grievances against

king, 150–151; *Notes on the State of Virginia,* 179; on emancipated slaves and citizenship, 179; and drafting of state constitution, 212n46
Jeremiah, Thomas (free African American pilot), 85–86, 92, 127
Johnson, Guy, *125;* and Indian relations with Britain before Lexington and Concord, 77; and Six Nations, 78–79; on Indians, British courting of, 84–85; and patriot news of using proxies, 97–98; and patriot rumors of encouraging cannibalism, 124–126, 167
Johnson, Sir William, 77
Johnston, Samuel, 45–46, 58, 89

Karonghyontye (Capt. David Hill), *125*
Kemp's Landing, 110
Kentucky, 177
Key, Francis Scott, 170–171, 179
Killbuck, John (Delaware Indian leader), 175, 176
King, Henry, 106–107

Lafayette, Gilbert du Motier, marquis de, 165–168
Lake Champlain, 78
Langdon, John, 139
Laurens, Henry, 74, 80, 86, 197n15
Lay, Benjamin, 51
Lee, Arthur, 74, 139
Lee, Gen. Charles, 116–117
Lee, Capt. John, 137
Lee, Richard Henry, 79, 110–111, 142, 143, 148
"Legend of Sleepy Hollow, The" (Irving), 173
Leonard, Daniel: as "Massachusettensis," 62–67
Leslie, Samuel, 110
Lexington and Concord: myth of, 68, 76; news of, coinciding with British threats to arm enslaved people, 71–76, 102; as turning point, 93, 100
Liberty Boys (N.J.), 43, 190n19

Literacy and orality, 34, 83, 111, 130
"Little declarations of independence,"
    151–153
Livingston, Philip, 190n14
Livingston, Robert, 48, 148
Livingston, William, 133–136, 143
London Coffee House, 27
Loudoun, Samuel, 133
Loyalists: counterargument of, to patriots,
    59–65; on unity as unlikely, 63–64

McCrea, Jane, 165, *166*
Maclay, William, 179–180, 182
Madison, James, 18–20, 105–106, 169–171,
    181–182
Magdalen (ship), 72–73
Malcolm, John, 63, 65–66
"Manifest destiny," 177–178
Mansfield, William Murray, 1st earl of,
    53–55
Martin, Josiah, 84, 89, 97–98, 101
Martin, Laughlin, 80
Maryland, 71–72, 75–76, 109
Maryland Journal, 15, 20, 171
Mason, George, 109
"Massachusettensis" (Daniel Leonard),
    62–67
Massachusetts: and history of religious
    intolerance, 42; and rumors of Natick
    slave rebellion, 69–71; and rumors of
    Framingham slave rebellion, 69–71. *See
    also* Boston; Salem (Mass.) committee
    of safety
Massachusetts Gazette, 61
Massachusetts General Court, 54
Massachusetts Government Act, 62
Mein, John, 13–14, 16, 59–60, 61
Merchant, George, 138–139
M'Fingal (Trumbull), 168
Miller, Henrich, 213n53
Mingo Indians, 108, 142
"Minos" (pseudonym), 112–114
Mohawk Indians, 77, 79
Montague, George, 202n8
Montgomery, Gen. Richard, 133

Morgan, Capt. Daniel, 139
Morgan, George, 142
Mount Vernon, 109

Natick Indians, 69
Native peoples. *See* Indians
Naturalization Act of 1790, 178–179, 183,
    184
New-England Chronicle, 117–118
New Hampshire, 48–49
New Jersey, 43, 174–175
New Jersey Assembly, 55, 58
New Light Congregationalists, 51–52
Newspapers: fabrication and manipula-
    tion of news stories by, 14–17; and
    meaning of freedom of the press, 15; as
    pro-patriot, 17–21; presses of, 18; geog-
    raphy of, 18–21, 27; production of,
    20–28; circulation and readership of,
    27, 31–35; new sources in, 27–28; ex-
    changes in, 28–31, 92–93, 99–100; on
    Indians as British proxies, 97–98, 145–
    146, 148, 150, 212n45; and reactions to
    news incorporated into patriot cause,
    98; and pairing of content, 101–102,
    105, 115–116, 127, 132, 145–146, 150,
    202n3, 212n45; and proxies, 115–116,
    131–136; on German mercenaries, 138–
    140; on germ warfare, 150; silence of,
    on Indians as patriot allies, 175–178
New York: and Green Mountain border
    dispute with N.H., 48–49; and anti-
    slavery movement, 55; and slave rebel-
    lion in Esopus, rumors of, 70, 73. *See
    also* Albany (N.Y.) committee of safety;
    Albany Congress (1754)
New York City: British occupation of, 155,
    171; response to Declaration of Inde-
    pendence in Long Island, 161–162
New-York Journal: and Sons of Liberty, 15,
    20; on Dunmore's proclamation, 112;
    and response to German mercenaries,
    142; and the Cedars, 146; and slave in-
    surrections, 198n26
New York Packet, 133

New York Provincial Congress, 79

Niles, Hezekiah, 1, 2, 5

North, Lord Frederick, 36–37

North Carolina: newspapers of, 20; relationship of, with South Carolina, 41; and Regulator movement, 44–46; and fear of link between patriot cause and slave insurrections, 86–91; and actual slave rebellions, 88–89. *See also* Wilmington (N.C.) committee of safety

"Novanglus" (John Adams), 65–67

Oneida Indians, 92, 175

Otis, James, 13, 52; and "cooking up" of news, 16, 30

Otter (ship), 102, 108, 202n8

Owen, David, 120

Paine, Thomas, 133, 171; *Common Sense*, 130–132

Patriot leaders: and metaphorical slavery, 52; and concern about alienation of public, 61; on Indians, 77–79; and loyalists, 80, 156; and shaping of news, 96–99, 123–127, 130, 131; on Dunmore's proclamation, 110–115; on army desertion, 117–119; and use of proxies, 147; on citizenship and republicanism, 183. *See also individual leaders*

Paxton Boys, 39, 47

Pemberton, Israel, 189n14

Pendleton, Edmund, 114, 141

Penn, John, 49–51

Pennsylvania: and Wyoming Valley dispute with Conn., 46–48; and border dispute with Va., 49–51; and murder of Indians, 177. *See also* Philadelphia

Pennsylvania committee of safety, 120

Pennsylvania Evening Post, 78–79; on Dunmore's proclamation, 120; and printing of Schuyler letter, 124; "Candidus" and "Sincerus" in, 131–132

Pennsylvania Gazette: on arrival of German mercenaries, 139

Pennsylvania Journal, 15, 27; subscription books for, 31–35; and printing of Stuart letters, 98; on proxies, 136; on German mercenaries' arrival, 139. *See also* Bradford, William

Pennsylvania Packet (Dunlap), 133, 158

Philadelphia: presses of, 18; hostility of, toward Mass., 42; and response to Dunmore's proclamation, 120; and "little declarations of independence," 151–153

Phile (Pfeil), Philip, 178–179

Pinkney, John. See *Virginia Gazette* (Pinkney)

Pipe, Captain (Delaware Indian), 175, 176

Pitt, William, 13

Pittsburgh: and Pa.–Va. border dispute, 50

Poor, Salem, 122

"Populus" (Samuel Adams), 14

Printers: as political actors, 15; official, of colonies, 15, 20; as keepers of secrets, 16–17, 27–28

Print shops: and patriot cause, 131

Proclamation Line. See Royal Proclamation of 1763 (Proclamation Line)

Providence Gazette, 138

Provincial Congress, 120

Pseudonyms: use of, in print, 16. *See also individual names*

Pullers (print shop laborers), 26–27, *26*

Purdie, Alexander. See *Virginia Gazette* (Purdie)

Quakers: and dispute with Puritans in Mass., 42, 189n14; and antislavery, 51, 55, 180–182; and gradual abolition, 173–174

Quincy, Josiah, Jr., 40–43, 46, 189n14

Racial ideology: eighteenth-century development of, 11–12, 183–184

Ramsay, David, 111

Randolph, Peyton, 73, 109

Regulator movement, 43–46

Republicanism: and white supremacy, ix, 12, 185. *See also* Citizenship

Respess, Thomas, 88

Revere, Paul: and myth of ride, 68–69

Rhode Island Assembly, 55

Richelieu River, 83

River Raisin Massacre, 169

Rivington, James, 18, 20, 60, 61, 64–65, 106

Rivington's New-York Gazetteer. See Rivington, James

Royal Proclamation of 1763 (Proclamation Line), 49

Rush, Benjamin, 42, 56–57, 121; *An Address to the Inhabitants of the British Settlements, on the Slavery of the Negroes in America,* 52–53

Russian soldiers: rumors of, 136

Rutledge, Edmund, 40, 147

St. Clair, Col. Arthur, 49–51, 158

St. Luc de la Corne, 79, 81

Salem, Peter, 69, 122–123

Salem (Mass.) committee of safety, 137

Sambo (enslaved person), 85–86

Schaw, Janet, 87

Schuyler, Gen. Philip, 124–126, 146, 149, 167

Scott, Lt. Col. Charles, 114–115

Seabury, Samuel, 59, 61–62, 64, 65

Sellers, William. See *Pennsylvania Gazette*

Seneca Indians, 142

Seven Years' War, 47, 52

Sewell, Jonathan, 62

Shadwell (enslaved person), 205n30

Sharp, Granville, 53

Shawnee Indians, 50, 108, 142, 177

Sherburne, Maj. Henry, 144, 149

Sherman, Roger, 143, 148

Shipley, Jonathan, 97, 123

Short, Henry, 212n45

Simmons, John, 75–76

"Sincerus" (Samuel Adams), 131–132

Six Nations, 78–79. See also Iroquois Indians

Slave insurrections: fear of, in South, 41,

71–74, 86–92; and antislavery movement, 58–59; fear of, and Lexington and Concord, 69–71, 74–76, 93; Indian involvement in, 70; publicizing of plots for, 70–71, 105–106; as linked to Dunmore, 72–74, 167; and class divisions among whites, 75–76; before Revolution, 105–106, 182–183; in Declaration of Independence, 113–114; fear of, as unfounded, 129; depictions of, in children's book, 167–168; abolitionism and legacy of, 173–175

Slave patrols, 73, 87, 88; equivalence of, to fighting British troops, 92–93

Slavery, 41, 51, 58–59; metaphorical, of patriots, 52

Slave trade, Atlantic: abolition of, 54–56, 180–182; in rough draft of Declaration of Independence, 156–157

Smallpox, 141, 143–144, 149–150

Smyth, Dr. John, 115

Society for the Relief of Free Negroes Unlawfully Held in Bondage, 57

Solomon (Stockbridge Indian leader), 77

Somerset case, 53–55

Sons of Liberty, 13, 15, 20

South Carolina: newspapers of Charleston, 20; and commitment to slavery, 40–41, 51; slaves as majority in, 41; fear of slave insurrections in, 41, 91–92; and Regulator movement, 43–44; on news of Lexington and Concord, 74–75; and newspaper reports on British arming of slaves, 79–81; and Stuart's meeting with Indians, 85; and slaves' running away to British troops, 85–86, 205n30; and raid on maroon community on Sullivan's Island, 119–120. *See also* Charleston (S.C.) committee of safety; Charleston (S.C.) council of safety

South Carolina committee of safety, 119–120

South-Carolina Gazette, 20, 80

Squire, Capt. Matthew, 105–107

Stamp Act, 15

"Star Spangled Banner" (Key), 170–171. *See also* Key, Francis Scott

Stewart, Charles, 53

Stewart, Lazarus, 47

Stiles, Ezra, 120

Stockbridge Indians, 77, 175

Stuart, Henry, 149, 150

Stuart, John: on patriot reaction to proxy rumors, 74, 127; and British courting of Indians, 84–85; warrant for, in Charleston, 86; letters of, published by patriots, 86, 98, 149; and patriot news of proxy use, 97–98

Sullivan, Gen. John, 175–176

Summary View of the Rights of British America, A (Jefferson), 56

Susquehanna Company, 47

Tamar (ship), 205n30

Taney, Roger B., 184

Taverns: reading aloud of newspapers in, 34

Tecumseh, 169

Thomas, Isaiah, 18, 45–46

Thornbrough, Col. Edward, 205n30

Timothy, Peter. See *South-Carolina Gazette*

Toney (enslaved person), 72

Towne, Benjamin. See *Pennsylvania Evening Post*

Townshend Duties, 13, 55

Treaty of Fort Stanwix, 47

Trumbull, John: *M'Fingal,* 168

Tryon, William, 44–46, 48

Tucker, Josiah, 46

Tudor, William, 96

Tuscarora Indians, 175

Tye, Colonel (formerly enslaved person), 173–174

Unity of colonies, unlikelihood of: overview of, 3–4; and previous attempts, 37–38; coastal vs. backcountry, 43–46;

and competition between colonies, 46–51; regional differences of, and slavery, 51–59, 128; and loyalist counterargument, 59–65

Virginia: newspapers of, 20; border dispute of, with Pa., 49–51; and debate in House of Burgesses on slavery, 54–55, 57; and threats of slave rebellion in Williamsburg, 72; fears of slave insurrections in, 72–74; hurricane in, 104–105

Virginia Assembly: and resolution on independence, 141

Virginia committee of safety, 109

Virginia Convention, 150–151

Virginia Gazette (Dixon), 28–29

Virginia Gazette (Dixon & Hunter), 150

Virginia Gazette (Pinkney), 115; on Dunmore's proclamation, 112–114

Virginia Gazette (Purdie), 126; exchanges in, 28–29; on slave insurrections' unifying patriot cause, 91; on Squire's harboring of slaves, 105–107; on Dunmore's Proclamation, 112; on Indians in Carolina backcountry, 149

Virginia Gazette, or the Norfolk Intelligencer: and press confiscated by Dunmore, 20, 107; on slaves' running away, 104, 105–107; on burning of Royal Navy ship, 105; on Indians, 198n3

Ward, Gen. Artemas, 137

Ward, Samuel, 119

War of 1812, 169–171

Warren, James, 64, 96, 146

Washington, George: myth of, 91; on Dunmore as threat, 102, 115; on Indians and plot with Dunmore, 107–108; and Connolly's plan, 109, 115; and Continental army, 117–119; and enslaved people's escape to Lord Dunmore, 119; and Blacks in Continental army, 121–123; and German mercenaries, 137–139,

171–172; on the Cedars, 145; authori-
zation of Indian employment by, 148–
149; and military invasion of Iroquois
country, 175–176; election of, to presi-
dency, 178–179
Washington, Lund, 109, 119
Watson, Ebenezer, 145–146
Wentworth, Benning, 48–49
What Think Ye of the Congress Now?
(Chandler), 64
Whipple, William, 146
White Eyes, Capt. (Delaware Indian
leader), 175, 176
Whiteness: and eighteenth-century racial
ideology, 172–173
White supremacy, ix, 12, 185
Wilkes, John, 47
Wilmington (N.C.) committee of safety,
89
Wilson, James, 171
Withington, Peter, 32–34

Women, colonial: as subscribers to *Pennsylvania Journal,* 31; literacy of, 34; as
purported victims of Indian attack, 99,
118, 142, 146, 165, 167–169, 174, 177; as
purported victims of slave rebellions,
113, 142, 146, 167, 174; as purported victims of British tyranny, 121; place of, in
society, 128–130; as purported victims
of German mercenaries, 171
Women, Indian: as victims of patriot
attack, 177. *See also* Indians
Wood, James, 108
Woodford, Col. William, 114, 116, 170
Woodmason, Charles, 39
Woolman, John, 51
Wyandot Indians, 108, 142, 169
Wyoming Valley dispute, 46–48
Wythe, George, 143, 147

Young, Dr. Thomas, 45–46